RAY DANTON

RAY DANTON: The Epitome of Cool

(a career retrospective)

by Joseph Fusco

BearManor Media
2019

Ray Danton: The Epitome of Cool (a career retrospective)

© 2019 Joseph Fusco

All rights reserved.

For information, address:

BearManor Fiction
P. O. Box 71426
Albany, GA 31708

bearmanormedia.com

Typesetting and layout by John Teehan

Published in the USA by BearManor Media

ISBN — 978-1-62933-442-4

Dedicated to Julie Adams

Special thanks to
Julia Brandner
whose guidance and inspiration
made this book possible

Table of Contents

Introduction 1

GOLDEN AGE OF TELEVISION

Live Anthologies: The Early Days 15
From Live Drama to Videotape 26
Gypsies, Soldiers, Card Sharps and Duelists 37

SUPPORTING ROLES

Hollywood Westerns 47
Romantic Archetypes 58
Career Men 66
Topical Soap Operas 74

AMERICAN PULP

Unknown Shades of Gray 83
The Dark Side of Justice 98
Albert Zugsmith's American Nightmare 112
The Signature Roles 122

WARNER BROTHERS TELEVISION

Urbane Private Eyes 139
The Outside Type 156
Western Prime 169
Prairie Spirits and Mixed Brands 183

Transitions

Bits and Pieces 195
A Reality Check 202
Last of the Classic Phase 210
The New Westerns 220
The Theater 235

Eurocines and Late 60's Americana

A Malaysian Pirate and Euro-Super Spies 239
More Spies and the Absurd Side of Things 253
European Gold 263
Network Relevance: The New American TV Demographic 273

The Disco Era

70's Overview 287
The Return to Hollywood 292
The New Age Technicolor Hipster 305
Indies, Vampires, Radio and the Stage 319

70's Nostalgia Bust

Bottom of the Barrel 335
The Twilight Mob: Crime Bosses, Con Men and Assassins 343
1975: Spin of the Coin 355
The Last Picture Show (with extras) 372

Law and Order Revue

Behind the TV Eye 383
Quincy, M.E (Pt. 1) 385
Quincy, ME (Pt.2) 397
Cagney and Lacey 411
Mickey Spillane's Mike Hammer 426

General Directory

The Crime Club 439
Family Values 449
Syndication and Cable 451

Afterword 467

List of Credits

Movies as an Actor 469
Television as an Actor 479
Movies as a Director 494
Television as a Director 495
Theater as an Actor 507
Theater as a Director 508

Acknowledgements 511
Endnotes 513
Index 515

A portrait of Ray Danton that accents his charm and bonhomie. 1960, Warner Bros. Dist. Corp.

Introduction

MENTION RAY DANTON and even the most astute modern film fans might not give you much of a response beyond his roles as Legs Diamond and George Raft. A handful of Fifties' nostalgia television buffs may recall his roles on the Warner Brothers circuit. Some aficionados of 60's European movies will mention his portrayal of Sandokan, the Malaysian pirate, or Lucky the Inscrutable, Jesus Franco's absurd debonair secret agent. There will be a few cult enthusiasts who will remember him as a director of three 70's horror movies. Ardent fans of *Quincy, M.E., The New Mike Hammer* and *Cagney and Lacey* will list his name among the show's recurring directors and consider him solely for that.

Ray Danton has worked in every facet of the performing arts. A prepubescent baritone enabled him to work as a child radio actor. Summer stock in his teen-age years culminated in appearing on the London stage before he was twenty. Live television in the Fifties introduced him to a burgeoning electronic audience. A contract with Universal-International in 1954 later produced a string of popular B's and a tenure at Warner Brothers yielded his trademark film, *The Rise and Fall of Legs Diamond*, plus a rogue's gallery for its' television division.

Stardom in Europe came in the form of fantasy heroes and James Bond clones. The Seventies were made up of low-budget independents, mob boss impersonations for the major networks and directing and producing independent films. A move behind the camera led to television production, where writer, director, producer and supervising producer were the cappers to his career.

Ray Danton was born in Queens, New York on September 19, 1931. He was the only son of Jack and Myrtle Caplan. His father was a haberdasher and he provided his family with a comfortable lifestyle during the Depression. The actor developed his trademark baritone when he was ten years old and started a career as a radio actor two years later after Nyla Mack, a producer for the NBC radio program *Let's Pretend*, heard him speaking to a group of other children during a public school assembly at P.S. 144 in Queens. Aside from the long-running children's show, *Let's Pretend*, his best known credit from this period is the juvenile quiz show, *Young Ideas*.

Like many aspiring actors from his time, Ray Danton did his time as a movie usher. His beat was the famed Radio City Music Hall. In 1947, Ray Danton graduated from Horace Mann Prep School and was accepted into Carnegie Tech. At night, he worked as a disc jockey and played semi-pro football on the weekends. He was enrolled at the school for two years but the curriculum bored him because he had learned most of the lessons from practical experience in radio and the Straw Hat Circuit. The faculty cited his irascible behavior as being a negative influence on the other students and asked him not to return in 1949. It didn't matter; by then, he had gained a foothold in the theater as a journeyman in summer stock productions.

Between 1947 and 1949, Danton worked as a stage manager and actor in summer productions of *Private Lives*, starring Tallulah Bankhead; *Happy Birthday*, starring Joan Blondell; *The Barretts of Wimpole Street*, with Susan Peters; and *Anna Lucasta*, starring Lizabeth Scott. Lady Sarah Churchill made her stage debut in a summer stock production during his apprenticeship, too.

Danton's journeyman's experience at the East Coast summer stock circuit at Oganaut, Princeton, Olney and other venues led him to be hired by Joshua Logan for his London production of *Mr. Roberts*. He was nineteen when he appeared as Wiley, a crewman, with Tyrone Power in the title role and Jackie Cooper as Ensign Pulver.

Letters written to Mary Morris, his acting coach at Carnegie Tech, during his London sojourn offer a glimpse into Ray Danton's personality. He was riding in a convertible, playing golf twice a week, and practicing gymnastics. Conducting himself as a cultured adult, he made adroit observations about the theatre world and life in general. The conqueror's line that exemplifies his arrogant triumph is that he "drank with the men and slept with the women." That included a J. Arthur Rank starlet.

After *Mr. Roberts* ended its run, Danton passed on an offer to star in a road show of *South Pacific* and a version of *A Streetcar Named Desire* produced by Laurence Olivier. He traveled to Paris, where he worked as a drummer in a night spot called The New Eve. The young actor was offered a role on Broadway when he received his draft notice. He opted for the infantry instead of becoming part of an entertainment unit, feeling that he did not "want to be another actor in khaki."

Ray Danton completed basic training at Ft. Benning, Georgia and served in Korea. Being an infantryman in such a rough terrain was not exactly an ideal situation and his many letters complained about the inclement weather. Sub-zero winters and sweltering summers were punctuated by tumultuous monsoons. Little did he realize how lucky he was because the Korean War started after he was transferred to Ft. Dix, New Jersey to finish his military obligation.

His service at the New Jersey military base was uneventful except for a broken leg that he suffered during a service football game. His

AP wire photo announcing the March 20 wedding of Julie Adams and Ray Danton. January 25, 1954, Associated Press.

recuperation included watching movies as a form of therapy. One film that he watched a dozen times starred Julie Adams. Little did he realize that one day he would not only star in a movie with her but would also become her husband.

Ray Danton received an honorable discharge after he recuperated from his football injury and returned to New York to act for three years on live television dramas. It was an appearance in an episode of the cop drama *Man behind the Badge* that earned him the attention of Aaron Rosenberg, a producer for Universal-International Pictures. The movie man met with the young actor in New York and persuaded him to fly to Hollywood for a screen test for a picture he was making, *Five Rivers to Cross*, later to become *Five Bridges to Cross*. As a result, the 22 year old stage and television actor was signed to a contract with Universal-International Pictures.

Ray Danton flew to Los Angeles and was met by Julie Adams, acting as an emissary for the studio. Adams was an established star, having started out in Lippert Westerns years before. Her Fifties' Universal-International credits include *Hollywood Story* ('51), *Bend of the River* ('52), *Francis Joins the WACS* ('54), *The Creature from the Black Lagoon* ('54), *The Looters* ('55), *The Private War of Major Benson* ('55), *Away All Boats* ('56) and *Slaughter on Tenth Avenue* ('57), among many others.

Julie Adams was one of the stars of *Five Bridges To Cross* (1955), the movie that Ray Danton was scheduled to make a screen test for. He got the part but eventually lost the role to Tony Curtis because the studio wanted a recognizable star instead of a newcomer. The slight was considered an insult to the actor's integrity and he considered returning to the East Coast but was dissuaded by Julie Adams. The upside to his disappointing start in Hollywood was that he dated and eventually wed Julie Adams. Their married life was showcased in fan magazines, a glimpse behind the scenes of another blissful Hollywood union. They were married for over twenty five years and became the parents of two sons, Steve and Mitchell.

Ray Danton arrived on a lot whose constellation included reigning stars, leftovers from better times and promising newcomers. Tony Curtis, Piper Laurie, Jeff Chandler, Audey Murphy and Francis the Talking Mule mixed with Abbott and Costello, James Stewart, Mickey Rooney and Fred MacMurray, who shared the sound stages with Rock Hudson, Mamie Van Doren, George Nader and an endless parade of others.

Universal-International was one of the many incarnations of the studio founded by Carl Laemmle in 1912. Financial crises forced Laemmle

George Nader (l) was an established contract player at Universal-International Pictures when Ray Danton (r) arrived on the lot. 1955, Universal Pictures Company, Inc.

to sell the studio in 1935. Ten years later, after the Deanna Durbin period, a merger with International Pictures forged a production schedule filled with Westerns, comedies, crime dramas and action adventures. Double bills had to be filled and Universal-International was the studio to do it.

Ray Danton made his film debut in *Chief Crazy Horse* in 1955, cast in the supporting role of the renegade Indian, Little Big Man. He considered it a routine western and earned his newcomer's dues when he broke his wrist during the filming of the movie. A wrist operation was needed and he wore a black glove to conceal his convalescing hand when he played Blackie in his next western feature, *The Spoilers*. During his maiden year in the movie business, he also made *The Looters* and was on loan out to MGM, where he made *I'll Cry Tomorrow*, for which he won the Golden Globe for Most Promising Newcomer. It was an honor he shared with Russ Tamblyn.

The Best Newcomer Award doubled as a road that was off the beaten track of stardom. It contains many powerful performances and is the achievement of a professional actor and director whose career touched every entertainment phase except the success it richly deserved. Obscurity often implies a lack of talent or insignificance but in the case of Ray Danton, it is a hidden gold mine of original performances from an alternate universe of a Hollywood that had ceased to exist.

Ray Danton's bid for Hollywood fame was through movie stardom. In 1955, he was one of the promising new faces at Universal-International and had his share of public appearances, magazine profiles

Ray Danton made his film debut at the renegade Indian, Little Big Man, in *Chief Crazy Horse*. 1954, Universal Pictures Company.

and fan clubs hungering for autographed glossies and apocryphal stories. The October, 1955 issue of Hollywood Stars featured him as part of the "Accent on Youth.. 12 Great Newcomers." The 12 Great Newcomers were Shirley MacLaine, Dick Davalos, Ben Cooper, Jayne Mansfield, Margia Dean, Shirley Jones, Ray Danton, Carol Ohmart, Dana Wynter, Roger Moore, Kathleen Case, and Perry Lopez.

Ray Danton's segment was titled "I've Changed My Mind about Hollywood."

"By nature I'm not a Mocambo or Ciro's boy", he is quoted as saying in the article. "My preferences run to little restaurants in our Valley neighborhood. We enjoy going to the movies, too, and my idea of real fun is going to the ranch."

The same profile has a byline to a rakish portrait of Ray Danton that reads, "This handsome and independent Broadwayite dreaded what would happen to him in glitter town but he's changed his tune."

On the opposite page, a snapshot shows a beaming Ray Danton and Julie Adams in their kitchen. He looks ebullient and wears an apron and holds a tray of food. She, too, is wearing an apron and is admiring the aroma of the tasty display. The photo captions reads, "Posing for fan layouts was a pet peeve of Ray's until Julie Adams helped him realize the fan books stir up interest in the stars among millions of movie fans."

Ray Danton was an actor who exemplified a particular Hollywood period even though he was not famous. He was a contract player during the demise of the studio system, a precarious time for the grooming of stars. He was also a free lance actor due to an outside working clause in his contracts. Like the big stars of his time, Ray Danton earned his share of press and publicity puff pieces announcing business deals, vacation plans, personal appearances, industry parties and movie and television contract signings. His name had its time in bold tintype, especially in the late 50's through the mid-60's: the Eisenhower-Camelot eras.

There were also press releases about his celebrity tennis tournaments. Ray Danton was considered one of the best tennis players in Hollywood and participated in tournaments and competitions well into the late 60's. The actor's marriage to Julie Adams made them a celebrity couple and they, too, generated their own favorable copy.

There was a time when the actor seemed ubiquitous because of his concurrent film, television and stage appearances.

Ray Danton's heyday was the Hollywood of slick hair, cigarette smoking, hard drinking and two-fisted negotiations. His sharp-edged

The role of David Tredman in *I'll Cry Tomorrow* earned Ray Danton the Golden Globe award for Best Newcomer. 1955, Screen Service Group.

baritone matched dark chiseled features, making him a natural for his roles as suave heroes or venal hustlers. He had the look of a sly fox and the smooth moves of a dancing thief. His confident attitude, serpentine movements, switchblade stare, and silver-tongued voice gave his characters a touch of menace and panache.

Although he is known primarily for his roles as hard-boiled tough guys, Ray Danton's identity is multi-layered. He has played heroic leads, romantic types and light comedic parts. But despite the charm, elegance, and humor of these roles, the dark side of Danton's persona is what stamped its imprimatur on his reputation. Often arrogant and cruel, his savage characters got what they wanted through avarice, deception and, sometimes, murder.

They had cutting edge personalities and were steely-eyed, icy nerved, smooth talking and fast moving. Sometimes, they were noble when the situation called for honor and personable when it was advantageous to be so. They could also be charming creeps and spineless weasels or manipulative sharpies and characters beyond redemption. They were men that women either loved or hated! The trouble is they could love the scoundrels and hate the heroes and that made for a confusing mélange with the romantic payoff being happiness or disaster.

Apparently, this was the case in real life, too. Ray Danton possessed the same cool, cocky and charismatic charm of his characters off screen. A general consensus among his contemporaries was that Ray Danton

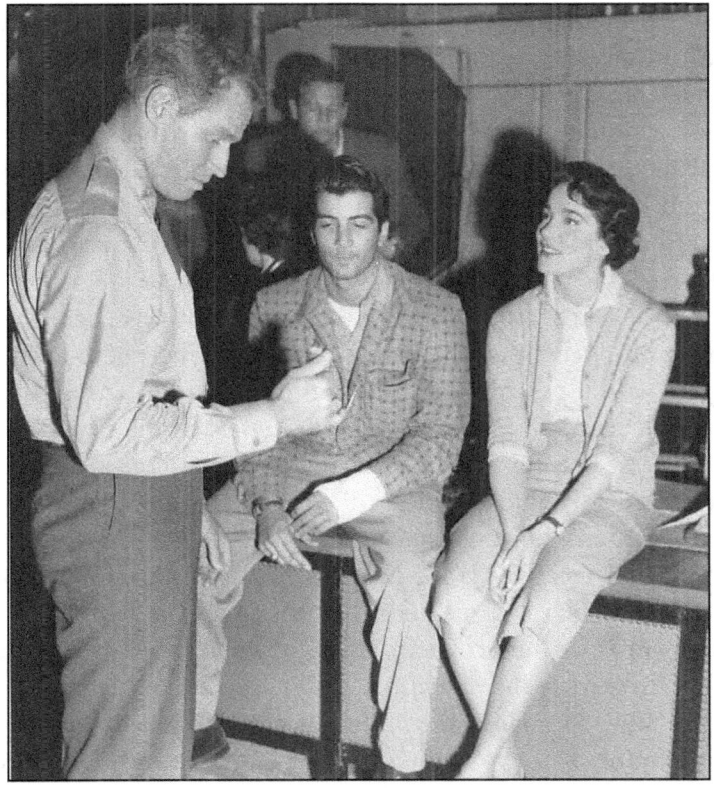

Ray Danton visits with wife Julie Adams and Charlton Heston on the set of *The Private War of Major Benson*. Danton sports a cast for a broken wrist suffered on the set of *Chief Crazy Horse*. 1955, Universal Pictures Company, Inc.

was an old school ladies' man that had no problem whatsoever attracting women; his trouble was alienating them because all he did was talk about himself. The Danton Ego is something that almost everyone who worked with him has agreed upon.

Ray Danton had a pointed style and straightforward manner that many people construed as assertive and egotistical (to say the least!). In an interview for the June, 1955 issue of Screen Stories (which featured a synopsis of *The Looters*), Ray Danton declared that he would like to win an Oscar before he was thirty. He did not consider himself arrogant, just ambitious and dedicated to his craft. It was something he said that should motivate other actors; if they didn't feel this way then why bother being in the business?

This take-no-prisoners attitude earned Ray Danton the reputation as being abrasive, self-assured and fiercely independent, not unlike his screen persona. Many of his friends and foes said that his assertive personality provided the basis for many bruised encounters, not only on a one-to-one level but with the studio production teams, too.

Ray Danton's insistent manner once caused him to be suspended by Universal-International when he refused to act in *Cult of the Cobra*. It was in his first year at the studio but he still defied the studio brass because he thought that the movie was beneath his talent. It was not unexpected considering his Golden Globe Best Newcomer award for *I'll Cry Tomorrow*.

He was also fired from Norman Taurog's *Fuzzy Pink Nightgown* when he told the producers that the audience wouldn't believe that the young kidnapper that he played would fall in love with his actress-victim, an older woman played by Jane Russell. He suggested that she be replaced with a younger actress. It was an arrogant move considering that the movie was being produced by Russ-Field, a production company owned by Jane Russell and her husband, Robert Waterfield. Ralph Meeker was hired to play his role. The trade papers announced that Ray Danton was replaced because he was considered too young for the part.

There are other humorous instances of the Danton ego, mainly with his facility for having his name inserted into some of his movies. In the *Beat Generation*, Stan Hess, the midnight rambler, jots down the address of his next victim. It is a house on Danton Street. He plays Oscar Wetzel, a mob enforcer, in *The Big Operator*. The killer sits in the gallery of a Senate Sub-Committee on labor corruption. The prosecutor asks crime kingpin Joe Braun (Mickey Rooney) about a house on Danton Drive. The second time he asks the question the camera pans across the gallery and Oscar Wetzel does a double take when the address is mentioned.

Ray Danton's European characters mention his name such in the conversation with a bound and gagged Pamela Tudor in the Italian espionage thriller, *You Only Die Once*. The most prominent use of the actor's name is in *Will Our Hero Find the World's Largest Diamond?* Jimmy Logan, the nerdish protagonist spy, enters a hotel lobby and hears Ray Danton being paged on the loudspeaker. An Arab bellman walks by carrying a placard with Ray Danton written on it and Jimmy Logan swerves in a Groucho-type of gait and is temporarily is distracted.

The self promotion continued into his directing period. In a Mike Hammer movie, technicians come out of the a recording studio and one of them has a question about a technical problem. His colleague answers, "Ask Ray Danton."

Ask Ray Danton, indeed, because the actor-director was an enigma. When you look at his career and compile a list of his best work, the result is a well-rounded collection of characters even though typecasting struck early and he was hard pressed to find a part outside of the menacing bone-crunching variety.

To look at a career from the other side of the shadows, track down means compiling a list of credits and matching them with sources that live off the beaten track of popular entertainment norms. There are film collectors whose appreciation of movies goes beyond search engine choices and top ten lists of commercial cyber-download chains. Their treasures are the movies that never made it to videotape or DVD and still exist on celluloid. In some collections, you will find 16mm prints of *The Looters* ('55), *Outside the Law* ('56) and *The Night Runner* ('57).

A Barcelona Lluvia de Estrellas gum card of Ray Danton illustrates the international influence of Hollywood. 1955, Editorial Bruguera, Barcelona.

During the 1950's, they were part of double bills and later found renewed life on 60's and 70's night owl television. Now, only film collectors and archivists know the place of these films in the Universal-International canon. Even to them, Ray Danton may have been an actor on the margins of the studio's lot. At least, they know and appreciate him, understanding how easy it was for a dark star like Danton to be overshadowed by the upbeat personalities of Tony Curtis, Rock Hudson, Rory Calhoun and Jeff Chandler.

The Rise and Fall of Legs Diamond exemplifies Ray Danton's explosive acting style. 1960, Warner Bros. Dist. Corp.

An initial search for Ray Danton produces his trademark film, *The Rise and Fall of Legs Diamond* ('60). The film's success is mainly due to Ray Danton's explosive performance but the movie's durability is due to its inclusion among Budd Boeticcher's best films, an ironic closure to his journeyman crime dramas as Oscar Boeticcher. It's the connection to Budd Boeticcher that gives the film its renewed periodic exposure.

Degree of connection is how to access Ray Danton; it is his relation to the stars and directors that he worked with that enables one to piece together his career. At first, such searches will turn up the perfunctory supporting roles in Warner Brothers films like *Onionhead* ('58), *The Ice Palace* ('60), *A Majority of One* ('62) and *The Chapman Report* ('62). An odd addition to the popular searches is the cult item, *Hannah, Queen of Vampires*, augmented by Ray Danton's direction in 1973.

To stop there is to dismiss Ray Danton as a marginal figure. Invisible status is the another irony of his career, an effect of bad timing. Ray Danton was a 50's contract player with a style and ego that were better suited for the screwball comedies of the 30's and the true blood *noirs* of the 40's. He was perfect for the suave Romeo roles, methodical anti-heroes and shady crime drama types of an earlier era.

Ray Danton had a chance to play these types in a few movies and plenty of television shows. The trouble is that a new method of acting had created a different type of anti-hero, a brooder with a tortured voice and a soul of anger. This style was exemplified by Marlon Brando, Montgomery Clift, and James Dean. After his arrival in Hollywood, Ray Danton collected the signatures of several re-located New York actors in a letter asking Elia Kazan to open a West Coast version of the Group Theatre but the innovative director declined the invitation.

By the early 60's, the old days went into suspended animation, ensuring oblivion as a career epitaph for all those who failed to achieve stardom during the eclipse of the studio system. Apropos of many contract players of his time, Ray Danton enjoyed renewed life on the late-night television movie circuit and prime time network shows of the late 60's and 70's. After that, it was a trek to Europe; it wasn't personal, that was the fate of his era of movie making and the Hollywood star system.

It is a major advantage for fans that Ray Danton augmented his film work with regular television appearances on many of the popular shows of his era. In over two decades, he acted in more than eighty television shows. It is the medium where Ray Danton gave some of his finest performances because he had more chances to play leading roles and to act in a variety of styles from to live drama to light comedy.

Ray Danton's film career has many notable performances but his mettle is tested by his television work. In the Fifties, he was an alternative to the corn-fed, beach-tanned, toothsome hero. During the Sixties, he was a retro-type of egotist going against the revolutionary spirit of the times. He ended his acting career in the Seventies offering parodies of the past as garish mop-topped hucksters and iron-fisted mob bosses.

His retinue of characters is impressive, even though they only exist in a shadow land that started with the 50's era of live television and ended with 80's cable productions helmed as a director. Collectors of vintage shows may recall appearances by Ray Danton just as well as T.V. buffs will

Ray Danton was well known and admired for his tennis game. He is pictured with fellow actors Robert Stack, Richard Anderson and Charlton Heston. AP, 1962.

list his credits as a director but it takes a career overview that focuses on what went on in between to really appreciate his unique style.

The final irony of Ray Danton's career is that many of the stars that once outshined him are now just as obscure in the world of the modern movie lover. Most black and white melodramas, Technicolor extravaganzas and television shows of yesteryear are negated by today's 3-D digital technology. There are the exceptions to the rule. Aside from a handful of actors that started in the old days and still have their mythology intact, few of yesterday's stars are getting the digital treatment. For the others, their careers exist piecemeal among the 16mm collectors, Eurocine lovers, devotees of 70's drive-in movies and television archivists.

Prime Time TV: The Golden Age

Live Television: The Early Days

Television gained ascendancy over radio during a transitional phase in America. It was 1950 and the post-war years had become The Cold War era and the specter of Communism redefined identity, manners and morals in America. This impacted the entertainment media as Senator Joseph McCarthy and his anti-Communist witch hunt affected Hollywood with a paranoia that was as devastating as the Senate's anti-trust suits a few years earlier.

The studio system was on its last legs and would continue to diminish during the decade. Declining revenue and public and official scrutiny hampered the creative and lucrative aspects of the film industry and the upstart medium of television took advantage of this by adapting many radio formats for visualization.

Anthologies, westerns, soap operas, situation comedies and crime dramas were grist for the mill during a period that has been dubbed The Golden Age of Television. Eventually, many of television's stars, directors, writers, and technical crews were migrants from the silver screen. Having been forced off the larger Hollywood canvas by a new generation of filmmakers, the old timers recycled their craft for television audiences. Because of this, the television dramas of the Fifties were like abridged movies.

The Golden Age appellation did not refer to television, in general, because the medium was frowned upon by culture mavens as being a general wasteland with vapid material serving as draws for sponsors. It was the sponsors who financed the shows and they often dictated the content, which meant that entries with the lowest common denominator were desired fare because the hucksters did not want their products to be associated with controversy.

The exception to the rule was the live anthology shows. They were produced and written by men and women who were conscious of the medium's power and they often battled with sponsors over censorship. The result may have been a mixed bag but much of the material was revolutionary and still holds up well today.

Before shows were filmed, they were broadcast live, making early television an electronic theater. This revolution was abetted by innovative producers like Fred Coe, who created one of the first and prestigious anthologies, *Philco-Goodyear Television Playhouse* and its variations. There were other giants, such as Martin Manulis, who invigorated *Climax* and *Danger* before launching the touchstone of live television, *Playhouse 90*. Other top-of-the line live broadcasts were *Studio One, Kraft Television Theatre* and *Robert Montgomery Presents*. The list seems endless.

Ray Danton entered the relatively new live television industry after his military discharge in 1951. His first role was a small part in the short-lived anthology series, *Starlight Theater*. In *An Act of God Notwithstanding*, the show's penultimate episode, he played Coles, one of the workers trapped in a power plant for two days as the technicians try to maintain electricity for a city during a blizzard. The subplot concerns a local doctor performing a Caesarian section on the wife of Ed Kennedy (Chester Morris), the foreman of the work crew.

The same year, the twenty year old actor appeared in two episodes of *Danger*, a live television anthology broadcast by CBS that lasted for five seasons. The stories were psychological dramas and murder mysteries with scripts supplied by writers that included Gore Vidal, Rod Serling, Paddy Chayefsky and Paul Monash. Other writers were the blacklisted Walter Bernstein and Abraham Polonsky, who wrote under pen names. Sidney Lumet, John Frankenheimer and Yul Brynner were some of the resident directors for the show. Two of the show's producers were Martin Ritt and William Dozier.

Each drama lasted twenty five minutes with five minutes of commercial time. It was a single camera setup broadcast by CBS. Besides being a proving ground for many actors, writers, directors and producers who eventually helped to shape their respective spheres, it showed a trail blazer in a different light before his ground breaking contribution to late night television. Steve Allen and Jayne Meadows appeared in two

A New York Times ad for *The Killer Scarf*. 1951, New York Times.

episodes of *Danger*. One was *Five Minutes to Die* (9/15/'53), written by Paul Monash. Allen wrote the second show, *Flamingo* (11/01/'53), about an Asian woman who falls in love with a dissolute musician.

The first episode that Ray Danton acted in was *The Killer Scarf* and starred Anne Bancroft when she used her original last name, Marno. *The Killer Scarf* is about Heidi (Anne Marno [Bancroft]), a young circus acrobat and the trials and tribulations of love and death. She is attracted to Carlo (Ray Danton), a virile animal trainer and this makes Fernandez (Gregory Morton), her guardian, jealous. He decides to prevent any budding romance by arranging for the trainer to be killed by one of his animals. He hopes to accomplish this by having a tiger become used to the trainer's scent by sniffing a scarf. The plan backfires when the acrobat wears the scarf as a good luck charm and walks too close to the tiger. She is attacked by the big cat and the guardian is killed when he tries to save her from the rampaging tiger.

The live show had an authentic circus ambience because it was filmed at Madison Square Garden where Ringling Brothers and Barnum and Bailey Circus was performing. Shots of circus performers and animals were intercut with the action of the drama. Stanley Prager also appeared as Irving, the hot dog vendor.

Ray Danton has a supporting part in *Marley's Ghost,* directed by Yul Brynner, who directed for the show until he signed to play the lead in *The King and I.* Despite its title, the episode had nothing to with *A Christmas Carol.* It told the story of a ghost writer (Rita Gam) to a famous author named Marley (Joseph Anthony). The ghost writer desires to step out of the shadows after ten years of being a ghost and the complications that ensue.

His next appearance was on the early innovative live half hour science-fiction show, *Out There,* which debuted the same year as *Tales of Tomorrow* and *Space Patrol.* The live program incorporated filmed special effects sequences in shows that were based on short stories written by premier science-fiction authors like Robert A. Heinlein, Ray Bradbury, Theodore Sturgeon, John D. McDonald, Murray Leinster, Frank Belknap Long and Milton Lesser. Some notable performers who appeared on the show were Rod Steiger, Kim Stanley, Leslie Nielson, Bethel Leslie, Robert Webber and Eileen Heckart.

The series appealed to adults and children but, despite its eclectic approach, failed to find a sponsor and folded after twelve episodes. It was surmised that its Sunday afternoon time slot contributed to the show's demise. There was speculation that the network was going to revive the program after its cancellation but it never came to fruition.

Ray Danton had a small part in the show's fourth episode, *Misfit,* adapted by Joseph A. Kramm from a Robert Heinlein short story. Danton played a member of the Earth Foreign Legion, an intergalactic squad whose latest mission is to shift the orbit of an asteroid so it can serve as space station and an emergency landing between Earth and Mars.

The play focuses on the angst of an astronaut who is a mathematical genius and can do computer-like computations in his head. The misfit is played by Robert Sylvester. Other actors in the cast are Wendell K. Phillips, Arthur Batanides, Jerry Paris, Gene Saks, and Eddie Hyans.

It was two years before Danton appeared on another live television anthology, *Kraft Theatre,* which was sponsored by the dairy company to sell its product, Cheese Whiz. It debuted in 1947 and ended its run in 1958. The show was similar to other anthologies of the time in that it presented adaptations of famous plays and novels along with presenting original productions. The show was resurrected as *Kraft Mystery Theater* in 1963 but was filmed and presented solely original works specifically written for the show.

To Live in Peace was adapted from the play by Giovacchino Forzano, an Italian playwright, librettist, stage director and film director. He was infamous for making propaganda films for Mussolini's National Fascist Party. Ironically, *To Live in Peace* is about a Utopia ruined by greed and ambition. The setting is a mountain village located near Siena, Italy in 1804. Don Geronimo is a priest who shepherds a flock of simple villagers who lead a peaceful life free from strife and ill-will.

This changes with the arrival of the French Army headed by a general. They are on a good will mission to seek help from the priest in locating a relative of Napoleon. He is needed to fill the vacancy of a high office in the French government. Their presence agitates the nobles and lawyers of the village and they become consumed with visions of power and grand delusions. Their chicanery, in turn, instills a greedy ambition among the villagers. Anne Bancroft stars in this comedy along with Florenz Ames, Doro Merande and Arnold Moss. Ray Danton plays a French corsair.

To Live in Peace has the distinction of being the first program broadcast in color. The night before the FCC gave the official go ahead for color broadcast, NBC televised this episode in what was then called 'compatible color.'

In 1954, Ray Danton signed a contract with Universal-International studios after he impressed Aaron Rosenberg, a producer for Universal-

Ray Danton (far left) played a French corsair in *To Live in Peace*, an NBC show that had the distinction of being the first television broadcast in color. 1951, J. Walter Thompson Agency.

International, with his performance in an episode of *Man behind the Badge*, a crime drama anthology hosted by Charles Bickford. He filmed two movies for the studio to be released the following year: *Chief Crazy Horse* and *The Looters*. Both roles featured Danton in the treacherous mode that would characterize him during his career.

In *Chief Crazy Horse*, Danton plays the renegade Indian, Little Big Man, a blood kinsman to Crazy Horse who is responsible for murdering the chief. It was *The Looters* that established the Danton persona. Pete Corder was a dashing, if bankrupt, bon vivant who becomes a murderous looter when he and the film's hero (portrayed by Rory Calhoun), attempt to rescue the survivors of a plane crash on Pike's Peak.

It was in March, 1955—a month before his movie debut in *Chief Crazy Horse*—that Ray Danton starred in *Hallmark Theater: The Pirate and the Lawyer*. The half hour show was a pre-cursor to the classic drama show sponsored by the greeting card company. Ray Danton portrayed Jean Lafitte, the New Orleans privateer who aided the colonies in the Battle of New Orleans.

Despite his assistance during the war, Governor Claiborne confiscated Lafitte's property. A distinguished lawyer named Edward Livingston took up Lafitte's case and argued on his behalf. The conflict is created because Livingston belongs to a family that had distinguished itself during the Revolutionary War. The resolution occurs when Livingston wins the case and Lafitte's citizenship is restored and he regains ownership of his confiscated property because of his valor in the Battle of New Orleans. Herbert Rudley played Edward Livingston, Douglas Dumbrille was Governor Claiborne and Andrew Duggan portrayed Andrew Jackson.

The month Ray Danton made his movie debut in *Chief Crazy Horse*, he had another starring role on television's *Lux Video Theatre*, a live drama show whose repertoire was mainly television adaptations of successful movies.

The series was a television adaptation of a successful radio program, Lux Radio Theater, which ran for 21 years. The CBS shows originated in 1950 from New York before moving to Hollywood two years later. It then became a one-hour show whose format was adapting popular films into abridged television shows. Like many anthology shows of the time, *Lux Video Theatre* has a series of host to introduce the episode and interview the performers. It broadcast its last show on September 25, 1959.

An Act of Murder was based on Universal-International's 1948 movie of the same name. The original film starred Frederic March, Florence Eldridge and Edmond O'Brien in the main roles. In the televised version, Thomas Mitchell, Ann Harding and Ray Danton played the leads. It is a story about euthanasia and the law.

Judge Cook (Thomas Mitchell) is a strict judge whose nickname is Old Man Maximum. He follows the letter of the law and shows no lenience towards defendants. His daughter loves public defender David Douglas (Ray Danton) who is at odds with his prospective father-in-law because of the way the judge has no sympathy for defendants. Cooke's understanding of the law changes drastically when he finds out that his wife, Cathy, (Ann Harding) has terminal brain cancer. He considers mercy killing but the consequences of a murder trial make him feel conflicted.

Ray Danton, Thomas Mitchell and Ann Harding starred in *An Act of Murder*, a television adaptation of the movie of the same name. 1955, J. Walter Thompson Agency.

Two months after starring in *The Pirate and The Lawyer*, Danton returned to *Hallmark Theater*. He had a supporting part in *The Promise*, the Greek legend of Damon and Pythias. The tale is a convoluted story about dedication and bravery that form the bonds of unbroken friendship. Marshall Thompson plays Pythias, who travels to Syracuse with his friend, Damon (Lamont Johnson). When Pythias is accused of sedition against the Greek tyrant Dionysius (Ian Keith) he asks Damon to take his place while he returns home to settle some personal matters.

Dionysius was intent on executing Damon because he believed that Pythias would not return. At the 11th hour, Pythias returns and explains to the tyrant that his ship was captured by pirates and he was thrown overboard. To keep his word, Pythias swam ashore and this courage and honesty warranted him and Damon a pardon from Dionysius, who retained both men as counselors to his court. Cathy Downs, Robert Brubaker and June Howard also appeared in the cast.

The Looters was released the same month as *The Promise* aired. It contained a powerful performance by Ray Danton, who all but steals the picture. Pete Corder remains one of the best performances of Danton's career, though one that helped to typecast him as a suave villain.

He resumed his television work with one more appearance on *Lux Video Theatre*, starring in *The Web*, another adaptation of a 1947 Universal-International movie. It is a taut murder mystery with twisted obsessions and double-crosses. In the movie, Andrew Colby (Vincent Price) is a tycoon who claims that he was threatened by Leopold Kroner (Fritz Leiber), a former employee of his company who was sentenced to five years in prison for embezzlement.

Kroner hires young attorney Bob Regan (Edmond O'Brien) as a bodyguard to protect him from Kroner. Regan shoots Kroner in self-defense when the ex-con shows up in Colby's hotel room. The bodyguard suspects that he was set-up because of his involvement with his employer's secretary-girlfriend, Noel Farady (Ella Raines).

In the television version, Raymond Burr plays the tycoon, Barton MacClane is the embezzler, Ray Danton portrays the attorney turned bodyguard and Arleen Whelan is the secretary-girlfriend. *The Web* was broadcast the same month that *The Spoilers* was released, along with a movie Danton made on loan out to MGM: *I'll Cry Tomorrow*.

In 1956, Ray Danton had his first starring role in *Outside the Law*, a gritty crime noir for his studio, Universal-International. He returned at the end of the year to appear in another telecast of *Lux Video Theatre* called *The Quick and the Dead*. He appears along with James Whitmore, Karen Steele and Keith Larsen in a western tale about paranoia and bad judgment. It deals with a wagon train of settlers who are being guided to their destination by a Sioux Indian. A gambler suspects that they will be betrayed by their guide and his suspicion breeds paranoia among his fellow travelers.

In 1957, Ray Danton starred in one more crime drama for Universal-International, *The Night Runner*, his last movie for Universal-International. His contract was renegotiated from a multi-picture deal to a yearly contract when it was mutually terminated. He appeared on stage with Don Taylor and Una Merkel in *Career*, performed at the La Jolla Playhouse and starred with Robert Ryan, John Ireland, Marilyn Erskine and Mary Astor in Jean Giradoux's *Tiger at the Gates* at the Sombrero Theatre in Phoenix, Arizona and the Ivar Theatre in Los Angeles. Ray Danton also found the time to star in *Happy Hunting* at the Sacramento Live Opera Theater during the summer.

Ray Danton returned to live television with *Studio 57: Always Open and Shut*. *Studio 57 (aka Heinz Studio 57)* was a rarity among early television anthologies because it was filmed. It was also broadcast by the short-lived DuMont Television Network, which lacked the large budgets of its rivals. As a result, its productions were modest and it could not rely on stunt casting, that is, the use of major film stars to attract viewers. A few of its performers did go on to become big stars, such as Paul Newman and Natalie Wood.

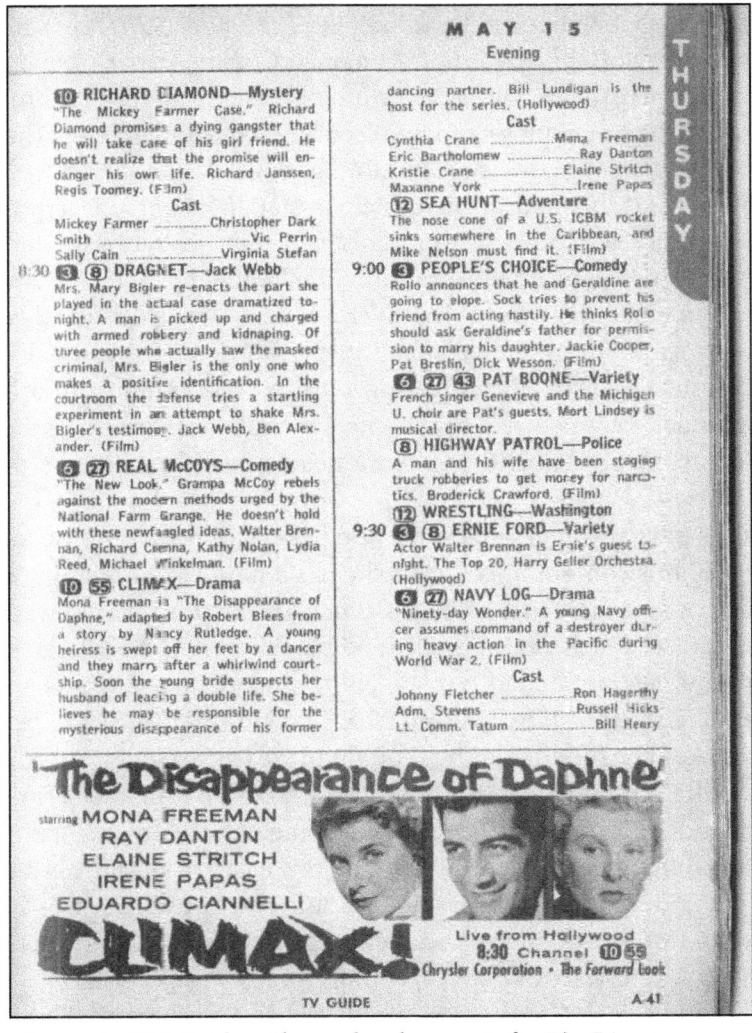

A page in T.V. Guide with an ad and synopsis for *The Disappearance of Daphne*. 1957, TV Guide.

In *Always Open and Shut*, Ray Danton and Scott Brady play two police officers who are partners whose prowl car covers a dangerous night beat. They are in love with the same woman and this adds tension to their partnership. The friends become enemies when the woman chooses Brady. Danton decks him and ends their friendship although they still remain partners.

It takes a crisis to find out if they can rise above personal feelings to fulfill their obligation to each other and the badges they wear. Scott Brady's character is caught in a deadly shootout when Danton risks his life to save him and heal the wounds to rise above the negative emotions.

Ray Danton continued to do live television and appeared in two episodes of *Climax!*, a popular live drama anthology: *The Sound of the Moon* and *The Disappearance of Daphne*. *Climax!* (renamed *Climax Mystery Theater*) was an early pioneer of color television technology. The episodes were broadcast in color but they were preserved on black and white kinescopes. The show originally had a solo host, Willian Lundigan, who later shared his duties with Mary Costa. It had an inauspicious start before pioneer producer Martin Manulis was brought in to bolster the show's ratings. One of his assets was using neophyte director John Frankenheimer.

In *Sound of the Moon*, Jan (Vera Miles) is a steel-willed airline stewardess who has handled many in-flight crises. A personal matter becomes unbearable for her, creating a sense of isolation from others as she continues her intensive flight into psychological terror. It happens when a passenger almost dies from a heart attack because she did not hear his cries for help.

Jan is partially deaf, a fact that she has concealed from the airlines. Her problem is compounded when she has a hard time accepting advice from three passengers who try to assist her. The doctor (Royal Dano) who saves the heart attack victim is curt and perfunctory in his diagnosis. An operation is recommended but she is too impatient and wants a short-term cure. His suggestion of using a hearing aid upsets her and personal vanity makes her shudder at the thought of wearing one.

It is the kind philosophical humor of Jazzman (Hoagy Carmichael) and his sideman (Ray Danton) that change the woman's life. Jan is especially emboldened after the sideman reveals to her that he is partially deaf. She is dumbfounded that he can still play music. It gives her the courage to face her dilemma and seek a solution, even if it means giving up her job as a stewardess.

There is a lot of tension to the drama, mainly due to Vera Miles' portrayal of anxiety-ridden stewardess. Hoagy Carmichael lends his easy going charm to his role of Jazzman, as does Ray Danton as his sideman. Royal Danc delivers an able portrait of the doctor who is on the spot, if not in the house. Buzz Kulik directed from a script by Irwin and Gwen Gielgud.

In *The Disappearance of Daphne*, Cynthia Crane (Mona Freeman) is a young heiress who is courted and swept off her feet by Eric Bartholomew (Ray Danton), a dancer. They become involved in a whirlwind romance that ends in marriage. Time passes and Cynthia begins to suspect her new husband of leading a double life. Before long, she believes that he may have been responsible for the mysterious disappearance of his former dance partner, Daphne.

Everybody wonders about what happened to Daphne once the question of her existence is brought up. Eric Bartholomew-the resolute rake replete with a mustache and goatee-is of a suspicious nature and this, in turn, makes everyone unnerved. hey begin to suspect each other until they focus their accusations at him.

Elaine Stritch plays the rich girl's sister and she is strong and straightforward in her suspicion about her new brother-in-law but it turns out that Irene Leleku-Papas (Irene Pappas), the former flame turned revenge queen, is the one who-done-it! Eduardo Cianelli and Jenny Hecht also star in the drama.

Ray Danton had the opportunity to act on one of the prestigious anthologies, *Studio One*. The CBS show ran from 1948 to 1958 and was always in Emmy contention from 1950 to 1958. It aired 466 shows, some of which were made into movies, like *1984, Twelve Angry Men*, and *Dino*. *Studio One* (and its variant titles) set a high bar for anthology show and was a precursor to *Playhouse 90*.

He starred with Amanda Blake and Barry Sullivan in *Tide of Corruption*. Barry Sullivan plays Edward Roberts, a young investigator for a Senate committee on corruption. He plans to make a name for himself by investigating the rackets empire of notorious gangster, Mr. Antony, played by Murvyn Vye.

The gangster counterpunches by digging into Roberts' past. He is rewarded with information regarding Roberts' mother, who once accepted help from a crooked politician. Antony uses this information to blackmail Roberts in order to derail the Senate investigation. Amanda Blake and Patricia Neal also starred in this drama, along with Ray Danton, who had a supporting role.

FROM LIVE DRAMAS TO VIDEOTAPE

Ray Danton was versatile and acted in a variety of styles and formats. Two examples of these divergent styles were two different live format shows that Danton appeared on in 1957. *Matinee Theater: Eye of the Storm* was an episode of a daily afternoon soap opera and *Playhouse 90: The Death of Manolete* was a bullfighter drama that was part of a celebrated weekly anthology series that boasted fine direction, writing and acting.

Matinee Theater was a live hour long daily afternoon soap opera created and produced by Albert McCleery. *Eye of the Storm* opens on a sweltering summer night in the country when Annie (Gloria Talbot) arrives at her sister Stella's (Marian Seldes) farm with her baby in tow. Stella is a bitter, hawkish spinster who resents Annie but allows her to stay because of the infant. The older sister is harsh because she lost Ben (Ray Danton), her beau, to Annie and was left to care for their senile father.

Despite Ben's boorish personality, Stella still believes that he is the ideal man. It is a fantasy that she clings to as her world fell apart-Maw is dead and Paw (William H. Vedder) is senile. Her only company is Lonnie (Dick Gardner), the happy-go-lucky ranch hand. The night of Annie's arrival, Lonnie takes her to a movie. On the way to town, they stop in a field, where she tells him the reason that she left home was her husband is a drinker and a wife-beater.

Back at the farm, Paw is asleep in his rocking chair and Stella is napping on the porch, her head resting on a column. Ben arrives, singing a carefree hiking song while clenching a cigar between his teeth. Dressed in a hound's tooth jacket with wide shoulders, he is a back wood's Romeo brimming with confidence. Stella awakes and acts as if she is still dreaming when she sees her former beau standing before her.

The rugged ne'er-do-well sweet talks Stella into taking off with him. He cons her into believing that he really loves her and that his marriage to Annie is a mistake. Stella tries to resist his advances but desperately wants to believe him because she still desires him. She realizes his con when they stop at a motel and he makes a slip of the tongue and tells her that he is doing this to provoke Annie.

Stella, distraught and irrational, returns to the farm and takes off into the woods with the baby. Annie and Lonnie return to the farm and find out that the baby is missing. Annie hears from Paw that Ben has arrived and suspects that he took the baby. Ben returns and, before long, he and

Annie have made up, much to Lonnie's chagrin. A brief confrontation between Ben and the ranch hand ends when the sheriff intervenes.

They are worried about the baby, whom they believe was kidnapped by a distraught Stella. Lonnie finds Stella and the baby in the woods. She confesses that, by taking the infant, she pretended that she was Ben's wife. She trumps Annie and Ben by planting doubts in their minds about possible infidelity on both their parts. Annie will never know whether Ben and Stella slept together at the hotel and Ben will never know whether Lonnie and Annie consummated their desire for each other in the field. The carefree Annie and Ben are crestfallen. A delirious Stella is ecstatic about her triumph.

"You brought it on yourselves", she tells the mercurial couple.

A Tennessee Williams wannabe on a late afternoon soap opera is an apt description of this teleplay. It's not that the principals-Marian Seldes, Gloria Talbott and Ray Danton-are bad; they bring their characters to vivid life in spite of some of the drama's heavy-handedness. It's just that they are watered down versions of the dysfunctional leads that are so often the focus of Williams' plays. There is some expertise to the writing because of the twist ending. The play could stand on its own if it wasn't compared to Tennessee Williams. It was the late fifties and it fit in with the "dysfunctional bucolic family" of the daily live soap opera conundrum.

Marian Seldes is fine as a woman drained of her life force. One doesn't appreciate her performance until the end, when she emerges from her room, refreshed and dressed in a polka-dotted dress. It is then that we realize how far she has fallen. At first, we suspect that she lost Ben because she is drab. We now know that this isn't the case.

Gloria Talbott is flirtatious as the younger sister Annie. She initially appears as a young innocent wronged by her overbearing husband. It isn't until the end of the play that we realize that she is an instigator. She plays the innocent to lure Lonnie into a false sense of infatuation. By the play's end, she has little regard for Lonnie's hurt feelings.

Ray Danton stands out as the rake, Ben. He is the epitome of the country Romeo, who is swift with a line, his fists, and his charm. We realize that his sensual qualities short-circuit the women who fall in love with him. He is the classic bad man who attracts "nice girls." He would return to Matinee Theater for *Button, Button*, a tense drama about the threat of nuclear annihilation.

Playhouse 90 was a watershed series that raised the standard for live dramas with the scope of its subject matter, breadth of its productions and the quality of talent in front of and behind the cameras. Ironically, its ambitious compass also predicated the demise of live television as the development of videotape enabled the shows to be broadcast to the West Coast without losing any technical quality because of inferior Kinescope process.

The show was grand in every way possible: its' duration was ninety minutes; it had big-time Hollywood stars performing; exorbitant pay scales for writers, directors and performers; and the ability to deal with mature subject matter in the way a novel or a play would. The program was an antidote to the bland network offerings that were merely vehicles for sponsors to hawk their goods.

Playhouse 90 produced 134 programs, many of them lost; however, those that remain include classic stories, some of which were made into equally powerful motion pictures. *Requiem for a Heavyweight, The Comedian, Days of Wine and Roses, The Miracle Worker*, and *Judgment at Nuremburg* are prime examples. Some of the top notch directors who honed their craft on the show are John Frankenheimer, George Roy Hill, Fieldler Cook, Delbert Mann, Robert Mulligan and Sidney Lumet.

The most successful program of its maiden season was *Requiem for a Heavyweight*, written by Rod Serling and directed by Ralph Nelson. It starred Jack Palance as 'Mountain' McClintock, an over-the-hill boxer who is exploited by Maish Rennick (Keenan Wynn), his unscrupulous manager and loved by the sensitive Grace Carney (Kim Hunter), a caring woman who works at an employment agency.

The episode won three Emmy Awards for Best Program, Best Acting, Best Writing, and Best Directing. *Playhouse 90* also garnered an Emmy for Best New Program. It was an auspicious start for this groundbreaking series.

It was the original intention of producer Martin Manulis to open the second season with, *A Town has Turned to Dust*, written by Rod Serling. Difficulties arose with the sponsor's objections to plot elements. Creative differences and client's revenues were the basis of much antagonism in a world where artistry and economics formed a strange and symbiotic partnership. Compromise was often the answer but, in the case of the second season's opener, there was also another factor to be considered: The General Electric's Theatre's plans to broadcast television's first bullfighting drama, *Cornada*, starring Tony Curtis. It was a filmed show already in the can and scheduled for broadcast.

One of *Playhouse 90's* aspirations was to push the envelope on forbidden material in an attempt to broaden American sensibilities.

Bullfighting was a prohibited subject because of the sport's brutal nature. Not to be outdone by a rival network, Martin Manulis gave the green light on the story of Manuel Rodriguez Manolete, a legendary bullfighter who died in the ring on August 28, 1947. The source material was to be *The Day Manolete was Killed*, a narrative album written by Barnaby Conrad, a bullfighting enthusiast.

The Death of Manolete is a live drama opens with the funeral of the greatest bullfighter of modern times-Manolete. Using pre-recorded footage of thronging crowds, the director cuts back and forth between the tape and the live action. The narrator tells the audience that they are witnessing a homage to a fallen hero. He recounts how the great Manolete was killed in an obscure arena. The bull sacrificed him to create a great memory. The scene dissolves to the beginning of Manolete's rise.

In a bar lined with the death masks of toreadors, Manolete sits at a table with Jose (Nehemiah Persoff), his manager. He is told that, one day he will be the reigning bullfighter. The young matador is self-effacing. He cannot believe that he will surpass the great Marquez. His hero-worship is reflected in his admiring comments on the bullfighter's latest fight.

Antonio (Ray Danton) and his manager, Peres (Robert Middleton) sit in a bar lined with the death masks of famous toreadors in *The Death of Manolete*. 1957, CBS (Columbia Broadcasting System).

Manolete's strength is that he can conquer fear itself! He illustrates this with his mastery over the bull. His style ignites the crowd. Manolete is now the best of his field and has become a celebrity. Exuberant crowds chant, "MAN-O-LET-E!, and carry him on their shoulders. In two years, he has fought 372 bulls.

The toll of success and public adulation was uncertainty and poor eyesight; the responsibility of maintaining his legend was persistence in fighting the bulls. Even the pleas of Augustias (Esther Manicotti), his mother, and Tani (Suzy Parker), his mistress, fall on deaf ears. Manolete's last fight is the reversal of his first one. Antonito (Ray Danton)—the new rival to Manolete's throne—does such an extraordinary job of handling the bull that he is presented with its ears as a prize. The crowd is ecstatic. Manolete knows that he will have to outdo Antonito. Jose tells him that he has nothing to prove.

Spain's greatest bullfighter performs the best fight of his career. The crowd rewards with an adulation that is deafening. It is his turn to kill the bull. As he taunts the bull, there is a miscue and he is gored.

On his deathbed, Manolete asks Jose if the bull died. Jose replies that it has died and Manolete was awarded the ears, the tail, and every other part of the bull as a prize. The bullfighter, blind and numb, sits up and declares that he can't feel anything. He drops to his bed. Manolete is dead and has become a legend.

The distraught manager leaves the room, brushes passed a troubled Antonito, and repeats, "We kept asking for more and more and more and…"

The narrator repeats his lines from the opening to remind the audience that Manolete was the quintessence of manhood. In death be became a legend and a god. The last shot is the tomb of Manolete. It is a monument to individual courage.

Director John Frankenheimer learned his art and craft directing live dramas like *The Death of Manolete*. It is a skillful production that incorporates filmed bits. Nothing lags, as was one of the demands of live drama. He gets what he can out of his actors and actresses.

Jack Palance was known for his tortured characters. Manolete is one of them. Although, self-effacing, he is burdened by life in the arena. For him, it is an escape from poverty and a way to achieve pride. Still, he is a tormented soul.

Nehemiah Persoff delivers an excellent performance as Manolete's manager. He is there for the whole ride and beyond it. Persoff often gave emotional and heartfelt performances. He is true to his style in this television drama.

Robert Middleton (as Perea, Antonito's manager) and Suzy Parker perform what is expected of them. They have supporting roles and do what they can with their limited stage time. Ray Danton has a small role as Antonito. He is a face in the bar until he emerges from the shadows to become the premier bullfighter. His look of anguish over the death of Manolete momentarily fills the screen towards the end of the teleplay. That is the extent of his acting. His bullfighting is part of the filmed bits that punctuate this bullfighting drama.

John Frankenheimer imbues his story with a melancholy light. His characters are people made from blood and sand. Their only hope of eternal life is immortality in the ring. An earthly monument and the choice parts of the bull are the rewards of a chosen few. Manolete ranks among the elite. Death in the ring gave him eternal life.

Unfortunately, the show was trounced by everyone, from the critics to the show's participants. Critics were quick to pan Jack Palance's tentative interpretation of a legend who emboldened the ethics of machismo. Oddly enough, that was Palance's criticism after he watched the West Coast kinescope version of the play. He regretted emphasizing the human side of the man and believed that he was wrong to show Manolete's inner torment and insecurities. He accepted blame for his miscue, something that John Frankenheimer said that he also bore responsibility for.

The other points of concern were miscues and technical errors, such as the shadow of the boom mike on the actors and the scenery or the sound of the camera dolly moving in some scenes. This is a shame because of John Frankenheimer's painstaking method of working. The director had cues for 110 film inserts, lined up 1,000 different camera shotand had seven cameras at his command at a time when four cameras were the standard.[1]

The harshest criticism was reserved for Suzy Parker, who was a super model before the term was coined. Ms. Parker was referred to as "the most photographed woman in the world" at the time and it was natural for her to try to become a film star. Her previous movie roles were limited to a line of dialogue and this was the first part that gave her a chance to emote. She never achieved her dream of being a screen star.

Ethel Winant, the casting director and unofficial producer (John Houseman's phrase), said that she flubbed when she cast Suzy Parker but her big regret is that it may have ruined any chance that the budding actress would have had to become a movie star. It was not only because of the model's flat performance but featuring an actress groomed for movie stardom in a television role was often seen as a kiss of death. [2]

The logic behind this thinking was that the audience would not pay to see a performer in a movie when they could see the same person on television for free. Pat Boone and Troy Donahue were perfect examples of this. Their promising film careers were cut short by successful television shows. The one notable exception to the rule is James Garner, who achieved success in both mediums and moved effortlessly between the two with regularity.

Towards the end of the Fifties, filmed dramas began to replace live performances. This was true for anthologies as well as drama shows that had a single theme and regular stars each week. Ray Danton had the opportunity to have his own television series when he filmed the pilot for *The Big Time*. The show was to be produced by Irving Brecher, who helmed the popular *People's Choice* starring Jackie Cooper, Patricia Breslin and Cleo the dog. Brecher was known for writing and directing his shows along with producing them. Unfortunately, *The Big Time* did not make the network schedule.

Ray Danton followed *The Big Time* with a starring role in *The Millionaire: The Eric Lodek Story*. The series centered on the benevolence of John Beresford Tipton, a multi-billionaire who lives on a 60,000 acres estate. He has an odd habit of giving away tax-free checks of a million dollars to complete strangers. He does this through his executive secretary, Michael Anthony (Marvin Miller).

Erik Lodek (Stephan Bekassy) is a Holocaust survivor who hits the jackpot when Michael Anthony visits him with the millionaire's blessing. The only condition is that he never discloses the benefactor or the amount of the check; not even to his wife and children. Lodek replies that he is single and childless-his family perished in a concentration camp during World War II.

The timid man with the weak heart is excited by his sudden found fortune. He will use part of it for a heart operation. The remainder will be used to establish a fund to help the impoverished children of the world. During a night drive, Lodek suffers a fatal heart attack.

Escaped convict, Ben Slade (Ray Danton), finds the dead man in his parked car by the side of the road. Slade's search of Lodek's body yields an identification card, a last will and testament claiming no relatives, and the check for a million dollars. The quick-thinking convict removes the wire-rim glasses from Lodek's face and wears them. He looks in the car's mirror and realizes that he will have to grey his temples if he is to impersonate Lodek.

Slade dresses in Lodek's clothes and places the dead body in his own car. He releases the brakes and pushes the car over a cliff. It crashes into the ravine and bursts into flames. An unrepentant Slade bids his farewell to his benefactor: "So long, Santa Claus."

Life as Eric Lodek is good for Ben Slade. It is a smooth run until he vacations in Mexico and meets Marika Franze (Chana Eden), a woman from Lodek's past. She is part of a family who was rescued by Lodek during the war. He is a hero to Marika because of her father's tales. Her father, who died years earlier, owned the hotel where Slade is staying. With no one there to expose him, Slade continues his charade as Lodek. The hero-worshipping young woman becomes attracted to him. Slade doesn't discourage Marika's advances.

One day, at poolside, she rubs tanning oil on his body. Marika conceals her shock when she rubs his arms and doesn't see a concentration camp number. The real Erik Lodek would have one because he was interned at the same camp as her father. She plays along with him until she has a chance to expose him.

Slade threatens her when he is confronted with her knowledge. He tells her that he can't allow her to live because she knows too much. They fight and he pulls a gun on her. She is saved when the door is forced open and the house detective shoots the gun out of his hand. A defeated Slade sits on the floor by the vanity chest. He is bewildered by the irony of his impersonation.

"I didn't kill him but nobody will believe me. I had it made-all the money in the world. I may hang for killing a man I never saw until after he was dead."

He pours himself a glass of champagne and makes a toast: "To freedom."

The Eric Lodek Story is another of *The Millionaire's* morality plays where irony is the author and the denouement is sour grapes. It is fitting that someone who has the arrogance to impersonate a Holocaust survivor should be condemned to death for his bold conceit. Ben Slade may have parlayed his roadside fortune into good times under the sun but it all ended in a self-imposed death sentence. A heart attack may have killed Eric Lodek but a shove over the cliff made it murder.

Ray Danton is a natural as the supercilious criminal turned adventurer. It is a pleasant irony that he should run into the benefactor of his good fortune. That is what spells doom for him-the humanitarian side of Lodek is what brings him down. The last shot of him toasting freedom is priceless. He has the look of a man poisoned by excess.

It's as if the Devil cast the sentence on Slade himself.

Ray Danton ended 1958 by signing a contract with Warner Brothers. He made his Warners' television debut as a Black Bart on the popular western, *Sugarfoot: Bunch Quitter*, starring Will Hutchins. The same year, Danton created some of his best early western characterizations in *Wagon Train: The Monte Britton Story*, *Bronco: Quest of the Thirty Dead* and *Yancy Derringer: An Ace Called Spade*.

A suspected deserter is the only hope for a wagon train stranded in the desert. The faded colors of a renegade colonel are a red flag to one of his former troops. A fast draw and an imposing bedside manner betray a legendary duelist. Monte Britton, Colonel Magrider and Stuart Spade are studies in the evolution of heroism into villainy.

Loretta Young was one of the many Hollywood screen stars who hosted an anthology series. One summer, her replacement show was *Decision* and seven of the shows aired were pilots for proposed series. *The Virginian* (James Drury), *The Tall Man* (Michael Rennie), *Indemnity* (Richard Kiley), *Stand and Deliver* (Louis Hayward), *Man Against Crime* (Darren McGavin), *Adventures of Mike Shayne* (Mark Stevens) and *Danger Game* (Ray Danton).

Long before Ray Danton emigrated to Europe to become part of the James Bond craze, he played a secret agent in *Danger Game* ('58), an unsuccessful pilot. In it, Danton plays Stagg, a U.S. undercover agent posing as a nightclub entertainer in the Far East. His mission is to covertly protect a missile expert who is visiting the region. There is an assassination plot on the expert's life and Danton pulls out all stops to prevent enemy agents from succeeding in their mission.

Ray Danton played secret agents –Stagg and Ralph Drake-in a television pilot and a cold war anthology series.

The next year he would play another secret agent in *Behind Closed Doors*. The show was an espionage anthology with a Cold War spy vs. spy theme. The episodes were based on real case files taken from the military intelligence case files. Bruce Gordon played Commander Matson, the host-narrator of the show. The real Commander Matson appeared in some of the show' episodes.

In *The Meeting*, U.S. spies learn that a new chief of the U.S.S.R. secret police has been appointed. Agent Ralph Drake (Ray Danton) goes to Austria to meet with Western agents from six Iron Curtain countries to find out more about the change and what it means to foreign intrigue.

They are Vilmas Kranitz (David Opatoshu), Zina (Virginia Gregg), Eliska Hurban (Judith Braun), Overbeck (Robert Warwick), Branka (Booth Colman) and Anton (Wolfe Barzell). Drake's rendezvous requires him to give the friendly spies information about Soviet agents that have infiltrated their ranks. He also has to collect their intelligence reports about secret plans the Soviets may have to turn the tide of the Cold War in their favor.

There is a double agent among them and he begins to methodically murder the agents. Four agents are killed before Drake uncovers the name of the Soviet agent from one of the intelligence reports of a slain spy. It is Vilmas Kranitz and he meets an untimely death in the Bavarian Alps after an unsuccessful shootout with Ralph Drake.

John Peyser has directed a taut thriller based on a teleplay by Robert C. Dennis. Most of the action is along the lines of a murder-mystery but this has always been a dependable angle in the plot development of espionage thrillers. Ray Danton was one of the first actors to portray a spy in a Cold War themed drama. The most notable example is Barry Nelson, who played Jimmy (James) Bond in a *Climax* production of *Casino Royale*, a pilot for a proposed series about Bond.

Ray Danton ended the decade with a part in another pilot, *Desilu Playhouse: Chez Rouge* ('58), with Janis Paige and Harry Guardino. It is a variation on the South American café with the international clientele a la Rick's in *Casablanca*. Paige plays the proprietress, a woman still entangled with a bothersome ex-husband.

Canal pilot Paul Conrad (Harry Guardino) is in love with the proprietress of a Panama night club, a woman known as the Redhead. But she has had bad luck with a previous marriage and is determined not to make another mistake. Unexpectedly, the Redhead's ex-husband Robert Mason (Ray Danton), who has been fighting with revolutionaries on a nearby island, turns up in Panama.

Robert Mason (Ray Danton), the revolutionary, seeks funds from his ex-wife (Janis Paige), who reluctantly aids him. 1959, Desilu Productions.

He needs money to finance the revolution and seeks financial assistance from his ex-wife. Danton is in good form as the island revolutionary. He cuts both ways with his idealism and hypocrisy. Ultimately, his biggest challenge is overcoming the influence of the canal pilot, an anarchic loner whose command of the seas secures him a greater freedom than anything Mason can win with a revolution.

Soon, the Redhead becomes confused about the men in her life and has to make a decision about choosing between the past and the future. Janis Paige, as the Redhead, sings "A Brand New Man."

GYPSIES, SOLDIERS, CARD SHARPS AND DUELISTS

As popular as big screen westerns may have been in the Fifties, the movies could not match the popularity of the genre on television. Western shows were among the most popular programmers during the 1950's. Eight out of the top ten shows of the 1958-1959 season were westerns. *The Lone Ranger, Hopalong Cassidy, The Cisco Kid* were among the many heroes who rode the West to right wrongs and set a moral standard for America's youth.

Given Ray Danton's celluloid reputation as a hard-boiled urban tough guy, it may be hard to believe that he also acted with equal effectiveness in westerns. It took the small screen to allow Danton a wider scope in his western characterizations. The tube's western craze phase provided plenty of opportunities to create interesting characters.

Ray Danton proved the point at Warner Brothers and backed it up with a powerful assortment of characters during the salad days of westerns, when shows like *Gunsmoke, Bonanza, Bat Masterson* and *Wagon Train* entertained America with stories about the old West.

One of the early popular western series was *Bat Masterson*, starring Gene Barry as the debonair and frontier-tough fashion plate. Only Jock Mahoney's *Yancy Derringer* rivaled him for fashion and grace. In the old West, these were unique traits, considering the raucous tempo of the times. The television series was loosely based on the memoirs of the real Bat Masterson.

In *The Romany Knives*, Bat Masterson saves Grasia (Frank Silvera), a gypsy king, from being shot in a street brawl with a rancher. The grateful gypsy takes Bat to his camp, where he is given the cold shoulder, especially from Antonio (Ray Danton), the leader-in-waiting.

Inside the gypsy king's tent, Bat is impressed by the opulent living quarters. The tent is decorated with expensive art objects taken from the world over. They drink wine from a California monastery in sterling silver goblets. Bat is told that he can select anything as a gift for saving the king's life. The dandy refuses to accept a gift because he says it's unnecessary. The king calls a raven-haired beauty named Leda (Chana O'Brien).

"You have a true eye for beauty", he tells Bat. "Leda puts to shame all the precious jewels of the world. Ah? If this is what you want, you can have it."

Antonio is enraged that the chief should give away Leda and challenges the old man's authority. The king is derisive of Antonio's boldness and states that his word is final and that the matter is ended.

Gene Barry played the debonair Bat Masterson in one of many hit series he had on television. 1958, ZIV Television Programs.

"That is not the end for me!", declares the defiant Antonio.

The king doesn't see things as being so complicated even though he is sworn by honor to keep his word to Bat Masterson. He has a proviso-"As a man of honor, I cannot go back on my word. I've given her to Masterson. She belongs to him. You have no honor. You made no contract."

Antonio is free to do what he wants and threatens to kill Bat. Although Bat Masterson is an erudite gentleman he is also a swift thinker and can match wits with a robust and demanding thief like Antonio. The gypsy is not a jilted suitor, but is a conniver who realizes that Leda is a heiress. He discovered that the day she was found as a baby, the only survivor of a stagecoach massacre. Her papers stated that she will inherit a fortune on her twenty first birthday. This is the cause of Antonio's ire.

Bat Masterson's cool and collected manner counter-balances Antonio's passionate and demanding behavior. That is why the vengeful gypsy is defeated by Masterson when he leaves Antonio and the anxious gypsy clan on a train platform as they watch with bemused admiration as a disguised Leda makes her getaway.

Antonio's passionate fire sets him up for laughs but the same cannot be said for Monty Britton. He is a loner who was once a leader of men and his shame was undeserved. That is why he suffers in silence. It is the code of the officer.

The Cavalry occupies a special place in the lore of the American West. Keepers of law and order that tamed the wild frontier, the Cavalry provided the material for endless tales of valor and shame. Heroism and cowardice are two frontier themes that never lose their edge. Monte Britton is branded with the stigma of cowardice despite being a war weary hero.

Ray Danton first appeared on *Wagon Train* in 1958, starring in an episode called *The Monte Britton Story*. The popular show enjoyed a long lifespan, starting out as an hour long black and white program and ending up as a ninety minute show shot in color. Ward Bond starred as Maj. Adams, the original wagon master, during the black and white years. John McIntire replaced Bond when he died and played Chris Hale when the show was revamped for its remaining tenure. Throughout its run, *Wagon Train* told stories that centered around an individual with a cross to bear or an interesting story to tell. The drama was created by the tension the star caused to the wagon train settlers.

In *The Monte Britton Story*, the wagon train is stranded in the desert. They are rationing their water and are at the point where bickering and bad blood is brewing.

Wagon Master Adams is a seasoned vet still burdened by the need to make decisions and he quells the disturbances.

Monty Britton, a stern loner, is sure there isn't any water ahead of the wagon train. If there was any water, the scout would have returned

Antonio swears revenge on Bat Masterson when the western dandy absconds with the grown-up foundling worth her weight in gold. 1958, ZIV Television Programs.

by now. The major asks him how he came to that conclusion. Britton tells him that he's seen maps. The major tells him that only surveyors and soldiers know how to read maps.

"I picked you for a soldier the first time I laid eyes on you", says the major.

Monty Britton's manner gives him away as a military man. He even tutored one of the boys in drill and ceremonies. Although he claims to be a failed farmer, general opinion is that he is a deserter.

Redmond (Claude Akins), one of the train, tells the major that he believes that Britton is a deserter because that's the only reason a man would deny ever having been in the army. Redmond likes to taunt Britton. He is proud to have been a soldier and makes it known that he served his full hitch. He goads Britton by telling him there's a bounty on deserters and "there's always someone ready to collect a bounty."

The gregarious Mr. Redmond invades Britton's space when he offers to add his antelope meat to Mrs. Britton's (Mona Freeman) stewpot. Later in the drama, when Britton catches him hoarding water, he antagonizes him by saying that his wife shares a drink from his canteen and is a lonely woman. They fight but the wagon master breaks it up.

The scout, Flint McCullough (Robert Horton), returns on foot. He is exhausted and delirious. His horse died drinking poisoned water. This upsets the camp. It becomes apparent to the major that he will have to send someone to Fort Pyoot. It is a dangerous trek but the only hope to getting water.

The reverend volunteers to make the ride but is considered too valuable to the wagon train. Britton knows the way and will make the voyage if he is given two canteens of water and the best horse in the camp. The major is apprehensive because he feels that there may be some credence to the desertion rumors. Instead, he wants Britton to give directions to Redmond.

The next morning, the camp verges on hysteria when it finds out that Monty Britton has taken the rest of the water and the best horse. Redmond cracks up and the disgusted major tells him to shut up. He talks to Britton's wife to get the lowdown on her husband. All she will say is that he was an officer and not a deserter. The major will have to get the rest of the story from him when he gets back.

At first, they are not sure but the truth dawns on them-Britton has succeeded in bringing the Cavalry to the rescue. The wagon train cheers as the Cavalry arrives, with a torn-up Britton strapped to a gurney. He

Like many popular shows and movies, *Wagon Train* had its own comic book series. Ward Bond and Robert Horton grace the cover as Major Adams and Flint McCullough. 1958, Revue Studios, Universal Television.

braved the sandstorm and made it by giving all of his water to his horse. The captain of the troop is Mrs. Britton's father and Monty Britton's enemy. He tells the major the story of Monty Britton.

Britton was once a lieutenant who was discharged after being court-martialed. He was deemed a coward when his first command was wiped out while retreating from a battle. A seasoned vet like the major can read between the lines.

"Are you sure that he wasn't obeying his last command?", he asks the captain.

He also states that there wasn't a court-martial that couldn't be reviewed. The captain agrees but says that Britton bolted before the review because of his stubborn pride.

"They say it takes pride to make a great officer", counters Major Adams.

Having made his point, the major gives his men an order: "Give a hand to Lt. Britton. He's gonna' need a lot of rest before he goes back on active duty."

The solitude of the desert is a perfect backdrop for the dwindling hope of the wagon train. It's lonely area is appropriate for the sandstorm that torments them at the peak of their weakness. The setting could also be used to describe the landscape of Monte Britton's soul.

Monte Britton is a man burdened by the qualities that make a man an unknown hero. The slow suicide of self-torment is Monte Britton's way. He is heroic in a masochistic Biblical sense. The loner is simultaneously a hero and a villain, made that way by a curse and an epiphany.

In *Wagon Train: The Monte Britton Story*, justice and character create a biblical pride that condemns a man to a private hell. The love of his wife keeps him steady although his stiff necked pride keeps stretching it to the breaking point. Fate and pride combine to create a hellish environment. Truth nurtures the soul but contempt torments the body. He is the lonesome hero, sparse with his words but brave and selfless.

Ray Danton could take his keen wit, cool charm and smooth refinement and twist them into a card sharp, a hired gun or a two-timing fore-flusher. Blackie from *The Spoilers* was the outline for the saloon rat and he evolved into card sharps and hired guns who gambled with their own lives as well as the lives of others.

Ray Danton uses some of Blackie's offbeat barroom charm for Clem, a gambler in *Trackdown: Sweetwater, Texas*, a smaller than a one-horse town that is a stretch of dust with minimalist sets and enough supporting players to give the impression of life. Bare essentials is the budgetary clause and it poses no problem because the half hour show is short and straight to the point.

Add a Texas Ranger, a crusty marshal, a stilted French saloon singer, a suave gambler, a traveling salesman and an orphaned baby and you have *"Sweetwater, Texas."*

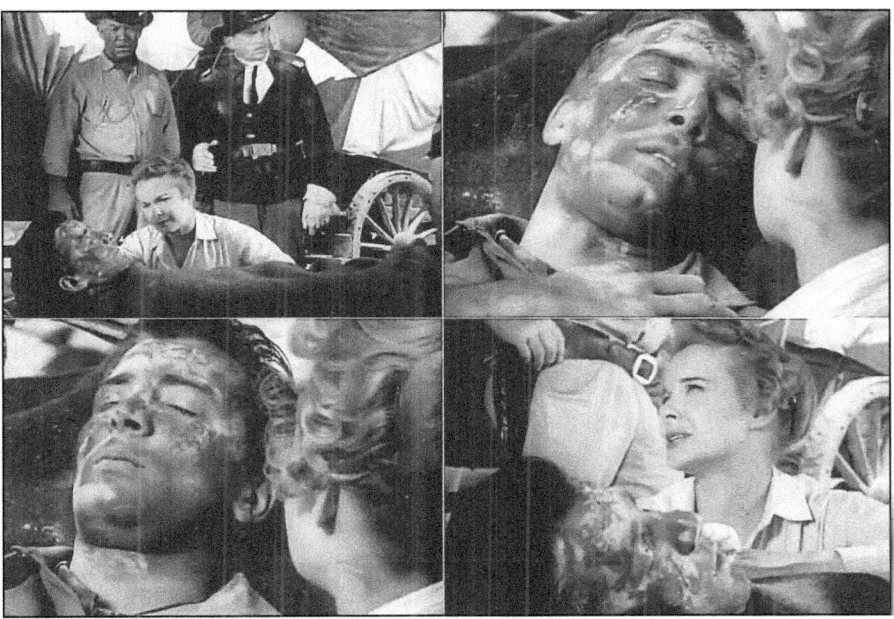

A series of shots showing Monty Britton's heroic quest to alert the Cavalry to the wagon train's plight. 1958, Revue Studios, Universal Television.

Not to forget the goofy doc who demands milk for the baby that is the only survivor of a stagecoach massacre.

Texas Ranger Hobey (Robert Culp) is the one who finds the child in the carnage. He rides into town where he encounters baffled looks and sarcastic comments. The saloon chanteuse (Chana O'Brien) ridicules his request for milk but he makes her feel guilty when she is told about the killings. Clem (Ray Danton), the gambler, takes the news in stride as he fleeces a nerdy traveling salesman (Paul Richards) at cards.

Later, in her room, the chanteuse confronts Clem about the fancy bracelet he gave her earlier in the day, implying that he may have pulled the stagecoach job during the time he was away from Sweetwater. She threatens to alert the law about her suspicions and Clem gives her an off screen beating.

Hobey the Ranger believes the show girl's suspicions about Clem when he visits her, sees the bruises and listens to her story about the bracelet. In the bar, Hobey confronts the gambler, who loses the bracelet to the salesman in a card game and conveniently reveals that the jewelry belonged to the man in the first place.

Texas Ranger Hobey directs his attention to the salesman, who breaks down and confesses to being a scavenger who rode upon the scene on his way into town and looted the belongings. He begs everyone to believe that he is innocent of the murders. The Texas Ranger makes sure that the salesman is on the next stagecoach out of town. Clem ignores his apologetic barroom honey and leaves the saloon. The Texas Ranger gives the woman the child to raise as her own.

Clem is the first of the polished western dandies played by Ray Danton. He is a card sharp who maintains his villainous status even after he is cleared of the murder suspicions. Danton's performance is one of the two "live" performances of the show; the other is Paul Birch's portrayal of the marshal. Birch brings his usual grit to the role. The other performances are stilted and self-conscious. Ray Danton had another opportunity to act with Birch in *Bronco: The Buckbrier Trail*.

Ray Danton broadens the character type with Len Farrell in *Lawman: Lily* ('59). Farrell is a shady card dealer who needs to make a big score so he can move to New Orleans with Annette, his fiancée. His plan is the same one that he used before in another town: lose a large amount of money to a patron and mug him in the alley at the end of the night. This time, the gambler is tough and pulls a knife on Len, only to be stabbed with his own blade.

Len Farrell's homicidal side is a step towards the hired gun. He is a lethal card sharp who isn't afraid to resort to killing. A step beyond killing to steal is to be paid to kill, the basis of a gunfighter's dilemma in another *Lawman* episode: *Yawkey*. He is the quintessence of the hired gunslinger that started with Stuart Spade in *Yancy Derringer: An Ace Called Spade*.

The opening shot establishes Yancy Derringer's (Jock Mahoney) formidable presence as he stands beneath a Bourbon Street sign. Dressed in riverboat gambler's regalia, he stares at the audience with a look of *bonhomie*. Behind his guise as a gambler and dandy, Derringer works as an agent for John

Yancy Derringer (Jock Mahoney) was a two-fisted fashion plate who helped the oppressed with the aid of his sidekick, the silent Indian Pahoo (X Brands). 1958, Derringer Productions, Desilu Studios.

Stuart Spade (Ray Danton) tries to settle a score with Yancy Derringer, a move that backfires on the duelist. 1958, Derringer Productions, Desilu Studios.

Colton (Kevin Hagen), a New Orleans bureaucrat. His sidekick is Pahoo (X Brands), the silent Indian.

In *An Ace Called Spade*, an insatiable thirst for revenge twists a widow's reasoning and distorts her concept of restoring lost honor. Crushed by the execution of her husband for cowardice, she aims to publicly humiliate Colton, the man who sentenced her spouse to death. Mrs. Lake (Joan Taylor) doesn't want him killed, only humiliated.

Cold to the touch, Stuart Spade promises the woman that his mark can't run-neither can she. He admits that he will use blackmail to get what he wants-a little private time with her. She stresses that the arrangement is strictly business; he insists that such arrangements are a part of business. Mrs. Lake calls off the deal and, to humor her, Spade agrees, especially when she tells him to keep the money.

The gunslinger has no intention of keeping his word. He plans to kill Colton in his unique way. It has to be accomplished within the rules of a duel. That is Spade's procedure because he is a duelist. A duel is the professional hit man's dream encounter. Under the pretext of defending a social wrong, the secret ambition of a contract killer is fulfilled. The duel is Spade's alibi-his job is done and sanctified by an old-world code of honor.

The setup begins when several attempts are made by Spade to provoke Colton. A final confrontation between Spade and Yancy Derringer ends when the hired gun is shot dead by Mrs. Lake. She kills him to protect her honor. In doing so, she is finally separated from her husband's dishonor. His memory has been neutralized and she has achieved independence by removing the last remnant of obligation to him-Stuart Spade. The duelist's death has liberated Lavinia Lake.

Stuart Spade is a fleshed out version of Danton's western dandy. He ranks among the best portrayals of this type. His arrogance is enhanced by the way he impresses his sycophants and intimidates his victims. There is an unintentional comic touch by his failed attempts to achieve his goal. As cool as Spade is, he can't outshine the lead, Yancy Derringer. It is his show and only he can excel at being daring, brave, romantic, and tough. Derringer is chief of the fashion-plated rogues and Spade is out of his league when he competes with him.

Supporting Roles

Hollywood Westerns

Ray Danton's good looks, deep voice and confident attitude gave him the potential to become a leading man but his dark countenance and angular features also fit the bill for shady types, criminals and Indians from central casting. He had dreams of being a star in an age when the hero was a toothsome and clean-cut mid-Western All-American type of lad. There were few exceptions.

Studios like MGM and Warner Brothers capitalized on his good looks and cast him as a romantic cad, usually in supporting roles. Ray Danton's early Hollywood career is filled with supporting parts in dramas, comedies, lightweight soaps and big budget escapist fare.

Ray Danton's concise approach, athletic bearing and threatening expression were perfect for the role that many novices had to cut their teeth on at Universal-International: the Hollywood version of the American Indian. Rock Hudson and Jeff Chandler are two of the Universal-International actors that played these parts early in their careers. It is in such a role that Ray Danton made his screen debut.

In *Chief Crazy Horse* ('55), he plays Little Big Man, the scorned and disgraced brave who fulfills a Lakota prophecy by being the kinsman who kills the Indian leader.

Crazy Horse (Victor Mature) is a man of destiny. He unites the Lakota tribes into a single fighting force, employing radical strategies that outwit his opponents. His unifying strength is also his weakness because he is vulnerable to a prophecy's dark side. His betrayer and executioner is his cousin, Little Big Man (Ray Danton), who is banished from the tribe after

Black Shawl (Susan Ball) and Chief Crazy Horse (Victor Mature) offer aid and comfort to Twist (John Lund), a wounded trapper who becomes their ally. 1954, Universal Pictures Company, Inc.

he insults Crazy Horse and Black Shawl (Suzan Ball), the chief's daughter, at a courting ceremony.

Little Big Man's banishment forces him to become a renegade. In order to survive, he will have to become a warrior of a different tribe. He is beyond the pale of betrayal, existing in the no-man's land of the mercenary. For a price, he has hired himself out as another rifle to cut down more of his blood kinsmen. This is his way of fighting Crazy Horse—to become a white man once removed.

The Mantz brothers are responsible for finalizing Little Big Man's corruption. They are merchants who take advantage of Little Big Man's plight by hiring him as a guide and sentry to raid the burial grounds. The more they use him to plunder the sacred burial grounds, the closer he gets to destroying the heart of the Indian nation—Chief Crazy Horse.

In a vain attempt to share the white man's power, the disgraced ex-warrior surrenders his identity. The Mantz brothers' gold greed matches

Little Big Man's thirst for revenge and redemption. They serve each other well until they are destroyed by the consequences of their greed.

The rest of the movie focuses on the white man's paranoia about Crazy Horse's ability in uniting the Lakota tribes in battle. More broken treaties and brutal skirmishes eventually erode the Lakota strength. Crazy Horse invents a new fighting strategy to defeat the omnipotent Cavalry. In the Battle of Little Big Horn, he uses decoys to lure and encircle the soldiers. Helpless and outnumbered, the soldiers are slaughtered by the braves that rush them from all sides.

The turning point of the power struggle is the Winter of the Seven Year Snow. Chief Crazy Horse finally submits to a plan that would allow his people to roam the plains during the hunting season but otherwise live on reservations. In an attempt to impress the authorities, Little Big Man sabotages the agreement by challenging Chief Crazy Horse as he is being led back to the general's quarters. In the heat of the moment, Little Big Man stabs Crazy Horse in the back with his rifle's bayonet. As Crazy Horse lies dying, his wife and father realize that the prophecy has come full circle. The chosen one who united the Lakota tribes is about to die from wound inflicted by a member of his own tribe. The film ends with a shot of the cloud filled sky where the warrior rode his horse in the child Crazy Horse's vision. The choir seals the gloom with its soothing voices.

Chief Crazy Horse is a morality play of the American West. Filmed in the Black Hills of Dakota, it is a respectful portrait of a great American general. The production is smooth and polished. The performers express the personality of their characters, being deftly directed by George Sherman. Combined with a breathtaking cinematography and seamless editing supported by a standard-but adequate-score, the movie is an American history primer, a Hollywood version of Golden Books.

The movie is a violent, yet anti-septic, version of the power play of the American West. It successfully conveys the mixed alliances, star crossed destinies, forked-tongue diplomacy and manifest destiny that made up the burgeoning frontier world.

As Chief Crazy Horse, Victor Mature looks as if he was carved out of a mountain. He speaks with the earnestness of a leader seeking a way to make the Lakotas victorious. Mature's tortured expressions convey the challenges faced by the warrior chief and give the character a vulnerability that underlies his strength, making his death tragic and noble.

Suzan Ball, as Black Shawl, is beautiful and her natural charm matches the majestic natural elements and belies the short tragic life of the actress who played the part. John Lund plays Major Twist, the noble white man-diplomat on horseback who pays his blood dues with two arrows on separate occasions.

Major Twist is bonded to Chief Crazy Horse but obligated to the government to seek a truce to the hostilities. In the end, he is a kinsman to the warrior chieftain. He becomes that the day he gave his goods to Crazy Horse in the courting ceremony. That's when he and Little Big Man exchange social standings in their respective societies.

Ray Danton makes his film debut as Little Big Man, the disgraced brave who fulfills a Lakota prophecy by being the kinsman who kills Crazy Horse. This is movie fiction because Crazy Horse was killed by a soldier while in captivity. Nevertheless, the change made for a compelling emotional element and it adds dimension to the character. His vengeful attitude rises out of his jealousy of the film's hero. Danton's hard-edged voice enhances the death threats that he swears.

Little Big Man is vain and ambitious. A grievous insult to Crazy Horse and his wife, Black Shawl during a courting ceremony earns him the contempt of the tribal chief.

Little Big Man (Ray Danton) and Chief Crazy Horse (Victor Mature) cross paths for the last time. 1954, Universal Pictures Company, Inc.

His banishment forces him to become a renegade. He is beyond the pale of betrayal, existing in the no-man's land of the mercenary. In the role of Little Big Man, Danton gets to play it tough, as well as cowardly because the part embodies ambition, betrayal, disgrace, and revenge.

It all spells self-destruction for Little Big Man. He degenerates from a Lakota brave to an accomplice to the robbery of sacred burial grounds. The transformation from fierce Indian brave to duplicitous soldier is emasculating. His final act of cowardice is the murder of Chief Crazy Horse at the peace talks.

He is the traitor who ties together all the loose ends of the prophecy in the film's final scene. From a warrior to a sellout, Little Big Man's revenge is basically on himself. His banishment means cancellation of his identity and total absorption into the movement that is decimating his people. His vengeful attitude rises out of his jealousy of the film's hero.

Robert F. Simon and James Westerfield play the greedy Mantz Brothers well. They dutifully convey the rascally greed of the businessmen who decimated the West for personal profit. Donald Randolph and David Janssen plays the Commissioner and his son, an army lieutenant. It is the son's death at Little Big Horn that impels the Commissioner to kill the Mantz Brothers before turning the gun on himself. He blames their greed and his compliance with the escalating hostilities between the Indians and the white man. The cast is filled out by Universal-International standbys like Dennis Weaver and Morris Ankrum.

Ray Danton had a supporting part in another Universal-International western, this one set off the beaten track in America's ice age. Rex Beach's *The Spoilers* has been filmed five times: in 1914, 1923, 1930, 1942, and in 1955. The last version is a Technicolor feast for the eyes that uses the Cinema-Scope process to bombard the senses with the wild, untamed frontier of turn-of-the century Nome, Alaska.

The time is 1899 and Nome is the site of one of the last great gold rushes. Nome is a mining town on the verge of being tamed by law and order. It has all of the necessities of a frontier town-a bank, a hotel, a sheriff's office, and an ornate saloon called the Northern. It is a place where brazen men, half-crazed by gold lust and personal ambition, reap and lose fortunes every day. Avarice, gambling, and bad judgment are the standard ways of losing one's good luck. A new way is to have the court system take away claims and award them to claim-jumpers.

In Nome, established claims are being challenged and the Claims Commission has tied up mine ownerships until a decision of ownership can be made. The old timers resent the intrusion of the federal government into their business. They want to settle their affairs the old-fashioned way- by stringing up the claim jumpers as if they were figs to be dried in the sun.

Two grizzly miners, Flapjack Simms (Wallace Ford) and Banty Jones (Forrest Lewis), lead the rebellion. Their mine has just been put into a litigious limbo by the new gold commissioner, Alex McNamara (Rory Calhoun). Overheated and itchy-fingered, they want to shoot him and the two spoilers who laid claim to their mine. Flapjack organizes a group of disgruntled miners at the Northern and they discuss implementing their own brand of justice. The owner of the Northern, Cherry Maloote (Anne Baxter), quells their anger.

Cherry Mallote is the blonde lady liberty of the Yukon. In Nome, she is a goddess to the salty miners whose claims are being stolen by the land commission. She soothes their anger with good humor and earth-shaking moves. Sliding down the handrail to head them off with a pass, Cherry's cunning genius saves the day for the hapless prospectors when she promises to visit the gold commissioner to straighten things out.

Alex MacNamara is impressed with Cherry's style. He assures her and the men that they will receive due process of the law once he's had a chance to review the claims. A federal judge is about to arrive and he will hear the cases and render a verdict. MacNamara assures them that they will learn to respect and trust him once they see that he is sincere and looking out for their best interests.

It is just a matter of time before it become apparent that he is the villain and his plans are to grab the mines through the courts. His scheme is to tie up the claims of the small mines then grant them to the original owners. This is to establish trust. His grand scheme is to takeover Nome's largest mine-the Miter, owned by Roy Glennister (Jeff Chandler) and his partner, Dextry (John McIntyre).

Roy Glennister is a rough hewn, two fisted muscle-headed hunk of tough guy. He is in love with Cherry but it is a romance fraught with games spiced with broadsides and blind swipes. The ordinarily obliging Cherry is miffed because of Glen's friendly attitude toward a shipboard companion, Miss Helen Chester (Barbara Britton), niece of the federal judge. She is another character who deceives everyone except Cherry with her holier-than-thou mid-eastern etiquette. She, too, is a compliant participant in the scheme to defraud the miners. At the movie's end, a sympathetic change of heart doesn't absolve her of her guilt.

Cherry Maloote (Anne Baxter) makes a point about love to Blackie (Ray Danton), her croupier and strong arm man. 1955, Universal Pictures Company, Inc.

Dextry is an old frontiersman. The only law he knows is natural law. He is guided by experience tempered by natural instinct. He doesn't trust municipal law. To him, it's unnatural; so are the guardians of the law. Dextry considers them artificial men in tailored suits who hide behind affidavits that guide their lives. That's why he greets them with a six-shooter that drills holes in an affidavit that puts his mine into the court's custody. He also booby-traps the mine with dynamite, a move that comes in handy in the final confrontation with the deputies.

The hallmark of the earlier versions of *The Spoilers* is the final barroom brawl between Glennister and McNamara. This version is no exception. They tear apart The Northern: balconies collapse, mirrors break, chairs are thrown, and showgirls scream. The combatants fly through the saloon doors and continue their match in the mud-strewn streets. Glennister lands the winning blow and stakes his claim to being the sole suitor of Cherry.

The Spoilers is an entertaining movie made by first rate craftsman and a cast that plays their parts well. Jeff Chandler and Anne Baxter are charismatic leads. Chandler is perfect as the two-fisted oaf who loves brandy and hard-boiled eggs. Anne Baxter is electrifying as the colorful woman who is described as being like a "sleek yacht or thoroughbred: beautiful but hard to handle." One gets the sense that the riches from his mine and her political connections will lay the groundwork as a power couple in the burgeoning city.

Rory Calhoun plays his usual rugged self; only, this time, he is on the wrong side of the law. He shows his talents as a charmer, a scoundrel, a leader, and a fighter. Calhoun's land grabber is a smoothie who is on the

A montage of the battle for the Miter. 1955, Universal Pictures Company, Inc.

winning end when he is swindling helpless miners. Glennister is another matter. Although he admits that they are both alike, he claims to have more larceny in his soul. That's his demise.

John McIntire is all grit "n" gristle as Dextry, the wizened curmudgeon. He is as honest as he is tough, symbolizing America's frontier spirit. Not one to take a fight lying down, he is in the thick of things, especially at the fight at the Miter. It is his detonation of the dynamite that saves the mine for him and Glennister.

Ray Danton is shifty and ruthless as Blackie. He secretly adores Cherry and connives to protect his boss' interests, except when it comes to her love for Glennister, whom he resents. In the scene where Glennister and Dextry try to retrieve their confiscated safe, Blacky shoots the marshal in the back after tipping him off about the plan. It is a murder that Glennister is arrested for. Blackie not only frames him for the death of the marshal but curses him with his dying breath after the train wreck at the mine.

In *The Spoilers*, Blackie has been neutered by his unrequited love for his boss, Cherry Maloote. He has the suave look and manner of the dependable boyfriend and the manipulative attitude of the roguish make-out artist who cancels out himself. At the decade's end, Ray Danton played a toned down version of Blackie in the recurring role of Nifty Cronin, a shifty saloon owner, in *The Alaskans,* a short lived television series set in Skagway, Alaska.

Barbara Britton is prim and low-key but this is to be expected when considering her part—dull shades of gray compared to the Technicolor character played by Anne Baxter. The rest of the cast is rounded out by a stable of venerable character actors: Wallace Ford and Forrest Lewis as Flapjack and Banty, with other roles played by Willis Bouchey, Carl Benton Reid, Roy Barcroft, Ruth Donnelly, and Bob Steele, among others.

Ray Danton returned to the high plains to play another type of warrior in *Yellowstone Kelly* for Warner Brothers in 1959. This time around, he is not a renegade although he has a rebellious streak that creases his skull with a fatal moon madness. The character is Seipai, the aggressive nephew of Gall, the tribal chief; unlike Little Big Man, Seipai is fierce and decisive. His passion is aroused by the Meeleewah, the Indian woman nursed back to health by Yellowstone Kelly. She is the spark that sets the fire that warms Kelly, spurns Gall and consumes Seipai.

Seipai is publicly humiliated by his uncle when he is throttled and brought to his knees for challenging the chief's edict about Mahleewah.

He raids the Kelly settlement and does the unthinkable by shooting Edd "Kookie" Byrnes in the stomach with an arrow. It gives the pop idol a chance to give a death speech like Elvis in *Love Me* Tender. No sleep is lost when Seipai loses to Yellowstone Kelly in a dramatic lightning filled moonlit shootout.

If anyone seems to be fashioned from nature's hard elements, it is Clint Walker. Equal parts Paul Bunyan and Rockie Mountains, he is the personification of the rugged western mountain man-a redwood with a face painted on it. Soft-spoken and courteous, he can cause an earthquake with his anger if riled by stupidity or injustice. If left alone, he is the lengthening prairie shadow of an autumn day.

Clint Walker is basically playing his Cheyenne character in *Yellowstone Kelly*, a brooding frontiersman who enjoys the solitude of nature to the company of men. His code of ethics has been sharpened by nature and transcends civilization.

Anse (Edd Byrnes), a young cowhand, Mahleewah (Andra Martin), an imperiled Indian maiden and Seipai (Ray Danton), a crazed Sioux warrior interrupt Yellowstone Kelly's solitary routine.

Kelly is drawn into a drama when he saves the life of Mahleewah, a wounded Arapaho maiden. She is the captive of the crazed Seipai, whose uncle, Gall (John Russell), was saved by Kelly seven years prior to the story. Gall's gratitude enables Kelly to set traps in the area.

Now, the score is settled and he has to prove himself by saving Mahleewah.

If he fails, his life is over. Kelly succeeds in removing a bullet from near the woman's spine. He is free to go but his troubles are not over: Seipai has sworn to kill Yellowstone Kelly. A triangle of antagonism exists: Gall considers Kelly his brother because of his honesty and integrity. Seipai hates him because he is a white man. Mahleewah turns Gall against Seipai because both men want her. Yellowstone Kelly complicates matters because the woman has chosen to be with him.

Yellowstone Kelly is a showcase for Warner Brothers' television performers. Edd Byrnes, who plays Anse Harper, was Kookie. He was on hiatus from *77 Sunset Strip* because of a salary dispute. It must have been agonizing for Kookie's fans to see their idol being shot in the stomach with an arrow by Seipai. However, his death scene is drawn out to elicit sorrow from his legion of fans.

John Russell, famed for his role on *Lawman*, plays the Indian Chief Gall. He shows more emotion as the chief than he does as Marshal

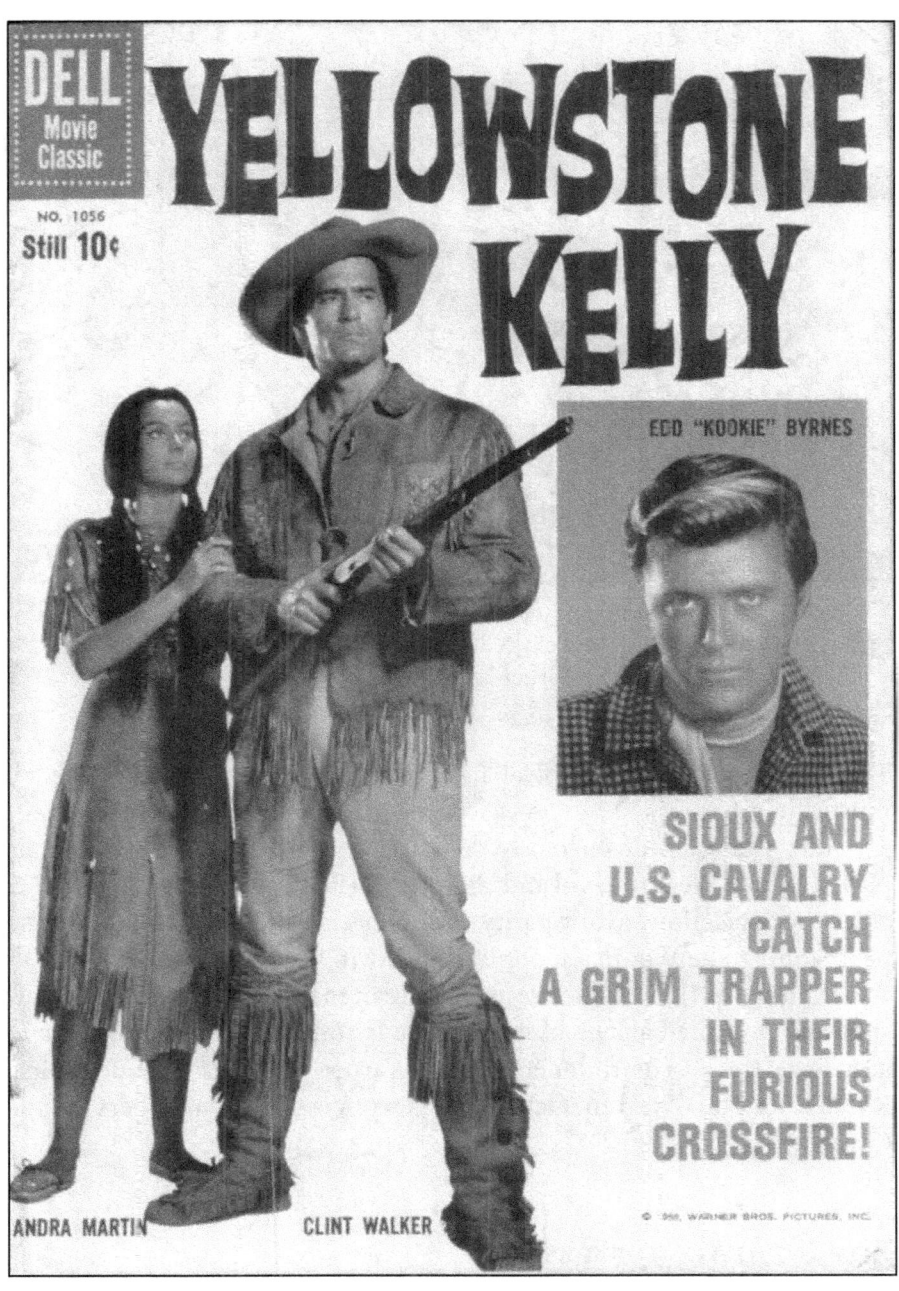

Dell Comics published a series of comics based on movies and television shows. The cover for *Yellowstone Kelly* features the stars, Andra Martin and Clint Walker with Edd Byrnes (inset). 1959, Dell Comics Group.

Chief Gall (John Russell) reminds his nephew, Seipai (Ray Danton), who rules the tribe while Yellowstone Kelly (Clint Walker) acknowledges the point. 1959, Warner Bros. Dist. Corp.

Troup. Troup is basically stoical and Gall is intense and without a pencil mustache.

Ray Danton was currently co-starring on *The Alaskans* when he played Seipai. He is forceful and warlike, constantly challenging the tribal chief with objections to any parity with Kelly. He attempts to sabotage the peace, only to be shot in a moonlit showdown with Yellowstone Kelly.

Andra Martin is seductive as the Indian maiden. It is easy to see how she can upset the balance of nature. She is soft and wise, yet torrid and arousing. The cast is rounded out by Warner standbys: Claude Akins, Rhodes Reason, Warren Oates and Gary Vinson as members of the Cavalry.

ROMANTIC ARCHETYPES

The best of Ray Danton's supporting roles are mainly secondary romantic types. David Tredman in *I'll Cry Tomorrow* ('55) and John Howard in *Too Much, Too Soon* ('58) are the best examples of opposing quixotic attitudes

Supporting Roles | 59

according to the code of Ray Danton. David Tredman is the sincere and dependable boyfriend and John Howard is the haughty conniver who can deliver the thrills. Both men serve as the basis for the charmers and scoundrels that form the cast of Ray Danton's early supporting roles.

In *I'll Cry Tomorrow*, Lillian Roth (Susan Hayward) is a siren whose inner demons swallow her soul and make her a slave to addiction. Her golden talent is tarnished over the years as her beauty becomes deformed because of the dark forces within. An arduous childhood leads to a successful career that is consumed by alcoholism. Broadway to Skid Row is the road map she travels. All that is left is a shadow play that is resuscitated by the help of concerned fellow travelers of the same dead end street.

A child actress driven by a domineering stage mother, Lillian learns early to save her tears for the next day. That is her demanding mother's advice, something that stifles the child and hampers her development as an adult. Her childhood is one long audition. There isn't any time for anything else.

She becomes a popular singer but her idyllic rise above the tears comes to a crashing halt when her true love, David Tredman (Ray Danton), dies of a brain tumor. It is the start of her dependence on alcohol. Her sorrow is strung along with career success and a succession of marriages.

Roth ultimately slips off the radar screen and takes up hiding on Skid Row, the purgatory of alcoholics. A bottle full of laughs is their salvation as they keep each other company in their world of self-loathing. It is a world that sucks the beauty out of Lillian. All that is left is a shattered rag doll on the verge of suicide.

She has literally dropped out of sight and—for two years-nobody knows what happened to her. It's not until she reads an ad in the paper seeking communication from her that she realizes how low she has sunk. A failed attempt to jump out of a window leads to a chance meeting with Burt McGuire (Eddie Albert), the guardian angel who runs a chapter of Alcoholics Anonymous.

On the popular show, "This Is Your Life", she is resurrected for a nationwide audience. Lillian Roth has faced her demons and conquered them. Now, she tells her inspired story to offer hope to those who have lost it.

Susan Hayward is a sex siren full of steel resolve. Beneath her beautiful exterior is a vulnerable child who never grew up. Although she doesn't really age through the years, Hayward's acting ability enables the audience to experience her crack-up. Her scenes as a drunkard are sad and harrowing. She has never been able to control her life and has lost her only love, David Tredman. It is a double stigma that has worn her down.

Hayward has a fine singing voice and she belts out, "Sing, You Sinners", "When the Red, Red Robin (Comes Bob, Bob, Bobbin' Along)", "Happiness is a Thing Called Joe", and, as part of a medley, "The Vagabond King Waltz."

In *I'll Cry Tomorrow*, Ray Danton plays it straight as the romantic interest, showing a side seldom seen in his stateside pictures. As the childhood friend and Roth's only love, Ray Danton's performance is suave, secure, and amiable. There aren't any traces of the cruelty and sadism that would exemplify his pulp years. Instead, his performance is likable and gives an indication of the type of leading man he would have been if his career went in that direction. David Tredman is the most conventional of Danton's romantic parts. He is a character calculated to please.

He is a successful entertainment lawyer who would like Lillian to be his wife. She does not have a problem in giving up her career for him. Lillian tells her mother that she'll continue to sing if she wants to but not as a professional. This causes her mother great pain because she sacrificed her life to live through her daughter. She does not want to be shut out of the starlight, even if she is only experiencing it vicariously. It does not matter because David is hospitalized and dies. He is gone a half hour into the film; so is Lillian's will to live.

Don Taylor, Richard Conte, and Eddie Albert play the other men in her life.

Wally (Don Taylor) is a good-natured sailor. He is a simpleton and a stumblebum who truly lucked-out when he met and married Lillian Roth. Of course, it was the liquor that twisted their senses, but-in the long run-it was Wally who got the better half of the relationship. She learned to Conga.

Tony Bardeman (Richard Conte) is charming and one feels good about Lillian falling in love with him. Initially, he is preventing her from drinking and offers a stern shoulder to lean on. The train compartment scene when he is transformed into a beast is shocking. He, too, is an alcoholic, an abusive one, at that. She learns the hard way that his periodic disappearances were not due to business trips; they were benders. After the discovery of his dark secret, it is a continuous descent in hell for Lillian. Tony is such a louse that he makes Wally seem like a lucky pick for any woman.

Katie Roth (Jo Van Fleet) is less than enthusiastic about hearing her daughter Lillian's (Susan Hayward) intention of giving up her musical career to marry David Tredman (Ray Danton). 1955, Screen Service Group.

Burt McGuire (Eddie Albert) displays warmth and compassion. He has been to hell and back. Instead of being bitter, he uses his experience to help others who have fallen into alcoholism. There is a touch of torment in between his smiles but he is able to control his inner demons. As the director of an Alcoholics Anonymous program, he helps Lillian regain her footing in life.

Ironically, it is Lillian's nurse, Ellen (Virginia Gregg), who introduces her to the bottle. It happens when Lillian has a minor breakdown because of David Tredman's death. It brings out a lot of resentment against her mother, who never wanted to get involved romantically because she was afraid it work short circuit her daughter's career and take away meaning for her own life.

Lillian refuses to spend time in a sanitarium to recuperate; instead, she opts for continuing her tour because it was arranged by David in the first place. After a confrontation, Kathy leaves and Nurse Ellen takes over as Lillian's assistant. One night, she gives her charge a bottle and tells her a couple of drinks will help her sleep. It also makes room for a succession of undesirable men.

Jo Van Fleet is a brilliant actress and her portrayal as Kathy Roth, the stage mother, has to be seen to be believed. She is the essence of the frustrated woman who tries to become reborn again through her daughter. In a confrontational scene between her character and Lillian she admits that she wanted her daughter to have all the things that she never had. In a sense she succeeded-her daughter became a fountainhead of demonic possession.

Margo has a small part as Selma and Henry Kulky, the former wrestler, and Timothy Carey, the future cult star, have small parts as derelicts. Daniel Mann's direction is direct and upfront. He blends excellent acting with a cinematography that uses light and shadows that vary with Lillian's state of mind. Mann balances the pace of the movie on the tempos created by the characters' downward spirals, making *I'll Cry Tomorrow* seem like an ashcan symphony where the alley cats and winos take over after the musicians have left the stage.

A trip to the other side of the sartorial lawyer is the spineless gigolo, starting with John Howard, the feral tennis bum in *Too Much, Too Soon* (58), the bio of Diana Barrymore. Danton's screen time is short but his impression is indelible as the opportunist who cashes in on the Barrymore name.

Too Much, Too Soon is a Gothic horror story set in Hollywood. It is about love distorted through a prism of fame and dissipation. Illusion passes for reality and hope is a substitute for despair. Heredity is a curse, not so much from the genetic standpoint but from the expectations of public adoration. Family tradition is a burden in popular culture and no one is more aware of it than the daughter of the legendary actor, John Barrymore.

Lost in the shadows of a neglected childhood, Diana Barrymore (Dorothy Malone) desperately seeks the love and acknowledgement of her father, the Great Profile (Errol Flynn). Fanzines and press clippings are her means of getting to know him. Somewhat resentful of her mother's obfuscation of the Barrymore myth, Diana constantly looks for ways to cement the paternal bond. It is incomprehensible that the greatest living actor may be out of her orbit and that he would rather be doing anything except play nursemaid to her.

A reunion on her father's yacht turns into humiliation when his pleasure-seeking friends pull aside in their yacht. Barrymore gives an

Ray Danton talks with Don Taylor and Susan Hayward on the set of
I'll Cry Tomorrow. 1955, Screen Service Group.

impassioned Shakespearian recitation. He gets so carried away that he tumbles overboard. His amused friends beg him to climb aboard and join their pleasure seeking. Barrymore apologizes to his daughter and swims towards the yacht.

Rejection only makes Diana seek her father with more determination. The closest thing she can do is become an actress. Ironically, it is through this ambition that Diana is reconciled with her father. At first, it is a picture book relationship until alcohol creeps its way back into Barrymore's life.

After her father's death, Diana inherits the curse. She returns to the empty mansion and picks up a gilded copy of Hamlet with her father's profile on the cover. Wiping the dust off the profile, she breaks down in tears.

At that point, she looks off to the side and sees her father's overcoat hanging on a coat rack. In the pocket is a bottle of booze. The rest of the movie is about a slow decline that includes a failed film career, a series of marriages, a burlesque routine and a stint in a home for wayward women.

Although Dorothy Malone is effective as Diana Barrymore, it is Errol Flynn who steals the picture. He is so efficient because he is playing himself-a celebrated actor and personality who has dissipated through too many decades of high living. Flynn is so worn out that you think that you are watching the Barrymore of the Great Man films that were made well beyond his prime.

Flynn's recitation of Shakespeare; his ugly drunken outburst in the shadows of the empty mansion; and his sentimental clinging to a past that never existed are masterful. It is hard to fill in for his character once he's gone. His portrayal of Barrymore is so brilliant that it unfairly overshadows Dorothy Malone's excellent acting.

Dorothy Malone successfully matures as the film progresses. She is actually believable as the young adolescent in her sailor suit, pouring over fanzines in the back of the limousine. She radiates an earthy sexuality as the young woman who arrives in Hollywood, hoping for a film career that will make her father proud of her. Malone handles Diana Barrymore's descent into alcoholism and madness successfully. It is heart breaking to watch, considering that the role model eventually committed suicide.

Efrem Zimbalist, Jr. plays Vincent Bryant, the actor who becomes her first husband. Zimbalist plays Bryant in the resolute and upright style he used for most of his career. He is upstaged by Ray Danton as John Howard, the tennis bum who moves in on his wife and becomes her second husband.

Danton has seldom been creepier, even though he is dressed like an all-American tennis pro. He was even coached by the former tennis pro, Tony Trabert. Ray Danton doesn't kill anybody or beat anyone up, yet his character is odious. John Howard is portrayed as an amoral egotist. Howard is a user who manipulates Diana Barrymore and discards her without any hint of emotion. He is a rude influence on Diana and does nothing to help her with her growing dependence on alcohol, a leech that disgusts her family the way Diana disgusts him.

The opportunist sees Diana dancing at a party, dressed only in a bathing suit, and zooms in on her. Forget that she is married, Howard wants her every way a man can have a woman. Their scenes together sizzle with a wicked sexuality.

It ends when they have a truthful conversation while he is practicing his volley in the driveway of their house. He explains his expectations to Diana while he lobs the ball off the wall. The conversation turns vicious and he traps her against the garage door, scaring her as he aims his volleys at her. The ball ricochets around her with the cutting edge of a carnival knife-thrower's precision. Howard makes his point when he bounces the ball off of Diana's face.

Diana Barrymore (Dorothy Malone) seeks approval from her father, the Great Profile, John Barrymore, played with gusto by Errol Flynn. 1958, Warner Bros. Dist. Corp.

Murray Hamilton plays Charlie Snow, a movie producer who borders on the neurotic. He is ruined when a dissolute Diana refuses to honor her picture contract. Failure to do so would weigh heavily on the producer's reputation with the major studios.

Martin Milner applies his innocent charm as Lincoln Forrester, a man without guile, the only person who loved Diana in a school boyish way. It is his reappearance at the end of the film as a balding but successful business man that bolsters Diana in her attempt to recover from her incarceration.

Ed Kemmer found out what it was like to act in a respectable movie before he discovered his future as a star of Grade-Z horror flicks like *Earth Versus The Spider* and *Giant From The Unknown*. He plays Robert Wilcox, a recovering alcoholic who meets Diana at a summer stock playhouse. They are married and are reduced to burnouts in a neon-lit fleabag hotel. Diana's new husband isn't any help to her anymore because he has backslid into being a vindictive drunkard. In a downbeat scene, he tries to revive Diana's numb response to her mother's death by throwing a drink into her face.

Barrymore's next stop is doing drunken impressions of celebrities in a burlesque house. After being fired, she stumbles along the street and stops in front of a drugstore. She mimics the women in the advertisements. When she glimpses her aged visage in the window's reflection, she becomes angry and smashes the glass and the displays. It costs her freedom when she is incarcerated in a health clinic for women.

A writer visits Diana with the idea of helping her write her autobiography. She is apprehensive because she doesn't want to relive her hellish life. Nevertheless, when she is released she decides to visit the writer.

CAREER MEN

Warner Brothers continued to capitalize on Ray Danton's good looks by casting him in supporting roles that could have been played by anyone. Having Ray Danton play the parts provided the heart throb factor for female movie fans and also allowed the studio to utilize its roster of supporting players.

Clem Marker and Ensign Higgins continue the genealogy of David Tredman and John Howard. Their vices and attributes have nothing to do

John Howard (Ray Danton) is an amoral tennis bum who puts the move on Diana Barrymore (Dorothy Malone) at a Hollywood pool party. 1958, Warner Bros. Dist. Corp.

with romance because their relationships have to do with their respective careers: the military and the judicial system. Ensign Higgins is the flip side of Marker when it comes to American jurisprudence. They are both clean cut Ivy League types on opposite sides of the law. The lawyer obeys the tenets of the law but the naval officer betrays his oath when he violates the maritime code.

Clem Marker, the defense attorney in *A Fever In The Blood*, is a case of pose and diction in black and white. His scenes are all courtroom bound and he delivers a convincing portrayal of a lawyer defending a client in a high profile case. Not only is his client accused of murdering his wife, he is the grandson of the retired governor. Another problem is Callahan, the DA (Jack Kelly). He wants to use the case to publicize and legitimize a possible run for the Senate.

A sweat covered brow mixed with a leer combines with heart palpitations, a sensual black negligee and a breath taking pillow crush to comprise the opening of *A Fever In The Blood*. This is the basis of a sensational murder case that will be tried by a DA, presided over by a judge (Efrem Zimbalist, Jr.), and monitored by a senator (Don Ameche) whose common bond is a run for the governor's mansion. The luridness of the trial makes it high profile, especially since the murder suspect is the nephew of ex-governor Thornwall.

An attempted bribe by the senator to the judge will be the deciding factor in the race. How it is handled by the three principles not only defines the characters but determines the outcome of the nomination. It will be made public when the trial gets out of hand and Mr. Marker (Ray Danton), the defense attorney, seeks a mistrial.

Political intrigue, courtroom dramatics, and sensational undercurrents make *A Fever In The Blood* another economy movie where you get more than what you paid for. Morality and righteous behavior is the backbone of the movie, a cautionary tale of greed and corruption.

A Fever In The Blood is a glossy soap opera where betrayal is the accepted code of behavior. The characters use each other to achieve their political ambitions. The degree of their friendliness is equal to the degree of their need to succeed. They are constantly making deals, only to break them later. The only exception is Judge Hoffman, and he is tarnished and almost ruined before he triumphs over his adversaries.

Their scruples are put to the test when the men are faced with temptations that may undermine or enhance their ambitions. In the end, only one man remains standing. The other two are defeated by their surrender to corruption. The senator dies from a heart attack and the prosecutor cancels himself; only the judge passes the test and wins the nomination for governor.

A Fever In The Blood is a capable thriller. It is borderline soap opera with the standard romantic subplots and grandiose power schemes. However, the political machinations make for good viewing. Don Ameche is extraordinary as the manipulative yet charming, Senator Simon. He is a quick-witted political animal who can smell the blood of the campaign and doesn't care what opponents he has to trounce, even if they are friends of the moment. He is aided in his downfall by his wife, played by Angie Dickenson. Her former love for Judge Hoffman rescues the underdog in the end and destroys his power hungry husband.

Jack Kelly's Dan Callahan is a loser from the start of his bid for the nomination. Strained, double-crossing and overly-confident, he sells himself short by trying the case and planning his campaign. He is stretched thin by a two-front battle plan. The fact that the outcome of the trial will determine his popularity and that the trial is presided over by Judge Hoffman, adds more pressure to his burden. He doesn't have what it takes to carry the weight of a war on two fronts.

Angie Dickenson is the blonde shadow of loves past, present, and future. A thinking trophy wife, she knows how to play her hand. Her former love for Hoffman sets her free. It is her break from the suddenly corrupt Senator that frees her from the past.

Ray Danton plays the prosecutor, Clem Marker, with a perfunctory effectiveness. It is a role that is limited to the courtroom scenes. He is capable as a jurist arguing his client's case against a prosecutor playing to the public via larger-than-life headlines. He uses all the right gestures and employs the right intonations for his objections and declarations. As the prosecutor's adversary, he holds his ground and argues a credible case against the state.

The supporting characters flesh out the cast. Carroll O'Connor, Parley Baer and Jesse White are effective as second bananas who wheel and deal on the side. Andra Martin is beautiful as a helpless witness being brow beaten on the stand and Rhodes Reason is a footnote in a role that is light years away from his starring roles in *This Island Earth* and *Kronos*.

Onionhead is a rough and tumble naval follow-up to *No Time for Sergeants*. Al Woods (Andy Griffith) may be rural but he's far cry from Will Stockdale. Stockdale is a good-natured country oaf—Lil' Abner in the Air Force. Al Woods is a brooding thinker, a man with an attitude who is not afraid to express it.

Although Al Woods is a young man, he is cynical beyond his years It's a toughness ingrown from coming from the wrong side of the tracks It is also a characteristic that helps him survive the pecking order of the Coast Guard. At one point, it's this abrasive distrust of authority that makes him jump the chain of command when he uncovers corruption in the mess accounts.

Jack Kelly plays Callahan, an ambitious D.A. who wants to use the political ramifications of his current case to launch a career in politics. 1961, Warner Bros. Dist. Corp.

Once he is a part of the military world, Woods becomes aware of the civilians who build their lives around servicemen. Chief of these is Stella (Felicia Farr), a beautiful blonde who comes off as a manipulative gold digger. She is supposed to be a world of sugar and spice. The truth is that she's another human trapped in a set of circumstances beyond her control.

Al Woods feels contempt towards her when she marries "Red" (Walther Matthau), the mess sergeant. He refuses to believe her speech giving her the right to seek security and benefits. Stella isn't the only platform for Al Woods' unctuous morality. The way he handles shipboard larceny also shows his self-centered attitude.

Once "Red" is transferred, Al becomes chief of the submarine galley. Woods is alert and observes the inferior goods that have been ordered. He also sees the expensive food that is delivered for the officers' mess. It is beginning to dawn on him that Ensign Higgins (Ray Danton) may be finagling with the accounts. Fearing widespread corruption among the officers, Woods bypasses the chain of command with his complaint.

Mr. Higgins is a by-the-book hard-headed officer. He makes sure that his sailors obey every "jot and tittle" of maritime code. Condescension is his social code and arrogance is his weakness.

Wartime battles on the coast relegate the mess hall scam to the back burner. It is when the captain (James Gregory) is implicated in dereliction of duty during the battle and possible indictment in the mess hall accusations that Woods retracts his charges and suffers penal justice.

This being Hollywood, the movie ends on an upbeat tone. Forlorn and dejected, Woods sits with his buddies in the bar, wondering about what could have happened to Jo (Erin O'Brien Moore), his small town sweetheart. Just then, she walks through the barroom doors. Al Woods is besides himself with worship. He is the complete opposite of the proud pig-headed lout who left Jo on the porch of the sorority house at the beginning of the movie.

After declaring his love for Jo, Al grabs her by the hand and leaves the bar, walking through puddles in his socks. Love has made him oblivious

Ray Danton plays Clem Marker, the defense attorney, in a politically explosive murder trial. 1961, Warner Bros. Dist. Corp.

The newbie (Andy Griffith) and the vet (Walter Matthau) share opinions and world views, including the right way to make cinnamon buns. 1958, Warner Bros. Dist. Corp.

to everything around him. Although his Coast Guard stint has taken a downward spiral, his personal life-which is what spurred him to enlist-is at an all time high.

Andy Griffith handles the comic side of his character as well as the dramatic aspects. Kitchen mishaps are a natural grist for laughs. Improbable situations like monstrous dough products and perfectly cooked gourmet meals are played for laughs. His portrayal of Al Woods is the stereotypical military chef and ranks with the best of them, as does his boss, "Red" Wildoe, played by Walter Matthau.

Even in the Fifties, Walter Matthau was a salty curmudgeon. His scenes with Woods are the atypical clash of the generations in the territorial mess hall. Wildoe's recipe for cinnamon buns is his answer to all of the kitchen's woes. He expresses the importance of cinnamon buns in a hilarious scene with Woods.

They are in a bar and stoned to the gills! Being drunk, they mangle the English language in an argument about the cinnamon bun recipe. It's the misanthrope versus the curmudgeon. They see eye-to-eye even though they are pie-eyed!

Felicia Farr excels as the fallen angel-Stella. She is a soiled pinup queen. Stella is controlling, coquettish, melodramatic and-yet!-vulnerable. As played by Ms. Farr, Stella is a barroom flower. Every man wants her, some men have her, yet no one possesses her. She marries Wildoe for security but still maintains her address in limbo because her husband is often away at sea.

Erin O'Brien is cherubic as the steadfast small town girl with a heart of compassion. She loses Al in the beginning, only to get him in the end. Like an old-time English fairy tale maiden, she waits while her suitor goes on his quest. Al Woods' rite of passage entitles him to win Jo's hand in marriage. It's an ancient courting ritual that still had relevance in Fifties' America.

The supporting characters in *Onionhead* help make the movie the success that it is. Not only do they fill in the gaps or help develop the plot, they are played by a cast of reliable performers. Ray Danton plays Ensign Higgins, a member of the officer corps who follows the book to the letter. Beneath his strict shipboard manner, he is an embezzler. He is one of Al Woods' chief antagonists.

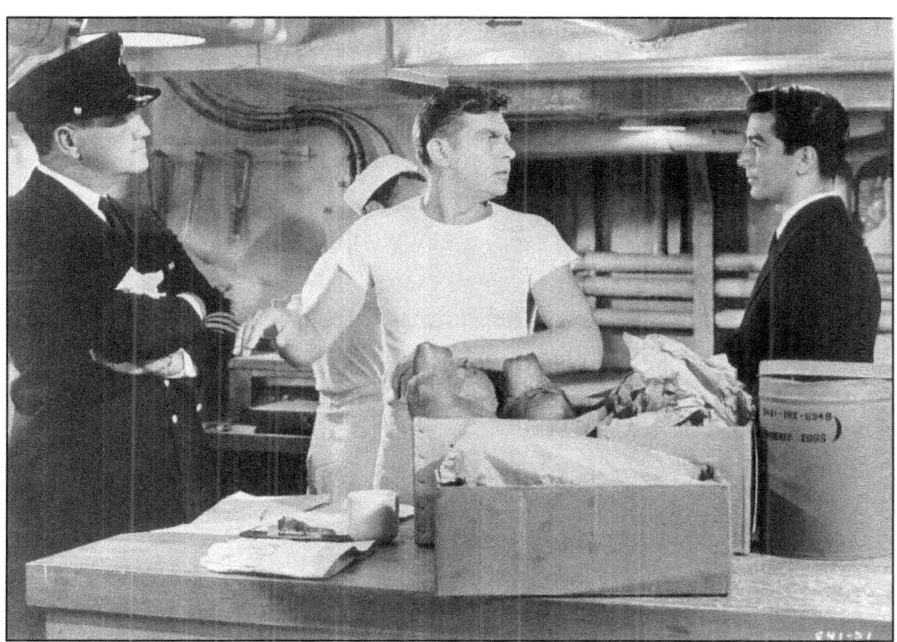

Ensign Higgins (Ray Danton) is challenged by Woods (Andy Griffith) about misappropriating mess hall funds. 1958, Warner Bros. Dist. Corp.

Ensign Higgins handles the mess accounts and finds them over the budget. His pretense is that incompetence has put the food budget in the red. He plans to straighten that out by making out the menus and ordering the foodstuffs. Woods, the mess sergeant, is alert and observes the inferior goods that have been ordered for the enlisted men. He also sees the expensive food that is delivered for the officers' mess. It is beginning to dawn on him that Ensign Higgins may be cooking the books.

There is a confrontational scene between Woods and Higgins in the captain's quarters. The ensign mistakenly believes that the captain will side with an officer. The captain believes Woods and supports the cook after he knocks the ensign down. The flustered and shocked officer appeals to the captain for a grievance but the commanding officer says nothing happened, he had just slipped. He adds a warning that he will have him court-martialed because there's no room in the service for men like him.

In the end, Woods, who gets the support of the "Skipper", played by James Gregory, exposes him. He, too, was playing the crusty old timer as far back as the Fifties. His shipboard character is the understandable yet garrulous veteran that Gregory played throughout his career.

Joey Bishop, Claude Akins, Joe Mantell, and Tige Andrews shine in smaller roles. They are the surefire comic relief. Bishop and Akins are kitchen helpers. Somewhat independent and streetwise, they are eventually kept in line by Woods. Mantell plays an aspiring barber who develops a hair tonic to help Woods' balding.

After being criticized by Ensign Higgins for hair in the food, Woods's head is shaved. Mantell's character has developed a tonic extracted from onion juice. His premise is that you never see a bald onion so if you apply the nutrients to a bald scalp, hair will grow. That's how we have the movie's title. Tige Andrews is one of the buddies from basic training and is seen in a few barroom scenes. He is good natured and willing to drink and fight with the best of them. That is why *Onionhead* is a very good service yarn. The characters are real and the performers draw you into their acting.

Topical Soap Operas

Television had supplanted the movies as the number one source of entertainment in America by 1960. Hollywood tried to compete with the small screen by creating new ways of presenting its films. Gimmicks like

Cinemascope, Cinerama and 3-D were grandiose ways of presenting epic stories culled from The Bible and world history. *The Ten Commandments, Ben-Hur* and *Spartacus* were some of the blockbusters that lured Americans away from their television sets. Like most trends there were scores of imitations and retreads. There was even a step towards dealing with mature material in soap opera formats.

Warner Brothers had achieved a brief resurgence in its popularity during the late 1950's because of their phenomenally successful schedule of television dramas and westerns. This success would continue into the early 60's. The studio, like the rest of the industry, still churned out big screen epics and soap opera melodramas. Two movies with larger-than-life subjects were *Ice Palace* and *The Chapman Report*.

Ice Palace was based on the novel by Edna Ferber, a Pulitzer Prize-winning playwright and novelist. Besides collaborating on several plays with George S. Kaufman, Ferber wrote many novels, some of which were turned into successful motion pictures. Among the books that were later made into films are *Show Boat* ('26), *Cimarron* ('29), *Saratoga Trunk* ('41), *Giant* ('52) and *Ice Palace* ('58).

The *Chapman Report* was loosely based on The Kinsey Report, which was actually two books written on male and female sexuality. *Sexual Behavior in the Human Male* was published in 1948 and *Sexual Behavior in the Human Female* followed in 1953. To call these sociological studies controversial would be a mild understatement. They proved that the United States was a space age-industrial society stuck in a Victorian social hierarchy. The fact that the movie was condemned by the Catholic Legion of Decency in 1962 showed how it was still difficult for society to accept the studies' findings.

Ray Danton had small parts in both films. He plays Bay Husack, a political pawn, in *Ice Palace* and Fred Linden, an acting coach on the make, in *The Chapman Report*. Bay Husack and Fred Linden are cads delineated by the class system. One has proper breeding and seeks to improve the blood line through marriage while the other is blue collar and lets evolution work through natural selection.

The political puppet and the acting coach use social mores as ways to achieve their ends, only one is considered a player with a well-articulated speech while the other drowns his loss in a whiskey bottle of garbled dialogue. They are pawns in social dramas where the leads carve out power blocks from the laws they exploit in their favor. Both men lose what they are after.

Romulus and Remus may have founded Rome, but it took Thor Storm and Zeb Kennedy to turn Alaska into the forty ninth state of the union. *Ice Palace* is their story, a sprawling epic of a friendship soured by betrayal; ambition turned deadly; and power plays that result in taming a wild frontier.

The film opens with an ode to Alaska. It is portrayed as a rugged frontier waiting to be tamed by modern Vikings. Zeb Kennedy (Richard Burton) is one of them. He is a man who believes that " a man's gotta reach for the sky even if he doesn't make it." His ambition is born out of the disappointment of being a returning war vet dealing with an unappreciative society. He does not realize that his rejection is due to being blackballed by his former boss, Einer Wendt (Barry Kelley), because the businessman does not want the volatile rough neck to curry his daughter Dorothy's (Martha Hyer) infatuation.

Thor Storm (Robert Ryan) is also a man used to adversity. The difference is he is also a man of faith, being the son of a missionary. He rescues Zeb after the hothead is thrown off a pier by a bunch of cannery roughnecks during a fight to preserve the honor of Wang (George Takei), a overworked laborer who breaks under the workload.

Robert Ryan, Carolyn Jones, Richard Burton and Martha Hyer comprise the power couples of *Ice Palace*. 1960, Warner Bros. Dist. Corp.

The conversation between the men aboard Thor's fishing boat defines both men but it is the action that follows which delineates their characters. The similarities attract both men to each other but it is their differences that combine to make a partnership in a cannery. Both men need each other because each has what the other lacks to make it in business.

Zeb Kennedy lacks Thor's social manner and trusting nature. Thor represents honesty and integrity, plus all the Christian virtues that make up a good seafaring man.

He has enough heart for both men. Conversely, Thor does not have Zeb's killer instinct or blind ambition. When they form their partnership, it is a melding of opposites.

This union also creates dissension when Thor becomes a tempest in a teapot after he is cuckolded by his fiancée Bridey (Carolyn Jones), the queen of the Fisherman's Ball.

She is the wedge that divides the partners after Thor brings home Zeb and her repressed instincts are aroused by the rough stranger. He is the innovator, conqueror, and builder and, in Zeb's presence. Thor Storm becomes a force of nature about to be tamed by industrialization. It's the radicalization factor that liberates the repressed Bridey.

Financing the cannery is a problem so Zeb returns to Seattle to seek help from his WW1 buddy, Jim Husack (Jim Backus). Husack lives a good life but is in no position to finance a cannery, especially since the new business will be competing with the established canneries. He inadvertently gives Zeb an idea when he tells him the real reason behind his blacklisting and that the boss' daughter still loves him. Zeb, forever the opportunist, marries her and returns to Baronoff, Alaska. But good news turns sour when Bridey becomes shocked at her hero's return. The reason is not lost on Thor and the partnership ends when he knocks Zeb to the ground and flees Baronoff in a dogsled.

After the betrayal, each man has absorbed enough of the other's qualities to become equals. That's when the power struggle begins. Kennedy becomes a powerful businessman hated by the fishing community because he works at cross-purposes with them. Thor lives in an Eskimo village after he suffered a mishap in the middle of the wilderness. He is rescued by an Eskimo, who accepts him as part of his family. Thor loses his wife in childhood and raises a son while Zeb marks out his territory and ruthless climb to the top. He is called Czar Kennedy and is still two-fisted, fast-forward, and on the prowl for new territories to conquer. He connives and manipulates, barking orders that eventually turn those around him into slaves.

One tried and true soap opera hook is letting the actors age as the time-span moves from one generation to the next and having the children of the warring ex-partners fall in love with each other. The different ethnic and financial background of the children also symbolizes the merging of cultures in the burgeoning Alaska.

If Zeb Kennedy ever felt contempt, it was for the native heritage of Alaska. He is a proud Welshman who considers himself above the rest even though he was kicked and booted about. In the long run, he is changed by the indigenous spirit of the land he has exploited.

Years later, Thor returns to Baronoff with his son. He resumes fishing and realizes that his former partner is about to rape and plunder the land because of his personal greed. He enters politics because he realizes that the only way Alaska can be saved from men like Zeb is to become a state.

A generation has passed by the time the men wield real power. Through the magic of soap opera conventions, the rivals' children-Christopher and Grace (Shirley Knight) elope. This, of course, enrages Zeb more than Thor, because Thor's son is half Eskimo. Tragedy claims the lives of the children during the time of their child's birth. Christopher is killed in a fight with a bear when he tries to bring his wife back to the city so she can give birth; when she does, death also claims her, leaving their child to grow up to be the perky blue-eyed blonde Christine (Diane McBain).

It is to her credit that Christine does not hide her Eskimo heritage, much to the consternation of grandfather Zeb, who forgets that he is an outsider to the land that made him rich. It is now the 1950's and Christine plays an important part to the plot development. She is equally divided between her grandfathers but wholly devoted to Bridey, who has become a nanny to the adversaries' children as retribution for her betrayal.

Many lives are affected by the rivalry between Kennedy and Storm. Some will profit by it; others will be destroyed. In every direction, the power of their hatred is seen and felt. People are used by Kennedy to block Storm's political rise. For him, Alaskan statehood would mean the reduction of his empire. One of the pawns he uses is Bay Husack (Ray Danton), the son of the only man that he trusts.

Bay Husack has become a business lawyer and is savvy when it comes to politics. He informs Zeb that statehood is inevitable but a middle-of-the road candidate may allay statehood for Zeb to consolidate his power instead of losing his empire to levees and taxes. Czar Kennedy plans to give Husack political clout by having him marry his granddaughter.

Supporting Roles | 79

Bay Husack's (Ray Danton) hopes of gaining power and prestige through a political marriage arranged by Zeb Kennedy are dashed by Bridey's (Carolyn Jones) meddling. 1960, Warner Bros. Dist. Corp.

Marrying a Kennedy family member would be leverage against his arch rival, Thor Storm, in the election determining Alaska's statehood, which he opposes. The plot goes according to the plan, a party is held, then all is exposed by the loose lips of Bay Husack's drunken ex-girlfriend. She implies that that the marriage may be political in nature. Aunt Bridey's tough questions contradict Kennedy and Husack, ruining the party, wedding plans and Kennedy's scheme to delay statehood.

Ice Palace would not be a soap opera without the final conflict and grand reconciliation. This happens when Thor's plane goes down in a snowstorm on the way to Washington to plead his final case for statehood before the legislature votes. The inclement weather discourages any rescue effort and all hope rests in the one man who knows the terrain like he does his own soul: Czar Kennedy.

"Czar" Kennedy's heroic effort to rescue his wounded enemy enables his arch-enemy to persuade the lawmakers to grant statehood to Alaska, something he bitterly fought. The saccharine ending has Thor Storm giving a radio address about universal cooperation and appreciation of nature's resources as the scenes fades into a panoramic montage of Alaska's beauty.

Although it is told in a straight forward manner, *The Ice Palace* comes off as hopelessly funny in some parts and amazingly artificial in others. The story of Alaskan statehood has all the elements of the soaps, including ham acting and dialogues rife with proverbs and heavy-handed sayings. It goes off in many directions, milking every cliché for what it's worth, including having the feuding men's children marry to create more tension like Romeo and Juliet. Another Warner's technical triumph and a crowd pleaser, *Ice Palace* is dazzling eye candy. If not taken seriously, it is enjoyable.

The same thing can be said about *The Chapman Report*. The nuclear age brought a major change in American mores. There wasn't a facet of society that remained untouched by modernization. Everything, from culture and politics to religion and lifestyles, was challenged and transformed in the process. One of the changes that eventually became one of the Sixties revolutions was sexual attitudes. The Kinsey Report helped to crack the façade of a self-proclaimed puritanical nation.

The Chapman Report is Hollywood's attempt to dramatize some of the juicier elements of the Kinsey Report's findings. Topics like extramarital sex, frigidity, and nymphomania are some of the plot elements of the movie. George Cukor, long heralded as a "woman's director", helmed the film, and provides the gloss for what is essentially a big budgeted large screen soap opera.

The sullen, square-jawed seriousness of Andrew Duggan's Dr. George C. Chapman is supposed to give the film a sense of professional approval. Before things get too out of hand with the sexcapades (early Sixties style!) of the four film heroines, the scene cuts to the professorial Dr. Chapman, who either clarifies a definition or explains a concept to a reporter. He is the film's stamp of approval. Otherwise, it is a tawdry (for its time!) soap opera. By today's standards, it is a drawing room comedy.

The four women are Kathleen Barclay (Jane Fonda), a frigid widow, Sarah Garnell (Shelly Winters), an adulterous suburban housewife, Naomi Shields (Clare Bloom), a self-hating nymphomaniac, and Teresa Harnish (Glynis Johns), a bohemian conducting sex research of her own.

Their stories were provocative and risqué enough to have caused concern among church groups, stamping the film off-limits to minors. To look at the movie today is to realize how sexually repressed society must have been. To consider most of the film's behavior as deviant is twisted in itself.

Efrem Zimbalist, Jr. plays Paul Radford, Dr. Chapman's assistant, and assumes the lead in the movie. He is one of the interviewer's who becomes involved with one of the interviewees-Kathleen Barclay, a frigid widow attached to a possessive and domineering father (Roy Roberts) whose opinions are the law. One thinks that he has a too-tight-a grip on his daughter. Is this the cause of her frigidity or is it the death of heroic husband, a race car tester who was killed in the line of duty?

The four principal women of *The Chapman Report*: Clare Bloom, Glynis Johns, Shelley Winters and Jane Fonda. 1962, Warner Bros. Dist. Group.

Naomi Shields thrives on good times but hates herself because of it. Used as a rag doll by the strangers she seduces, her story is used as an escape hatch for the frustrated peepers in the audience. What would eventually be seen as sexual emancipation is portrayed as sinful living. It is mainly because of the guilty aftermath that traps the woman in a world of self-hatred.

Teresa Harnish is a bohemian who actually goes out on a limb because of her intellectual husband (John Dehner), a bargain-basement Hugh Hefner. He is an older scholarly man and she is a scatterbrained blonde easily impressed by his pseudo-intellectual indulgences like bad poetry. Ty Hardin plays the beach boy who becomes part of their game.

Ray Danton is amusing as Fred Linden, a fifth rate acting teacher whose seductions work with the desperate and lonely housewives in his acting group. One of them is Sarah Garnell. Her husband, Frank (Harold Stone), may be satisfied with suburbia but she isn't. What she needs is a fast-talking show biz hot body with a bottle of Scotch in his briefcase and an extra berth in his bunk. Before long, she is having a torrid affair with Linden. She slowly realizes that she is one of many housewives that take private lessons on his houseboat.

Fred Linden is a pickled version of John Howard. His actress is an amateur and so is he when it comes to amoral deception as one of the cads

A lobby card set of *The Chapman Report*. 1962, Warner Bros. Dist. Group.

in *The Chapman Report*. Acting lessons, a yacht and bottles of Scotch are all he needs to bed some of his acting students, the latest being a lovelorn suburban housewife played by Shelley Winters.

She is one of the four women whose secret vices make up the storyline of the movie, a big budget color extravaganza based on the Kinsey Report. Linden is smooth like Howard but lacks the cruelty, opting for a superficial charm that melts into drunken confusion at a bar when he gets the icy kiss off from his conquest.

If anything, the film is an ancient reminder of the role women's sexuality played in the nuclear age. The opinions, attitudes, and perspectives of the women are all related to a single motivational point: their husbands. It is the men in their lives that define the four principals. Do they act the way they do because of or in spite of their feelings about men?

American Pulp

THE DARKER SHADES OF GRAY

The 1950's as a decade was often considered staid and placid because of the way it has been preserved by old television shows and newspaper ads. Orthodoxy was perceived to be the antidote to anarchy and strict censorship and moral codes seemed to assure a secure and stable domestic life.

There were challengers to the system and the plastic model of conformity was confronted by the ethos of the anti-hero. He was someone you could root for even though he was up to no good and his dark character began to cross over to the other side of the moral compass thanks to a new style of character interpretation popularized by the Method School.

This change in attitude gave latitude to creating characters whose blend of virtues and vices were arbitrary to the norm and its' moral codes. The trickle-down effect from the groundbreaking movies and performances was apparent in B-movies, especially crime dramas and detective thrillers.

During the 1950's, Ray Danton hit his stride in a series of solid B's that introduced a different kind of dark, kinetic personality. *The Looters* ('55), *Outside The Law* ('56), *The Night Runner* ('57), and *Tarawa Beachhead* ('58) established the Danton attitude: cool, menacing, and slick to the touch.

Pete Corder, Johnny Salvo, Roy Turner and Joel Brady are characters whose emotional makeup are blends of contradictory characteristics. They are men who have performed good deeds and committed heinous acts. Heroes with larceny in their souls, they are dark brothers who can be interpreted in a variety of lights. Their fates are determined by their state of mind the moment they perform the act that defines their motives.

Although Roy Turner appears to be the odd man out, his repressed maniacal side is what bonds him with the others. At times, the others display Turner's ineffectual attitude. At the beginning of *The Looters*, Pete Corder is humbled by his bad luck. In a hotel declaration of love, Johnny Salvo shows his soft side in *Outside the Law*. Cpt. Joel Brady's prelude to wartime heroics in *Tarawa Beachhead* is a momentary comfort zone of shell-shocked catatonia.

Combined, these four characters are early members of Ray Danton's fraternity of backhanded redemption. They are the basis for all such characters that followed, including Legs Diamond and George Raft.

Abner Biberman was a prolific character actor whose most known role is Chota, the murderous Thuggee in *Gunga Din* ('39). In the 1950's, he became an acting coach and head of casting for Universal-International before becoming a director for the studio. Biberman specialized in directing intense dramas that were offbeat and somewhat lurid. The twisted part of the human soul was his terrain and he explored it without flinching or settling for happy endings. Ray Danton starred in two early Abner Biberman films, *The Looters* and *The Night Runner*.

In *The Looters*, a hero, a villain, an inamorata, a good Joe, and an ambitious stooge are embarking on new phases of their lives when they find themselves in a plane crash survival drama set in the Rocky Mountains. The theme of the Good Samaritan seduced by greed gives the movie its serrated edges.

Jesse Hill (Rory Calhoun) has taken refuge in the mountains after a sour romance. He is a man who is remote on the outside but has enough compassion to risk his life for strangers in peril. His mountain ranger experience qualifies him as a guide and his daily challenge is dealing with the seasons and the rugged terrain. He resents the Army's yearly artillery practice but is powerless to stop them from using Pepper Valley as a target area. It is an inconvenience that will turn into his salvation.

Pete Corder (Ray Danton) is a washed up adventurer, hustler, and cad hoping to for one more score on the Riviera. After WW II, he was a smuggler along the Spanish border, the companion of a rich Brazilian millionairess, and a Las Vegas gigolo. Rock bottom is being the most broke man imaginable. That is how he cashes in his ticket as the man who saved Jesse's life in the war: guilt through bankruptcy and self-pity.

Sheryl Gregory (Julie Adams) is an adult model whose attempt to return to her small town home turned her into a tawdry pin-up queen for

Poster for *The Looters*, a searing crime thriller disguised as an outdoor survival adventure. 1955, Universal Pictures Company, Inc.

the boys. She is hoping for one more crack at the big time in New York City. Cynical and prone to sarcasm, she is as much of an object as the strongbox of money that sets off the madness.

Newly retired Chief Petty Officer Stan Leppich (Frank Faylen) is Brooklyn all the way and can't wait to get home because his wife has been "waiting a long time for the big furlough." He is personable, practical, and a model of shipboard chivalry on dry land. Two-fisted retaliation is his final attitude but he is kept in check by the gun-toting looters.

Pete Corder was Ray Danton's hard-boiled tough guy and remains one of his best characters. 1955, Universal Pictures Company, Inc.

George Parkinson (Thomas Gomez) is a spent brokerage clerk passing himself off as a financial consultant. He is the one who triggers the insanity when he finds a stash of Treasury money and gives himself away by trying to bribe Hill into taking him back to Manitou. It takes the outdoors to bring out the Wall Street mountain lion in Parkinson. Soft, cuddly, and obscenely greedy, the brokerage clerk unwittingly becomes Pete Corder's dupe.

The adventure begins when Corder visits Hill, his wartime buddy, in the Rocky Mountains. Before any link can be made there is an airplane crash on Pike's Peak. The men hitch their mountain climbing gear and become a rescue team. It is a common goal that leads to a fork in the road when temptation appears in the form of a small fortune in Treasury loot found in the plane wreck by Parkinson.

A fundamental rule of crisis movies is that the disaster brings out the best and worst in people. Personalities change, motives become apparent, and sympathies are transferred. The race with time is a factor and it is a given that not all of the principals will survive.

Things are further complicated by the burden of the incidental conscience—a wounded peripheral figure whose support for survival is a test to the humanitarian instincts of the survivors. In this case, it's Red (Rod Williams), the co-pilot who suffers a skull fracture in the plane crash. The semi-conscious co-pilot is the weak link in the survivor chain and will be jettisoned by the cruelest player in the survival sweepstakes.

It is betrayal that aids Jesse Hill, along with a map of the artillery site. Parkinson has been cut out of the action and Corder is outsmarted by a clever ploy by his former partner.

Rory Calhoun is good as Jesse Hill, the hero. He is toughened by his outdoor experience and honed into a rough hewed personality by the mountains. Hill carries the wounds of a betrayed lover and covers the scars with his tough guy personality. However, his pain has not made him bitter. He still lends a helping hand—first to Pete Corder—then to the survivors of the plane crash.

Ray Danton shines as Pete Corder. It is his second big screen role and it remains one of his best parts. Corder is the basis for all the in-your-face characters Ray Danton would play in his career. His theme song is a jaunty French folk tune that he whistles throughout the movie. It is an ominous death hymn.

Sharp, confident, and arrogant to a fault, Pete Corder is a classic study in evil. Twisted by his desire to keep the loot and eliminate the

The madness begins when Parkinson (Thomas Gomez), a broke timid clerk posing as a big-time investor, refuses to relinquish the Treasury money that he has found in the plane wreck. 1955, Universal Pictures Company, Inc.

witnesses, he is a war hero turned peace time looter. His willingness to kill Hill and the survivors shows the depths of his depravity. What makes it vainglorious is that it is all for a second run for fun in the Riviera sun.

Pete Corder's shady personality is evident from his introduction in the film's opening. He is a dark figure who enters a cabin and lights a fire before removing a rifle from its rack. It is the way he cocks the rifle after he settles into a comfortable chair that it apparent that the stranger is trouble. The credits roll and the music plays an interlude that consists of variations on the French folk tune that is Pete Corder's theme song, death march and leitmotif.

Assurance settles in after he is introduced as Jessie's wartime buddy. Sympathy is elicited by his hard luck story. Admiration colors his good deed of saving Jesse's life in WWII combat. Discomfort returns when he eyeballs Jesse's home while whistling his theme song after Jesse pledges his support.

The lure of Treasury money found in a mountaintop plane crash is what corrupts Pete Corder. He is a war hero who rejects honor when he values money and power above the welfare of people. A noble past is bartered by an illicit opportunity to buy a false future. His interest is the lives he has to sacrifice to make his dream come true.

The only chance of survival for the hostages is pinned on mountain man Jesse Hill, a wartime buddy who offers help to the destitute Corder at the outset of the movie before being betrayed over the money. Negotiating the terrain is less of a problem to Hill than dealing the twisted ambition of his ex-ally. He knows that Corder plans to execute everyone once they're out of the wilderness.

The most haunting display of Corder's depravity is during the nightfall campfire scene after he and Parkinson and taken the others as hostages. His failed attempt at reconciliation with Jesse while refilling the canteens ends with his brutal rifle butt retaliation to his ex-friend's chin at the expense of Parkinson's loyalty; his chilling testimony of mutual need and trust to Parkinson will lead to his partner's murder; and his concern about Red's fragile health results in a shadow pantomime of the co-pilot's death.

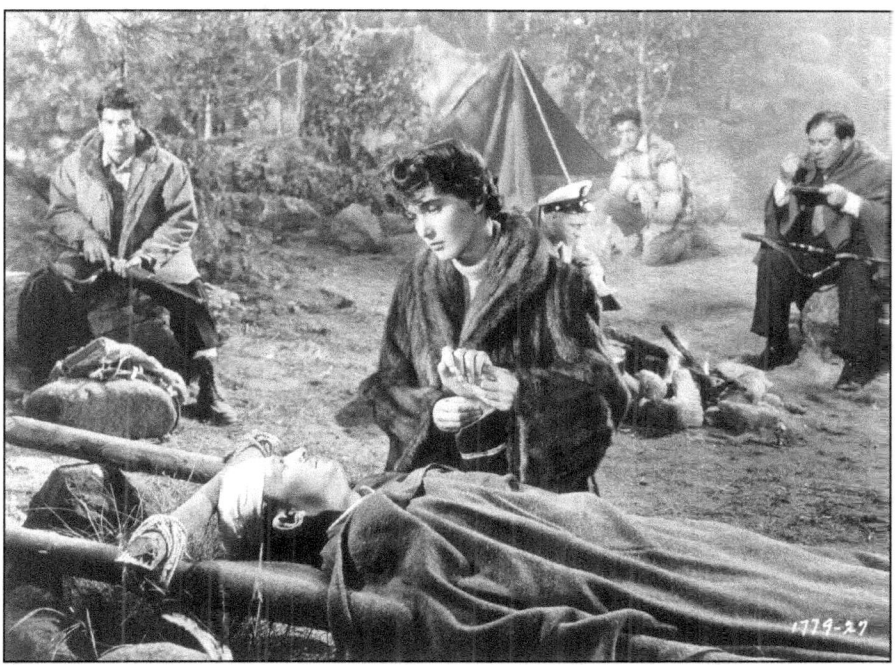

Pete Corder has struck an unholy alliance with Parkinson to share the money and has to find a way to eliminate the players, starting with Red, the wounded co-pilot.
1955, Universal Pictures Company, Inc.

Julie Adams is simultaneously cold-blooded and torrid as Sheryl Gregory. Usually, Ms. Adams exudes a cool and suave sensuality; as the pin-up queen, she is defensive and withering in her appraisal of men. Her sultry expression to Red's come-on line in the beginning of the movie is hot enough to turn the plane into a comet. Corder's grand scheme means nothing to Sheryl Gregory. Her disdain for him is evident from the beginning, when Corder outstays his welcome kiss and later suggests intimate sleeping arrangements. Sheryl's only concern is her mink coat.

"You wear it like a badge of honor", he tells her before the terror starts.

It's true, but that changes after the adventure ends in an explosive climax. She is the character who changes the most and she regains her self-respect, mainly because of the bravery she displays throughout the ordeal. She is her own woman and contributes her share of resistance to the looters. When the smokes clears, her mink coat is left behind on the battlefield. She does not need it anymore.

Cheryl is the one who turns the tide by pretending to seduce Parkinson so she can take his rifle from him as they near their destination. It is futile because Corder has removed the bullets because he says that he felt that his partner was getting sloppy. The real reason was that they were coming near the end of their journey and Parkinson's name was on the hit list. His protests forces Corder to collect his dividends a little early with a pull of the trigger that sends a shot that cracks into an echo in Pepper Valley.

Frank Faylen is one of the highlights of the movie. Faylen specialized in playing working class stiffs with a sense of justice. The only thing that matters to him is returning home to be with his wife. His character doesn't have any social airs. He has a working-class appreciation of Sheryl's career. To him, she's a famous model; it doesn't matter that she's a pin-up queen. She's worth risking his life for.

Thomas Gomez gives an intense performance as the brokerage clerk who is destroyed by greed. Parkinson is pretentious because he tries to be more than what he is. The Treasury money makes him realize how much he hates his life. Even on the plane, he lies to the other passengers when he claims to be an investment counselor.

Rod Williams as Red is a character on a gurney. His only lines are when he comes on to Sheryl and tries to calm the passengers during the turbulence. Russ Conway plays the commander of the Howitzer maneuvers. His battalion is a modern day Cavalry unit to the rescue. John

The lurid title card for *The Night Runner*, a disturbing drama about mental illness and 50's Americana. 1957, Universal Pictures Company, Inc.

Stephenson is his second in command. The rest of the acting credit goes to the matte-mountains for the outdoor scenes of the rescue climb.

Abner Biberman again shows his proclivity for bizarre character studies with *The Night Runner*, based on a short story by Owen Cameron and published by Cosmopolitan in 1955. The film's weirdness is similar to the strangeness of a film Biberman would make the next year called *Floodtide* ('58). Both have seaside settings and deal with psychological quirks. Roy Turner (Ray Danton) could have been the disturbed child in *Floodtide*.

The Night Runner is a strange and unpleasant movie that is one of the seedlings of the motel madmen movies that was perfected in *Pyscho* ('60) and revived periodically over the decades. In this version of madness in obscurity, the madman is the protagonist. The prematurely released patient and soon-to-be seaside maniac is Roy Turner, who was treated at Woodvale State Hospital because of attempted murder.

Too much work, unfair treatment on the job, and a negative family background took their toll when he tried to kill a stranger on the street. Institutional overcrowding forces the system to release the half-cured patient with a doctor's admonition that he is to avoid confrontational situations with a "no stress-no strain" mantra.

This proves to be a tall order for Roy Turner. He takes a train to Los Angeles to apply for a job as a draughtsman but is unable to deal with routine application questions on a job interview. Confusion and anxiety impel him to bolt from the employment office and he collides with a young couple when he runs out of the building. Unable to handle the confrontation, Turner attempts to strike the man before he is dissuaded by the woman's passionate pleas. Instead, he runs into the traffic and becomes more confused by the ramblings of the big city.

Turner is lost and is inspired to leave the city by a window display in a Greyhound office. He boards a bus and finds refuge in a quaint seaside hamlet. Roy Turner's entrance into the static life of the hermetic beachfront is a salve to the inhabitants' loneliness. They may appear to be assisting Turner to life at their speed but they actually need his existence for their survival. The banal characters and the endless boredom of the sedate beachfront life will create an evil that is far more oppressive than anything Turner carries within his tortured soul. The seemingly sane surroundings of the seaside motel will spell doom for Roy Turner and result in a return to his homicidal nature.

Loren Mayes (Willis Bouchey) and his daughter, Susan (Coleen Miller) run the motel where Turner rents a cottage. Loren Mayes is a single father with a suspicious nature and bitter disposition. He is crusty and morose, distrusting Turner from the moment he arrives. Shrewd observations from years of running a motel give him the impression that the new guest is trouble. It's not until his violent death that the viewer \

Susan Mayes (Coleen Miller) mirrors Turner's madness in a canvas that depicts a fearful reminder of repressed painful memories. 1957, Universal Pictures Company, Inc.

realizes that he was right in his low assessment of the mysterious guest with no car.

Susan is young and her beauty charms the introverted new tenant. She combines all of the positive elements of the seashore haven: sea breezes and natural beauty. She is twenty two years old and lives a sheltered life. Painting seascapes is her means of escape and she fantasizes about traveling around the world to see what it is like. Roy Turner is a suitor for Susan's untested chastity and has become a challenge to Loren Mayes' bitter isolation.

Hank Hansen (Harry Jackson) is the friendly mechanic in the middle of nowhere. His roadside business is his only connection to the outside world. He needs another man to talk to and finds one in Roy Turner. One wonders how many innocent bus passengers he has persuaded into going to the motel for their final unraveling. Amy (Merry Anders), his pregnant wife, is sweet and charming and her desire—beside odd food combinations—is to see Susan paired off with Roy.

The only other character who is detached from Turner is Officer Wallace (Robert Anderson) of the Highway Patrol. He witnesses a Turner outburst when the stranger breaks a bust during a polite inquiry about his history. Susan's willingness to understand his anger prevents the scene from being totally bizarre. And it is bizarre, to say the least. He, too, distrusts Turner from the start but keeps his distance. It must have been a mixed pleasure to arrest and detain the rival of Susan's affection on murder charges.

Susan makes Roy Turner's transition to the civilian world smooth and steady. With her guidance, he gets a job at an engineering firm five miles down the road.

Her innocence is what short circuits Turner. She doesn't understand madness and believes that her infatuation is really love. This insistence is what forces Turner to assume a guise of normalcy.

Glimpses into his history reveal sordid episodes that twisted his personality. One such incident is recounted to Susan when she takes a break from painting one of her seascapes. A sky full of seagulls reminds Turner of his childhood hobby of raising birds. He lived on the Atlantic seaboard and raised cranes, sandpipers and seagulls. His favorite pet was a seagull named Bulls Eye, who was so commanding in flight that it was poetic. The bird was shot for sport by a mean old man-his father.

The disturbed look on Susan's face shows her discomfort yet it does nothing to dampen her enthusiasm for the stranger. It only makes her sympathetic to him. Because of Susan's support, Roy Turner is able to fake normalcy but it is under the watchful eye of Susan's father

Loren Mayes eventually drives Roy Turner over the edge with his mean-spirited meddling. The stressful situation that Roy Turner was told to avoid is confronted dead-on. Loren Mayes opens a letter addressed to Turner from his doctor. He learns that his guest is a former patient at the state hospital and demands that he leave while Susan is running an errand. Mayes will allow Turner one shred of dignity by allowing him to leave without being exposed as a lunatic, to use Mayes harsh description, which is accompanied by pointing to his head.

Turner reluctantly agrees but has a breakdown as he walks away from the motel. He buckles and the camera angles tilts to the sound of brash brass chords. Turner does an about face and returns to the motel. The sly grin he shows is an indication of his descent into madness. He bludgeons Mayes with a football trophy while the man is watching a television western.

American Pulp | 95

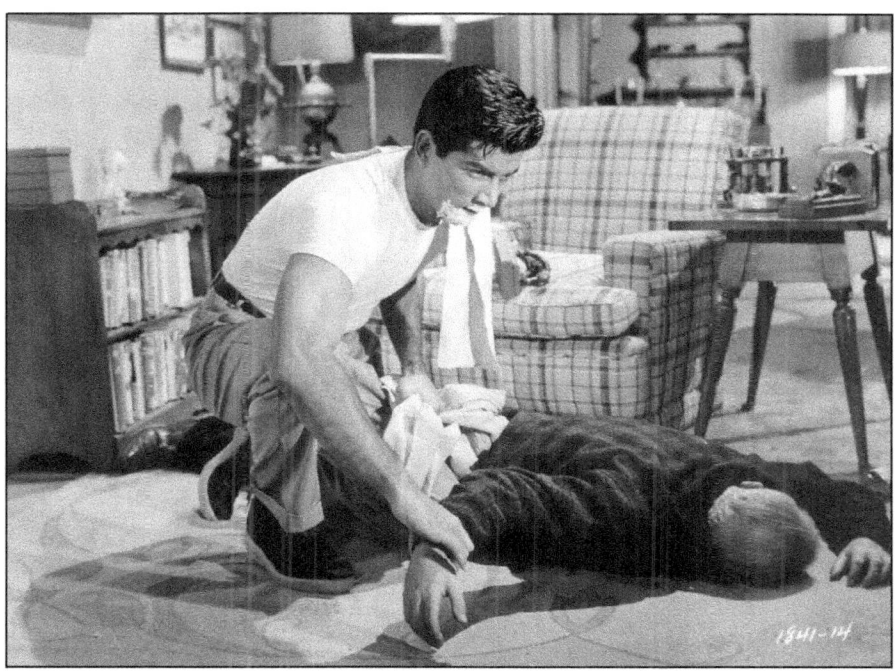

Roy Turner examines the crime scene, pretending to be an innocent spectator alerted by another guest's anguished scream. 1957, Universal Pictures Company, Inc.

At the point of Turner's crossover into madness, the film becomes a horror movie. The movie is mostly sunshine and boredom until the climatic descent into terror. Picnics, walks on the beach and friendly chatter comprise most of the movie before the dramatic rupture. The only hints of madness are in the film's introduction when the panel of psychiatric personnel evaluates Turner's mental condition in light of a new busload of arriving patients and release him because of necessity. He also shows his tentative social skills when he cannot deal with a job interview or when he mishandles bumping into a stranger by grabbing him by the lapels before fleeing into a crowd.

Part of Turner's dementia is being able to hide behind a guise of control after he has committed the murder. A middle-aged couple enters the motel to register a minute after the murder and Turners assumes the role of motel manager. He dissuades the couple by telling him that the plumbing is faulty. This scene eerily foreshadows Norman Bates in *Psycho*.

He has enough presence of mind to make the murder seem like a robbery gone bad. As he hatches the plan to mislead the police the television western shows a cattle stampede to reflect Turner's agitated state of mind. Turner also helps Susan run the motel as if nothing happened. It is the appearance of minute clues that begin to peck away at his disguise. A five dollar bill stained with nail polish, Loren's watch buried in the garden and partially filled out register receipt turn Susan into a detective.

Abner Biberman directs Ray Danton and Coleen Miller in the final beachfront meltdown scene. 1957, Universal Pictures Company, Inc.

She believes that the police can use the receipt in their investigation, reasoning that if the couple did not register at the motel they would have gone somewhere else. This eats away at Turner and he decides to kill her. It is then that we realize that Roy Turner is not an innocent victim of circumstance.

He is-indeed-a monster who hid under good intentions. He takes Susan out for a walk and confuses her with a rambling speech accusing her father of messing with their romance and comes to the conclusion that he has to kill her, too. A violent dip in the ocean brings the point home to Susan while a disillusioned Turner strolls along the beach.

His murderous delirium is shocked into sanity by the sight of a seagull, a symbol of his painful childhood. He saves Susan from his darker self in a last act of heroism and carries her back to the motel where he telephones Officer Wallace to turn himself in. Turner ambles out to the porch to sit in Loren Mayes' rocking chair. A medium shot focuses on Turner's confused silence as it surrenders to empty space.

Roy Turner was doomed from the start because the cards were stacked against him. The audience sympathizes with him because his descent into madness is inevitable. Watching him arrive there is half the drama. He is affable and laid back until he is pushed to the brink of madness. Unable to adjust to his new environment, Turner self-destructs and leaves misery as a reminder of his dashed hopes.

The natural order drives him insane by making him confront his original nature. Meekness and timid reactions give way to a temporary swell of violence that claims a life. Turner accepts the evil within himself when he resorts to killing. He is partially absolved when he undoes his murder attempt on Susan at the end of the film.

His deceit is a lie to himself that makes him crack wide open at the end when guilty mementoes come to life and perform a citizen's arrest on his repressed memories. The surrender to justice is a walk in the gray area that surrounds his darkness, an absolution of irony, freedom and madness.

To appreciate the bold subject matter, one should be aware of how mental illness was viewed by society at the time *The Night Runner* was made. Shock treatment and lobotomies were standard procedures for altering extreme patients' behavior and Thorazine was just introduced as a pharmaceutical way to deal with the illness. There were not any outpatient programs or halfway houses to help the recovering patients to re-adjust to daily life in the community.

Negative public perception stigmatized anyone who sought psychiatric treatment and people who resided in sanitariums were branded for life. Loren Mayes' scornful attitude is indicative of the perception, including using the derisive word, 'lunatic' to describe Roy Turner. Society was just stepping out of its medieval attitude about mental illness during the 1950's.

The movie appears to be an apologia for Roy Turner only because we view it with modern sensibilities. One need only consider two of the movie's lobby cards to see that the film is meant to be a topical horror story. One reads, "Released Mental Patient Hunted In Terror Attack!", "Are inmates turned loose too soon?", "Berserk suspect tortures victim." Another states, IT HAPPENED TO AN INNOCENT GIRL…it could happen to you!" and "She gave her love to a man the State Asylum turned loose too soon!"

The Dark Sides of Justice

In *Outside the Law* ('56) and *Tarawa Beachhead* ('58), wartime heroes deal with their battle scars in different ways. Johnny Salvo uses them to buy a clean slate and a solid reputation. Lt. Joel Brady cashes in his reputation for the big brass ring. Both men collect dividends on their heroics, only one capitalizes on a debt.

Johnny Salvo redeems himself and restores honor to the family name when he busts a counterfeiting ring in *Outside The Law*. He would have been an ex-con for the rest of his life if the government didn't need his services. An official pardon washes away the blood of the old lady he ran over with his hotrod.

Lt. Joel Brady thinks that being a war hero is the key to success back home in *Tarawa Beachhead*. He would be a murderer if he didn't work for Uncle Sam under conditions extraneous to the law. His Medal of Honor is the headstone of the man he kills in combat. It becomes his new coat-of-arms when he marries into the slain man's family.

Outside the Law and *Tarawa Beachhead* are two contrasting studies in heroism directed by Jack Arnold and Paul Wendkos. Both are done in light and shadows, yet one is hopeful and the other is mooted by despair.

Because of its truncated length, Jack Arnold's *Outside The Law* is fast moving and jam-packed with all of the elements of assembly line crime dramas sweetened by a plot full of lonely characters and settings in the parameters of daily life.

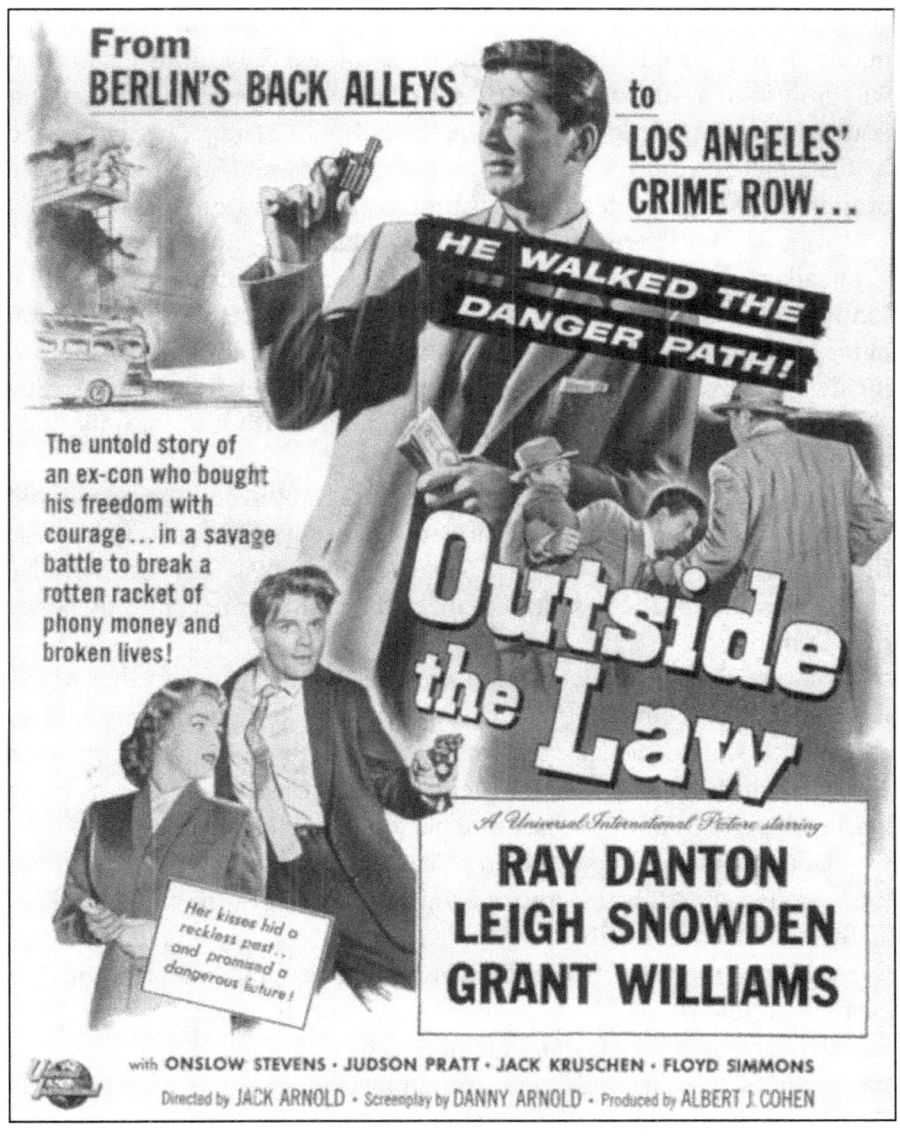

Outside the Law is a fast-paced crime drama with sympathetic characters, snappy dialogue, imaginative direction and a smoky musical score by Henry Mancini. 1956, Universal Pictures Company, Inc.

Johnny Salvo (Ray Danton) was a juvenile delinquent chaptered into the Army because of vehicular manslaughter. Now, he is a decorated war veteran called upon by the Treasury Department to help crack open a counterfeiting ring. The common link is Harry Craver, a convicted counterfeiter, bunkmate of Salvo's in San Quentin and murdered Army buddy in post-war Berlin. His death has drawn Salvo into a case that will grant him a full pardon and restored citizenship rights. Salvo's quest is to wipe away one identity and replace it with a new one. He has to be blackmailed to do it. It is a coercion of a different sort-removal of a burden placed by a system that has him by the reputation.

Alec Conrad (Onslow Stevens) is the burnt out Treasury agent who calls the shots in the counterfeiting case. His added burden is that Johnny Salvo is his estranged son. Salvo, who uses his mother's maiden name, feels betrayed because his father failed to aid him after the hotrod incident. The new conflict is over Maria Craven (Leigh Snowden). She was married to Harry for nine months and lived with him for only three because of his overseas duty.

Salvo has to find a way to track the criminals by becoming acquainted with Maria Craven. He needs to romance her to get information because the head T-man believes that she is part of the racket. Salvo falls in love with her while on the case and realizes that she is innocent. His father doesn't think so.

Maria Craven is the ice blonde who melts in the arms of Salvo. Maria is sexy without being sultry and has a soft-spoken charm to her. Her character is walking a legal tightrope because she is peripherally involved with the counterfeiters. One of them, Dan Kastner, would like to bring her in deeper. His motives are more personal than business.

Don Kastner (Grant Williams) has a faded California beach bum look that is perfect for the crooked con artist trying to rip off Uncle Sam. He hates Johnny Salvo for his entrance into Maria Craven's life. Kastner warns him to stay away from Maria and supervises the hotel beating. His desire is so intense that he tells Maria that if she decides to go with Salvo he will kill them both. Kastner attempts to do that in the climatic scene at the bus station but wounds Alec Conrad instead.

These are the main characters in what is essentially a quest drama for Johnny Salvo. The ex-con-war hero has to clear his name, forgive his father and save the woman that he loves from the long arm of the law. Johnny Salvo is the quintessential pulp movie hero: star-crossed and branded by society as a louse but willing to provide a service to the government for official redemption.

Attitude and pose is what gives Johnny Salvo his muscles. Salvo is wisecracking with authority, tough with the villains, and romantic with his leading lady. It is comical the way he emasculates his father with his

Johnny Salvo is given a chance to change his destiny if he can deal with his past in *Outside the Law*. The character is one of Ray Danton's clear cut good guys despite his spotty past and juvenile crime record of a vehicular manslaughter rap. 1956, Universal Pictures Company, Inc.

withering criticism. Nevertheless, the chief T-man gets the job done, including taking a bullet meant for his son in the film's climax. Ray Danton's performance earns him a place in the section on out-of-the way crime drama heroes; he even suffers a beating in a neon-lit hotel room.

The film traces the T-men's attempts to crack the counterfeiting ring. We meet dupes, accomplices, and anonymous heroes who work around the clock to see that justice is done. The action takes place in settings as diverse as post-war Berlin and a Spanish restaurant in Hollywood. In between there are early morning stakeouts, a romantic interlude at the Spanish restaurant, conferences at headquarters, and a final confrontation at a bus station. Hard work and crisp calculations finally pinpoint the source of the illegal printing operation and the brains behind the West Coast wing.

It is the colorful characters that give the movie its breath and personality. Milo (Mel Welles) is a shifty philosophical middleman in the counterfeiting operation. He is married to Mama Gomez (Amapola Del Vando), a lifelong friend of Maria's who runs a Spanish restaurant. Milo sits at the bar and drinks the wine when he is not pestering the customers.

He is the second Papa Gomez and ones sense that Maria's friend and confidante married him out of loneliness. Milo is the 'bait and switch' man of the operation.

His opinion of a jacks-of-all trades is a sound philosophical piece and the sarcasm that covers his pithy diatribes is poisoned honey. It is Milo who telephones Don Kastner to inform him of the date between Johnny and Maria. This sets up Salvo's hotel beating that follows his dinner date.

Phil Schwartz (Jack Kruschen) is a good-natured but tough T-Man with a bum stomach calmed by his special pills. He keeps things light with his humorous jibes but is observant and tough when the situation calls for it. He runs the stakeout that nails Milo but not before a well-placed crowbar creases his skull.

Maury Saxton (Judson Pratt) is Alec Conrad's brusque right-hand man. He is cynical but logical and reluctantly offers advice to Alec Conrad and how to approach his reconciliation with his estranged son. He knows that Salvo's connection to Harry Craven is a coincidence that Conrad uses to bring his son back into his life. Still, he keeps his distance and uses clear judgment to make the calls that help nab the counterfeiters.

Phillip Boorman (Raymond Bailey) is a smug, beady eyed businessman who runs an import-export firm that comes under suspicion because of the large amount of paper it uses. The feds believe that a firm that size would not need such a large inventory and the amount of drawback entries on their records seem to suggest that they feds are right. They are.

The Pulenskis (Kaaren Verne and Maurice Doner) are a diminutive immigrant couple who are questioned by Conrad to find out about the counterfeit money they deposited in a bank account. It turns out that they were given the funny money by a friendly stranger in London who swindled them when he converted their currency to American dollars. They are almost Munchkin like in appearance and behavior. The husband is soft-spoken to the point of being apologetic. He ends the meeting with saying, "I am sorry if we caused you any trouble" despite the fact that his life has turned into a nightmare.

Jack Arnold, whose other early credits include *The Creature from the Black Lagoon, The Incredible Shrinking Man, and It Came From Outer Space*, gives *Outside the Law* its heart and soul. His clever and poetic command of camera moves and angles, plus the use of the smoky music washes create a dreamy otherworldly feel for the movie.

A crisp screenplay written by his brother, Danny, adds to the two-fisted quality of the movie.

Arnold is known primarily for his science-fiction movies but he directed several crime dramas besides *Outside the Law*, like *Girls in the*

Johnny Salvo and Maria Craven deal with Treasury agents and counterfeiters, not to mention a psychotic henchman, a brow beating chief T-Man and the uncertainty of new love. 1956, Universal Pictures Company, Inc.

Night ('53), *The Glass Web* ('53), *Man in the Shadow* ('57), *The Tattered Web* ('57) and *High School Confidential* ('58).

He was also a director for a television show that he produced for Blake Edwards, *Mr. Lucky* ('59-'60) , along with directing episodes for Edwards' other crime drama show, *Peter Gunn* ('59-'60).

He displays a dreamy style in *Outside the Law* that is enhanced by the musical score. One is his striking visual effects is the use of back-projection in the scene where Milo tries to make a getaway. He has just slugged one of the T-Men with a crowbar and attempts to drive away before he is shot to death by another agent. The image of the heroic T-Man rushing in front of the van is a filmed backdrop and the contrast between Milo and the projected image is eye-catching.

The love scenes between Johnny Salvo and Maria Craven are also handled with sensitivity and are compelling instead of mawkish. They add a subtle dimension to the movie which makes it a cut above the usual low budget crime drama quickie. They first spend time on a hillside overlooking a valley while they exchange family history. It is a night time scene and one senses that a connection is being made between the couple. The lethal triangle is reinforced when they drive away followed by Kastner and nasty mood music.

The scene in Mama Gomez's restaurant is one of the highlights of the movie, not only because of the introduction of the picaresque Mama Gomez and Milo. We also have Aluísio Ferreira serenading the customers with his lyrical guitar playing. Even the shot of his left hand playing out of sync with the music adds charm to the movie.

The couple dance on the veranda to the dreamy accordion strains of the movie's theme song. Maria tells Johnny that he has lonely eyes, "Deep with no bottoms." It is when they share their first kiss, which is interrupted by Mama Gomez when she tells them that their dinner is getting cold. It is a golden moment, especially when it is followed by the scene of them kissing in the car outside of the hotel. It is the leitmotif played in a smoky jazzy burlesque grind that gives the scene the stamp of approval. It is one of the many reasons why this film is a minor gem.

Their love comes out in the open in the hotel scene where Maria finds refuge in Johnny after Don Kastner promises to kill her if she leaves him. They hash out their differences and Johnny comes clean about his mission. Salvo and Maria declare their love for each other and seal it with a classic movie embrace and kiss. It is done in a straight forward manner a combination of hope and trust in a hotel room. It is Jack Arnold's

American movies played worldwide. *Outside the Law* headlines at the Regal Theater in Bombay, India. 1956, Trade Magazine.

direction and the cinematography of Irving Glassner that gives the scene its impact.

The rousing finale is a shootout in a bus station where Johnny Salvo and Don Kastner fire at each other, stalk one another through the rows of parked buses, and trade jabs and crowbars in a one-on-one confrontation. Kastner may be able to break Salvo's grip but is shot dead by one of the cops who arrive in a squad car. The film ends with Johnny, his father and Maria settling their scores.

The closing credits add to the good feeling because of its use of the old fashioned technique of showing film clips of the characters with the names of the actors superimposed under the images. What makes the closing credits so powerful is the *leitmotif* played with gusto and authority.

Henry Mancini co-scored the film and his contributions are familiar smoky jazz riffs and sound washes that highlight many of the scenes. His best piece is a sensual *leitmotif* played in a variety of musical styles and tempos to enhance the growing romance between Johnny Salvo and Maria Craven. It also creates a dreamy ambiance for the closing credit shots of the main characters.

Honor and heroism are also examined in *Tarawa Beachhead,* a sharp, edgy movie that packs a lot of action and emotion within a seventy-seven

A lobby card set for *Tarawa Beachhead*, a stark and bleak war drama that examines the definition of heroism on the battlefield. 1958, Columbia Pictures Corp.

minute time frame. Its stark intro is a series of shots sans music: a battleship's big guns blasting, a fleet of amphibious crafts landing, and a dead soldier floating face down in the surf. It's a fight in the Pacific and, instead of being heralded by martial music, it assaults the eyes with the storming of a Pacific paradise turned into a raging inferno: Guadacanal-1942.

On the island, Lt. Joel Brady (Ray Danton) tells Sergeant Sloan (Kerwin Mathews), his platoon sergeant, that the troops will have to take the caves that they have encountered. They don't know whether or not enemy machine gun nests inhabit the mountain caves. Lt. Brady radios the rear with the news of the caves but refuses all offers of assistance

Lt. Joe Brady thinks that being a war hero is a way to get the key to success back home. He uses morality to justify the fact that he is beyond morality. The battlefield is the legislator of the private sector. Becoming a war hero is the ticket to being a success in the civilian world. It becomes apparent to Sloan that Lt. Brady is possessed by the desire for war glory.

A bloody battle wins the caves but leads to an insurmountable Japanese ambush on the road ahead. Only three soldiers survive to flee into the jungle: Lt. Brady, Sgt. Sloan, and Pvt. Johnny Campbell (John Baer). It is during a tense scene with the three of them hiding in the brush that the private bolts and is shot dead by Lt. Brady.

Was the shooting accidental or intentional? Did Lt. Brady hope to silence Campbell, whose hatred is caused by the senseless deaths of his friends in the campaign for the caves? Could it be possible that the tense lieutenant was lost in a reverie broken by the sound of the rustling elephant grass?

Sgt. Sloan accuses Lt. Brady of murder. Brady protests and maintains his innocence. The men have become adversaries but, to the viewer, these labels are ambivalent. Sgt. Tom Sloan could be the film's hero because he wants to avenge Johnny Campbell's death. From another perspective, Lt. Joel Brady might be a hero, too. Surviving two intense battles may have blurred his nerves with a faulty night vision. Campbell's death could be perceived as a casualty of war.

Nothing is said about the incident in the commander's tent when Sloan and Brady give their stories on the platoon wipeout, an ordeal that earns a promotion for the men. From that moment onward, Cpt. Joe Brady and Lt. Tom Sloan play a game of cat-and-mouse with rules arranged by fate and coincidence. Brady's ambition versus Sloan's conscience is the basis for the friction between the two men. The rest of the movie consists of their run-ins and the buildup of tensions and animosities.

The struggle Sloan has is with his conscience. He spends the rest of the movie debating himself about bringing charges against Brady. The irony of chance and scriptwriting has the two men running into each other in peacetime and in war. The loser is Johnny Campbell because his memory is used to impose on his family, whose lives are altered by the appearance of the two survivors.

Capt. Joel Brady is an ambivalent hero-villain depending on your perspective of war. 1958, Columbia Pictures Corp.

Lt. Sloan visits Johnny Campbell's family in New Zealand to present his widow Ruth (Julie Adams) with a letter he found on the dead private's body. The only problem is that Captain Brady made his acquaintance first and is dating Paula (Karen Sharpe), the dead man's sister-in-law. This does not sit well with Sloan and creates an air of tension that is noticeable to the family.

The men play it cool for appearances sake but Sloan makes it clear that he still plans on bringing charges against Brady, who scoffs at

Lt. Joel Brady warns Sgt. Sloan about pressing the issue about the soldier he shot dead under the duress of combat. They may have lost the caves but they gained commissions in the field so Brady feels that they should both be grateful. 1958, Columbia Pictures Corp.

his accuser's scorn. Time only weakens the charges and there is really no case in what would be considered a casualty of war; still, Sloan persists in his harassment of Brady.

In *Tarawa Beachhead*, Kerwin Mathews gets star billing but his righteous lead is no match for Ray Danton's steely-nerved Brady. In every scene they do together, Danton dwarfs Mathews. Sloan always gets cut down after delivering a blistering tongue lashing to Brady, whose retort is a sardonic grin and a dose of dry wisdom. Sloan doesn't have what it takes to bring Brady down-only Fate can do that.

Joel Brady is razor-sharp in his ruthlessness. He knows what he wants and goes after it double time. His plans are to exploit the war because it is his ticket to success. Cunning and arrogant, nothing stands in his way to getting the key to the city.
    Brady's battle ribbons and wedding band link him to success and upward mobility. Hypocrisy befits the officer as he ingratiates himself into the family of the man he killed in combat. He is a heroic link to their fallen family member; that's why they accept him as an in-law after he marries Paula.
    Sloan may ponder the desire to press charges and Brady may talk about good cowboys and desperadoes but the differentiation isn't so easily discernible. In this movie, irony is the final arbiter when Brady is killed in combat and Sloan is forced to acknowledge that maybe it is guys like Brady that win the war or maybe they start them.
    Julie Adams gives a sensitive performance as Ruth, the war widow on the verge of a new love affair. Her heart can't take another combat loss yet it needs the love offered by the sensitive and caring Sloan when he visits Campbell's family in New Zealand to present his letter. The burgeoning love affair is carried out against a backdrop of war. Only time will tell whether the affair will come to fruition and whether Sloan will settle in New Zealand, as is the wish of Ruth's father, Casey (Russell Thorsen).
    Ms. Adams' sophisticated sensuality is a contrast to Paula, her sister-in-law, played by Karen Sharpe. She is kittenish in her sexuality. Her voice and her moves are torrid yet her attitude is virginal. She hangs out at the officer's club and teases her fan club, which includes soldiers of every age. They know that she is leading them on but they don't care. She lifts their morale and that's all they have during wartime.
    Paula is dating Brady, who has preceded Sloan in his offer of condolences. A private word of warning with Brady opens old wounds. In an ominously lit hotel room, Brady tells Paula, his wife-to-be, about the basis of the friction between the men. It's their philosophy of war-they differ in the way they believe it can be won. After a thoughtful pause, Brady scoffs, "Tom Sloan-the man who plays God."
    Onslow Stevens is his usual brusque self, this time as Commanding General Nathan Keller. Keller is a no-nonsense commander who gives Sloan all the combat he can eat. He teaches the young officer about the war, just like Joel Brady does. He cautions the young officer about making charges that cannot be substantiated. His battle weary war wisdom broadens Sloan's philosophy about combat. It is something that is brought

Sloan is mortified to find the he was proceeded by Brady, who has settled into the comfort of the New Zealand family of the man he killed in combat. 1958, Columbia Pictures Corp.

home in the last shot of the movie where the surviving soldiers' rout step along the beach while Taps plays for all the soldiers that got the keys to the city but didn't live to use them.

Paul Wendkos had a talent for getting the most out of the least, meaning that he directed small, low-budget films that left a strong impression on the viewer. This was evident from his debut feature film, *The Burglar*, a powerful portrait of a brilliant but ill-fated jewel thief played by Dan Duryea. Wendkos only directed a handful of films and television shows and never went on to anything big. However small his resume may be, it is still impressive. *Tarawa Beachhead* may not occupy a high rank in the canon of war films, but it still stands tall and looks good, mainly due to his expert direction and a searing performance by Ray Danton.

Despite the quality of this production, it lay on the shelves for two years after it was made by Morningside Productions. Columbia Pictures optioned the picture and released it to little fanfare. The trade papers noted with sarcastic glee that it was successfully re-released, only because it was shown on the same bill with several popular Three Stooges shorts, the ones with Joe Besser, no less.

ALBERT ZUGSMITH'S AMERICAN NIGHTMARE

Albert Zugsmith was a colorful Hollywood director and producer who was known for his eclectic credits. He produced classics like *The Incredible Shrinking Man* and *Touch of Evil* for Universal-International and a series of exploitation films with Mamie Van Doren for MGM with one exception, which was made for his old studio. The credit for the classics goes to their directors, Jack Arnold and Orson Welles. The credit for his topical comedy-melodramas can be equally shared between the producer and his star, Mamie Van Doren. Zugsmith also produced many two-fisted crime dramas and odd exotic-themed films.

The Mamie Van Doren films were considered shocking for their time and had titles like *High School Confidential* ('58), *The Beat Generation* ('59), *The Big Operator*('59), *Girls Town*('59), *The Private Lives of Adam and Eve*('60), *College Confidential* ('60) and *Sex Kittens Go to College* ('60). They were stigmatized for being condemned by The Catholic Legion of Decency. It was if Cardinal Spellman got a perverse thrill out of hounding Mamie Van Doren. Now, these exploitation films may seem like drawing room comedies but they stand as valid commentaries on the hypocrisy and corruption that roiled underneath the placid and ideal American Dream. They presaged the social revolution that was to break out in the late 60's and can be viewed as social satires.

In 1955, Danton's first year in pictures included three journeymen roles for Universal-International: Little Big Man in *Chief Crazy Horse*, Pete Corder in *The Looters* and Blackie in *The Spoilers*. The same year saw him as David Tredman, the first role to present Danton as a romantic actor, in MGM's *I'll Cry Tomorrow*.

Danton's success with this role at MGM impelled him to seek a change in studios but Universal-International held steadfast to its contract with Danton. It is an ironic note that, years later, during his stay at Warner Brothers, Danton returned to MGM for two films-*The Beat Generation* and *The Big Operator*-that were more brutal and downbeat than any of the pulps he did for Universal-International. It was strange compensation for a failed screen test for a major role in *Ben-Hur*, the reason for his return to MGM.

His characters—Stan Hess and Oscar Wetzel—are extremists in a post-war consumer society that denies its decadent side. They are two mutated versions of the attitudinal outsider-Stan Hess, a perverse beatnik in *The Beat Generation* and Oscar Wetzel, a cold-blooded rackets enforcer in *The Big Operator*.

The movies are cheesy period piece peepshows that teased and shocked audiences with their taboo subject matter. They have all of the

A press book cover for *The Beat Generation* captures the film's luridness. 1959, National Screen Service Group.

elements of Zugsmith's best productions: cheap sensuality, brutal sadism, and warped emotions. Stan Hess is the Aspirin Kid, an ersatz beatnik whose tortured soul harbors a harsh secret. Oscar Wetzel is a brutal mob enforcer who is dark, noxious and vicious.

Stan Hess is actually Arthur Garret, a dissolute young man who expresses himself in Hollywood's contrived beatnik lingo. Jack Kerouac had popularized the counter-culture movement with his book, "On the Road." Hollywood lost no time in creating stereotypes to capitalize on the youth movement. Stan Hess is the dark side of Maynard G. Krebs, the beatnik played by Bob Denver on TV's, *The Many Loves of Dobie Gillis*. However, Stan Hess was no lovable space cadet. By the film's end, his terror-kidnapping scheme has been ruined and he needs a frenzied mob to provide him cover for an aquatic getaway. To incite his sycophants, Hess does a beat rap on rockets to the moon.

Oscar Wetzel is a cobra with a pencil-mustache. His beady eyes are cold and remote. He oversees union boss Joe Braun's terror network when it comes to getting information and removing obstacles. Supervising the removal of a witness played by Charles Chaplin, Jr. via a cement mixer and setting Mel Torme on fire are parts of Wetzel's resume.

The Beat Generation opens with Louis Armstrong singing the title song. It is an ambling, sorrowful blues tune about the nihilism of the beats. While he sings, the camera captures the styled hipsters in various modes of confused delirium. Chief of the beats is Arthur Garrett (Ray Danton) nee Stan Hess. He sits at a table, reading a book by Schopenhauer and waxes philosophical about the vicissitudes of love. His partner, a young blonde haired girl, is disconcerted because she is leaving and won't be missed by him.

"Everybody's gotta move ", says Hess in beatnik meter. " I mean, you can't stand still for the next mushroom cloud. Now, you dig?"

What follows is the sickness that lies beneath the beatnik façade. It starts with a hula-hoop, hi-fi jazz, and a knock at the door. Stan Hess is no longer a beatnik but a well-dressed young man wanting to repay a loan to a woman's husband. Convincing her to let him in to write a check is his set-up.

Stan Hess is the Aspirin Kid, a rapist whose sickness illuminates the moral rot within Sgt. Dave Culloran (Steve Cochran), the detective trying to capture him. Sgt. Culloran and Hess stalk each other, using women as bait to whet their appetite.

Sgt. Dave Culloran is a two-fisted, no-nonsense type of guy. Humor is foreign to him and self-torment is his regular perspective. He is a loving, if

Georgia Altera (Mamie Van Doren) frustrates Sgt. Culloran (Steve Cochran) and his partner, Jake (Jackie Coogan) with her festive mood during their interview. Her flustered husband (Ray Anthony) stares at a sketch of the rapist they are searching for. 1959, National Screen Service Group.

suspicious, husband. He often questions women's motives and blames the victims of these assaults for the consequences. As the movie progresses, it becomes apparent that Sgt. Culloran is the flip side of Stan Hess.

When *The Beat Generation* was released, it must have seemed that audiences were peering through a looking glass at a society of fallen people. To them, the beatniks were lost because of their anarchic lifestyle and the rape victims lost their status in proper society when they were molested. A dark angel represents each side. For the beat generation, it's the Aspirin Kid; for society proper, it's Sgt. Dave Culloran.

Misogyny is viewed from both sides of the law. Sgt. Culloran is a cop who suspects the worst of all women because his first wife was unfaithful. Stan Hess hates women because of his parents' failed marriage and his father's penchant for marrying young women. The common juncture for the men is when the Aspirin Kid attacks Culloran's wife, Francie (Fay Spain).

Their neutral ground is Georgia Altera (Mamie Van Doren), a sultry potential victim of a copycat rambler. Culloran's sickness is manifested when he hounds Georgia Altera so she can lead him to Hess. Today, no cop would be able to get away with that type of harassment. The film justifies it when Altera breaks down and tells Culloran that she was meeting with someone whom she believes is the Aspirin Kid, not knowing that it is Art Jester (Chris Mitchum), Hess's disciple, used as a copycat to confuse the police.

Although harsh and brutal, *The Beat Generation* makes a profound point with the equation of a rapist and a macho cop because of their misogyny. It also boldly handles the liberation of Culloran's wife, Francie, who achieves independence when she cancels her husband and the rapist by declaring her unborn child to be "my baby."

Steve Cochran plays the two-fisted macho cop to perfection. He is attitudinal and full of a bitterness that he disguises behind a front of sincerity. His inability to sympathize with his wife's dilemma makes him a stone man. He plays the sanctified twin to Ray Danton's damned character.

Stan Hess (Ray Danton) kidnaps Georgia Altera (Mamie van Doren) but she is too much for him to handle. 1959, National Screen Service Group.

At first, Danton appears to be comical as he recites his lines with the exaggerated hipness of the Fifties screen beatnik. His performance deepens when he shows the impetus for his behavior. Late in the film, he dispenses with the beatnik charade when the game of tag between him and the detective turns violent.

Fay Spain's character development as the cop's wife has the most magnitude of any character in the film. She goes from a middle-class housewife to a fallen angel demonized by her rape. The burden liberates her from the hypocrisy of societal conventions. She is a resurrected goddess by the end of the film.

Mamie Van Doren, as always, is alluring and mesmerizing. She provides a comic turn within a vile tale. Her Georgia Altera is a sexually liberated woman lacking fear.

Even when Hess kidnaps her, she doesn't abandon rationale thinking. She makes pointed remarks about the similarity between the cop and the rapist.

Sgt. Culloran (Steve Cochran) captures Stan Hess (Ray Danton) after an underwater sea chase. Georgia Altera (Mamie Van Doren) is unimpressed because she feels that both men are equal because of their misogyny. 1959, National Screen Service Group.

Jackie Coogan, as the cop's sidekick, is the voice of reason within the macho world of cops and robbers. He is balanced and enjoys the benefits of a healthy marriage. His character keeps Halloran grounded in reality, having the guts to force his partner to face his woman-hating impulses.

William Schallert gives an understated performance as a self-righteous priest who calmly delivers an unctious speech to Francie about the sanctity of life even though he is cut off from the world at large. He dispassionately talks about God while tending to his garden.

On a minor note, the movie is also interesting because of the supporting cast. That includes B-movie icons, faded celebrities, and perennial supporting players. Among them are Louis Armstrong, James Mitchum, Irish McCalla, Charles Chaplin, Jr., Regina Carroll, Vampira, "Slapsie" Maxie Rosenbloom, Grabowski, and Sid Melton in drag.

Albert Zugsmith's topicality was piqued by The Kefauver Senate Hearings on labor corruption and he produced a couple of movies that capitalized a trend encouraged by *On The Waterfront*, which set the tone for similarly themed movies that followed it in the Fifties. The typical plot has a tyrannical union boss with underworld muscle exploiting the workers until the vulnerable hero destroys him. Along the way, examples of the boss' two-fisted earnestness are illustrated to make comeuppance more enjoyable.

Zugsmith's variations on the labor theme are *Slaughter on 10th Avenue* and *The Big Operator*. In *The Big Operator,* Albert Zugsmith reassembles most of his cast from *The Beat Generation* and adds Mickey Rooney as the heavy. The result is a corrupt labor union movie with the Zugsmith trademarks: sleaze, exploitation, and violence.

Little Joe Braun (Mickey Rooney) is a pint-sized terror to

Poster for *The Big Operator*, a brutal and sadistic exploitation movie about labor corruption. 1959, National Screen Service Group.

the union workers that he squeezes to make a profit and pad his cushion as the boss of the Precision Tool Union. It is amusing to see big burly bent-nosed types taking orders from the pint-sized Joe Braun. He smokes a cigar that's almost as big as he is and makes threats that are even bigger. Always the finagler, he finds a person's soft spot and rubs it raw. With the enforcer Oscar Wetzel (Ray Danton) at his command, he controls his union with fear.

Napoleonic in stature and intent, Little Joe is on the brink of ruin although he doesn't know it yet. His downfall will be the square jawed quiz show winner and all around nice guy, Bill Gibson (Steve Cochran), who works at the tool plant with his shadow, Fred MacAfee (Mel Torme). Their wives, Mary (Mamie Van Doren) and Alice (Ziva Rodann), are the best of friends, as are their sons.

Gibson doesn't buy any of Joe's attempts to lure him into the union hierarchy. At first, he thinks that Joe wants to hire him for muscle, then wonders why he would want him for a front office job. It becomes more quizzical when he finds out that Fred McAfee was offered the same deal.

It boils down to Gibson seeing Braun and Wetzel together in front of the union hall before a meeting. Currently under investigation by the Senate, Braun could be convicted of perjury if it is found out that he lied about their association, which he claimed was non-existent. The men find out about the connection while they are watching the televised hearings and Braun denies having known Wetzel.

Braun has already bought the loyalty of the other workers because of a deal he coerced out of a client. They now have a longer vacation and better benefits. At the union meeting, MacAfee is adamant in his resistance to Braun's attempts to buy the men.

Little Joe expels MacAfee from the union and Wetzel, using his own initiative, later sets him on fire.

The "human torch" scene is indicative of the mood invoked by this film. It is bleak, sleazy, and cheap, yet it draws you in with a perverse fascination. Oscar Wetzel is the beady-eyed enforcer of notorious crime boss, Little Joe. The movie opens with his character knocking out Bill Tragg (Charles Chaplin, Jr.), the Union Treasurer and watching him put into a cement mixer. The credits roll over the cement mixer as it churns to a pounding big band arrangement by Van Alexander.

Mickey Rooney is alternately funny and frightening as the cruel labor boss. His performance is over-the-top. Whether he is bossing around stooges like Ed Brannell (Jackie Coogan), his right hand man at the union hall and his lawyer Phil Cernak (Lawrence Dobkin) or chewing out Oscar Wetzel for setting McAfee on fire without his permission, Rooney's ire chews the scenery and spits it in the audience's face.

Bill Gibson is a firm, yet loving, husband and father. His righteous indignation turns to mania when Timmy (Jay North), his son, is kid-

Little Joe Braun (Mickey Rooney) tries to bribe (Bill Gibson (Steve Cochran) to become one of his stooges while wife Mary (Mamie Van Doren) dazzles him with her sensuality. 1959, National Screen Service Group.

napped. Along with his posse, he cleans out the house and apprehends Joe Braun.

Mamie Van Doren plays the suburban housewife well. Even being clean-cut and perky doesn't diminish her sexuality. Her radiance is enhanced by Joe Braun's visit to the house. He lights up like a bulb when she enters the room. His compliments are cleverly disguised innuendoes.

Her innocent suburban existence is a bone for Little Joe to chew on. He is cut down to size before he does too much damage to her life. In the end, she is just as tough as the men are when they storm the kidnap-house. She even knocks Wetzel unconscious with a whiskey bottle over his head in the film's climatic fight scene.

Fred McAfee is the eager beaver-next door neighbor. He is the Fifties' prototype regular guy-best friend. Mel Torme's folksy portrayal is so annoying that one actually applauds Wetzel for setting him on fire. One senses that he likes to live in Bill's shadow because it's a comfortable place to be.

Ray Danton is barbaric as Oscar Wetzel. A pencil mustache adds to the sleaziness of the character. His work is precise and cuts to the bone.

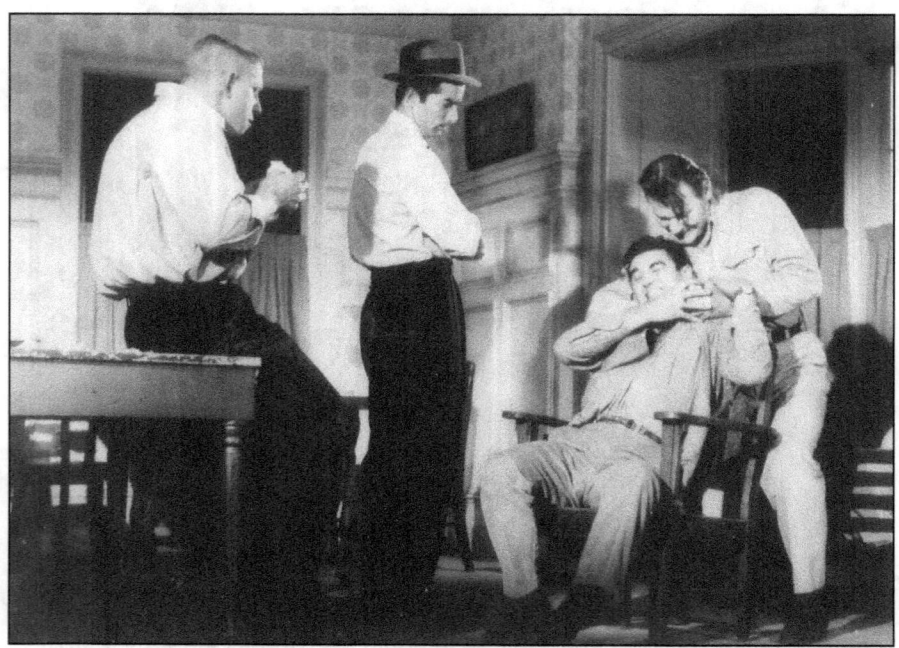

Leo Gordon gives Bill Gibson (Steve Cochran) while Grabowski and Ray Danton egg him on. 1959, National Screen Service Group.

Jim Backus, Mel Torme and Steve Cochran try to enlist the aid of two horny teenagers in tracking down the whereabouts of Little Joe's hideout. 1959, National Screen Service Group.

Cruel and cold to the touch, he supervises a gang of goons that includes Leo Gordon and Grabowski as Danny Scanzi and Lou Green, respectively. They are vicious, lethal, and more than willing to break any bone or grind anyone into paste. The gang exemplifies the Zugsmith touch because they are repellent.

They torture Bill Gibson in a scene that is so sadistic that it is laughable, especially with the way a nonchalant Oscar Wetzel stands by, somewhat bored except for when he leaves his mark with a lit cigarette. As brutal as they are, the enforcers are no match for Gibson. He can identify Scanzi by a ring that he wears and has no trouble pointing the finger at Green because of his cold. Gibson is also observant in a way that has him making mental notes on the sounds that he hears as he is driven to the hideout. His observations also include smells, jukebox music and the amount of steps that lead to the lair.

The Big Operator is full of ironies and cynicism, even down to point of having Gibson's son played by Jay North, the future Dennis the Menace of television. The scene of the boy being lured into the car by the kidnappers is unsettling because they are wearing Halloween masks and toss bags of candy on the ground. The boy, like a pigeon, picks up the bags that lead to the car where the men snatch him and take him to their lair. They even threaten to kill him if Gibson does not lie on the witness stand.

As with *The Beat Generation*, *The Big Operator* has its character actors and cameos. Jackie Coogan, Jim Backus, Lawrence Dobkin and Irish McCalla lend a hand in supporting roles and there are appearances by Vampira, Ziva Rodann, Ray Anthony, Don 'Red' Barry and Billy Daniels. They round out the seediness that is brought home by a brassy big band soundtrack by Van Alexander.

The Signature Roles

In 1955—Ray Danton's Hollywood debut year—he remarked in a magazine profile that he would like to win an Oscar by the time he was thirty. Five years later, he was frustrated by his status as a contract player at Warner Brothers. This led to resentment on his behalf and it affected his personal and professional life. Budd Boeticcher was a friend of Julie Adams and he visited her on the set of *Maverick*. They discussed her husband's discontent and he tried to assuage the difficulties by offering Ray Danton the lead in *The Rise and Fall of Legs Diamond*.

The director rigged the screen tests by shooting the other actors over their shoulders as they played their scenes with Karen Steele, who played Legs Diamond's wife in the movie. Ray Danton was the only actor who faced the camera in his screen test and this led Jack Warner to remark that "he's the only sonofabitch who knows what he is doing." That is how Ray Danton got to make his trademark film.[3]

Despite Budd Boetticher's magnanimity the shooting was not without friction.

The director remarked that the reason Ray Danton made such a great Legs Diamond is that "they were both charming bastards." The filmmaker described himself as a courteous individual who took as well as he gave. Even still, he said that the only two actors that he hated were Gilbert Roland and Ray Danton.

Boeticcher tells the story of directing the crime syndicate takeover scene that occurs at the end of the movie. He was called away from the set for a phone call. When he returned, he found Ray Danton directing Frank de Kova's crime kingpin and the other make believe gangsters in the shifting of power scene. This prompted Budd Boetticher to have two chairs made, one with actor printed on the back and the other displaying director. The next day, the director reiterated to his star what that meant.

Nevertheless, Ray Danton's style peaked with *The Rise and Fall of Legs Diamond*. Although the movie is directed by Budd Boetticher in a sparse fashion, written by Joseph Landon in a snappy manner that alters some gangster history of the times, and lensed by Lucien Ballard in the style of 1920's silent movies, it is not a paean to the film genre that Warner's had perfected in the Thirties, as one might expect.

The press book cover for *The Rise and Fall of Legs Diamond*, often considered Ray Danton's crowning achievement. 1959, Warner Bros. Dist. Corp.

The reason for Budd Boetticher's change of perspective was his disillusionment with the subject matter as his research and preparation progressed. Years after the movie was made, the director gave an interview with Bertrand Tavernier and said that, "Legs Diamond was a big hoax. In real life Diamond was a son of a bitch, probably the worst man who ever lived.

"As I progressed in my research I realized I couldn't possibly make a film out of it, and I didn't want to. I'd seen the crowds of films like *Scarface* [Howard Hawks, 1932] and I decided the public would be sick of all those mass killings and bursts of machine-gun fire. So I decided to make a comedy out of it, a real comedy about Legs Diamond and Alice; I mean that inside a serious framework I adopted a comic style and a comic tone, treating tragic scenes in quite a light manner, with gags."[4]

There is a lot of humor in the movie but it is dark and sardonic; how could it not be considering the subject matter? And much of the credit for that goes to Ray Danton's bold and aggressive acting style and the way it railroads everyone that gets in his way. Budd Boeticher's rapid fire movie chronicles Jack "Legs" Diamond's criminal career from petty thief to crime kingpin until his shooting death in a syndicate arranged hit. His direction is tight and nothing is wasted in the way he develops his characters and gets to the point of each scene without meandering.

Aided by nimble editing and effective cinematography, Budd Boetticher doesn't miss a step from the opening scene of the Diamond brothers arriving in New York to the closing setup of the detective forcing a street urchin to look at the dead gangster to prove that he was mortal. Each character, from Diamond down to a star-crossed cab driver, serves a purpose. No one and nothing is superfluous.

It begins when Legs Diamond and Eddie (Warren Oates), his tubercular brother, arrive in New York and witness a failed jewelry store robbery. The thieves are shot dead in a getaway attempt but that does not deter Diamond from planning a robbery of his own. Agile thinking and shrewd observation help him to improve on the robbery and he accomplishes this by finding a stooge in Alice Schiffer (Karen Steele), a beautiful but naïve dance instructor.

Diamond is bold at his first dance lesson when he asks her for a date, apologizing for his brazenness because he is new to the city and lonely. Alice is polite in turning down his advances by telling him that she has a dance competition that night. He weasels his way into her company by injuring her dance partner and takes his place in a contest where the couple wins a trophy. He tops the night by taking her to a movie in a theater that is located next door to the jewelry shop.

Legs Diamond (Ray Danton) defends himself from assassins after they gunned down his boss. Later, he will exact his revenge. 1959, Warner Bros. Dist. Corp.

The robbery is conducted on a bathroom break, in front of a cop who peers into the window and sees Diamond sweeping up as a janitor. He even gets through a dragnet led by Lt. Moody (Simon Oakland), the taciturn detective who will hound him throughout the movie. Arrogance and ingenuity work against the gangster when he is later caught and sent to prison.

This is not a problem because he has a stooge in Alice, whom he contacts years after dumping her. His teary-eyed invocation for help appeals to her and she vouches for him so he can get a job as a dance instructor at the studio where she works. It is a cover for a new scheme that is the gangster's pattern for success: he steals from thieves because they can't rely on the police for justice. He starts with a petty ante job of robbing a fence and ends with the usurpation of Arnold Rothstein's (Robert Lowery) criminal empire.

Legs Diamond's method for triumph is using people as steppingstones for his climb to the top. He ascends the ranks of the criminal underworld by hustling from one scam to another with the grace of a dancer and the dexterity of a fighter. He is cold hearted about whom he uses and totally bold when executing his plans. Diamond doesn't disguise his ambition- he telegraphs it. The mobster's conceit is bolstered by his feelings of invincibility from surviving multiple assassination attempts. Because of his belief that he can't be killed, it's not a problem for him to make enemies.

It is a character weakness to encourage Legs Diamond's forceful ambition because he always secures one job while keeping his eye on his next climb to the top. It is suicide for Arnold Rothstein to give Diamond his first big break because the fledgling gangster's ambition is a flame that will turn into a raging bonfire.

Arnold Rothstein is the gangster who fixed the 1918 World Series and caused the Black Sox scandal. He is amused by the way Legs Diamond tangles with his bodyguards to get an audience with him. Instead of being let into the inner circle, Diamond is given the job of bodyguard to Little Augie (Sid Melton), one of Rothstein's satellites. The jovial gangster is amused by Diamond's sense of humor and dies laughing after he is murdered by the McDermitt Brothers.

He locates his old Army sergeant, Joe Cassidy (Gordon Jones), and pays the bewildered man to teach him how to shoot with both hands. It is Diamond's retaliation that earns him the reputation of a two-fisted shooter who cannot be killed and this is what earns him a second audience

Legs Diamond (Ray Danton) relies on Alice Shiffer (Karen Steele) once again after he is wounded in another assassination attempt. 1959, Warner Bros. Dist. Corp.

with Arnold Rothstein, much to the consternation of Matt Moran (Joseph Rushkin), Rothstein's chief bodyguard.

It is Rothstein who gives Diamond the nickname, 'Legs', but it was not because of Diamond's skill as a dancer, like the movie suggests. The real Legs Diamond got the nickname because he started out as a "snatch and run" thief in New York's garment district. One senses that Rothstein tolerates Diamond because the gangster reminds the aging crime lord of himself at a younger age. He is not totally enamored by Diamond. After the aspiring mobster makes inroads with Monica Drake (Elaine Stewart), his smoldering moll, he sets up Diamond in a drug bust.

To show him who the boss is, Rothstein gives Diamond a pocket watch as a token of his gratitude. It holds a glassine packet of heroin that lands Diamond in jail after he is ratted out by Rothstein and arrested by Lt. Moody. The aspiring gangster is sprung the next day as an example of the crime kingpin's power. It is a fatal lesson for Rothstein.

Diamond shows his gratitude for Rothstein's guidance by murdering his boss after incapacitating his bodyguards, Matt Moran and Fats Walsh (Judson Pratt) with spiked liquor. He waits until the other mobsters carve up Rothstein's empire before moving in for his percentage. At first, the gangsters, led by Leo "The Butcher" Bremer (Jesse White), are amused by the announcement of his protection racket. They humiliate him and threaten him at the meeting but their mirth turns into despair when Diamond sabotages their businesses.

He does this by romancing Dixie (Diane [Dyan] Cannon in her first role) and pumping her for information. Before long, Legs Diamond is the mob kingpin after he reduces Bremer to a crawling weasel begging for mercy as the new boss points his Tommy-Gun at him in front of the other gangsters.

This infuriates Matt Moran, whose intense hatred for Diamond was formed the first time Diamond tried to broach the inner circle. Moran does everything he can to destroy Diamond, including killing Eddie when he is left to fend for himself. It is to no avail because Diamond is too smart for him and winds up turning an assassination attempt against Moran, who winds up dead in the street along with two other gunmen.

Joseph Ruskin exudes pure menace as Matt Moran. His enmity with Diamond eventually costs him his life. The score is settled eleven years later when Danton and Ruskin played small parts in the television movie, *Banyon* ('71). Ruskin's hit man liquidates Danton's character, a gangster recently released from the penitentiary.

Legs Diamond's success had more to do with the opportunities of the times than his genius. He rules like a ruthless dictator, using fear as a motivation. Like most dictators, he is undone when his forces fail to back him up in a formidable confrontation.

In the fast-paced world of gangsters, loyalties shift as fast as new deals are made. It is a Darwinian world where the strong feed on the weak. It is a matter of time before the predators become the prey. Arnold Rothstein falls to Legs Diamond, just as Diamond will fall to the emerging crime syndicate.

When Prohibition ends, a new syndicate is born. He learns about this during a European vacation with his wife, who he has reduced to a stammering alcoholic. A newsreel announces the end of Prohibition and this concerns him when he returns to find his empire has crumbled. This is the movie's main weakness because it seems that scenes chronicling the decline were edited. It would seem unlikely that Diamond's criminal empire would collapse during the duration of a vacation but, in the movie, it happens.

He returns to New York and is invited to a meeting by the Syndicate where he is told by the cool and calculating Chairman (Frank de Kova) that he is washed up, something that is unfathomable to him. The syndicate is

Legs Diamond (Ray Danton) surveys his crime empire when he becomes the undisputed crime pin after he murders Arnold Rothstein. 1959, Warner Bros. Dist. Corp.

amused by his arrogance in the same way the petty racketeers were after they divided Arnold Rothstein's empire among themselves. However, the new syndicate is not a clique of street hoodlums; they are a well-oiled machine that operates like a big business with a board of directors.

Legs Diamond is considered a garish dinosaur and his bodyguard (Judson Pratt) and chauffeur (Gordon Jones) desert him, reducing the once-invincible crime baron to a scared child. The irony of his cold-heartedness is the haughtiness that blinds him. He doesn't know that his invincibility is ensured by the love of those close to him: Alice, his trusting wife, and Eddie, his sickly brother.

Alone in an Albany hotel room, Legs Diamond still thinks that he can reach into the past and rely on a former stooge to help him out. This time, the stooge is Monica, the double-crossed paramour from the Rothstein days and she returns to arrange his death by hired guns.

As Legs Diamond, Ray Danton combines the best (and worst) elements of his dark-sided characters. He succeeds in showing the many sides of Diamond. He is charming as a conniving rake, ferocious as a rackets boss and pathetic as a man who has lost his grip on power. In his most notable role, Danton is ferocious to a fault. Eating people as if they were candies, he never flinches at the candy wrappers that are really former friends and foes. Everyone is a foil for Legs Diamond, from Alice, the blonde foil who eventually becomes his wife to Eddie, the sickly brother who is sacrificed to hedge the gangster's odds against being killed.

In Diamond's world, people are used and tossed aside once they have served a purpose. Along the way, enemies and innocent bystanders die and make a red carpet for his rise to the top. They add up to a violent and bloody payback when their betrayal ultimately betrays him. In the end, the crime kingpin is left alone and that makes him vulnerable.

In *The Rise and Fall of Legs Diamond*, Danton's performance is sharp, clean, and right on the money and the film created a buzz for Ray Danton and there was the sparkle of star potential. The trade papers were filled with accolades, he was the toast of London, and it was speculated that he would replace Sydney Chaplin in *Laurette* starring Judy Holliday on Broadway. He even met with director Otto Preminger in New York and they discussed a role in his upcoming *Exodus*. Ray Danton had an option for Warner Brothers, who were select about why or to whom they would loan their players.

The Rise and Fall of Legs Diamond did inspire a swell of gangster movies in its wake: *Pretty Boy Floyd* (1960), *Studs Lonigan* (1960), *Portrait of a Mobster* (1961), *Mad Dog Coll* (1961), and *King of the Roaring 20's: The Story of Arnold Rothstein* (1961). This trend also included another movie with an outstanding performance by Ray Danton: *The George Raft Story*.

George Raft's life was highlighted in "Out of My Past", a series of articles for The Saturday Evening Post. This stirred up interest in the life of the former movie star and, for awhile, two major studios-Paramount and 20th Century Fox-were interested. Raft was excited and even suggested that Tony Curtis play him in the screen biography. Both studios lost interest in the project and it was eventually taken on by Allied Artists.

Allied Artists was formerly Monogram Pictures, a poverty row studio that changed its name because it sounded prestigious. It was home to quickie producer Sam Katzman and provided work in the 40's for a fading Bela Lugosi. Its crowning achievement was that it produced the successful and long-running comedy series of The Eastside Kids/Bowery Boys with Leo Gorcey and Huntz Hall.

Producer Ben Schwalb took over the reins of The Bowery Boys movies after Jan Grippo retired. *The George Raft Story* was an attempt to change his gears and he eventually went on to produce *Tickle Me*, an Elvis Presley movie that also starred Julie Adams. He did not try to get Tony Curtis for the role of George Raft but he did hire Ray Danton.

Like most Hollywood biographies, *The George Raft Story* is mostly fiction but that doesn't detract from Ray Danton's electrifying performance. His gifts for dancing, romancing, and ego-glorification are showcased in a movie that details George Raft's career as a supper club hoofer and his rise as a Hollywood star. It also shows his slow descent into obscurity, with a stop at revolution era Cuba and an ending with an offer of a cameo in *Some Like It Hot*.

Stylized and exaggerated, *The George Raft Story* is less a biopic than it is a menagerie of movie genres. It is a gangster movie blended with biography, musical dance numbers, and backstage Hollywood exposes. Its assemblage of different styles adds vitality to the movie, keeping it moving at a brisk pace. Another element of its success is the incorporation of original gangster film standbys, such as impressive montages and a musical theme with the urban mood of George Gershwin's *Rhapsody In Blue* and Aaron Copeland's *Slaughter On Tenth Avenue*

A hoofer by vocation, Raft (Ray Danton) dances his way out of New York's Hell Kitchen. Using a variety of dance partners to jump from one circuit to the next, he builds a solid reputation as a nightclub dancer. The

Spanish poster for *The George Raft Story*. The film may not be George Raft but it is definitely Ray Danton all the way! 1961, Allied Artists Pictures Corp.

rackets-controlled environment makes it easy for him to get sidetracked into crime. Sponsored by mobsters, it is profitable for him to earn extra money doing small jobs.

Bad blood leads to an altercation that nearly kills Raft so the boss, Frank Donatella (Joe Di Santis), decides it's time for him to head West with Texas Guinnan (Barbara Nichols), the legendary nightclub hostess. Raft breaks into the movies and his early roles are dancing parts but, due to his dogged determination, he gets bigger and better roles. One of them is *Scarface*, which makes him a star and earns him a personal audience with Al Capone (Neville Brand), who gives the film his stamp of approval.

Scarface leads to stardom and the problems of being an individualist in the public eye. Raft is from the lower Eastside slums with a boorish attitude developed from a childhood of dancing for nickels and dimes. For Raft, money is power and he wants plenty of it. In Hollywood, he gets both, which is his reward and liability.

Commercial viability grants him an audience with the producers but his private self is a matter to contend with. Raft is hot-tempered, two-fisted, and his loyalty to his hoodlum friends, especially racketeer Benny "Bugsy" Siegal (Brad Dexter), are the excuses used by the producers to ease him out of the Hollywood picture.

Raft becomes less in demand and drifts off into obscurity. His slow descent is a lonely escapade. Danton effectively portrays a man who refuses to change as his world crumbles around him. He moves from a mansion to a small apartment without a trace of self-pity or remorse.

Salvation is a Cuban casino named after him. Flying down to Havana, George Raft's ego is boosted when he is received as a semi-star on the tropical circuit. As a figurehead for the casino, he signs autographs and enjoys the company of a bevy of beautiful women. It is an idyllic existence that ends with Castro's revolution. Then, it's back to the obscurity of Hollywood.

The movie ends on an upbeat note: Sam (Herschel Bernardi), his ex-agent, pays him a visit to offer him a small role in *Some Like It Hot*. At first, he balks because it is a gangster role. He relents and ends the movie by making suggestions on how the part ought to be played. The Raft ego emerges, once more, in a humorous ending to a roller coast ride of a movie.

In *The George Raft Story*, Jayne Mansfield, Julie London, Margo Moore and Barry Chase provide the passionate fireworks. Jayne Mansfield plays Lisa Lang, a successful larger-than-life actress based on Betty Grable. She comes off more like Mae West than Betty Grable and brings out the cold-hearted heel in George Raft, along with glorifying his insecurities and foibles. Her criticism about the hoodlums who leech off him is sound but it is too much for Raft to bear.

She seems like a harpy but she is right in her assessment of Raft's soft-hearted affection for his cronies and his self-destructive attitude toward the studio moguls. They bicker and fight constantly when they are not affectionate but it ends badly when Raft's mother (Argentina Brunetti) dies and he curtly dismisses Lang from his life. It seems that his mother is the only woman that he felt warmth for, even to the point where he

One of George Raft's early non-dancing gigs is driving for Frenchie (Robert Strauss), a bootlegger. Moxie (Frank Gorshin), his friend, goes along for the ride. 1961, Allied Artists Pictures Corp.

refuses to speak a movie line about the death of his character's mother.

One of his early dance partners is Sheila Patton (Julie London), a smoky-voiced singer who sings a torch song, "Lonely Gal." Sheila loves him but is nothing more than a dance partner and lover to the mercurial hothead. She zeroes in on his insecurities, something that he does not appreciate. Once she has served her purpose, she is gone from his life.

One of the woman that he does not use is Texas Guinan (Barbara Nichols), the notorious nightclub performer. Barbara Nichols performs "You've Got to See Mama Every Night", in a raucous tempo and upbeat speakeasy mode. Its fits her style perfectly and gives the impression that she is not the type of woman to be messed with unless it's with her consent.

Raft takes advantage of his connection to her only because it is the wish of his boss, nightclub owner Frankie Donatella (Joe Di Santis). The mobster protects Raft from the hostility of Jerry Fitzpatrick (Jack Lambert), a psychotic con newly released from prison.

Donatella has hired Fitzpatrick as muscle and it would defeat the purpose of being a successful boss having two of his men at each other's throats. The fissure is caused by Fitzpatrick's simian-like desire for Ruth

Harris (Margo Moore), the sweet blonde-haired cigarette girl. Ruth may be a naïve ingénue from the Mid-West but she is more sensual than all of the movie's women. Yet she is the only woman that George Raft does not try to take advantage of. In fact, he risks his life for her.

George Raft clashes with the psycho-killer and even survives an attempt on his life, not before humiliating Fitzpatrick by beating him up, along with one of his men. The sparks fly between the actors and their scenes together are electrifying. Donatella needs Fitzpatrick to do the type of jobs Raft won't do (read: murder) so he tells his subordinate to go to Hollywood with Texas Guinan.

It is his dancing that gets the attention of Milton (Frank Albertson), a movie director, when he and his partner, June Tyler (Barrie Chase), break out from a crowd of dancers and cut up the rug. It is June who encourages Raft after he becomes dejected because of loneliness and fading opportunities. She sticks with him as he makes a name for himself in Hollywood.

Barrie Chase became Fred Astaire's last dance partner and in the trailers for the movie she is billed as The Bolero Girl. She and Ray Danton recreate the famous dance from the movie of the same name. Although Ray Danton is fine in his tap-dancing sequence, his *Bolero* is stilted, although one hardly notices because of the grace and beauty of Barry Chase. Of course, June Tyler is jettisoned once Raft becomes a big star and first lays eyes on Lisa Lang (Jayne Mansfield).

One of the movies many benefits is the colorful cast of supporting players. The only annoying act is the Coney Island comedy duo of Pepper and Brand. They are a fifth-rate Martin and Lewis misfire who have way too much screen time for their act.

Frank Gorshin is entertaining as Moxie Cusack, an oddball and a gopher who is a leftover from Raft's New York days. Herschel Bernardi gives a heartfelt performance as Sam, Raft's faithful and long-suffering manager. They provide ballast to the star's volatile personality and he totters on the brink of obscurity when he jeopardizes his relationship with them.

Jack Albertson is Milton, the director who picks Raft out of a crowd of extras to participate in a fight scene. He also directs *Scarface*, George Raft's breakout movie. That would make him Howard Hawks in real/reel life. In his breakout role, George Raft plays Rinaldo, an underling to Tony Camonte, the mob kingpin played by Paul Muni in the 1932 movie.

They are filming Rinaldo's death scene, which includes Raft's flipping of the coin which became his trademark. In fact, the British title of the film is *Spin of the Coin*. It is one of the best scenes of the movie because George Raft lends credibility to the role when he explains to Milton how he would portray the death of the mobster. He objects to the script's stilted portrayal and when he is asked if he ever saw a gangster die, Raft replies, "Yeah. They don't die any different from anybody else." Ray Danton delivers this line with chilling effectiveness highlighted by a close up of his disturbed visage.

Brad Dexter and Robert Strauss are also on hand as gangsters. Brad Dexter plays the notorious Benny "Bugsy" Siegal with more charm than menace. The friendship is one instant where the movie is not fiction. They were friends until the gangster's shooting death. Robert Strauss is colorful as Frenchy, but, then, when has Strauss not been colorful? Frenchy is an affable bootlegger who is introduced to Raft by Moxie. He likes the young man's style and hires him as a wheelman for a midnight booze run. This is George Raft's initiation into the world of crime or so says the movie.

George Raft denounced the movie after it was released, claiming that it exaggerated his underworld connections. Raft was a big star and lost his fortune due to profligacy and to, what many insiders asserted, illiteracy. He was broke when he sold the rights of his life to Allied Artists. It would

George Raft's (Ray Danton) Hollywood lifestyle includes a fling with famous actress Lisa Lang (Jayne Mansfield), based on Betty Grable. 1961, Allied Artists Pictures Corp.

not be exaggerating to say that some bad career choices also had a hand in his eclipse as a star.

A notable omission is glossing over Raft's refusal to star in *High Sierra* and *The Maltese Falcon*, two films that propelled Humphrey Bogart to stardom. George Raft later turned down *Double Indemnity* by Billy Wilder, who later cast him as a mobster in his comedy, *Some Like It Hot*. There is no mention of James Cagney or Humphrey Bogart or reasonable facsimiles, either; nor of other co-stars at Warner Brothers.

The movie also doesn't acknowledge Raft's steady work in the Forties and Fifties. The bio gives the impression that Raft went from stardom to obscurity. His career may have been eclipsed by Humphrey Bogart by the mid-Forties but he still accrued a formidable resume. Some films from the mid-Forties onwards are *Johnny Angel* ('45), *Mr. Ace* ('46), *Nocturne* ('46), *Race Street* ('48), *Outpost in Morocco* ('49) and *Johnny Allegro* ('49).

The real George Raft shows up on the set to give the cast a few pointers on hoofing. He later denounced the movie, claiming that it exaggerated his underworld connections. 1961, Allied Artists Pictures Corp.

He found steady work in the Fifties, mainly in low-budget crime dramas like *Loan Shark* ('52), *I'll Get You* ('52), *Rogue Cop* ('54), *Black Widow* ('54) and *A Bullet for Joey* ('54). George Raft had a production company that produced his television show, *I'm the Law*, which ran for twenty-six episodes in 1953. He even had his first star cameo in *Around the World in Eighty Days* ('56).

The George Raft Story received mixed reviews from the critics, depending on their feelings about the movie's subject. However, Ray Danton's performance was applauded and there was even talk of him playing Joe DiMaggio in an independent biopic that never materialized.

The George Raft Story makes an appropriate companion piece to *The Rise and Fall of Legs Diamond*. The characters are alike because they are wise guys who scheme and dance their way in and out of women's hearts to nab the snares of profits and success. They also use crime and show business as means to an end. Each man puts an accent on different means.

In movie anthologies and film biographies, Ray Danton is often shown as Legs Diamond and George Raft. They are considered the highlights of his career. Both characters are larger than life and Danton's performances are broader than his other dramatic roles. That doesn't mean that they are better. His earlier pulp roles have shadings and subtleties that his trademark roles don't have room for.

The Rise and Falls of Legs Diamond and *The George Raft Story* are violent cartoons in monochrome. That is one reason why they are Danton's most popular roles—they are broad stroked characterizations in the gangster genre, a perennial crowd pleaser. The films are entertaining because the subject matter never fails when handled properly, including the two essential elements that set the screen on fire: scorching women and hot-tempered gangsters.

The Rise and Fall of Legs Diamond and *The George Raft Story* have energy levels twice the normal speed of most movies. They are frames for Ray Danton to hang his personality on and that is what gives the movies their manic pace and unique stamps. The movies may not be accurate biographies but they are the best examples of Ray Danton's dynamic acting style.

Ray Danton's portrayals of Legs Diamond and George Raft exemplify the style he developed with his previous characters. His signature roles may seem retrograde because of their eras but Ray Danton plays his most noted characters like they were modern Caesars. Their stories could be seen as allegories of the American frontier at the beginning of a new age. They are the family members who made it to the dawn of Camelot.

Warner Brothers Television

Urbane Private Eyes

Warner Brothers was a blockbuster studio and its power carried over to the small screen. A good deal of its television success was due to Jack Warner's son-in-law, William T. Orr. The former actor was executive producer of the many of the popular westerns and private eye dramas of the late Fifties and early Sixties. Any television viewer from that period will remember the Wm. T. Orr credits, along with the song writing credits of the talented team, Mack David and Jerry Livingston. Together, they

Jack Warner and his son-in-law, executive producer William T. Orr (center), headline their television gold mine, the television division of Warner Brothers. They pose with the stars of their successful drama and western series. 1959, Warner Bros. Television.

churned out an impressive array of entertaining hit shows with catchy theme songs.

As bright as it may have been for viewers, the Warner Brothers' system was deemed as indentured servitude by many of its contract players, Ray Danton included. Stars did not receive residuals from merchandising and they often had to share a part of their personal appearance fees with the studio. This was the cause of the court battles fought by Clint Walker, James Garner and Edd Byrnes.

They were contract players and paid a flat salary. Ray Danton was one of the highest paid actors on the lot mainly because he was one of the busiest. He earned a thousand dollars a week by acting in three projects simultaneously. It was not unusual for him to film a western in the morning, a drama in the afternoon and work on a film, such as *The Rise and Fall of Legs Diamond*, at night.

The quick shooting schedule for the television shows included three days for a thirty minute show or six days for an hour long program. Scripts were sometimes recycled and transposed from one show to another. The contract players rotated among the shows and also appeared in the studio's movies for a flat fee, often for scale.[5]

So economical and penny pinching was the studio's treatment of its television division that offices were threadbare and it was not unusual for different personnel to share the same office. It should not be surprising because the television arm of the studio was considered the bastard child of a noble man since its inception.

Jack Warner had a rabid hatred for television. His antipathy extended to refusing to show a television set in his movies or allowing anyone in his presence to utter the word. He reluctantly agreed to enter the field because the television networks were courting the major studios to provide programs for broadcast.

It was apparent by the early 1950's that television was not a temporary curiosity piece because of the revenue it generated. Advertising rates had doubled and broadcast signals were strong enough to reach more than ten million television sets. In 1954, Warner Brothers tested the waters by producing two shows for the new medium, *Casablanca* and *Warner Brothers Presents*. ABC is the network that cut a deal with the studio; at the time, the network lagged behind NBC, CBS, and DuMont, which eventually fell by the wayside.[6]

By 1960, Warner Brothers had ten hit shows on the ABC schedule and Jack Warner finally changed his mind about television, mainly because the

Warner Brothers capitalized on their television success by featuring their stars in other media. Here is A Christmas recording featuring several popular Warners' stars, including Ray Danton.

television section financed the movie studio with its revenues, including overseas syndication. Much of this had to do with Wm. T. Orr's genius. It still did not change Jack Warner's mind about upgrading the working conditions of his employees.

At a cursory glance, Ray Danton's stay at Warners' appears to be a mixed blessing. He was the star of his best-known film but also appeared in a number of faceless supporting roles that stood out because of his assured cockiness. *The Rise and Fall of Legs Diamond* may show Danton at his best but most of his supporting roles were inane, with John Howard in *Too Much, Too Soon* (58), being an exception.

All his other screen roles were in supporting capacities in big-budget soap operas and wide screen epics. In some of them, Ray Danton's billing was a couple of notches below the stars; this was the case with the two hours plus Warners' extravaganzas where his parts were often in support of the supporting players. The only exception is *A Majority of One* directed by Mervyn LeRoy. He gets third billing in a comedy starring Alec Guinness and Rosalind Russell.

Warner Brothers was true to the studio system's policy of utilizing its contract players to their fullest extent. This included work on the studio's successful primetime television shows. Ray Danton's work from this period was his television equivalent of his big screen pulp roles. The difference was his characterizations were more varied on television.

The afterglow of Legs Diamond affected Danton's roles on *Bourbon Street Beat, Surfside Six,* and *The Roaring 20's.* Duke Powell, Marty Hartman, and Dandy Brady are cut from the same mold as Diamond, only mixed with a better sense of judgment and respect.

Duke Powell is the blighted expatriate club owner in *Bourbon Street Beat: Last Exit* ('60). He has fled the United States to avoid being tried for murder. Is he guilty? It takes a manhunt to find out. *Surfside Six: Country Gentleman* ('60) casts him as Marty Hartman, a former mobster trying to buy his way into Miami society. His past won't allow it and is almost the ruination of him. *The Roaring 20's: White Carnation* ('60) is a gangster tale where he plays Dandy Brady, a club owner double crossed by his faded luck. His winning charm has washed out and there is nothing to aid him in his quest for revenge.

Bourbon Street Beat aired from 1959 to 1960. It starred Richard Long and Andrew Duggan as New Orleans detectives Rex Randolph and Cal Calhoun. Arlene Howell portrayed their socially-correct southern secretary, Melody Lee, and Van Williams played Kenny Madison, the law student who was also their leg man. Despite the romantic backdrop of New Orleans, the show was short lived, although it did have a certain Cajun flair to it.

In *Last Exit*, Rex Randolph is given a $2,000 retainer by Raoul Roulas (Damien O'Flynn) to go to San Marcos, South America and find his benefactor's daughter, plus bring his son's alleged murderer to justice. Amanda Hale (Joan Marshall), his daughter, is a singer who used the South American leg of her tour to find Duke Powell (Ray Danton), who fled the states after he was accused of murdering Rene, Amanda's brother and Roulas' son.

At the South American casino, Randolph becomes puzzled when the star attraction is Amanda Hale. His confusion is heightened when she

The New Orleans flavor of *Bourbon Street Beat* was provided by Richard Long, Eddie Cole, Van Williams, Arlene Howell and Andrew Duggan (l-r). 1960, Warner Bros. Television.

directs the passion of her love songs at Duke Powell, who sits at his table, sipping a drink while listening to his favorite canary sing. It doesn't make sense to Randolph.

The next morning, Randolph has coffee with Amanda. He reveals his identity and tells the singer about her father's concern. She explains to him that it was her intention to attract Powell and turn him over to the authorities. Instead, she fell in love with him and does not believe that he killed her brother. Randolph tells her that she has to make sure or else she will be dogged by guilt for the rest of her life. The following day Amanda leaves for the States. Powell, unable to live without her, packs his bags to follow. He is asked by Randolph whether he is innocent or guilty.

"Guilty", replies Powell. "But I'm not sure of what."

The drama reaches its climax at the Roulas' country home. Amanda and Duke have been lured there by Anita (Madlyn Rhue), Rene's widow. She plans to kill them and end the case of her husband's murder. She confesses her guilt to Amanda when she has a confrontation with Duke Powell. He uses his charm to disarm the woman who was once in love with him and committed murder to prove it.

From the jazzy theme to its stark woodcut graphics of a French Quarter lamppost and its glow, *Bourbon Street Beat* is a detective show with an attitude. *Last Exit* is a quickie-film noir where mistaken identities

Duke Powell (Ray Danton) sits at a table and is mesmerized by the singing of his favorite chanteuse. 1960, Warner Bros. Television.

and unwarranted guilt confuse the viewer into believing that guilt is in the eye of the beholder. Weighing in at fifty minutes, it is packed with enough essential elements to match the qualifications of the genre. Not only is it filmed in harsh and contrasting tones, the episode is filled with dark and fascinating personalities.

Duke Powell is an expatriate club owner in South America. He is wanted for murder in the States. Amanda Hale is the victim's vengeance-seeking sister. She has tracked Duke Powell and poses as a singer at his club in San Marcos. Rex Randolph is a New Orleans private eye hired to locate Amanda and extradite Powell back to the States.

The cast is rounded out by an assortment of roughnecks, from the wisecracking croupiers to scar faced assassins. Even Randolph's employer, Raoul Roulas, has poison in his veins. Being a wheelchair bound old man who has lost his male heir has turned him into a bitter and vengeful person.

In *Last Exit*, Ray Danton assumes many of the classic anti-hero poses. A white dinner jacket and a drink are props for his coolness when he sits at a table and drinks while being mesmerized by the singer he loves. After an unsuccessful attempt on his life, he grits his teeth with macho aplomb when she applies liquor as an anti-septic to treat a knife wound. He flashes a sly grin when he taps private eye Rex Randolph on the stomach and tells him that's he guilty, although he doesn't know of what.

Like most anti-heroes, it's love that has turned Powell into an expatriate on the run from the American law. It is also love that redeems him. He won't admit it, but it's chivalrous code of honor that impels him to bear the blame for a murder he didn't commit. Powell would rather live in exile than betray his code of honor.

Marty Hartman also refuses to betray his code of honor when he tries to make a successful shift into another social league in *Surfside Six : Country Gentleman*. This series was the last Warner Brothers' detective show to be created in the wake of *77 Sunset Strip's* success. This time around, the detective agency operated out of a Miami houseboat and the detectives were three surfer-boy types played by Troy Donahue, Lee Paterson and Van Williams, who had moved to Miami from New Orleans after *Bourbon Street Beat* was cancelled. Diane McBain and Cha Cha O'Brien were the female leads. *Surfside Six* was not as popular as *77 Sunset Strip* or *Hawaiian Eye* but did last longer than *Bourbon Street Beat*.

In *Country Gentleman*, Marty Hartman is an ex-east coast gangster trying to go straight in Miami. His dreams of becoming part of the Miami jet set are crushed when he is rejected by Commodore Gladstone (Robert Burton), a high society scion. Initially, Gladstone is happy to do business with Hartman but changes his attitude when Roger Fielding (John Hubbard), a gossip columnist, dredges up the ex-hoodlum's unsavory past in his newspaper column.

Commodore Gladstone refers to the "goon tactics" that fascinated him and the "misconception of the purchasing power of money" when he tells the social climbing hoodlum that "money will buy a whole lot of

Troy Donahue, Cha Cha O'Brien, Lee Paterson, Diane McBain and Van Williams (l-r) were the youthful stars of *Surfside Six*. 1960, Warner Bros. Television.

things in this world but it won't buy an ex-convict and racketeer social acceptance."

The next morning, a dead Commodore Gladstone is fished out of the bay. His associate, Alan Abbott (Fred Wayne), hires Dan Thorn (Lee Paterson), a private investigator, to scrutinize Hartman, whom he believes has motive because of the money he lost when the commodore pulled out of their deal and the death threats made against him at the club.

Thorn, the man responsible for sending Hartman to Sing-Sing, visits him at his Glass Dome Mansion and is impressed with the change in the ex-convict's life although he is not sure that it is genuine. Hartman agrees that his new digs are a "step up from free room and board on the Hudson" and also swears that he has gone straight. Hartman insists that he was tired of his old ways and wanted to change so he could enjoy life without looking over his shoulder. Thorn has his doubts because of the presence of Stinger (Frank De Kova), an old world bodyguard.

Stinger speaks out of the side of his mouth and settles arguments with a beating. He is critical of his boss's change in lifestyle. Revenge is a way of life with him and he feels uncomfortable in his new role as a gentleman's gentleman. Answering the phone politely and making canapés is not his forte; breaking kneecaps is, along with outfitting double crossers with cement shoes. He is out of place and will be the one who prevents Marty Hartman from making a smooth transition to Miami high society.

Thorn is convinced that Hartman murdered the commodore when Fielding is murdered and the tire tracks to Hartman's car are found near the boat where the columnist was killed. He also finds out that Hartman is broke and would have stand to gain the Gladstone fortune if he married Paula, his daughter. His theory falls apart when he confronts the country gentleman.

Stinger, unwilling to see his boss accused, admits to the murders. He didn't mean to kill anyone. All he wanted to do was warn them. It tore him up to see his boss fall from his pedestal. He remembers the old days in New York: fights at the Garden, sitting at the head of the table at meetings, and having everyone come to him for favors. To see the boss smoking a pipe instead of his trademark cigar worried Stinger that his boss had gone soft; that went for making canapés for socials or watching the boss falling for Paula Gladstone, a society dame. Stinger, blinded by confusion, pulls a gun on Thorn and Hartman tries to take it away from him. The gunsel is shot to death in the struggle.

Marty Hartman (Ray Danton) has traded his fedora and cigar for an ascot and a pipe in attempt to ingratiate himself into Miami's high society social set. It does not bode well for him. 1960, Warner Bros. Television.

"You did him a favor", says Thorn. "It would have meant the chair."

A stunned Marty Hartman stares into space and says," He thought he was doing me a favor."

Marty Hartman was too honest for the high society that he wanted to be a part of. It was just another social bracket where crime and avarice manipulated the deals. The sordid deaths of the Commodore and Fielding attest to that. They were more in Stinger's social class than in the company of Marty Hartman. His attempt to lead a legitimate life in the eyes of the law is smeared by the people who rejected him. It takes a simian to bring out the jungle swag in the society mavens that he was trying to impress. An unlit pipe is Marty Hartman's booby prize for losing at a game he had no business playing.

Wm. T. Orr also capitalized on the gangster genre which Warner Brothers honed to perfection in the 30's when the huge success of Desilu's *The Untouchables* revived the gangster tradition for television. *The Roaring 20's* was a rousing show centering around the exploits of Pinky Pinkham (Dorothy Provine), a speakeasy entertainer and Pat Garrison (Donald May), a newspaperman.

The vivacious Dorothy Provine played the irrepressible flapper, Pinky Pinkham, in *The Roaring 20's*. Here, she is flanked by two newsmen played by Donald May and Rex Reason. 1960, Warner Bros. Television.

In *White Carnation*, Dandy Dan Brady (Ray Danton) is a successful club owner framed for murder by a mobster named Ben Dorechal (Frank De Kova). Dandy has served three years in Sing-Sing and his upcoming release is cause for concern for three people: Ben Dorechal, Pinky Pinkham, and Sammee (Adam Williams).

It appears as if nothing's changed about Dandy. He still has his charm and swagger and is full of promises of success in the big time. Reality sinks in when Pinky tells him that Dorechal is downstairs.

It takes on an ugly air when he meets Garrison and pulls a reluctant Sammee out of the shadows. Sammee's was beaten and disfigured by Dorechal's goons and his shame pains Dandy, who promises a revenge that will consume Dorechal and get back their old club. Sammee is pleased and believes that it will be like old times.

While in sequestration, Dandy's spirit is awakened by Sammee's dice. He rolls a seven and realizes the old magic is still there. The friends leave for a night on the town. Sammee asks him if he could go along for the ride to the top. Dandy wouldn't have it any other way. Dandy is too happy to notice the limo turning the corner and heading their way. Sammee shields his friend as they are sprayed with machine gun fire. The goons succeed in killing Sammee but only wound Dandy.

A wounded Dandy enters Pinky's dressing room by breaking the fire escape window. He is armed and makes a phone call to Dorechel. The gangster's champagne celebration of his former partner's death is ruined by the call. He agrees to a meeting when Dandy tells him: "You're afraid of me. I'm afraid of you. That's how wars start. Whataya' say we open a new deck of cards?"

Pinky (Dorothy Provine) tends to the wounded Dandy (Ray Danton), who was shot in an assassination attempt that killed his buddy, Sammee. 1960, Warner Bros. Television.

Dorechel arrives at the club and Garrison sees him for a final word. In the dressing room, a severely wounded Dandy uses all of his energy to make it to his meeting with Dorechel. The club patrons scream in terror when they see the bloodied Dandy brandishing a revolver. A shocked Dorechel is caught by surprise and tries to escape.

"This is for Sammee", declares a defiant Dandy as he shoots his enemy. Dandy is mowed down by Dorechel's machine gun toting thugs. An hysterical Pinky tearfully listens to Dandy's dying declaration of love for her.

"This is the way it's gotta be", are his last words.

Pinky returns to the stage to sing, "The Man I Love."

The White Carnation is a gangster movie in a capsule. Dandy is a charismatic character who has lost his magic and doesn't realize it. Three years in Sing-Sing hasn't deterred his ambition to regain his nightclub from his ex-partner. Time has solidified Dorechal's power and the match is basically a man against the mob setup.

Once removed from the action, Dandy has become meaningless, a relic that fails to regain its relevance. To reclaim what is rightfully his is within Dandy's province of rights. His revenge is justified because it is backed by righteous indignation. The official declaration of Dandy's innocence is the system's exoneration, not his.

Dandy dies because he can't see the changes around him. He is the same but the new circumstances are different. His dying declaration acknowledges that. Dandy bluffs himself into thinking that he can still roll sevens. His last crap game ended with a chorus of Tommy-Guns.

Robert Altman's direction is tight and atmospheric. There is a scene when Dandy eludes Dorechal's henchmen by ducking into the chorus girls' dressing room while Pinky is singing a feel-good song at the club. He leaves by the ally exit while, behind him, a silhouette of the flappers beating up the gangsters animates a window that looks like a large, luminous screen. The smug look and sly grin of Dandy's conquest is masterfully captured as he puts on his hat and struts out of the danger zone. It is a great moment and shows why Ray Danton should have been a star.

Hawaiian Eye was the first show inspired by the success of *77 Sunset Strip*. It was a private eye show set in Hawaii and starred Anthony Eisley and Robert Conrad as Tracey Steele and Tom Lopaka. Their agency was called Hawaiian Eye and it operated out of the Hawaiian Village Hotel.

Tracey Steele (Anthony Eisley), Cricket Blake (Connie Stevens), Tom Lapaka (Robert Conrad), and Kim (Poncie Ponce) made *Hawaiian Eye* a fan favorite that rivaled *77 Sunset Strip* in popularity. 1959, Warner Bros. Television.

They investigated crimes and mysteries when not providing security for the hotel. The two dashing detectives were aided by two of the hotel's employees: Cricket (Connie Stevens) the photographer and lounge singer and Kim Quisado (Poncie Ponce), the irrepressible ukulele-playing cab driver. The show had a successful run that started in 1959 and lasted until 1963.

Crimes of passion have long since been the staples of private detective dramas. The eternal triangle and its ugly consequences is the theme of two episodes: *Murder, Anyone?* and *I Wed Three Wives*. Ray Danton plays Barry Logan and Mark Hamilton, two Janus-faced lovers. The three points of the first triangle are David and Sarah Crane topped by Barry Logan. The second triangle is made up of the three former wives of film actor Mark Hamilton.

The opening scene of *Murder, Anyone?* exemplifies the torrid romance between Barry Logan and Sarah Crane (Julie Adams). A tropical storm whips the palm trees into a frenzy. In the midst of the torrential rains, a man makes his way to a phone booth and makes a call to Sarah Crane.

She says that he has dialed a wrong number and hangs up. Her husband, tries to soothe her shattered nerves. She insists that it is a crank caller but it is her lover, Barry Logan.

The violent storm, the shady pretext of communication, the apprehension of the wife and the vehement concern of the cuckold are the elements of this illicit romance.

The concerned husband hires the hotel's private investigator, Tom Lopaka to check out the calls. The detective surmises that it might be a harmless crank, someone with a grudge against his wife, or a caller threatening the former occupant of the hotel room.

"There's no such thing as a harmless crank", insists David Crane (Herbert Rudley). "If he's a crank, he's dangerous."

Tom Lopaka agrees to take the case and advises his partners that discretion is necessary. At the hotel, Cricket, the singer, is excited about the upcoming tennis tournament because it will feature the first love of her life-Barry Logan. She barely can control her emotions. Barry Logan is an amateur tennis player. He works as a salesman for Mr. Crane and is the one romancing his wife.

Barry Logan is apprehensive about Sarah telling her husband about the affair. She hasn't any qualms about divorcing her husband to marry Barry. Logan doesn't want to be hasty. He is mindful that he is David Crane's employee and protégée. Believing that the matter should be given time to work things out, Barry prepares for his tennis match.

At a meeting with Barry, Sarah tells him that David knows. She feels free because she no longer has to live a lie. Barry is livid because he sees his career go up in smoke. Sarah is shocked and hurt when Barry tells her that his priority is winning the tennis match. Now that David knows about the affair, he will cut Barry off, crushing any hopes he may have of a successful future as a business man and tennis player.

That evening, David confronts Barry in the forest. He threatens the cad with a revolver. They fight and Barry knocks out the older man when he hits him and he stumbles backwards, cracking his head on a stone. The next day, the police find him but he is not unconscious-he is dead!

The police want to arrest Barry Logan but Cricket supplies an airtight alibi. Tom Lopaka convinces the inspector to let Barry play in the tennis match. He is not convinced that the player is guilty of the murder. He has a plan to ferret out the real killer, whom he believes to be Crane's partner, Mike Cornell (Richard Garland). He asks Cricket to help him with his scheme.

In "Murder, Anyone?", Ray Danton and Julie Adams work together again. This time, they play lovers. Danton's character is a clean-cut all-American type who is weak-kneed at the prospect of consummating his relationship with his boss's wife.

Julie Adams is the aggressor who gladly ends her marriage to be with Logan. Her strength cancels out Logan's weakness. In the end, they lose what they are after. His promising tennis career is without a sponsor and she loses both of the men in her life.

Herbert Rudley's portrayal of the cuckolded husband is touching because he doesn't deserve what he gets. He is good to those around him: his wife, Barry, and his partner. They betray him and set him up for his own death. Illicit love, closet jealousy and blind ambition club him to death. Only one of them will get the blame-the cane-wielding partner, who-for years-has harbored a secret love for his partner's wife.

In *I Wed Three Wives,* Cricket is ecstatic because the famous actor, Mark Hamilton, is coming to Hawaii and will be staying at the hotel.

The secret rendezvous of Barry Logan (Ray Danton) and Sarah Crane (Julie Adams) is threatened by an advancing cuckolded husband. 1960, Warner Bros. Television.

Mark Hamilton (Ray Danton) is bedeviled by Mavis (Kasey Rogers), one of his ex-wives after she corners the errant actor. 1960, Warner Bros. Television.

According to her, he is the "most exciting man in the world." Hawaii will be his last stop in a publicity junket that started in Paris, continued in Mexico, and will end in Hawaii.

He is usually unflappable; the only person who gets on his nerves is Henry (Barney Phillips), his business manager. He does this by reminding him of his financial vulnerability. It could land him in jail. The threat doesn't faze the star because he believes that he is invincible.

Totally exhausted from making three pictures in Europe, Hamilton expects privacy that will be assured by Tracey Steele, private eye. What he'll get is an adventure with the Mrs. Hamilton club, comprised of three ex-wives looking for back alimony payments.

They consider themselves three steppingstones in his career: Sharon (Lenore Roberts) made him an actor, Nora (Jeanne Baird) made him a father, and Mavis (Kasey Rogers) made him a star. Now, they have to plot to get what's coming to them: back alimony.

The ex-wives have arrived in Hawaii and try several methods to reach him. They succeed and kidnap the star to hide in their rented apartment. That's where he uses his charm to weaken his ex-wives as they guard him, one at a time. Tracey Steele and Sy Bliss (Tommy Farrell), his agent, have been frantically searching for Mark Hamilton after they find the cottage empty.

The detective uses his investigative skills to track the women down at their rented apartment. They arrive just as a gunshot rings out and break into the apartment to find an unharmed Mark Hamilton. The star refuses to press kidnapping charges and is taken back to the Lagoon Cottage, where they find Henry slumped over in a chair. He has been murdered.

Connie Stevens was a popular ingénue in films and television during the late 50's and early 60's before becoming a successful business entrepreneur.

Tracey Steele interrogates the women, trying to find out whether they still love him. It is obvious that there is some residual feelings towards the cold-hearted actor. Steele's plan is to convince them that the actor no longer has any love for them. In fact, he believes that he may be using them as a cover for Henry's murder. It is his hunch that one of them let Hamilton sweet talk himself into getting away for the time it took to murder the business manager.

There is nothing left to say when one ex tells Steele that she gave him the keys to the car during her watch. He was gone long enough to murder Henry, who had threatened the star with revealing his three bogus holding companies in Switzerland. A band of cops emerges from the bushes and arrests Mark Hamilton for the murder of his business manager. The episode ends with Cricket singing one of her torch songs at the Shell Bar.

If you get a kick at of Danton's arrogant characters, then you'll like Mark Hamilton. It's full steam ahead for him; only he not sailing but riding a steam roller. He opts for that instead of the gravy train because he can run over more people with the roller.

The story is about his rise and fall. The audience meets him at the height of his success. His European movie, *Apollo*, has cracked the million dollar mark. It's ironic that, for Hamilton, European success spelled super-stardom. For Ray Danton, it would become a step removed from Hollywood. Some of his European efforts would be excellent, but certainly no *Apollo* loomed on his horizon.

THE OUTSIDE TYPE

Ray Danton stepped outside of type for five unique roles: Senor Velazquez in *77 Sunset Strip: A Nice Social Evening* ('57), Johnny Manetti in *77 Sunset Strip: A Bargain in Tombs* ('61); Danny Rome in *Surfside Six: The Frightened Canary* ('60); Harry Shayne in *The Roaring 20's: The Vamp* ('61); and Hugo Petra in *The Gallant Men: Operation Secret*.

77 Sunset Strip started a trend when it glamorized the private eye genre by taking it out of a hard-boiled urban setting and moving it to a glamorous location. In this case, the milieu was California's Sunset Strip. The two stars were Efrem Zimbalist, Jr. and Roger Smith as Stu Bailey and Jeff Spencer, two former government agents who now walked the beat as private investigators.

They were aided by a hip parking lot attendant named Kookie, played by Edd Byrnes. The show had a great theme song and it didn't hurt that Kookie was a cultural phenomenon, that is, until Kookie's fame eclipsed Byrnes' career when he walked off the set in a salary dispute with Jack Warner.

The show suffered from his year long suspension and it didn't recover much when Byrnes returned as a revamped and mature Kookie sans the hipster lingo and hair combing routine. The show had a healthy run from 1958 to 1964, when it was cancelled after major revisions that saw most of the cast let go to make it a Stu Bailey adventure show. A slew of shows were developed at Warner Brothers because of *77 Sunset Strip* much in the same way the studio's many popular westerns were inspired by *Cheyenne*.

77 Sunset Strip was the show that started a series of hip private eye shows for Warner Brothers. Stu Bailey (Efrem Zimbalist, Jr.), Jeff Spencer (Roger Smith), and teen idol, Kookie (Edd Byrnes) scored big with their trailblazing version of the West Coast private eye tradition. 1958, Warner Bros. Television.

In *77 Sunset Strip: A Nice Social Evening*, Stuart Bailey is hired by the State Department to keep an eye on Senor Velazquez, a popular South American playboy visiting the United States. It is rumored that there is a plot to assassinate him to incite tension between the two hemispheres. Velazquez, who is resented by some of his countrymen for his pro-American loyalties, believes that the State Department has an over-active imagination.

Senor Velazquez is a thrill-seeking playboy who believes that life is a parade. He likes to stand on the sidelines and throw green confetti. His generosity has garnered an impressive entourage, mostly beautiful women. Every night is Mardi Gras for him and Stuart Bailey fears that he may die in his pursuit of American wildlife before an assassin kills him.

Top: Party animal, Senor Velasquez (Ray Danton) pounds the pagan skins while nightclubbing. Bottom: Senor Valasquez (Ray Danton) assures Stu Bailey (Efrem Zimbalist, Jr.) that nobody is trying to kill him while his dates-Dorothy Provine (l) and Arlene Howell (r)- size him up for dinner. 1958, Warner Bros. Television.

A montage of his nightclubbing establishes his partygoers' personality. He drinks, dances, jokes and plays the congas with a forceful energy that takes him from one club to the next with Stuart Bailey and the company of bodacious beauties. Although he refuses to believe that his life is in danger, there is an element of suspense when his car, driven by Bailey, is forced off the road one night. Bailey tells the State Department man that it wasn't an accident-the other driver probably thought that Senor Valazquez was at the wheel.

Everything comes to a head on a birthday party thrown by Senor Velazquez for himself on his yacht. To cover the enormity of the job, Stu Bailey enlists the aid of his partner, Jeff Spencer and Kookie. They deduce that his method of murdering the playboy will be using a bomb hidden in the birthday cake.

On deck, Senor Valazquez is leading the revelers in a conga line. He is surrounded by women, whom he asks to blow out the candles with him on the count of three. Before the countdown is complete, Bailey, Spencer, and Kookie rush through the crowd, grab the cake and toss it overboard.

A distraught Valazquez is confused by their actions until he is stunned by an explosion that creates a liquid mushroom cloud. It is then that the carefree and supercilious playboy realizes that there was a plot against his life. The story ends with him thanking the disembarking crowd for attending his party. He has special thanks for Stuart Bailey and jokingly rues the loss of his beautiful cake.

Ray Danton breaks with type when he portrays the South American playboy. Replacing menace with comical charm, he creates an easygoing and likeable character. The piece is like the nightclub comedies of the Thirties and Forties. Gold diggers abound, trying to snare his loot. In an unlikely turn of events, one of his girlfriends ties him down.

As Stuart Bailey, Efrem Zimbalist, Jr. plays the same stanch character that has typified his performances over the decades. His deadpan expressions and flustered mannerisms make him the perfect straight man to Danton's comical Velazquez.

Edd Byrnes pulls out all stops as Kookie, the pop icon. His hipster's lingo and elastic body language add spice and pizzazz to the proceedings. Kookie was coolness personified for the Baby Boomers, providing a serious alternative to Maynard G. Krebbs (Bob Denver) of *The Many Loves of Dobie Gillis*.

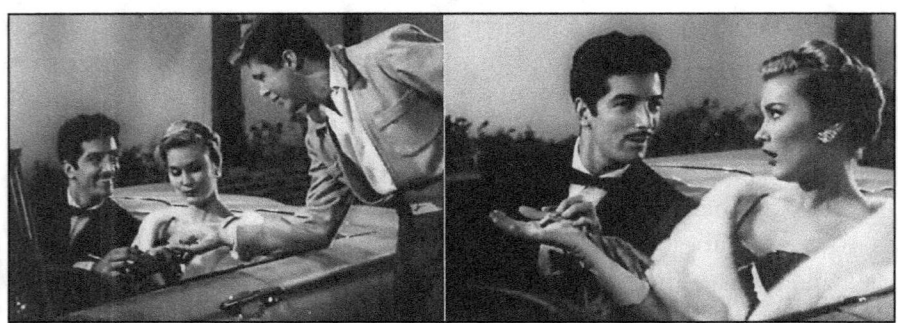

Kookie (Edd Byrnes) lays it on for the South American playboy. For once, the brunette trumps the blonde in the gold digger's game. 1958, Warner Bros. Television.

Velazquez is a magnet for beautiful women. That is what gives this episode the flavor of a screwball comedy. The gorgeous Dorothy Provine heads a list of beauties vying for Senor Velazquez's attention. Among them is Arlene Howell as a money-hungry Southern belle who snares him in the end. Provine plays an intelligent blonde and Howell is a ditzy brunette in a refreshing role reversal of female stereotypes.

There is enough menace to qualify it as a drama. The threats to Stu Bailey's life and the time bomb-inside-the cake are examples of the melodramatic touches. Overall, Danton's comical touch keeps the episode light.

Ray Danton returned to *77 Sunset Strip* to appear in *A Bargain in Tombs*, a Stu Bailey mystery involving the looting of ancient Roman artifacts in Italy. The private investigator's European vacation is interrupted by a plea for help from Delphine de Janville (Linda Watkins), a Kentucky matron reduced to spending her money on gigolos. Her latest, Armand, is a polo enthusiast. He is disappointed in her because the polo ponies that she bought for him are nags.

Bailey was recommended to her by a stateside friend after he found her missing husband in a cement mixer. The dowager's heiress niece, Miss Kenniston is missing in Rome and she was last seen by her aunt at the airport. Stu accepts the case, claiming that he owes himself a visit to the Eternal City. His investigation leads him to the Via Biscionne, the niece's last known residence.

He finds out that Miss Kenniston had a roommate, Julia Maltby (Louise Fletcher), so he leaves his address with the landlord hoping to make contact with the woman. A street urchin named Guido (Bart Braverman) is eavesdropping and cuts himself in on the action. Stu learns that Ms. Maltby is an archeology student who works for the rakish Johnny Manetti (Ray Danton). They are involved in an archeology project involving a tomb, along with Marta (Lisa Gaye), Guido's beautiful sister.

Marta is attracted to Stu but is reticent in talking to him. Her apprehension about discussing Johnny Manetti and the project interest him more than what she may say about Julia Maltby. The air of mystery makes him more determined to get to the bottom of things. Coincidence assumes its role in the story when Stu almost runs over the man he is looking for as he speeds down a narrow street. A heated argument ensues before the men realize that they are old war buddies. Manetti, once a black market operative, used to be Stu's driver during his OSS days and the feel good charm between the men returns, if only for a moment.

Stu later sours on Johnny when he finds out that his war buddy is a minor figure in an illegal archeology dig run by a seedy and suspicious man named Sebastian (Al Ruscio). The master mind is worried about Stu's snooping and he orders Johnny Manetti to kill his old war buddy. Johnny refuses and is cut out of the deal for his loyalty.

Stu awakens in the middle of the night and realizes that Ms. Malti is Miss Kenniston in disguise. He gets her to realize that the dig is illegal and that her employers aims are not trustworthy; furthermore, she will have outlived her usefulness when they no longer need her expertise in appraising and cataloguing the artifacts.

Things come to a head when Stu tries to break up the transportation of the stolen artifacts. Sebastian traps Stu Bailey and Julia Maltby in the tomb but Manetti gets even by saving Stu's life by taking the bullet that was supposed to snuff out his life.

A Bargain in Tombs is a good adventure story and has an Old World charm about it because of the Roman locale. The episode was directed by Reginald le Borg, a resident director for Warner Brothers television after being a veteran of Hollywood B-Movies. His best known efforts are Lon Chaney, Jr's *Inner Sanctum* Mysteries, a number of Joe Palooka movies and a couple of Bowery Boys features.

Louise Fletcher was a mainly television actress until she dropped out of sight in 1963. She resumed her acting career ten years later and won the best Supporting Actress Oscar for her portrayal of Nurse Ratchett in *One Flew Over the Cuckoo's Nest* in 1975. Guido adds cheerfulness to the yarn and is played by Bart Braverman, who later became a recognizable face to fans of 70's television. His most noted part was Binzer on *Vega$*, starring Robert Urich. Braverman is still active in movies and television.

Lisa Gaye was a hard working television actress who undeservedly lived in the shadow of her well known sister, Debra Paget. Her considerable beauty and magnetism brightened many television shows and a handful of movies before she retired in 1970. She was one of the regulars of *How to Marry a Millionaire* and often appeared on *Perry Mason*. Al Ruscio had an impressive resume in television and movies, often playing brusque gangsters. He handled mob parts with ease and, this time around, he

Warner Brothers took out this ad recommending Ray Danton for an Emmy nomination for his role as Danny Rome. 1960, Warner Bros. Television.

gets to boss around Ray Danton as the underling who gets duped before redeeming himself with some last minute heroics.

Johnny Manetti has the casual charm of many of Ray Danton's characters. He fits in well with the Rome environment. However, he lacks the touch of menace and bravado that would make his villain the master mind of the smuggling operation. It is a nice change of pace for Ray Danton.

He still gets to flash his sly grin and crack a few jokes but also does a bit of groveling when he tries to regain Stu's respect or talk Sebastian out of keeping his share of the percentage. His change of affiliation gives him a shade of heroics and he comes out ahead of Sebastian, even if it does not absolve him of duplicity.

Duplicitous would be a positive character trait for Danny Rome, a popular and obnoxious nightclub comic in *Surfside Six: The Frightened Canary*. He is like a barracuda on dry land. His large appetite for living includes consuming people like they were appetizers. The sad thing is they are mostly willing sycophants. Occasionally, there are innocent victims; one of them is Nina Landis (Nina Shipman).

Landis is an aspiring nightclub singer whose career comes to a screeching halt after she knocks out Rome in the alley behind an Italian restaurant. The comic was beating up her boyfriend, who was unable to defend himself because he was being held by Moran (Hal Baylor), Rome's bodyguard. The fight was over Rome's risqué behavior towards Nina.

The newspaper photo of the unconscious Rome is enough to rile the comic. He starts an all-out assault to derail her career. The harassment starts with threatening phone messages and funeral wreaths, continues with a dead canary in a jewelry box, and culminates in having every club owner in town blackball her.

Rome is intoxicated by his domination of Nina Landis. He even turns Eddie (Robert Ridgely), her boyfriend, into a gopher by promising to launch his singing career. The boyfriend doesn't mind being a patsy. His forced laughter and voluntary bootlicking is his way of paying dues to Rome. He even tolerates the comic's critique of him as a non-talent whose high point in life is to run errands for him.

Nina Landis is aided by Sandy (Troy Donahue), the all-too-cool beach boy/private eye with the California tan and wavy blond hair. He is the man who trips up Danny Rome into stumbling into a trap he set for Nina Landis. It will make his last standup a routine before the judge in a murder case.

Danny Rome is Ray Danton's most bizarre role. He is a synthesis of Jerry Lewis and Dean Martin. Although Rome is vicious, he is also hilarious. No one has to put up with his cruel vanity but his hangers-on choose to do so. A washed-up gag writer exemplifies the results of crossing Rome. He is drunk to the point of incoherence and his black balling has led him back to Rome on his knees. The comic delights in taunting him with promises of reconciliation. It will never happen but it gives the alcoholic hope.

Retribution comes in crossing his bodyguard, Moran, when the hired muscle refuses to lean on Nina Landis. Rome makes the mistake of insulting Moran. He tells him they are not friends because Moran is beneath him. The bodyguard's feelings are hurt and he takes it out on Rome in the form of a beating. He turns his back on the comic and is stabbed with a pair of scissors.

The comic's way out is to cart the corpse over to Nina Landis' place in an attempt to frame her. Instead, he trips himself when he visits the pad, pretends to be broken up by the death of his employee, and lets slip that Moran was killed with a pair of scissors.

The police inspector questions Rome about how he knew about the method of murder. The comic insists that he must have heard someone in the room mention it.

Danny Rome is arrested for the murder of Moran. The blacklist has been lifted and Nina finds work as a singer after giving her loafing ex-boyfriend the brush off when he wants to return to her side.

Another departure from type is Harry Shayne, the wily master of ballyhoo in *The Roaring 20's: The Vamp* ('61). The episode is a nod to the silent film days and the emphasis is on screwball comedy and slapstick payoffs. Harry Shayne is a Hollywood press agent who is in trouble with producer, Max Felix (Alex Jerry). Felix is upset because his star, Zelda Valmy (Mari Blanchard), believes the ballyhoo about her receiving a $10,000.00 a weekly salary for her next picture. They are dancing at The Charleston Club after the successful premiere of her latest silent movie triumph, "The Vamp", when she brings up Shayne's column.

Felix vainly tries to explain the value of publicity as a means of stirring up public interest.

"You mean, I'm not worth it?", she asks Felix.

The proud producer replies, "A contract is a contract."

So is an exit.

Harry Shayne (Ray Danton) has a brainstorm when he watches a preview audience laugh at his discovery for all of the wrong reasons. 1961, Warner Bros. Television.

"You can contact me: general delivery-care of the world", are her parting words as she leaves.

A livid Felix fires Harry Shayne in front of the publicist's friend, Pat Garrison.

The next morning, Garrison and a hung-over Shayne have breakfast at a local greasy spoon when they read the headlines announcing Zelda Valme is quitting pictures. This delights Harry because it will give him a chance to implement his new scheme: create a new star out of an anonymous nobody.

"I'll take the first pretty little doll I lay my eyes on and build her into a bigger star[than Zelda Valme]."

The anonymous nobody happens to be Helen Collins (Grace Gaynor), the clumsy waitress at the café where they are having breakfast. She is understandably suspicious of his proposition. It's not until Pat Garrison-a celebrity to her-vouches for Harry that Helen Collins believes that she is going to be the next Vamp.

What follows is a comic lesson in show-biz hype. Harry teaches her a variety of Vamp looks and gestures, among them the "treat me like dirt" look and the "make me grovel at your feet" expression. He also bribes the port commissioner and the captain of a pilot boat with cases of bootleg gin to escort his newest discovery into New York. She is Mara Nari, the mystery woman from Baghdad, Persia.

Things begin to unravel for Mara Nari and Harry Shayne on the first day of shooting her first picture. Not only can't she act, she is humiliated when Zelma and Max show up. Mara Nari is playing a harem scene when Zelma throws several pies into her face. She continues to emote, not knowing what is going on. The scene ends when Zelma and Max approach the stage and reveal Harry's con.

The next day, Harry is hurt, yet fascinated, by Max, Zelda, and the film crew as they laugh at Mara Nari's rushes. After the screening, he sneaks into the projection room and steals the can of film after it is placed there by the projectionist. Harry Shayne sends the rushes to Mack Sennett and stardom follows.

Helen Collins' first film, *Baggy Pants*, is a big hit at its New York premiere. The packed movie house howls with laughter as she disguises herself as a man, steals a necklace, outmaneuvers a locomotive (well, almost) and is chased by a troop of New York City cops. It is first rate slapstick comedy and a tribute to Charles Chaplin, Buster Keaton, Ben Turpin and The Keystone Cops at their zenith. In the end, Harry Shayne's ballyhoo is unnecessary because he has discovered the real thing-genuine comic genius.

War dramas were a popular American favorite and *The Gallant Men* was a short-lived series about Conley Wright (Robert McQueeny), an Ernie Pyle-type of war correspondent traveling with an infantry outfit. Their weekly exploits chronicled the horrific mission of the foot soldiers portrayed by the show's stars, which included William Reynolds, Richard X. Slattery and Eddie Fontaine. Each episode had a guest star to highlight a story. Unfortunately, the show had to compete with the more popular *Combat!* starring Vic Morrow and Rick Jason. *The Gallant Men* lasted one season.

Ray Danton's last appearance for Warner Brothers' television was as the star of a television pilot, an episode of *The Gallant Men* called *Operation Secret*. A couple of years earlier, he had filmed another pilot for Warner Brothers called *Solitaire*. It starred Ray Danton as a globe-trotting adventurer who wiles away his idle hours playing the card game. John Van Dreelen and Kathleen Crowley co-starred.

In *Operation Secret*, Ray Danton plays an American OSS officer who is a master-of-disguise. He is a ringer who infiltrates strategic points in enemy territory to aid the Allies and thwart the Axis Powers. The Solerno landing of the Americans has him posing as Hugo Petra, a ruined count who is the guest of an Italian countess in a Nazi-occupied zone.

The Nazi General Kile (Albert Paulsen) is suspicious of him and tries to use Countess Loren (Maria Machado), the owner of a occupied villa, to expose him. She is part shadow, part flower and acts as is if she is resigned to the Occupation. There is a touch of defiance in her submission and the persistent Nazi commandant likes to play a cat-and-mouse game with Petra and the countess. He loses two times around when the information that he extracts from Petra turns out to be a lie, as does the existence of a ringer that no one can expose.

The stark logo for *The Gallant Men*, an excellent-if short-lived war drama. 1963, Warner Bros. Television.

Petra allegedly winds up in a crypt in the countess' wine cellar. That is how the episode begins when the infantry storms the villa and Conley Wright encounters the countess praying at the crypt of the fallen soldier. The incongruity of finding an American officer in a Nazi-occupied zone about to be invaded by the Allies is the war correspondent's cause for investigation. The unknown soldier's dog tags serve as the starting point in a story that is told in flashbacks.

Wright puts together a story from the recollections supplied by Major Neumann (George Gaynes), a content Nazi officer P.O.W. convalescing in an Allied hospital; Gladenza (Vito Scotti), an ardent Italian resistance fighter sated with the usual Mediterranean verve, wild gesticulations and passionate elocution; and Sgt. Harry Motley (Tony Farrell), a bewildered mechanic working at an airfield where he saw the clandestine operation unfold.

Robert Altman shows that he belongs to the generation of film makers who were influenced by *Citizen Kane*. The moody flashbacks give the story its riveting point because Petra is a puzzle waiting to be pieced together. Too bad the final portrait is a masquerade but that is the stock of his trade.

In *Operation Secret*, Hugo Petra (Ray Danton) assumes the identity of a murdered Nazi officer while a freedom fighter (Vito Scotti) encourages him in his impersonation. 1963, Warner Bros. Television.

A puppeteer named Storm (Earl Hammond) speaks through an American G.I. marionette named Pally and provides a mysterious element to the plot, which hints that the unknown soldier's identity may have died in Salerno but the soldier lives on. He gives Pally the marionette to Wright and it sits with the war correspondent in a jeep when the episode ends with Petra stumbling along with a group of German P.O.W.'s. Getting a cigarette light from Wright is part of his chameleon mission as Pally plays the patsy that sets the war correspondent to thinking about faces and masquerades.

Ray Danton plays it heroic this time around and he makes a good action hero. This show can be added to the list of American secret agents that Ray Danton played on television before his European sojourn. Petra is a two-fisted charmer and his toughness is demonstrated by the sheer insanity of the operation that smuggled him into Salerno.

WESTERN PRIME

The success of the Warner Brothers dramas was matched by a popular roster of western shows like *Sugarfoot, Bronco, Lawman, Colt .45, Cheyenne and Maverick*. Their folklore, too, was celebrated with catchy and likable themes by the resident tunesmiths, Mack David and Jerry Livingston being the most notable.

Black Barts are shifty trail hustlers who cash in on their conceit by becoming the faceless tombstones of Boot Hill ambitions. Ray Danton played Black Barts in episodes of *Sugarfoot* and *Cheyenne*. The Black Bart Club—Blacky Rude, Duke McGann, and Marshal Lestrade—have a need act to act larcenous and wreak havoc. These sagebrush characters are star-crossed and lethal. Blacky Rude is a cowboy who plans to sell secret information about a cattle herd to a cattle rustler in *Sugarfoot: Bunch Quitter*. Duke McGann dreams of gaining power by monopolizing the

The blockbuster lineup of Warner Brothers incomparable western stars. 1960, Warner Bros. Television.

water supply in *Sugarfoot: The Wild Bunch*. Marshal Lestrade doubles as a card sharp-hunting guide in *Cheyenne: Savage Breed*.

Sugarfoot was one of the early successful TV westerns for Warner Brothers. It was based on a 1954 movie, *The Boy from Oklahoma*, starring Will Rogers, Jr. He played Tom Brewster, a cowpoke who refused to wear a shooting iron, instead electing to subdue his opponents with his roping skills.

Will Hutchins played Tom Brewster on television. He was a fledgling lawyer and greenhorn who earned the name *Sugarfoot*. Unlike his big screen model, Hutchins occasionally resorted to using a gun although he preferred to use his wits to take down the bad guys. *Sugarfoot* ran from 1957 to 1961.

In *Sugarfoot: Bunch Quitter*, Otto Jardine (Frank Furguson) is organizing a cattle drive to an unknown destination. The air of mystery makes it hard to replace one of his hired hands when the man is hurt in a bronco busting performance arranged by Blacky Rude. Blacky is a hustler, someone who goes from town-to-town with his wild mare to stage contests for wages. His dim-witted partner, Yamp Dooley (George O'Hanlon), is an alcoholic whose presence makes Blacky feel superior.

The drifter has honed his survival skills to the point where he can root out the best opportunity of any given moment. Word has gotten around that rancher Otto Jardine has bought a herd of cattle for cash but is having a hard time hiring men to make the drive because he refuses to divulge the destination.

Will Hutchins played Tom Brewster with an infectious but righteous naïveté in *Sugarfoot*, one of Warner Brothers popular westerns. 1957, Warner Bros. Television.

The drifter surmises that the air of mystery is due to Jardine's fear that a certain cattle rustler might steal the herd. All Blacky has to do is get a job for him and Yamp, find out the destination of the cattle drive and sell the information to whomever is the local bandit.

Blacky is as charming as he is larcenous and he uses his charisma to lure Jardine's daughter, Dale (Cathy Case), as a way to gain the old man's confidence. He carries her packages when he first sees her in town and wrangles a date with her at the local dance even though she has promised to go with Tom Brewster.

Mr. Jardine is not very trusting; neither is his foreman, Slim Jackson (Tylor McVey). They need two men because they are short and it is a rough ride. Slim is wary of Yamp and is told by Blacky that he will vouch for his partner. Slim asks, "Who will vouch for you?" Blacky's icy reply is, "Me. I vouch for me."

Yamp doesn't want to go on the cattle drive; neither does Blacky. He's interested because he knows that it's not an ordinary cattle drive on account of the destination being kept a secret. Blacky tells Yamp that the secrecy is meant to prevent a Mr. X from finding out about the route.

Blacky Rude (Ray Danton) invents a story that will clear him of murder on the range. Otto Jardine (Frank Ferguson), Dale (Cathy Case) and Yamp (George O'Hanlon) are hooked by his lying tale. 1957, Warner Bros. Television.

Mr. X-he presumes-is a cattle rustler. It is his intention to find out the destination of the cattle drive so he can sell the information to Mr. X.

Trouble ensues because Blacky's mare is a bunch quitter, a horse that strays from the pact and leads a few horses with it. This causes friction between Blacky and Slim and the foreman is shot dead in a showdown. Blacky swears that it is self defense but Tom Brewster eventually exposes him as a liar and murderer.

A doctor is summoned and is apprehensive about aiding the wounded Slim because he does not know anything about the cattle drive. He believes that the air of mystery jeopardizes his fee. Blacky overhears Tom Brewster give the doctor the secret information and later ambushes the doctor to retrieve the information from his notebook.

The Wisdom River Basin is tough country and the Circle J. ranch is where he and Yamp ride to tell Jardine about the mishap. He does this to allay any ill will against him, hoping that his alibi will grant him a reprieve from Slim's friends. He also has the chance to kindle the budding romance with Dale, who has fallen in love with him and unwittingly gives him the name of the cattle rustler.

Blacky is set to make his deal for a thousand dollars and does not intend to split it with his partner. To disarm Yamp, Blacky breaks a bottle of whiskey over his partner's head, knocking him out. He uses the distraction to meet with the rustlers and make a deal for a thousand dollars.

Brewster shows up at the ranch to tell Mr. Jardine that the cattle drive is heading their way. He also accuses Blacky of murdering Slim, Jardine's foreman. His proof is the shell casings found in Slim's gun; they were store bought and Slim always made his own. Blacky, not wanting to stand trial, rides off with Brewster in hot pursuit.

The race ends when the riders and their horses plummet off a broken bridge. They fall into a lake and fight each other. When fists fail, Blacky resorts to using a knife. Both of the men are submerged in the scuffle; only Brewster emerges from the lake. Blacky becomes a waterlogged memory. The cattle drive ends with the men kidding Brewster about being a green trail boss. He jokingly tells them that they were pretty lame, too.

In *The Wild Bunch*, Morgan's Ford is supposed to be a nice friendly town but when Tom Brewster reaches the outskirts he sees someone being chased by a bunch of hooligans. Brewster doesn't know that the man was the schoolteacher and he is next in line for the job.

The original job opening is for a law clerk but he is told by Mr. Markham, his prospective employer, that the town has shrunk to the point that there isn't enough work for him, let alone a clerk. Brewster noticed the boarded up houses and shut-down businesses on his way to Markham's home. Jenny (Connie Stevens), Markham's beautiful daughter, suggests that Brewster take the latest vacancy of school teacher. He gladly accepts.

The job isn't as easy as Brewster expects. The town bully, Ken Savage (Troy Donahue), is also a violent version of the class cut-up. His father, John Savage (Morris Ankrum), is the local baron and is locked in a struggle with the homesteaders who are trying to establish new lives for themselves. Savage has built a dam that prevents the homesteaders from getting the water they need. That is the reason for the exodus from Morgan's Ford. Another reason is the mounting body count due to the town marauders that are led by his son and nephew, Duke McGann.

Duke McGann's dark personality is streaked by an ambition that enables him to exert power over the invalid John Savage. He is a bad influence on his younger cousin, who has become a hellion that no one dares to mess with. Brewster finds this out the first day in class when the seventeen year old disrupts the class. They have a fist fight that spills into the yard, where Savage knocks Brewster unconscious. Brewster's twisted body entwined in the children's swing is a reminder that he is not teaching fresh faced kids.

Surprisingly, Brewster gets a sympathetic ear from John Savage. The old man tells his unruly son that he will have to stay in school until he is eighteen. The disappointed teenager storms out of the house. Brewster uses this as an opportunity to tell John Savage that it is futile to try to quash the spread of the homesteaders. For every one that he kills, three will takes his place. He will have to learn to live with them.

Duke McGann tells his uncle that three or four rifleman can handle the homesteaders. Savage tells him that he disagrees because Brewster is right: he can't stop the spread of the homesteaders and co-existence is the only solution to the tension.

McGann refuses to listen when his uncle tells him that there's plenty for all.

"That's not enough for me", snaps Duke.

Savage tells him that he's had enough of his violent ways. It was McGann's ideas to build the dam and use violence against the homesteaders. Savage orders his nephew to obey but the headstrong

Duke McCann (Ray Danton) enjoys a little rest and relaxation before he instigates a range war that he hopes will net him the water rights to the valley. 1959, Warner Bros. Television.

McGann is insubordinate. The heated argument causes Savage to collapse from a heart attack. McGann finds this amusing. McGann gathers his gunmen and they ride out to the damn. Duke and the boys take their positions.

"Fire at my signal", commands Duke.

Ken follows his cousin once he finds out what's he's up to.

"I'm running things now", insists Duke.

Ken shouts, "Ambush!", at the homesteaders and they run for cover.

Duke shoots his cousin in the shoulder. There is a shootout and Duke's gunmen are killed. Brewster tends to the wounded Ken, who warns his former enemy that Duke is about to shoot him. Brewster spins around and shoots Duke. Black Bart may have been one of the family but his bid to become the new land baron only bought him a plot in potter's field. The bad influence on the town hellion is history, along with the war against the homesteaders.

Familiar faces appear in *The Wild Bunch*. Teen icons Troy Donahue and Connie Stevens have starring roles. Veteran Morris Ankrum has a colorful role as the elder Savage, a land baron confined to a wheel chair. He has a great scene with Danton when Black Bart disobeys his order. The nephew tells him to get it down himself and Ankrum, trying to rise to the occasion, collapses.

An interesting aside is that at the beginning of the episode, Troy Donahue shouts, "Take that, Mr. Peckinpah", to the school teacher he and his gang have run out of town.

Nine years later, Sam Peckinpah broke ground with his violent western, *The Wild Bunch*.

Lawman starred John Russell as marshal Dan Troop and Peter Brown as Deputy Johnny McKay. They were two law men who kept the peace in Laramie. A saloon called The Bird Cage was the atmospheric watering hole run by Lili Merrill, played by Peggie Castle. The show ran from 1958 to 1962.

In *Lawman: Lily*, Laramie has a new saloon and restaurant: The Bird Cage. It is owned and run by Lily (Peggy Castle), a vivacious, two-fisted blonde chanteuse. Her portrait resembles Goya's, "Maji", and she constantly tells the bartender that it has to be hung a little more to the left. She is supervising the set-up of her club when Annette (Nan Peterson), one of her showgirls, tells her that someone is waiting to see her in the alley. It is Annette's boyfriend, Len, who was dismissed from Lily's

John Russell, Peter Brown and Peggy Castle were the stars of *Lawman*. 1959, Warner Bros. Television.

employment because he was involved in some shady business that resulted with her being run out of another town. He plays on her sympathies, citing a marriage proposal to Annette as a means of going straight.

"Len, get your table and set up", says a sympathetic Lily.

The patrons go wild when Lily sings a song about wanting a man. In her vocabulary, man is spelled m-o-n-e-y. Everyone is enjoying themselves, except a gambler who tells Len that he's had enough card-playing for the evening. The bartender thinks that Barney, the timber wolf has had enough, too. The deputy escorts his friend outside to get some fresh air. He leaves him parked on a bench in front of the saloon. Len and Annette also leave for a breath of fresh air.

The next morning, Barney wakes up in the alley way with empty pockets. He runs to the marshal's office to complain. Marshal Troop visits Lily to make an accusation about Len, who was seen leaving the saloon after Barney. He looks like a fool when Johnny runs in and tells him that Barney found his money in one of his boots. Outside, the marshal warns Barney that he has until the count of three to get out of his sight.

Len is upset at being accused and takes to drinking to calm his nerves. He tells Annette that he can't live like that. What he needs is a big score so he and Annette can move to New Orleans and start a new life. His idea is to fleece the gambler when he returns to the saloon that night. Annette is against his plans but goes along because she loves him.

Len Farrell (Ray Danton) is a shifty gambler who resorts to murder to reclaim money lost to a lucky mark. 1959, Warner Bros. Television.

Marshal Troop (John Russell) is quick on the draw and it's not in cards for Len to cash in with a winning hand. 1959, Warner Bros. Television.

After a night of playing cards, he loses an impressive amount to the gambler. He waits outside, where he mugs the man. The gambler is tough and pulls a knife on Len, only to be stabbed with his own blade.

He has enough strength to drag himself to the sidewalk, where he collapses. The deputy finds him and runs to get the marshal. The lawman heads to the saloon and accuses Lily of the crime. Annette comes to her defense and fingers Len. The card sharp fires at the marshal but is shot by the lawman. He fires a second shot that grazes Annette. The marshal finishes the job with a second shot that kills Len. The card sharp falls down the stairs.

A cynical Lily asks Marshal Troup if he is going to arrest Annette.
"She's not the first woman who fell in love with the wrong man."
Lily is surprised.
"Now, how about that drink?", he asks.
"I'll join you."
The marshal tells Lily that her portrait is too far to the left.
"I'll fix it", she promises.

Ray Danton returned to *Lawman* for *Yawkey*, a character that combined elements of the gambler and Black Bart with the characteristics of a duelist. Yawkey is a faded gunslinger impeccably dressed in black, his funeral suit. It still doesn't alter the fact that he is a top marksman with one more notch to make: Marshal Troup (John Russell). In *Lawman: Yawkey* ('60) the price of infamy is a tip of the coward's hand when a hired killer has a crisis and deals with it accordingly: he chooses to curse someone else with the domain name of myth.

Yawkey faced his destiny when he was seventeen years old. He found out that he wasn't afraid to die. The revelation spawned his vocation: gunslinger. To date, Yawkey had twenty seven killings to bolster his fearsome reputation. The duelist seeks the twenty eighth notch when he rides into Laramie. At the Bird Cage, the gunslinger orders whiskey and has a message for Jake the bartender to deliver to Marshal Troup: be ready for a showdown at half past three.

The marshal is curious why Yawkey wants to kill him.
"It's nothing personal", replies the gunman. "It's just the way things have to be."

The deputy wants to know how the marshal feels. Marshal Troup tells him that it's his moment of truth and there's nothing that he can do about it. Lily, the saloonkeeper, is worried. She witnessed three of Yawkey's showdowns and doesn't have much faith in the marshal's abilities. Yawkey

Yawkey (Ray Danton) is a hired gunslinger with a nihilistic view of life and death. To him, they are one and the same. 1960, Warner Bros. Television.

is asked why the marshal has to die and he tells her, "Because I say so, ma'am."

Deputy Johnny McKay draws his gun and demands that Yawkey leave town.

"Let me tell you something, son", says the gunman without looking at him. " I can draw my pistol, fire twice, and put both shots between your eyes before you can think to pull that trigger and that's a fact, son. Don't try me."

Yawkey doesn't have to make eye contact to drive home his point. His monotone voice says it all. At the appointed time, the townspeople line the street as the duelists take their places. The marshal asks Yawkey, "Before we start, do you mind telling me why?"

"It's a nice day to die, marshal."

They strike their pose and draw their weapons. Yawkey is faster but the marshal's shot reaches its mark. The fearsome gunman collapses and the marshal rushes to his side. He holds the dying gunman and asks, "You had me beat-why didn't you pull the trigger?"

"I did", replies Yawkey.

His gun is empty.

"I thought of killing myself but I'm not the kind", he tells the marshal and proceeds to give the reason why he decided to die. Yawkey could no longer bear the burden of his legend. His life had become a series of duels with comers of all ages. From boys to men, he would have to fight them all. Now, he would end his career at the other end of the bullet. He chose Marshal Troup because the lawman had a reputation of integrity.

"I'm sorry for making you the man who killed Yawkey. I don't envy you and that's a fact."

Yawkey makes the marshal promise him that he won't allow the press to take pictures of him. He always hated people staring at him. The marshal obliges and Yawkey dies.

A child picks up Yawkey's gun as the duelist is being carried away. Marshal Troup goes into the saloon for a drink. A townsman toasts him, "To Marshal Troup-the man who killed Yawkey."

The marshal is disgusted by the adulation and pours the drink back into the bottle. He leaves the saloon and sees the child practicing his draw with Yawkey's gun. He confiscates the weapon as the child protests.

Yawkey's torment creates a western legend that adds a new twist to justice.
1960, Warner Bros. Television.

Without saying a word, he walks away from the angry child and the hero-worshipping crowd.

Yawkey is a man drained of vigor. His will to live is sapped and his solution is suicide once removed. He wants to die from a bullet of a man with integrity. His compliment of Marshal Troup is also the lawman's curse. By including the marshal in his own legend, Yawkey has created another myth. The man who shot Yawkey will carry the tag as a scarlet mark.

Marshal Troup is an unassuming man. He does his job, which is to enforce the law. To accept challenges like Yawkey's are part of his job. His disgust at the town's toast is an indication of his quest for anonymity. The lawman doesn't take any credit for shooting the gunslinger. He hates the connotations. His sense of valor compels him to take away Yawkey's gun from a child who found it in the street. The boy was practicing his draw as a homage to the gunslinger. It is a reality that sickens the marshal.

Ray Danton played other characters that combined elements of the gambler, the duelist and the Black Bart type. One was Marshal Lestrade and he appeared on *Cheyenne: Savage Breed*. *Cheyenne* was the first series produced by Warner Brothers when it broke into the television market. It was also television's first hour long prime time western.

Clint Walker played the title character and he was the essence of the westerner: tall, broad shouldered, muscular and silent until riled. He also had a strong moral code which he displayed in each story. The character got his name from the Indian tribe that slaughtered his parents but raised him. He roamed the West and assumed a variety of jobs in his travels.

The show spawned two other westerns, *Sugarfoot* and *Bronco*. For awhile, they rotated under the aegis of *The Cheyenne Show*. The change was due to Clint Walker leaving the show in a contract dispute. He did not receive any residuals from merchandising, had to kick back half of his personal appearance fees to Warner Brothers, and could only record music under the Warner Brothers label. He reached an agreement with the studio and returned to work. It was one of the few times that an actor battled Jack Warner and won. Is it any surprise? Who ever won a contest against Cheyenne?

In *Savage Breed*, Cheyenne is hired as a buffalo guide for a hunting party. He is mystified because the land is void of buffalo. One day, while scouting he finds out why: somebody has been scaring off the herds. He realizes this when he finally spots a herd that is scared off by a gunshot. In the brushes, he sees someone riding away.

The Cheyenne Show starring Clint Walker started a western cycle for Warner Brothers that rivaled its private eye franchise. 1960, Warner Bros. Television.

His suspicion centers on Marshal Lestrade of Dodge City. All he does is stay in camp and beat everyone at poker. His biggest sucker is Senator Leland Carr (Carlyle Mitchell), the man who financed the hunting trip. Cheyenne returns to camp and accuses the marshal. The hotheaded lawman jumps on the mountain man and they fight. The senator breaks up the fight and the marshal fires Cheyenne.

The senator tells the marshal, "This isn't Dodge City; it's Indian country."

He wants Cheyenne to stay. The marshal relents, only to warn Cheyenne that only one of them is going to survive the ride back to Dodge City. Marshal Lestrade wants everyone to know that there hasn't been any Indian trouble in Kansas for years.

The scene cuts to a band of rampaging Sioux Indians raiding a farm. The marshal wants to bolt but Cheyenne advises against it. They won't have a chance against the Indians if they are caught in open country. They stand a better chance of surviving if they take refuge in the rocks.

Marshal Lestrade is annoyed that Cheyenne is wise to his crooked wilderness poker games. Empty prairies, a sudden stampede and vengeful Indians add up to his undoing. 1960, Warner Bros. Television.

They have enough food, water, and ammunition to survive until the army shows up.

Dull Knife (Michael Keep), a Sioux chief and two warriors ride into camp to demand the horses. The marshal is intent on fighting. He is backed up by the majority of the party. Cheyenne thinks that it is unwise. He believes that Dull Knife is sincere in his promise to spare the party in return for fresh horses.

"Nothin' doin'", says Marshal Lestrade. "Dull Knife is not after horses; he's after scalps."

One thing leads to another and everyone begins to betray each other. There is a final showdown between Cheyenne and Marshal Lestrade. They draw and the marshal is shot dead. After the party buries the dead, Senator Carr is saddened by the body count, which he blames on the Sioux.

"The Sioux didn't kill them. Dull Knife kept his word", Cheyenne says.

"The word of a savage", huffs the senator.

"The savages were back in the rocks…with us", says a sober-minded Cheyenne.

The survivors mount their rigs, ready to return to what they call civilization.

Ray Danton's last Warner Brothers' villians were on *Colt .45* and *Temple Houston*. Wade Preston was the star of *Colt .45* and he contended with Ray Danton as Kane in *The Bounty List*. He plays a gunslinger turned bounty hunter intent on collecting the ransoms placed on his former cohorts' heads. Sam is after one of the men but he wants to take him alive. Kane does not matter because wanted: dead or alive is his credo, too.

As Martin Royale on *Temple Houston: The Case for William Gotch*, he plays a devious gambler who obtains a ranch through dubious means. It takes the legal skill of lawyer Temple Houston (Jeffrey Hunter)—the son of Sam Houston—to rectify the misdeed. Temple Houston was aided by James Best and Richard Jaeckal as William Gotch and Coley. Jack Elam played George Taggart, the rancher who is helped by Temple Houston.

Prairie Spirits and Mixed Brands

Ray Danton may have created a list of dastardly varmints with no redeeming value on the Warner Brothers' back lot but he also portrayed a handful of characters with mixed alliances and agendas that were unpopular to the growth of a frontier land that would culminate in the policy of Manifest Destiny. Colonel Bill Magrider and Don Felipe are heroes of the soil and land and identity is what defines them. It is the adherence to a national boundary that ignites their sympathies and causes.

Myths and ciphers are what changed the West. Colonel Bill Magrider is a hero who left his myth in the dust of a crumbling aristocracy. Don Felipe is a proud blueblood about to be given a forced transfusion of red, white and blue. The proud Mexican is at the beginning of his fight while the cynical Southerner is at the end of his.

Col. Bill Magrider and Don Filipe are similar men at different junctures of a crisis. It is a matter of the presence or absence of hope. Don Felipe has it and the colonel doesn't. It is not a matter of character strengths or flaws; it is a matter of timing. Pre-crisis and aftermath are the reasons behind the dubious titles of hero and villain that would ordinarily be applied to the colonel and the don.

Bronco was created out of the contractual dispute between Clint Walker and Warner

Ty Hardin played Bronco Layne, a former Confederate soldier who wandered through the West, in a series that was spun off of *The Cheyenne Show*. 1958, Warner Bros. Television.

Brothers. Ty Hardin was brought into the show as Bronco Layne, an ex-Confederate captain who traveled throughout the West in search of adventure. *Bronco* became a separate show when Walker returned to *Cheyenne.*

Bronco: Quest of the Thirty Dead, is a tale of wonder tarnished by vain glory and tainted ambition. It is the saga of a revered Civil War hero who becomes a tragic myth when ideals clash and the larger-than-life figure crashes and burns. That is the legend of Bill McGrider (Ray Danton), a man whom Bronco Layne lionizes at the end of the story with a sobering tribute.

Col. Bill McGrider was an inspiration to the men of McGrider's Raiders, a band of elite Confederate soldiers who fought with a manic zeal for the Stars and Bars. For Bronco, everything changed the day the colonel bolted with a band of renegades to leave the war for the others to fight. Although Layne is disgusted with his fallen idol for replacing duty and honor with personal profit, he still has profound respect for the man.

His former commanding officer is a Confederate idol who breaks ranks with the secessionists and becomes the ringleader of a bandit outfit. Disillusioned by the North's impending victory, Col. Magrider crosses over to the other side of the law. Since the war, he has been terrorizing the countryside with his brigand of Mexican bandits. Paco (Jay Novello), his right hand man, is a ratty range rider, fond of drinking and killing but he knows the ways of the gringo and this make him invaluable to his boss.

Fate reunites the men when Bronco Layne works undercover for a railroad after a train wreck kills thirty passengers, his best friend Jim Brandt (Peter Breck) being one of them. He, too, was riding the train and was to serve as best man at Jim's wedding. Bronco survived the carnage with intent to find the saboteur that arranged the head-on collision between two locomotives. The chief suspect is his former commanding officer, Colonel Bill Magrider.

Months after convalescing, Layne becomes intrigued when Irene Lang (Beverly Lang), Jim's ex-fiancée, shows up at his hotel room with a message from his former commanding officer. He is warned not to pursue the matter and this increases his pursuit for justice, especially because he does not believe that the Colonel is responsible for the wreck. This is later confirmed when Bronco finds out that the man who delivered the message to Irene is an imposter.

Bronco receives another warning about staying out of the matter, this time from the chief of the railroad detectives, P.J. Mohler (Tol Avery).

He is an imposing brute with a threatening manner that disguises his real intention for keeping Bronco off of the train. Mohler is adamant about Layne not riding on the train and deputizes two men to make sure that the head strong young man obeys his advice. Of course, the admonition falls on deaf ears because Bronco hides and appears after the train ride has started.

Anonymity isn't Colonel Bill Magrider's style; neither is impersonation and false witness. He rides the same train as Bronco Layne in his own attempt

Colonel Bill McGrider hijacks a train to clear his name in a fatal train wreck disaster. He now commands an army of Mexican outlaws and has to contend with Bronco, his former right hand man. 1958, Warner Bros. Television.

to clear his name. McGrider takes advantage of the confusion created when Mohler's men get into a confrontation with Bronco after he confronts the imposter and real murderer. Mohler shoots the man dead on the pretext that he was reaching for Bronco's gun. The real Bill McGrider appears, aided by his gang of cut throats, who have been disguised as passengers.

He holds hostage Pearson (Willis Bouchey), the railroad president, Mohler, the detective, Irene and his former pupil. They ride in style and enjoy the gentleman's amenities provided by the Pearson's private car. Fine food and Napoleon Brandy make refined companions on a ride that will end badly for either Bronco or Col. McGrider.

McGrider likes to needle Mohler because the chief of detectives was his partner on the previous train robberies. He and the chief of detectives had a deal to split the take until Mohler decided to go solo and frame McGrider with the fatal train wreck. This costs Mohler his life in a dramatic showdown when McGrider pays him off with a fistful of dollars and a bullet to the belly.

After an elegant dinner and a sentimental conversation about dedication and betrayal, McGrider and Layne settle their differences with a showdown. Intents and purposes become irrelevant when the pupil and the teacher square off in a duel tinged with a little bit of reminiscing and chest beating. It is ironic fate that McGrider should meet his end with a showdown with his star pupil.

Afterwards, Layne is not bitter or angry, just disappointed and heartbroken. At the story's conclusion, Pearson offers Bronco a job as chief of detectives but is turned down. Irene still can't believe that Bronco still has a high regard for his former commanding officer. Bronco does not regret or feel confused about his adulation. He tells Irene and Pearson, "There's something to be said about a man who became a sergeant at 20, a major at 23, a colonel at 26 and a legend at 30."

It is a fitting tribute to a fallen hero, a larger-than-life man who fell face forward into the primordial mud because he had feet of clay.

Maverick was a rare western, an oater that had a sense of humor and two alternating leads (James Garner and Jack Kelly). They were shifty gamblers and con artists with intense self-preservation instincts that allowed them to avoid confrontations at any costs. However, when left with little or no wiggle room to elude an opponent, they could be fierce enough to win any confrontation.

James Garner played Bret Maverick and Jack Kelly was his brother Bart. Garner had always been a fan favorite because of his unique acting style, which combined self-effacing humor with a bedeviling machismo. James Garner earned headlines when he walked off the series in a dispute with the studio. Unlike Clint Walker, Garner did not win his suit but was allowed to exit the series and leave Warner Brothers to pursue a successful career in movies and on television.

In *Maverick: State of Siege* ('60), Bart Maverick (Jack Kelly) finds himself in the middle of a blood feud when he visits Don Felipe at his hacienda. They became acquaintances when Maverick saved the hidalgo's life in a poker game gone bad. Don Felipe accused a card player of dealing from the bottom. To protect a false sense of honor, the player drew his gun and was beaten to the draw by Don Felipe's knife. The man's partner was going to shoot Don Felipe in the back when Maverick averted the shot. In appreciation, Don Felipe extended his hospitality to Maverick should the card sharp ever find himself in the vicinity of the Santa Rita Grande.

Bret (James Garner) and Bart (Jack Kelly) Maverick are brothers with nimble hands and quick draws. *Maverick* was a light-hearted western played with sophisticated wit by its stars.

Maverick is delayed on the way to El Paso when his stage is detained because of an Apache war party ahead. The dandy uses a fresh horse to ride to the nearby hacienda. He is given a cold welcome and finds the place to be cold and remote. The only occupants, besides Don Felipe, are Yaquito (Ref Sanchez) and Mamacita (Bella Bruck).

Yaquito is a non-smiling pampas Indian who is Don Felipe's bodyguard. Mamocita is the housekeeper. Don Felipe begrudgingly extends his hospitality to Maverick, who is invited to spend the night. A night's sleep in a comfortable bed is interrupted by the hasty arrival of a woman and her father.

Maverick deduces that the woman is Soledad (Lisa Gaye), Don Felipe's betrothed because they have a heated argument and shows throws vases at him, aside from calling off their engagement. Don Manuel (Ice Di Santis), her father, is wounded and appears to be a man of great importance. Intrigue turns to inconvenience when Maverick is told that he has to leave.

He is hesitant about leaving the comfort of his large bed and is told by Don Felipe ,"By leaving now, you will lose a few hours sleep; if you wait-it may be your life."

Maverick gets the point but it is too late! He is fired upon by a brigand outside the hacienda walls.

"All I wanted was a good night's sleep", is Maverick's refrain as he reloads his gun.

Yaquito aids him in returning to the safety of the fortress. Once he is inside, he learns that the attackers are led by Don Felipe's compadre, Don Lopez (Raul De Leon). Lopez tells Don Felipe that he wants to talk under a flag of truce.

"Since when do we need a flag of truce to speak?", asked a puzzled Don Felipe.

Outside, Don Lopez tells him about their movement's betrayal by the revered Don Manuel. Maverick learns that the two dons are plotting a revolution to reclaim the land that was annexed by the United States government. Their leader, Don Manuel, absconded with the funds, electing to use the money to finance a revolution in Mexico. The arms he purchased were given to his insurgents to propel him to power as the new president in Mexico. Maverick reminds them that this is now American territory and what they are planning is treason.

Don Felipe (Ray Danton) his his betrothed, Soledad (Lisa Gaye), confront her father, Don Manuel (Joe Di Santis) about missing funds needed for the revolution. 1961, Warner Bros. Television.

Don Manuel will hear none of this.

"For betrayal, we demand death", he vehemently proclaims.

Don Manuel tells Don Felipe that he understands his conflicted loyalties because Don Manuel is the father of his betrothed. Nevertheless, if he doesn't surrender Don Manuel, the insurgents will raid the villa. Don Felipe is amused by the threats because his hacienda is a fortress that can withstand any conventional attack. Don Lopez is not impressed and Don Lopez throws the flag in the dust. Don Felipe picks it up.

The siege is on. The men shoot the insurgents as they bound over the wall.

"Just my luck to be caught up in a local feud", says Maverick.

Don Felipe replies, "Why should that bother you, Senor Maverick. It will be easier for you gringos to steal our land. Isn't that true?"

Maverick suggests that Don Felipe give up Don Manuel. Don Felipe speaks of the honor of sanctuary. There is a cessation in the fire and Don Felipe speaks with his mentor. Don Manuel finally confesses that he used the money for a greater cause-to seize power in Mexico. He describes himself as a Yankee fighter and gringo hater. He chastises his followers for not listening to his prediction that there is no justice in the Yankee courts.

Don Felipe is a hero burdened by destiny. He stands on the line of demarcation that separates the Old World from the new, having been cheated out of his inheritance by the Northern land grabbers. Don Felipe is a proud hidalgo whose land has been swallowed by the American courts. He fights a second battle to protect his estate from his fellow revolutionaries in a siege. Don Felipe, at the behest of Maverick, will appeal the land grab in an American law court. It is a move that will either restore his power or destroy his honor.

The roles of the hero and villain are combined in Jess Larkin, a federal prisoner about to be lynched in *Bronco: The Buckbrier Trail*. His belief in truth and justice is so strong that he is willing to risk death by hanging to see that the law is served.

Bronco Layne is hired to escort Jess Larkin (Ray Danton), a dangerous criminal to stand trial for murder. Unfortunately, the supposedly secret mission is well-known in the town. A leak has spoiled the element of surprise and just about everyone knows Bronco Layne's name and mission.

Marshal Pete Kilgore (Paul Birch) is a cautious lawman and he is flustered about the blown cover. He has been occupied hiding behind the locked doors of his office, anxiously awaiting Layne's arrival so he can be rid of his prisoner. The town is in an uproar and there is talk of lynching

Don Felipe (Ray Danton) defends the honor of his title and his right to the ownership of the land that has been declared null and void. 1961, Warner Bros. Television.

Larkin. Marshal Kilgore's plan is to have Bronco leave immediately with his prisoner, the last thing the town would expect, especially with Layne's luggage in tow at the hotel and his horse resting in the stable. Marshal Kilgore instructs Bronco to take the Buckbrier Trail.

Jess Larkin is a slick and oily villain. Shaggy haired and silver-tongued, he has a sharp retort for every insult or threat. Impending death does not phase him and he itches for a chance to take down a lawman or two on his way to the gallows. He has a western villain's typical disdain for the law and does not believe that Bronco will suceed in escorting him to stand trial. Bronco disagrees and they depart on their midnight run.

Their solitary trek is intercepted by a Cavalry troop led by Lt. Blyden (Mike Road), who tells Bronco that he has orders to relieve him of his prisoner. Bronco refuses to surrender his prisoner until the orders are produced and becomes suspicious when he is presented with butcher's paper with orders hastily scribbled in pencil. The officer assures Bronco that the orders are real and are an example of his commanding officer's eccentric personality.

Bronco is not convinced but it does not matter because the officer tells him that he and his men are renegade soldiers and they have been hired to kidnap Larkin. Lt. Blyden tells him that Larkin is the ex-partner of their employer and he needs Larkin because he knows where the buried gold is located. Bronco is subdued and Larkin is relieved of his manacles. He knocks Bronco to the ground, takes a revolver from the renegade officer and fires two shots at the prone man.

When Larkin and the ex-soldiers arrive at the hideout, it is revealed that he is really a deputy and not a lawbreaker. He is shot and left to die by the roadside until Bronco finds him. They seek help at the cabin of Norton Gillespie (Denver Pyle) and his daughter, Ruth (Sandra Gale Bettin). Larkin is well enough to ride with Bronco to alert Marshal Kilgore, who is escorting the real prisoner.

The marshal is ambushed at the relay station but Larkin and Layne lead a successful counter-trap. All goes well until it is learned that Ruth is being held hostage at the cabin. A standoff turns into a gun battle and

The Alaskans starred Roger Moore, Dorothy Provine and Jeff York as three adventurers during the turn-of-the century Gold Rush in Alaska. 1959, Warner Bros. Television.

Ruth is saved, the prisoner is escorted to trial and Larkin can resume his identity as a U.S. marshal.

Ray Danton was able to have time on a regular series when he played a toned down version of Blackie, his character in *The Spoilers*, in the short-lived role of Nifty Cronin in *The Alaskans*. It was a single season series

Nifty Cronin was a larcenous saloon owner who could never quite best Silky Harris (Roger Moore), Rocky Shaw (Dorothy Provine) and Reno McKee (Jeff York). 1959, Warner Bros. Television.

set in Skagway about the exploits of three profiteers named Silky Harris (Roger Moore), Rocky Shaw (Dorothy Provine) and Reno McKee (Jeff York.) For thirty-seven episodes, the con man, dancehall queen, and gold miner schemed to carve out a piece of the new frontier for themselves. They always had competition. During the early part of the show's run, the chief spoiler was Nifty Cronin, who was aided by Fantan (Frank De Kova), a corrupt Eskimo.

Nifty Cronin was larcenous but it was tempered by a cool sense of humor. He was more crafty than cruel and had a way of wheedling out of a con turned sour. His character-a villain, to be sure-added flippancy to the show and displayed Ray Danton's good timing for comedy.

The Alaskans occasionally recycled scripts from other Warners' western shows because of the writers' strike of 1960. It was also a springboard to *Maverick* for Roger Moore, who briefly played Beauregard Maverick, an English cousin in the family of con-artists, who was called upon to keep the show going after James Garner's departure.

He called *The Alaskans*, "my most appalling series ever." Not only did he dislike filming the Alaskan scenery on the Burbank back lots but found it stifling to wear winter gear during the long, hot summer.

Ray Danton was introduced as Nifty in the second episode, *Cheating Cheaters*. The story deals with the saloon owner agreeing to ship gold dust to the States for Silky, Reno and a number of other miners. The ship sinks and various attempts are made to recover the payload.

Aided by Fantan, he spies on the men when they search the lake for the booty. Reno McKee, in a diver's outfit, combs the depths for the sunken treasure. Fantan, at the behest of Cronin, shoots the air hose that enables him to breath. It takes more than Cronin's treachery to kill McKee.

The miners succeed in raising the chest and are baffled when it is empty. Nifty confesses that the gold dust was never on board. He had hoarded it in an effort to keep it for himself should the miners believe his claim that their gold lie on the bottom of the lake.

Waylaying other people's plans seemed to be in Nifty's nature, as evidenced by his skullduggery in *The Petticoat Crew*. Silky Harris buys an old, broken down paddlewheel boat so he can transport a crew of dancing girls to town. He has a schedule to keep but it is sabotaged by Nifty, who wants the girls for his saloon. The paddlewheel boat becomes adrift at sea and the only way for the men and the dancing girls to stay alive is to roast the turkeys Silky has bought as part of an agricultural business.

Nifty Cronin's last appearance on *The Alaskans* was at the end of 1959. In *The Golden Fleece*, Nifty plays shifty landlord when he threatens to slap a foreclosure notice on Silky and Reno for non-payment of the mortgage on their mining claim. The sub-plot is a human interest story of a baby that is abandoned on their property and the tough guys attempt to raise money by staging a Name That Baby Contest. The heroes win and Nifty's plans are dashed. All his attempts to become rich have failed and Nifty Cronin was gone after three episodes.

Transitions

BITS AND PIECES

Warner Brothers was similar to Universal-International in that the studio did not really capitalize or utilize its star potential. Ray Danton's electric star performance in *The Rise and Fall of Legs Diamond* and his stellar television appearances merely led to the studio giving him the big screen roles of the bland Jerome Black, an upwardly mobile petty bureaucrat, in *A Majority of One* ('61) and the nondescript Fred Vitale ('63), a computer genius whose engagement is threatened by his doting mother, in *F.B.I. Code 98*, a project released several years after it was made.

In the film adaptation of the stage play, *A Majority of One*, Ray Danton plays a repressed xenophobe, a son-in-law who objects to his Brooklyn mothers-in-law's intention to marry a wealthy Japanese widower. He is a diplomat whose liberal veneer masks a racial hypocrisy when he deals with a situation for which there are no rehearsed lines.

Culture clash and racism are handled with humor in *A Majority of One*. The unlikely pairing of a Jewish widow from Brooklyn and a Japanese widower makes for an interesting combination that doesn't elicit approval from the woman's daughter and son-in-law. Besides squeezing laughs from problems arising from acculturation and opinions based on nationalistic sentiments, the movie also skewers a liberal's pretense of being free from prejudice and having an entitlement of moral superiority.

Mrs. Jacoby (Rosalind Russel) is the stereotypical lower eastside Jewish mother that has been celebrated in stories, movies, songs, and comedy routines. She is the center of the universe, the hub that sustains the spokes that emanate from her radiance. The maternal symbol of the triumph of the immigrants, this urban mother, alone, has the right to

Mrs. Jacoby (Rosalind Russell) and the Blacks (Ray Danton and Madlyn Rhue) make the on-board acquaintance of Mr. Koichi (Alec Guinness). 1961, Warner Bros. Dist. Group.

converse with the immortals and pass this information along to others as wisdom.

In *A Majority of One*, she represents tradition, something that is being threatened by the change of the nuclear age. Her daughter (Madlyn Rhue) is married to Jerome Black (Ray Danton), a rising star in the diplomat corps. His promotion is the impetus that starts the action in the movie. The announcement of his promotion and transfer to Japan is met with bemusement followed by heartache.

Jacoby is a product of the old world. Japan is the still the country that tried to engineer a world takeover. To bring the cataclysm closer to home, Jacoby lost her son during the war. The wounds are still fresh and acknowledgement of her children moving to Japan won't help them heal. To compound matters, Jacoby fends off isolation by agreeing to move with them.

It is the fear of obscurity that compels Jacoby to make this monumental decision. Her best friend is moving out of the neighborhood because of changing demographics. She would be the last of her age. In order not to lose meaning, she agrees to live in the world of her enemy, if only to be close with all the family that she has.

Jacoby is forced to confront her hatred when she meets Mr. Koichi (Alec Guiness) on the shipboard cruise. He senses her hostility and asks her if it has to do with his nationality. She tells him that it does and recounts the story of her son's death in the war. She recites the letter from the Secretary of State, word by word. In turn, Mr. Koichi tells Jacoby about how his son died in combat and his daughter, a nurse, was killed at Hiroshima.

It is a nervous moment for the two of them but it has become a connection that will bring them closer as the movie progresses. The differences in culture provide some laughs; situations force them to explain things to each other. They begin to have an effect on each other-she uses Japanese phrases and he uses Smith Brothers cough drops.

The discordant familial ring exposes the Blacks' racial hypocrisy. At the start of the movie, Jacoby's friend tells them that she is leaving the neighborhoods because of "undesirables." When Jerome Black understands what she means, he reminds her that-not so long ago-the same neighborhood didn't accept Jews. The friend tries to explain her comment but the righteous Blacks put her in her place.

It's an admirable thing to do but serves only to set the Blacks up when they have a hard time accepting Jacoby's love for Koichi. The couple that had preached about accepting differences among people now have a difficult time accepting eastern customs within their family.

A Majority of One looks like a film stage play, at times, and it can be plodding, too. At two hours and twenty minutes, there are times when tedium can demand a pause from viewing. The length of the movie gives it an embalmed feeling. A little editing wouldn't have hurt it. But within this long time frame are impressive bits and worthwhile routines.

The movie belongs to the stars, Rosalind Russell and Alec Guinness. Their characters are stock characters given individuality through the expertise of the veteran performers. Occasionally, their talent shines through the heavy handedness and bad make-up. They have some good bits as solos and with each other.

Rosalind Russell's Jacoby is a fish out of water. In typical Brooklyn style, she influences others to adopt some of her attitudes. She, in turn,

The title of the movie may be from Rudyard Kipling but the film's message repudiates another one of his sayings as evidenced by the successful blending of cultures: New York's lower eastside and aristocratic Japan. 1961, Warner Bros. Dist. Group.

adopts kimonos and a bun hair style. Alec Guinness projects dignity, majesty, and strength. He is a magnificent figure whose home life is an austere, yet pleasant environment. His garden is breathtakingly beautiful with sculpted bushes and crystal waterfalls.

Ray Danton and Madlyn Rhue play the uptight, upwardly mobile couple of the new America. Service to the government has afforded them the chance to rise above their Brooklyn street origins. They serve their employers well in the hopes of receiving a rising status in the community.

Ray Danton is frivolous worry wart as Jerome Black. A go-getter as in subordinate hoping for a berth in middle-management, his bootlicking is futile unless Mr. Koichi likes him. Madlyn Rhue is the subservient Fifties housewife making a grand entry into the nuclear age. She is supportive of her husband, although her love for her mother is paramount.

Warner Brothers was still competing with other studios in a time of major change, but its once invincible television annex was about to go through major changes that would make its phenomenal success a recent memory. ABC suddenly lost faith in the Wm. T. Orr machine and was dissatisfied with the ten Warner Brothers shows it had on its primetime schedule. The older successful shows were running out of the steam and the new offerings were less than mediocre.

Wm. T. Orr and Hugh Benson, his head of production, were fired and actor-producer-director Jack Webb was brought in to clean house. He immediately dissembled Wm. T. Orr's operation in a massacre, only retaining a severely revamped *77 Sunset Strip*. In its last season, the old show literally became a new show and should have been given a different title even though its star, Efrem Zimbalist, Jr. as Stu Bailey, was retained. The series had a new theme and Bailey was now an international private investigator. The new streamlined 77 Sunset Strip lasted one more season. None of the Jack Webb's Warner Brothers' shows were successful and

Fred Vitale (Ray Danton) uncovers the suitcase bomb in mid-flight. His partners, Robert P. Cannon (Jack Kelly [l]), Alan W. Nichols (Andrew Duggan) and his fiancé (Merry Anders) watch him disarm it. 1962, Warner Bros. Dist. Corp.

his reign as a creative force was the complete opposite of Wm. T. Orr's residence.

This left some residual programs from the old regime; one of them was *F.B.I. Code 98*, originally filmed in 1960 as a television pilot and shelved. Three years later, after the suspension of Warner Brothers' television unit, it was issued as a movie. The padding is what sinks it because it consists of dryly-narrated documentary styled information about F.B.I. procedures. *F.B.I. Code 98* is another Warner Brothers' ensemble piece. This time, the Warner's' crew demonstrates the efficiency of the F.B.I. in tracking a mad bomber.

Ray Danton's character is a geek, of sorts, along the line of Jerome Black. He, too, works for the government and is a mama's boy. His name is Fred Vitale, a computer genius who is one-third of a powerful electronics firm that has contracts with the government. *FBI Code 98* is the tale of the trio being the target of a mad bomber's rage.

Vitale is more level headed than Black and actually has the wits to disarm a booby-trapped valise in mid-air. He is considered soft because his mother dotes over him and it is something that he hasn't resolved to his fiancé's satisfaction. It's a surprise that the film's stars—Jack Kelly, Ray Danton and Andrew Duggan—didn't sue to prevent the movie from being released. Instead, they were released from their contracts after the movie went into circulation, along with everyone else at Warner Brothers' television division.

The film opens with a shot of the bomber assembling his apparatus. The narrator sternly tells the audience that when a nefarious idea is regulated to the mind, it is not a crime. It is when the idea is realized that a crime is committed. When the crime threatens national security, it is a job for the F.B.I.

The subjects of the bomber's discontent are the three geniuses that started a revolutionary computer company in a California garage. They are Robert P. Cannon (Jack Kelly), Fred Vitale (Ray Danton), and Alan W. Nichols (Andrew Duggan). Now, their company has expanded into a major business that has vital contracts with the United States government. The stern narrator informs the audience that it will be a blow to national security if these men were eliminated.

The non-action continues as a gopher (Eddie Ryder) picks up the suitcases for the men. He is to deliver them to the airport. Of course, the bomber is following him. At one point, he parks in a basement garage. He replaces one of the men's valises with a look alike suitcase that contains the bomb. It is set to go off in mid-air.

The bomb that would have rocked the plane out of the sky is discovered by accident. Fred Vitale's secretary and fiancé (Merry Anders) spills coffee on Cannon. He discovers the bomb in his suitcase when he opens it for a change of clothing. Tension fills the cabin when the three men and woman sense their lives are about to come to an end.

Fred Vitale, the electronics genius, deftly disarms the bomb by severing the proper wires. The bomb is rendered useless, the usual suspects are fingered and the F.B.I. is called in to investigate. We are introduced to the FBI's exhaustive resources. Through an intelligence network supported by a militaristic chain-of-command, the FBI is able to pursue any type of investigation. In this case, experts are called in to examine the bomb, interview witnesses, and piece together the information to come up with a suspect: Joseph Peterson (Vaughn Taylor), a weasel of an employee whose motive is revenge.

His son was fired from the company for being an incompetent and moved away to start a new life as a television repair man. His wife died ten months earlier so he lives a lonely life and he blames Cannon, Vitale and Nichols for it. Hampered by anger and bitterness, he is no match for

Phil Carey leads his G-Men into action as they track down the mad bomber. 1962, Warner Bros. Dist. Corp.

the quick-witted lawmen. They disarm him and remove one more nut from the gears of a society that is supposed to run smoothly because it is a democracy. You have the men of *F.B.I. Code 98* to thank for that.

Despite the general disaffection with the movie, there are things that are noteworthy about it. One of them is Leslie H. Martinson's original direction, which is unencumbered by the lugubrious narration. His direction has the punch of his other television episodes yet Martinson's style earned the enmity of Ray Danton, whose constant clashes with the director caused Stanley Niss, the producer, to visit the set to sort things out.

Another noteworthy aspect of the film is the supporting cast. The chief agent is Philip Carey, star of *The Time Travelers* and *Screaming Mimi* and a stream of other credits. He is the granite bulwark agent in charge. Merry Anders, also a star of *The Time Travelers*, appeared with Ray Danton in *The Night Runner*. William Reynolds plays an FBI agent, much like the one he would soon play on television in *The F.B.I.*

Eddie Ryder, as a company driver, gives an amusing performance. He is a solid working-class individual in the midst of computer wizards. He is happy with a routine that is relieved by bowling night and drinking beer. Jack Cassidy is refreshing as the knave who is carrying on an affair with one of his bosses' wives. He is the same energetic, brassy go-getter that he played in his all-too-brief career.

Kathleen Crowley is stunning is her role as the cheating wife. In this movie, she is dolled up to look like a trophy of upper-class suburbia. It is a bitchy sensuality compounded by the helplessness of being neglected. As the bomber and Crowley's kidnapper, Vaughn Taylor is amusing because he stands out as an oddball, especially when we are considering this is Cold War America and almost everyone had a cookie cutter look to them.

A Reprise and a Reality Check

It was 1961 and Ray Danton was in negotiations with Warner Brothers for a new contract that included outside appearances. There were loan outs to other studios and appearances on televisions shows outside of Warners' purview but, despite his full schedule, his status at the studio and his luck as a free lancer were emblemized by a reprise and a reality check.

The reprise is Legs Diamond, who makes a cameo in *Portrait of a Mobster* ('61), starring Vic Morrow as Dutch Shultz. The reality check is a loan out to 20th Century Fox as Captain Frank in the war epic, *The Longest Day* ('62). According to Hedda Hopper's column, the only reason that Warner Brothers allowed Ray Danton to appear in *The Longest Day* was so he could plug *A Majority of One* in Scotland, where he was to film his scenes.

In 1961, Ray Danton returns as Legs Diamond in *Portrait of a Mobster* but he is not as hungry and feline as he was in *The Rise and Fall of Legs Diamond*. Here, he is more poised and relaxed. He has the polish of a successful businessman. The only time he loses his temper is when he is scolding Schultz for being impetuous. It is something that ends with his assassination.

The year before, he turned in a crackerjack performance as the title character in *The Rise and Fall of Legs Diamond*. To continue its retro-gangster revival, Warner Bros. made *Portrait of a Mobster* ('61), starring Vic Morrow.

Vic Morrow borrows Sheldon Leonard's intonations, swipes Marlon Brando's smirk, and mimics Boris Karloff's method of intimidation for the role of Dutch Schultz. A smalltime hood from the Bronx, the Dutchman is rough cut, uncouth, and uncontrollable. It's a wonder that his short fuse doesn't cause him to immediately self-destruct, considering that his is a world of attitude and blood lust.

Portrait of a Mobster is done in a Roaring Twenties' devil-may-care chaos style. Prohibition is the driving force behind the rackets' power and booze, bribery and blood was the currency that made the juice flow. Because of the money involved, certain strata within law enforcement and City Hall are on the bootleggers' payroll in a power scheme where the body count is high and the catbird seat is a musical chair. For a time in the Twenties, it was Dutch Schultz's turn to sit in the musical chair.

Arthur Fligelheimer starts out as a rough Bronx hood with his sidekick, Bo Wetzel (Norman Alden). The first step into the big time is to become Legs Diamond's (Ray Danton) bodyguards and this is accomplished the old-fashioned way-by beating up the bodyguards in front of Diamond. Offended because Diamond ridicules his birth name, Dutch Schultz and Bo Wetzel demolish the bodyguards. Shortly thereafter, they are on the payroll. This is similar to the way Legs Diamond gained access to Arnold Rothstein.

In *The Rise and Fall of Legs Diamond*, the up-and-coming gangster uses his boss as a steppingstone. Dutch Schultz does the same with Legs Diamond, only he is nowhere near as smooth as his boss was with

Dutch Shultz (Vic Morrow) intimidates Iris Murphy (Leslie Parrish), a cop's wife, into becoming his moll. 1961, Warner Bros. Dist. Corp.

Rothstein. Schultz is headstrong and argumentative. It is a matter of time before an overheated Schultz quits to go on his own.

From the moment of the split, Schultz becomes a target. Ultimately, he wins the contest when he shoots Legs Diamond from a window. The sharp gangster is cut down in the street, unlike the death in his own movie, where he is shot by a gunsel in a hotel room.

Dutch Schultz is the undisputed king of the underworld and Vic Morrow lets the whole world know it with his larger-than-life portrayal. He is a blond simian from the outer borough whose lust for power takes him to the center of the action in downtown New York. The Dutchmen is one of the kings of the Roaring Twenties and his empire is one of seizure, conquest, and expansion.

His ability to adapt to changing times is illustrated by his entrance in the numbers racket. The repeal of the Prohibition is the death knell for many mob kingpins. Dutch Schultz survives by stealing the Harlem numbers business. Not shown but mentioned, the takeover is characteristic of the street smart and savvy business attitudes of the blond simian.

Portrait of a Mobster also has a series of miniatures related to the main subject.

They are the supporting roles that-when added up-contribute to Schultz's downfall. Always corrupting others to satisfy his lust for power, he is ultimately corrupted when he betrays his own lucky charm-Bo Wetzel. It is the final betrayal that rescinds all offers of redemption. Damnation is his penance, the price paid for corrupting so many people along the way.

Dutch Shultz's demonic nature is represented by the way he effects the lives of Frank Brennan (Peter Breck) and his wife, Iris Murphy (Leslie Parrish). His devilish accomplishments include killing Murphy's father, dominating her husband, possessing her, and ruining their marriage in the process.

When he first meets Iris Murphy, he is struck by her class and charm. After he owns her, she becomes a boozer and a tramp. He discards her like a used up flapper. The same goes for her husband.

Once an honest cop, Frank Brennan is broken by his inability to pay the bills and please his wife. He is framed in a bribery scam and coerced into becoming a bagman by his precinct captain. His first job is to pick up a payment for the captain; when he arrives he is paid by Schultz. The look

Legs Diamond (Ray Danton) reads about the young Turk's campaign to carve out a crime empire for himself. 1961, Warner Bros. Dist. Corp.

he gives Brennan is a coldhearted stare of conquest. The detective's next job is as a welcome mat in reverse for his wife.

Iris' descent into alcoholism and idiocy is sad to watch. When her husband fails to give her the things she needs, she replaces him with the hoodlum. This soap opera subplot is played out against the main drama-control of the rackets' fiefdom.

As is fitting for a gangster movie, there are colorful supporting roles played by the usual suspects. Ray Danton reprises his role as Legs Diamond. Norman Alden plays Schultz's lifelong lieutenant-Bo Wetzel. Frank de Kova plays the mobster who makes a deal with the fading Schultz to buy his way out of obscurity. Part of the deal involves setting up his loyal underlings, including Bo Wetzel. The contentious relationship between Schutlz and the Italian mob culminates in the final scene.

The boys are playing a friendly game of poker. At the appointed time, Dutch Schulz heads to the men's room. De Kova's goons arrive and machine gun the players. They have to add an extra hit to their list but a

None other than the Duke (John Wayne) will lead the Normandy invasion in *The Longest Day*. 1962, 20th Century Fox Film Corp.

funny thing happens to them on the way to the men's room-two of them are killed by Schultz. The third flees.

It doesn't matter. Destiny includes Schultz in the tally when he is shot by Bo Wetzel, whose blurred vision only sees a man with a gun approaching him. The dying Wetzel believes that it is one of the goons. It is Schultz that he shoots and the circle of betrayal is completed.

It is fitting that Dutch Schultz is gunned down by his trusted lieutenant. To agree to de Kova's demands of erasure is to insure his own death. Schultz always told Bo that he was his lucky charm. Bo was the reason that Dutch was alive; to betray this fidelity deserves betrayal in return. In the end, the streetwise hustler who rose to the top of the rackets winds up a crumpled Judas on a barroom floor.

Ray Danton went from a reprise of his most notable role to playing a part in a cast of thousands. His role in *The Longest Day* is characteristic of his place in the Hollywood constellation. He was a minor star compared to the giants of the industry; but, then so were most of the other faces in the multitudinous cast. It was an eclectic, motley and amorphous bunch under the aegis of giants like John Wayne (Lt. Col. Benjamin Vandervoort), Henry Fonda (Brig. Gen. Theodore Roosevelt, Jr.) and Robert Mitchum (Brig. General Norman Cota); still, Ray Danton carried his weight and stormed Omaha Beach with the best of them.

The Longest Day is a marathon of war stories strung together under the aegis of D-Day. Of course, it's really an all-star extravaganza, an excuse for Hollywood's finest to compete with international stars in a patriotic re-enactment of the invasion that changed the course of the war. Anyway you look at it, it is a production achievement on behalf of Daryl F. Zanuck, who assembled forty-eight stars among a cast of millions to be handled by five directors.

D-Day will be the decisive campaign of the war and it will include many prestigious actors and actresses from the host countries that fought in the war. They take the place of the real soldiers who fought the battles. It is a matter of spotting the star and matching him/her to the role, which becomes secondary to the player.

The main recognition goes to John Wayne and Henry Fonda as larger-than-life heroes. The Duke plays himself (in a manner of speaking) and Fonda is a son and namesake of Teddy Roosevelt. Robert Mitchum and Robert Ryan (Brig. Gen. James M. Gavin) are heroes, too. Mitchum storms the beach at the end and survives the carnage. He clenches a cigar between his teeth as he offers closing remarks about the war.

Captain Frank (Ray Danton) and Brig. General Norman Cota (Robert Mitchum) before the invasion.1962, 20th Century Fox Film Corp.

Ray Danton plays Captain Frank, *aide-de-camp* to tough guy Robert Mitchum. He shares screen time with Mitchum, Eddie Albert (Col. Thompson), and John Wayne, plus battalions of extras on Omaha Beach. In the Hollywood pecking order, this may seem logical but one can't help but think that John Wayne couldn't play Lucky the Inscrutable, Eddie Albert would be a tenth-rate Legs Diamond, and audiences would offer hoots of derision to Robert Mitchum as Sandokan the pirate.

The masses that make up the enlisted personal are teen idols like Paul Anka, Sal Mineo, Fabian, George Segal and Tommy Sands. The others are established stars of the time like Robert Wagner, Red Buttons, Jeffrey Hunter, Steve Forrest and Richard Beymer as Pvt. Dutch Shultz.

Henry Grace makes a convincing replica of Gen. Dwight D. Eisenhower. Curt Jurgens still remained an anonymous German actor to the average movie goer; so did Gert Frobe until a couple of years later when he played the titular role in *Goldfinger*. Most of the international cast probably drew blanks at the time, too.

Arletty and Jean-Louis Barrault appear in the segment filmed in Colleville, a French town under siege. Barrault plays Father Louis

Roulliard and gives an impassioned sermon about resistance from the pulpit and Arletty, ironically, plays a character named Mrs. Barrault. They still evoked the grace and beauty of their masterpiece, *Les Enfants du Paradis,* made during the actual French Occupation.

The mayor is played by Bourvil and Irina Demich plays a French Resistance fighter. Sean Connery and Peter Lawford are British soldiers, as is one of the stars, Richard Burton. Other stiff upper lip soldiers are Richard Todd, Leo Genn and Kenneth More.

For three hours, international contingents plot and battle each other in efforts to salvage a stake of the world in the closing days of World War II. The movie is an astounding piece of story-telling.

Ray Danton may have been able to promote *A Majority of One* while he was making *The Longest Day* but it did neither the actor nor the studio any good. After *A Majority of One* and *The Longest Day* had played, *F.B.I. Code 98* was finally released without fanfare and Ray Danton's days at Warner Brothers were numbered, along with most of the of the actors, actresses and behind the scenes personnel who enjoyed the successes of the glory years of the late 50's and early 60's.

Television's growth supplanted the movies as the number one entertainment medium but it also changed the politics of its own makeup, as well. The 60's domino effect of the studio system's demise included a big shakeup of Warner Brothers' television division and its personal. In his case, Ray Danton suspended negotiations with the studio for a seven year contract with outside rights. He was going to use his agency, The William Morris Agency, to negotiate a deal with an Italian producer to make a film overseas.

A press junket for *The Longest Day* has star Henry Fonda (c) flanked by the youth contingent: Robert Wagner, Fabian, Sal Mineo, Roddy McDowell, Ray Danton and Tommy Sands. 1962, 20th Century Fox Film Corp.

Last of the Classic Phase

Talk shows were a relatively new phenomena in the early 1960's. They were pioneered in the late 50's by Steve Allen with his Tonight Show format and Joe Franklin with his early morning/late night repeat routine. The programs were video versions of fan magazines where stars were interviewed by a host, usually seated behind a desk. In some cases, they were interviewed in their homes or on a movie set as was the case with *Here's Hollywood*. Ray Danton appeared on *The Joe Franklin Show* ('61), *Here's Hollywood* ('61) and *That Regis Philbin Show* ('64).

He also taught at The Actor's Studio for a spell before signing a contract with Revue Studios, the television division of Universal Studios. His roles from this period are a departure from his brash and straightforward style. His characters still had their shady dimensions, only introspection was now a part of their style.

One of Ray Danton's strongest performances from this period is Magnus Repp in *The Dick Powell Show: The Hook* ('62). Special Agent Collin Maese (Robert Loggia) is frustrated in his pursuit of narcotics czar, Magnus Repp. For Maese, Repp is a puzzle waiting to be taken apart. The San Diego narcotics merchant seems untouchable. Maese's superior tells him that he has to find his hook.

An exhaustive study of Repp's dossier leads Maese to a startling conclusion: the time spent at San Quentin must have been intentional. Maese's reasoning is based on Repp's comment that nothing ever happens to him unless he wants it to. His clean record is a testimony to his cleverness. Further research reveals that he was the cellmate of Mac Thane, the reigning narcotics czar of his era. Maese concludes that Repp set himself up for incarceration so he could be tutored by the best junk man in the business: Mac Thane (Ed Begley).

Collin Maese has found his hook: Mac Thane. Thane is a throwback to the Capone era. He is a product of Prohibition racketeering and a survivor in the age of drug dealing. His time in San Quentin is stretched beyond the limits of his sentencing because of fights that always occur before he is to be paroled. Maese concludes that these fights were arranged by Repp to keep his former mentor behind bars. Maese arranges for his release. The agent wants Repp to believe that Mac Thane plans to reclaim his heroin empire. It works: Repp is nervous about his gang's enthusiasm about Thane's return.

There is no cause for alarm. Mac Thane arrives with big ideas that are clichés left over from the Capone era. It doesn't take long for the gangsters

Meese and Repp are confrontational and cast no shadows in their mastery of the hunt. It is a game of dares where only one of them will cross the finish line. 1962, Four Star Productions.

to realize that Mac Thane is senile. Repp's only recourse is to humor the old man by setting him up with a suite of offices, a gaggle of young secretaries, and dead files whose dates have been changed to the present. When Maese finds out that Thane is senile, he believes that his plan has failed. He improvises a new one that will use Thane's senility to his advantage.

Collin Maese and Magnus Repp are intense individuals whose tenacity and resilience create a force field of electricity. The electrical currents are strong because of the forceful personalities of the lead characters. Loggia's portrayal is strong enough to match Danton's. That's what makes their scenes together so good. Their anger and dry wit bounce off each other. It is a street attitude split in two directions.

Robert Loggia's Maese is confrontational. He can afford to be that way because he is backed by the law. Danton's Repp, while reptilian, has to be pokerfaced and economical in word and deed. He, too, is kinetic and deadly. Circumstances dictate that he has to be discreet in how he shows it.

"I'm the kind that cries inside", says Repp when he is accused of being stoical about the toll in lives his product takes. The interrogation is a hostile confrontation between two strong willed individuals. Repp controls his emotions and hides his eyes behind bubble-lensed sunglasses. Maese is threatening and belligerent.

"Nobody touches me", boasts Repp. "Nothing happens to me that I don't want to happen."

Maese calls him "an animal that looks human."

Before he leaves the agent's office, Repp asks Maese, "Do you really know how the animal fights? I don't think you have the slightest idea."

The hunt is on.

They form a formidable circle complementing each other. Both men have a touch of the other in their own soul. That's why they understand each other. Repp tells Maese that he doesn't think that he knows how the wild beast hunts. It doesn't matter because Repp is a reptile. The only beast is Mac Thane and he is a bull without horns.

Ed Begly is outstanding as Mac Thane, the senile former narcotics king. In prison, he taught Repp everything he knew about the business. Now, he lives in a world of the Twenties yet generates fear and concern until the final sting is played. It is Repp who doesn't know how the wild beast hunts. They use decoys and deception to confuse their prey. Mac Thane destroys his protégée and doesn't even know it.

The attitudinal Maese is skeptical about receiving an award for killing a man. His superior tells him that it's more than that and justifies it with Biblical logic. Maese will continue to be skeptical because it is part of his makeup. His in-your-face attitude will serve Uncle Sam well. The conflict will always make him an ambivalent hero. It will probably drive him crazy one day.

Crazy is a polite description of Warren Price, a Walter Mitty-type whose grandiose image of himself is related to listeners in a jam-packed anecdotes of historical wonder and statistical awe. He is a winning raconteur who rivets his audience with tales of derring-do but the trouble is the stories are false, the products of an overactive imagination and an under-developed ego. That is the premise of *Wide Country: The Bravest Man in the World*.

Price's lying takes a near-fatal turn when he meets Andy Guthrie (Andrew Prine) and Mitch Guthrie (Earl Holliman), the famous rodeo rider of *Wide Country*. The show was a modern western about a famous rodeo rider and his younger brother. It centered around a rodeo and the characters that participated in the events of the week. For Warren Price, his story starts when he accidentally meets Andy at a stop over for a bus change.

Warren Price mesmerizes his fellow bus passengers with his heroic exploits at Inchon. 1962, Gemini Productions.

Andy's pocket had been picked and Price heroically chases the thief, tackles him, and knocks him out. As Andy helps Warren pack the spilled contents of an open valise, he picks up a copy of Warren Price's autobiography: "The Bravest Man In The World."

Andy is so impressed that he wants Warren to stay over. He can't believe that he's talking to a war hero and football star from Annapolis. When he hears that Warren also rode in rodeos, he sets him up with a job at the arena.

Mitch isn't so impressed with Warren. Andy is miffed and-to back up his point-gives Mitch a copy of "The Bravest Man In The World." It is after Mitch reads the book that he is convinced that Warren is a fake. He checks references to incidents and doesn't find any sources to back up the stories. Mitch confronts him about the masquerade and is punched in the face for his inquiry.

Warren's meek and longsuffering wife visits Mitch and Andy and apologizes for his behavior. There is a brief clinical explanation of the world inhabited by the pathological liar. To try to help the Prices, Mitch arranges for Warren to work as a ranch hand at the Callahan Ranch.

Trouble starts when Anita (Yvonne Craig), Callahan's (Ford Rainey) daughter, hears of Warren's exploits when he takes the cowpokes out for beer after he was thrown from a horse. The tales that mesmerize them are of his Inchon exploits. Anita gets him started when her father expresses interest in the war heroics.

Mitch, Andy, and the wife wait for Warren to arrive for a celebration. After two hours of waiting, she gets a call Warren was hired as the ranch's foreman. Mitch has to warn Callahan of Warren's problem before any real damage is done.

At the ranch, Anita and her father listen with rapt attention as Warren spins another one of his tales. Her world comes crashing down when Mitch arrives and delicately tries to get Warren away by telling him that his wife wants to see him.

Anita, unaware that he was married, has a fit after Mitch leaves. She moves away from Warren, trips on an inflatable raft, hits her head on the diving board, and falls into the pool unconscious. Warren -crippled by his fear of water-is unable to jump into the pool. He can't reach her with his outstretched arm so he frantically chases after Mitch. The heroic cowboy runs back to the pool, throws off his cowboy hat, and dives in to save the young woman from drowning.

The next scene is the questioning and breakdown of Warren Price by the police. His wife listens in shame as the inspector slowly breaks him down by poking holes into his story and proving that he is a fraud. He does this by comparing his wartime heroics with the inaction at the swimming pool.

Warren slowly falls apart as he catches himself falling into his lies. He stops in mid-sentence when he uses his stock phrases. His locations and heroics become mixed up with each other. Fumbling cigarettes and alibis, he finally confesses that he can't swim and breaks down.

The episode ends on an upbeat note. Mitch arranges for Warren to really work as a ranch hand for a friend in San Diego. After they help his wife board the bus, Mitch and Andy smile and bid Warren Price good luck as he boards the bus.

Danton's performance is broad and he gets to touch many bases of his screen persona. He portrays the macho tough guy with ease and returns to the schizophrenic terrain of *The Night Runner*. He mixes both styles to evoke humor and pathos. Mitch's challenge causes Warren to unravel. He is exposed as a fake when he can't rescue the woman who fell into the pool and was knocked unconscious. His final unraveling comes

Ray Danton and Andrew Prine take a break from filming and enjoy some downtime at the commissary. 1962, TV Guide.

under interrogation about the incident, when he is accused of pushing the young woman into the pool.

Despite the changing styles in movies and on television, Danton continued to star in pilots that never made the networks' schedules. *Solitaire* and *Entre Nous* are two pilots that never made the fall schedule. *Solitaire* was about another international agent who wiles away his private time playing the popular card game.

Entre Nous was based on the movie, *To Catch A Thief*, starring Cary Grant. Danton assumed the role of the Riviera jewel thief. In both cases, his smooth style failed to ignite roles that proved to be successful for stars in later decades. The secret agent and suave jewel thief later became popular to the point of cliché.

Ray Danton returned to type when he appeared on *Redigo*, the new name of *Empire*, starring Richard Egan. In *The Thin Line*, Jim Redigo (Richard Egan) hires a prison parolee and then learns the man is a potential killer. Redigo tries to help him stay out of trouble with the parole board despite his flip attitude.

In 1963, Ray Danton co-starred on his last anthology show, *Kraft Theater*. It was a revamped version of the live anthology. Now, it broadcast filmed dramas. He plays a lawyer in *Talk to My Partner*. Joanna

Ray Danton played an elegant jewel thief in an unsold pilot, *Entre Nous*, based on *To Catch a Thief*.

Moore plays Hilary Snow, a neophyte corporation lawyer who is asked by the Legal Assistance League to defend a Japanese Gardener accused of wholesale robberies. She gets legal assistance from Brig Hazard (Ray Danton), one of the firm's junior partners.

Ray Danton's last appearance on a dramatic show before his departure for Europe was on *Arrest and Trial*. Before there was the long running popularity of *Law and Order* and its spin-offs, there was the short lived curiosity known as *Arrest and Trial*. The show was divided into two parts; the first was the commission of a crime and the arrest of the criminals. The second part dealt with the criminal trial. Chuck Connors played John Egan, a lawyer and Ben Gazzara was Det. Anderson.

Brig Hazard (Ray Danton) goes over a brief with Hilary Snow (Joanna Moore) in the legal drama, *Talk to My Partner*. 1963, Revue Studios.

In *The Black Flower*, Rick Tobin (Dewey Martin) returns home after spending seven years in San Quentin for second-degree murder. He protected Jess Malloy (Ray Danton), his adulterous boss, from an angry husband when he delivered the knock-out punch that sent his victim to his death.

Tobin is intimidated by the outside world. Everything is too large for him: the crowds, the cars, the apartment, even the bed. He tells his wife that he could stretch out his arms and touch the walls of his prison cell. When she wakes up in the middle of the night to an empty bed, she finds Rick sleeping in the bathroom. There, he can touch the walls when he stretches out his arms.

Tobin doesn't allow himself time to adjust to the outside. He becomes paranoid and makes excuses to persecute himself. At a celebration at Jess's club, he doesn't want to dance but insists that his wife dance with Malloy. Then, he thinks they are dancing too close. His replacement at the club infers that there is an affair between Malloy and Ellen. This sends Rick Tobin into a tailspin. The drinks flow like water and he rides a river of self-pity until he is out of control. In the space of twenty four hours, he fails to return home and is fired from his new job without spending a day at work.

Ex-convicts often gravitate to other ex-convicts. Rick Tobin is no exception. He seeks out his former cellmate, Hobie Osborne. Hobie works at an amusement park called Kiddie's Fun Land. They take a ride on the kiddie train and discuss their plans for the future. Both agree to pull a robbery. Hobie has a real gun and gives Rick a cap pistol.

"If the job goes wrong, the rap is lighter."

The job does go wrong.

Jess Malloy doesn't want a life on the lam for Ellen. He relents at her insistence and tells her to let him handle the details. She tells him that Rick is hiding out at a twenty four hour movie house. After Ellen leaves the club, Malloy tells Heidi the singer to make a call to the cops. She gives them the hot tip about Rick Tobin's hideaway. Sgt. Anderson (Ben Gazzara), his original arresting officer, slaps the cuffs on him a second time.

John Egan (Chuck Connors) is a high-powered attorney who likes to practice his putting in his office and relax in a steam room by himself. He can pick and choose his own cases and doesn't have a care in the world. He is fascinated by the Tobin case and decides to take it when he is visited by Ellen Tobin. A blank check sent before by Jess Malloy doesn't hurt matters but it is Ellen's sincerity that makes him lean towards taking the case.

Rick Tobin (Dewey Martin) has second thoughts about his former boss,
Jeff Molloy (Ray Danton), a man he served a manslaughter rap for.
1964, Revue Studios, Universal Television.

Jess Malloy seems to be a benefactor up until the point when he betrays Tobin by having one of his workers drop a dime on him with the police. He thinks that this will clear the way for him with Ellen, who he assumes would prefer him because of his power and connections.

In the office, Malloy explains his reasons to Ellen for turning Rick in. He is in love with Ellen and doesn't want her to spend her life with a loser. When he kisses her, she recoils in horror. Malloy loses all semblance of control and attacks her. He slaps her around, pushes her across, the room, and knocks her to the ground. Egan walks into the office and sees Malloy battering Ellen. A couple of well-placed punches demolishes Malloy and Ellen is taken to the hospital.

Egan gets special permission for Rick to visit Ellen in the hospital. It is then that Rick Tobin realizes that his wife has been faithful and truly loves him for who he is.

Jess Malloy never meant anything to her other than being an individual helping friends through hard times. Jess Malloy is one of Ray Danton's repugnant characters. He has characteristics of Stan Hess and Oscar Wetzel and there is a sleaziness to him that would make him welcome in a world processed by Albert Zugsmith. He appears to be concerned and helpful but his real intention is to crowd out Tobin and claim Ellen for himself. His rejection brings out the cowardly lion in him and he is tamed and shamed by the tall square-jawed Texas lawyer. His world comes crashing down when his abuse reveals him to be a venal coward. It takes a healthy dose of Egan's rugged righteousness to keep him in check.

The Black Flower was the last urban drama Danton starred in before leaving for Europe. Luckily, Jess Malloy was not Ray Danton's last American performance before his departure. That distinction would be his excellent portrayal of Jeb Stark, the ruthless boss of a pre-Las Vegas desert gambling hell in *Wagon Train: The Stark Bluff Story*.

THE NEW WESTERNS

In the years preceding Ray Danton's '64 departure to Europe, a stream of westerns, a series of hard-hitting dramas and a pilot for a war show gave him the opportunity to create more powerful characters before he left Hollywood.

After the golden years and before the European exodus, Danton's roles were on the last of the westerns. The westerns of the 60's had greater thematic depth than many of the sagebrush sagas of genre's halcyon days and he played the ruthless frontier gigolo Vince Jackson on *Laramie: The Fortune Hunter*.

Ray Danton combined the qualities of the gambler and duelist to create a lethal Romeo named Vince Jackson. He a ruthless frontier gigolo in *Laramie: The Fortune Hunter*. *Laramie* was filmed in color and ran for four years. It starred John Smith as Slim Sherman and Robert Fuller as Jess Harper.

Vince Jackson is quick on the draw and specializes in serenading the proper daughters of wealthy men in pay-for-profit schemes: hasty elopements annulled by hefty blackmail payments. Suave and smooth in his dandy's regalia, the eloquent speaking and ever-confident Jackson is a study in contrast to his partner, Hutch Davis (Peter Whitney), a vile and slovenly ignoramus. Davis aided Jackson five years earlier when he was released from prison for a confidence rap.

Jackson impresses Kitty McAllen (Carolyn Craig) and her father (Parley Baer) with his intelligent conversation and charming manners.

It's a matter of charm and intelligence versus dusty trails and savvy as Jackson horns in on Kitty's suitor, Slim. The timing is perfect because of a row between the lovers.

Although Vince Jackson is a lover, he is not unacquainted with firearms. The episode opens with him squaring off with a disgruntled father (Willis Bouchey) in a showdown in another town. He appears to ease Slim out of the picture as he plays with Kitty's inexperience.

Slim and Jess may not have the social airs of Vince Jackson but what they possess is an understanding of human nature. At the saloon, they get the lowdown on Vince Jackson from Opal, a new showgirl who knew him from his Cheyenne days. She tells them about his elopement-blackmail routine. When he relates the news to Kitty, she insists that he is the gentleman that Slim could never be. An overheated Kitty returns to the ranch to find a forceful Jackson waiting for her. She is powerless to rebuff his advances and agrees to immediately elope with him.

Slim Jackson (Ray Danton) has little sympathy for a father (Willis Bouchey) seeking to defend his daughter's violated honor. Jackson does not shoot to kill. He merely blows the buttons off the father's vest. 1962, Revue Studios.

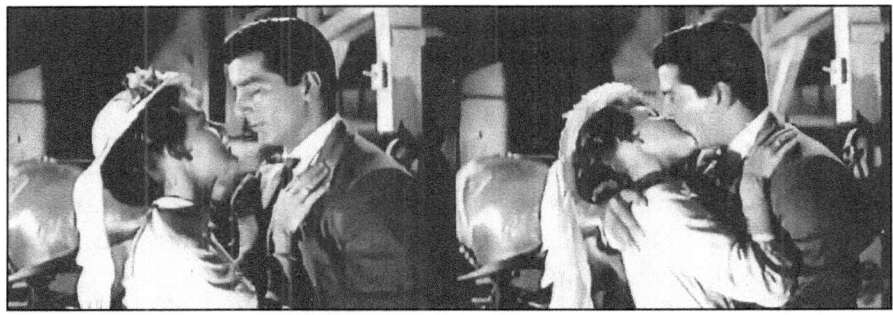

Slim Jackson tries to score with a mining engineer's daughter but he is fouled up for the last time. 1962, Revue Studios.

Slim pursues Vince Jackson in a classic chase scene. Kitty attempts to prevent Vince from killing Slim and is shoved off the buggy by Jackson. There is an off screen buggy crash. Jackson survives and has a gunfight with Slim, who prevails when he fatally wounds the cad. The episode concludes with Kitty being sent to college. In the long run, Slim will be Kitty's first crush-the two-fisted hero who saved the pure maiden from the dark villain. Five years after playing Vince Jackson on *Laramie*, Danton played a Jackson-type in *The Big Valley: Devil's Masquerade* ('67). He is Reed Clayton, the boss behind a mail order bride scheme. Anne Helm plays his lure. John Douchette is the mark. Clayton, too, is unmasked and dispatched in the show's finale.

Ray Danton played another Cavalry officer on *The Virginian* in 1962. The show originally aired as a half-hour pilot- summer replacement show for The Loretta Young Show in 1959. It didn't become a regular show until 1962 when it was expanded to ninety minutes and shot in color.

The Virginian told the tale of the Westerners, rugged mountain men who tamed the West with their brute strength. The Virginian was played by James Drury and his sidekicks were two ranch hands, Trampas (Doug McClure) and Steve (Gary Clarke). Pippa Scott provided the brains and beauty in the form of Molly, the newspaper editor.

Unlike Monty Britton of *Wagon Train*, brave and selfless are not character descriptions for Lt. Drex of *Riff-Raff*. Lt. Drex is a West Point graduate who is hungry for combat medals that he can use to cash in respectability in the private sector. In that, he is reminiscent of Lt. Joel Brady in *Tarawa Beachhead*. Lt. Drex is a pompous bore from West Point who is taught a lesson in humility and combat tactics by a group of mountain men.

The making of legends is spoofed in *Riff-Raff*. Teddy Roosevelt's ride up San Juan Hill with his Rough Riders is lampooned. The power of the press is examined in a lighthearted way. The story also ridicules the differences between the officer corps and the non-commissioned fighting men.

The disparate elements that make up the Army are a reflection of society's class system. The officer corps is comprised of college educated men while the enlistees are the working class, otherwise known as riff-raff. The officer corps does the thinking and most of the fighting is accomplished by the enlistees. This episode illustrates the practicality of wisdom over the abstract theories of intellect.

Trampas and Steve join the Army after Molly, the newspaper editor, ridicules them for not knowing about the Spanish-American War.

The Virginian tracks them down and is talked into enlisting by Teddy Roosevelt, who is impressed with the rough and tumble ways of the Westerners.

Lt. Drex (Ray Danton) is dismayed at having to deal with the roughnecks. In a conference with Captain Langhorne (Don Durant), he calls the westerners dumb animals. He suggests that Trampas be chaptered out. The captain disagrees, believing that their savvy prairie ways will make them excellent soldiers if their energy can be harnessed.

A polo match is Lt. Drex's suggestion of establishing social bearing and the captain agrees much to their dismay when they are humiliated in defeat. A game of breeding turns into a lethal brawl on horseback and the westerners re-define the rules of the game and adjust the score with their sense of justice and survival tactics.

Lt. Drex earns a black eye for his idea but it is that ferocious fighting spirit that Captain Langhorne wants to harness to fight the Cuban battle. The West Point graduate has a broader picture of the war. It is his main chance to exploit it for a grander scheme. War has given this country its top men-George Washington, Andrew Jackson, and Zachary Taylor. Lt. Drex encourages the captain to take the medals and get the field promotions because somebody is going to hit it big in this war.

The lieutenant sees the war from a broader perspective in the Cuban jungle, where he and the troops are hacking their way through thick brush when it is decided that a scouting party should go ahead to negotiate the terrain. The party consists of Lt. Drex and the westerners. They reach an open plain that is protected by cannon fire. It is the objective of the lieutenant to have his men take out the cannon. His plan is to have them cross the open country and charge the hill.

The forward command is given and the ten men make a valiant charge. The lieutenant is wounded in the action. They retreat to cover where the Virginian suggests an alternative plan. He tells them that the men can crawl through the grass and make it to the hilltop to disarm the cannon. All they will need is a little diversion to help them. The lieutenant gives his approval.

The mountain men kill the soldiers and disarm the cannon.
The Virginian runs down the hilltop to meet the captain, who tells him that they make "a good blend-western ingenuity and army tactics." He looks at the advancing soldiers and says that the Rough Riders were successful.

"Rough Riders?", asks the Virginian as he points to the foot soldiers.

Lt. Drex is a combat warrior posed for victory. 1962, Revue Studios.

Trampas complains, " I still say we should have used horses."

Ray Danton's sly acting style also embodied humorous elements. Sometimes, the laughs were nervous because they were provoked by sadism; other times, they were straight from the belly because they were caused by genuine comedy. The latter is the case with *Death Valley Days: The Wooing of Perilous Pauline*.

Death Valley Days started as a radio program in 1930 and made the transition to television, where it was broadcast from 1952 to 1975 for a total of 558 episodes. It had five hosts: Stanley Andrews, Ronald Reagan, Robert Taylor, Dale Robertson and Merle Haggard. The show was so popular that it was repackaged in reruns under different titles and new hosts which included John Payne, Will Rogers, Jr., Ray Milland and Rory Calhoun. Dale Robertson even resumed his hosting chores for one of the syndicated incarnations.

The Wooing of Perilous Pauline is the saga of Pauline Cushman (Paula Raymond), a legend in her own time. She was raised by Indians, was a genuine Southern belle, and acted as a Northern spy during the Civil War. She lives in an obscure Arizona mining town, far from the fray of fame and fortune. Her only friend is a trusty bullwhip that she uses whenever she has to make a point.

Pauline is a hellfire considered too hot to handle by many men. There was a time when her honor was defended by generals, vice-presidents and presidents. Now, a peach fuzz faced boy is the only ardent admirer whose ready to risk life and limb for her. She is a hellion that most men are afraid of courting. That changes with the arrival of Jeremiah Fryer (Ray Danton) and his friend, Frank Miller (Eddie Ryder).

The western spitfire intrigues the men when they see her in action. Whether it is the way she makes men dance to the snap of her whip or intimidating mule drivers to back down from her, Pauline has a fiercely independent nature that impels Jere to bet Frank one hundred dollars that he can marry her in a week.

Jere is a man from a good family and has a solid education. He thinks that he can impress Pauline with his deft phrases and florid poetry. Calling her "a garden in the middle of the desert" only gets him crowned with a plate of food. He tips a broken piece of china on his head like it was a hat.

The arrogant Fryer gets Pauline's attention by aggressively wooing her and letting her know that he is doing her a favor. His hook is that he can take her or leave her and this loquacious attitude riles the frontier hellion. From then onward, he is in control. He sweeps her up in his arms in front of the townsfolk. She commands him to put her down and he drops her.

He finally gets her to succumb to his offbeat charm. At their wedding, a drunken Frank Miller hands a hundred dollar bill to a nervous Jere in front of Pauline. Outraged that their marriage was the result of a wager, she grabs her trusty bullwhip and chases Jere and Frank into the street. So ends the wooing of Perilous Pauline.

Ray Danton is a total cut-up as Jere Fryer. He is spry and deftly handles the slapstick bits he has to perform when he invokes Pauline's

The boisterous Jere Fryer meets his match in Perilous Pauline.
1964, Flying A Productions.

ire. He also possesses expert comic timing when he delivers his punch lines with Eddie Ryder acting as his sidekick. The two actors appeared in *Tarawa Beachhead*, released in 1958.

The 60's westerns also gave Ray Danton the opportunity to create a series of powerful characters before he left Hollywood, including a broader perspective of his American Indian portrayals. Chief Four Thumbs is a tour-de-force of exiled heroics in *Empire: The Four Thumbs Story*. He is Four Thumbs, a cursed hero whose combat experiences in the Korean War have left him shell-shocked. Zeb Stark is a robber baron of a different type in the Old West. He is a mixed-blooded town tyrant in *Wagon Train: The Stark Bluff Story* ('63). In *Wagon Train: The Molly Kincaid Story* ('62), he plays John Kincaid, the white shadow that defines Four Thumbs and Zeb Stark.

In *Empire: The Four Thumbs Story*, a shell-shocked Indian has a clearer view of destiny than those around him. He fights a war on two fronts: Korea and the old West. His spirit is committed to joining his ancestors in their standoff with the Cavalry. That is how his saga ends, a death that is welcomed by his brother, a "modern" Indian and rued by Redigo, his old platoon sergeant in the war.

During a bloody battle in Korea, Four Thumbs was cut off from the unit, which was wiped out. He survived for six days without food or water, like his grandfather did against the U.S. Cavalry. Four Thumbs gave the orders and carried them out, holding his position but losing his mind.

Now, he is a man twice robbed of his identity. In war and on the peaceful home front, Four Thumbs has lost the essence that made him a man. Shell shocked and wracked by survivor's guilt, he lives inside a lonely hell. His cell is his extended body, but his mind is an over wound clock ready to spring.

Redigo (Richard Egan) was his platoon sergeant in Korea and periodically visits Four Thumbs in his room at the Veterans' Memorial Hospital. Flashbacks of the war cloud Redigo's head when he enters the facility. Pleasant chatter turns to the war and Redigo reminisces about the time Four Thumbs rode into the Army camp dressed in full warrior regalia. He had saddled up with his deer rifle and was accompanied by a couple of braves, ready to raid Peking and Moscow. Four Thumbs triumphantly declared that the Navajos were the greatest warriors on earth.

Now, Redigo reminds his old friend that, "This is New Mexico. We left Korea for the Korean people." It does not matter to Four Thumbs because he is still fighting everything and everybody. It is his violent impulses that keep him confined to the hospital. Even the doctor acknowledges that Four Thumbs is still fighting a war from within and he makes it impossible for the staff to treat him. All Four Thumbs can ask Redigo is, "What kind of place is this for an Indian?"

It is after Redigo leaves that Four Thumbs overpowers an attendant and escapes from his solitary cell. It does not take long for news of Four Thumbs' escape and tussle with Bird Johnson, a rancher, to reach Redigo. A search party is put together with Redigo leading the way. The copter pilot is Rabbit Stockings (Rudy Solari), Four Thumbs' brother. Rabbit Stockings considers himself a modern Indian and has contempt for brother. Four Thumbs refuses to relinquish the old ways because it

Four Thumbs is comforted by his father, a chief who cannot understand why his son has been driven mad. 1963, Screen Gems Television.

would be subjugating himself to the white man's culture. Not only is Four Thumbs fighting the war in Korea, he still bears arms against the new order, just like his ancestor did against the Cavalry.

Redigo has no clue to where Four Thumbs may be heading but it is no mystery to Rabbit Stockings. He says, "Do you know where he's going? He is heading straight to you because you are his commanding officer. You're all he has."

Rabbit Stockings contempt and shame for his brother because he believes that, "My brother is the kind of Indian that makes your people say the Indians can't grow up. He's going to bring a lot of trouble."

With the help of Redigo, he returns to his tribe. He has convinced the rancher, the state troopers and the doctors that the best place for Four Thumbs to be is on the reservation. Four Thumbs returns to the reservation and feels at peace when he remarks, "I can talk to the ground."

The next day, he is shocked to see the commercialization that has corrupted his people. The reservation has become a tourist attraction and he can't deal with sharing the tribe's precious secrets for money. Ceremonial dancing, painting sacred symbols and posing for pictures with the white tourists pushes him to the brink of madness and he beats up a tourist that has been harassing his father for a photo. The fight escalates and Four Thumbs breaks the man's camera before the authorities gang up on him. He escapes arrest by retreating into the desert.

Four Thumbs retreats into the hills for a standoff. The Chief thinks that he is fighting the battle of his ancestors. He knows that they have a place reserved for him. All he has to do to join them is to confront the modern Cavalry.

Four Thumbs creates sanity in a world whose madness is disguised as moral superiority. His madness gives him a vision that helps him locate his ancestors. To be like them, he has to meet them on their own grounds. Four Thumbs is killed in an alteration with Bird Johnson.

Redigo buries the Chief with his ancestors. He plants his rifle in the burial ground and is rebuked by Rabbit Stockings, who thinks that it is a trivial gesture, even though his ancestors burial mounds have similar headstones. He believes that it is the waste of a perfectly good rifle but Redigo leaves the monument as it is. As the sun sets, Four Thumbs belatedly takes his place besides his fallen ancestors. Redigo looks up at the sky and is reminded of something that Four Thumbs once told him.

"He is right. You can see the whole world from here."

Four Thumbs (Ray Danton) tells Redigo (Richard Egan) to look at the desert and see the images of his ancestors and the Cavalry 1963, Screen Gems Television.

Ray Danton gives a tour-de-force performance as Four Thumbs. The subtleties and nuances he imbues the character with create a true portrait of tragedy. It is the glory of the Old West fading into the industrial age. It is possibly the most emotional and expansive performance Ray Danton has ever given.

He plays Four Thumbs as a defeated man clinging to a noble ideal that redeems his madness with a clear vision of pride and tradition. The Korean War may have unsettled Four Thumbs and destroyed his personality but his Navajo blood made him more sane than anyone around him, including Redigo.

Four Thumbs' head was in the clouds and his feet firmly planted on the terrain when he made his final sacrifice. His grave is on the sacred burial grounds of his ancestral heroes who held the mount for six days against the Cavalry. Four Thumbs' addition to the sacred grounds is akin to adding another face to Mount Rushmore.

The Stark Bluff Story is the last of Ray Danton's great Hollywood performances. Zeb Stark ranks among his fiercest portrayals of his mania-driven power mongers. The story takes place in an Old West Las Vegas-a pleasure town ruled by excess controlled by a tyrant. As before, the despot will be destroyed by his own secrets.

All that needs to be known about Stark Bluff is summed up in the opening scene when the trailblazers sit around the camp fire and jawbone about their next stop. Charlie the cook (Frank McGrath) says, "Rough, tough and I do mean wild-no place like Stark Bluff!" but its' history is summed up by Cooper Smith (Robert Fuller).

It was once beaver country until it was settled by Eben Stark, who opened up a trading post in the wilderness. He persuaded the Indians to work for him for trinkets and whiskey. To assuage the growing resentment against him, Stark married the daughter of a Sioux chief. Despite his hardened character, no one meant more to him than his wife. He turned his back on civilization and eventually built a town on his fortune before he was killed in a barroom brawl.

Although he bequeathed the town to his wife Ogala (Carman D'Antonio), the town was run by his son, Zeb. Zeb Stark is an angry man who blames other people for his twisted emotions. His mother disagrees and tells him, "Two good bloods don't make bad-you poisoned yourself." It is of no import to him—his anger dominates a town in the middle of the desert and his paradise is hell for his subjects. He rules his desert empire before being destroyed by his own hubris.

Wagon Master Chris Hale (John McIntire) informs his crew that they will bypass the town because it is a den of iniquity. He has even learned that Judge Pike (Stanley Adams), a passenger from a previous journey, has "sold his soul for a pint" of whiskey. He tells Duke Shannon (Scott [Denny] Miller) that he will ride into town to pick up the mail and see if there are any passengers for the wagon train. Hale confiscates his silver with the admonition: "There's no sinning in that town without money." A flustered Duke replies, "That's like leading a horse to water and not letting him drink." Little does he realize that he is more like a steer being led to the slaughterhouse.

Zeb Stark is introduced in his den of iniquity: the saloon and gambling casino. He cuts a sharp figure with his angular features, long hair, and well-tailored suit. His face is cold and void of emotions. It has the calculating look of a rattler waiting to strike. he ruler walks from table to table, collecting bags of money to store in his safe. He gives a cold stare to Jefferson, his angelic black singing piano player. The man is chained to the piano stool.

Stark's mother, an Indian princess who inherited the town-is dominated by her son. Zeb Stark has a dark-sided charm that is twisted into ugliness by his hatred. He believes that his mixed blood has poisoned him. He hopes to purify it by marrying the blonde haired Suzy Durfee (Jean Hale), widow of the newspaper publisher who was killed in the arson fire that gutted his office.

Suzy works off her husband's debts as a book keeper at the saloon. Zeb Stark wants to control her because it is his desire to make her his wife. Ogala admonishes him, expressing her disapproval of his plans to marry the widow of the newspaper publisher. Zeb Stark has a sour attitude and doesn't care what his desert fiefdom will think of a mixed marriage.

Duke Shannon rides into town and the first thing that he notices is the gutted newspaper office. Ralph and Suzy were passengers on the wagon train the previous year and elected to set up their newspaper in Stark Bluff. Duke riles Sheriff Pincus (Peter Whitney) with his sarcastic meddling, especially when the cowboy finds out that Ralph died in the blaze. It unsettles him when he finds out that there are no legal records of the fire. What really sets Duke over the edge is finding out that Suzy is working off her husband's debts as Zeb Stark's book keeper.

The sheriff's discontent is nothing compared to Zeb Stark's anger when he finds the stranger and Suzy making plans for her escape. Stark arranges a confrontation between his bartender/deputy and Shannon. When Shannon shoots the bartender in self-defense, he is arrested and charged with attempted robbery and the murder of a lawman.

This pleases the sheriff, who relishes needling his prisoner about going to gallows if he is not lynched by the townsfolk. Shannon's only hope rests in Jefferson (Hari Rhodes), a freed slave who is still a slave in a Stark Bluff jail when he is not playing the piano in the saloon. He has murdered a white man for trying to steal another child to be sold at the slave auction. Jefferson is kept alive because of his musical talents and the service he provides at the saloon.

Jefferson owes nothing to anyone and the only person he has empathy for is Zeb Stark's mother. She tells them that they understand each other because they are basically members of two oppressed groups: African-

Zeb Stark and Suzy (Jean Hale) face a mutinous crew that object to his marriage plans. 1964, Revue Studios, Universal Television.

Americans and the American-Indians. Jefferson tells Duke, "His momma was born to rule over her people-just like me." They provide a moral support for each other because they also share a hatred for Zeb Stark.

It is Jefferson's assistance in arranging a sting to outwit Sheriff Pincus that makes Zeb Stark vulnerable. The sheriff leads a posse into the wilderness to hunt down the escaped Shannon, not knowing that he is still in town.

Zeb Stark's balance of power shifts when he is crossed by the people he dominated, namely his mother and Judge Pike, who loses his life but regains his self-respect in his freedom gambit. Ogala eradicates the family shame with a single bullet. Zeb Stark dies without leaving an heir but having the breath to curse his life.

The Stark Bluff Story is a powerful episode whose undercurrents are rife with the stark realities of the Old West. Beneath the Hollywood sheen, the brutal existence of the American Indian and the dilemma of the freed African slaves is displayed for those with discerning sensibilities. Ray Danton ably blends the discontent and misery with his portrayal of the bitter and vengeful Zeb Stark. There is no bottom to his depravity, which includes murder, deception, and intimidation. He even beats his mother so that she will put her mark on the wedding affidavit.

His counter actions with Judge Pike are a study in politics. Stanley Adams gives a brilliant performance as the judge who sold his sold for a bottle of the blessed sour mash. His senses are numb to the commands of his cruel boss but he is obedient in a robotic manservant manner. That is what has costs the judge his self-respect and ensures his death when he reclaims it in the story's bar room showdown.

It is fitting that Howard Christie was the producer for *The Stark Bluff Story*. He produced *The Looters*, which contained Ray Danton's first memorable Hollywood villain, Pete Corder. Zeb Stark would be his last full-fledged Hollywood villain.

The Apaches figure once more in *Wagon Train: The Molly Kincaid Story* ('63). This time, Ray Danton is on the other end of the American identity. He plays John Kincaid, a man whose wife was abducted by Apaches.

Racial identity and societal mores are examined in this drama. Molly Kincaid (Carolyn Jones) was kidnapped by the Apaches thirteen years before she returned to white society. In the intervening years, her memory was deified by her husband, a man whose cowardly behavior the day of the Indian raid saved his life but ruined hers. Their daughter, Martha (Brenda Scott), is raised with the false story of that fateful day and pays daily tribute to her mother by laying fresh flowers at her grave.

Molly Kincaid returns to seek vengeance and is overshadowed by the saintly image that took her place. The stately grave and church built in her honor contradict the slave tattoos that mar her face. She may be revered in death but she is hated in life. No one believes that she is human because of her time spent with the Apaches. If not for the perseverance of Kate Crowley (Barbara Stanwyck), revenge would have been accomplished and the life of her family totally ruined.

Kate Crowley is a desert flower. She is a woman toughened by being independent in a frontier society. She wears blue jeans, carries a bullwhip and doesn't back down from any man, no matter how two-fisted and ornery he may be. She is so tough that she tames a lynch mob with her whip when Molly and her adopted son, Rome (Fabian), arrive in town and are accused of horse rustling.

John Kincaid, the subject of her revenge, is a respected businessman with a lovely daughter. People are touched by his tributes to his dead wife yet their scorn her as an Apache war prize. He feels the same way about Molly. Kincaid doesn't want his daughter to see her mother like that and is content to let her worship a false image of her.

A prairie couple prepares for the possibility of an Apache attack which, when it happens, ends with Molly being kidnapped. 1963, Revue Studios, Universal Television.

She returns to fill a void in Kincaid's life and it restores the valor that he lost the day of the Apache raid. 1963, Revue Studios, Universal Television.

Carolyn Jones gives a bravura performance as Molly Kincaid. She effortlessly blends the Indian and the white woman into a single identity. Brenda Scott gives a sensitive performance as the young woman who discovers that her mother is Indian captive that has upset the town. Fabian, the teen idol, plays Rome, Molly's adopted son, also a kidnapped white.

Extra praise goes to Barbara Stanwyck as the gregarious Kate Crowley. She can kick butt and still remain ladylike. She was the star of an earlier Wagon Train episode, *The Kate Crowley Story*. At one point, she is taming an angry mob with a bullwhip and, at another, she is extolling the virtue of drinking beer out of cut glass. Ms. Stanwyck brings her movie magic to television and would have crowded everyone off the screen if not for the performance of Carolyn Jones.

Ray Danton gives John Kincaid a hollow personality. Danton is wearing his grey-at-the temples look he used for awhile during his post-Warner Brothers phase. He is pomp and circumstance justified by the hallowed memory of a wife he abandoned during an Apache raid. He pays the price for his pretense when he is exposed as a fraud. Forgiveness is the arbiter that reunites the estranged couple.

A feral Fabian is along for the ride.

THE THEATER

The theater had always been a second home to Ray Danton so it was not unusual for him to return to the boards, especially considering the changes that the movie industry was going through due to the increasing popularity of television. In 1962, Ray Danton returned to the stage in Jean Anouilh's *Becket,* performed at the famed Pasadena Playhouse. Ross Martin played Thomas Becket and Ray Danton assumed the role of Henry II, Duke of Normandy and King of England.

The play recounts the conflict between two former best friends whose rift defined the separation of church and state. Becket renounces his worldly ways when he is made Archbishop of Canterbury and creates a rift when he becomes an ascetic and preserves the power of the Church against the worldly kingdom of the king. He is ultimately assassinated by nobles from the royal court, impelling the king to become contrite and to seek penance.

Ray Danton and Ross Martin had similar acting styles, the difference being Martin was able to show his versatility through a gift for mimicry and impersonation, which became his typecasting. Despite their similarity, the actors were able to create enough tension between their characters by delineating intentions and motivations.

"The King, an exuberant, earthy, shrewd creature of primitive impulses is played with great insight and power by Ray Danton", wrote the Herald-Examiner. The Hollywood reporter stated, "Ray Danton plays the King as an ignorant crude minded primeval man, one of the last of the Dark Ages' chieftains! A difficult part to make sympathetic, but Danton makes it winning." And the Starr News declared that, "Danton's King is at once selfish, spoiled, degenerate, lonely, amusing, and pitiable."

Ross Martin was also able to muster a collection of favorable reviews. The best of these was The Los Angeles Times', "Ross Martin dominates a huge cast because he succeeds in imparting simply the complex personality of Becket. Martin takes accurate, circumspect measure of this man and his catastrophic inner struggle."

Ray Danton also had an opportunity to display his singing voice in *110 in the Shade* when he replaced Robert Horton in the lead role of Starbuck for the road show of the musical. N. Richard Nash wrote the book for the 1963 musical version of his 1954 play, *The Rainmaker,* which also served as the basis for the film starring Burt Lancaster as Starbuck. Harvey Schmidt composed the music, the lyrics provided by Tom Jones, the choreography was directed by Agnes de Mille and David Merrick was the producer.

It tells the story of Starbuck, a traveling con man who charms the people of a drought stricken town in the Texas Panhandle that he can produce rain. The plot also deals with effect he has on Lizzie Currie (Inga Swenson), a spinster, and how it changes her relationship with Sheriff File (Stephen Douglass), a reluctant divorcee.

Ad for a performance of *Becket* at The Pasadena Playhouse. 1962, Pasadena Playhouse.

Starbuck has one hundred dollar price tag for his services, which include having the town folk beating drums in an ancient rain making ceremony. His natural charm does not end there as he tries to work his magic on the plain Jane who believes that she will never marry. Unlike Ray Danton's other con artists, this character delivers on his promises, not only bringing rain to the county but causing Lizzie's lonely soul to blossom and bear fruit.

Will Geer, Lesley Ann Warren and Gretchen Cryer appeared in supporting roles. The original play ran for 330 performances at The Broadhurst Theatre and received several Tony nominations. Ray Danton solo songs included, "The Rain Song", "You're Not Foolin' Me", "Melisande", and "Wonderful Music."

Another musical, *Carnival*, followed in 1964. The play was based on *Lilli*, a 1954 French film starring Leslie Caron about an orphan who finds a home with a carnival and reluctantly falls in love with a lame Puppeteer named Paul, played by Mel Ferrer. The film, in turn, was based on a Paul Gallico short story called, "The Seven Souls of Clement O'Reilly."

"Lilli" capitalized on Leslie Caron's dancing abilities and produced a hit song, "Hi-Lilli-Hi-Lo." It was David Merrick's idea to turn the movie into a stage musical and he accomplished that with the help of song writer Bob Merrill, dancer Gower Champion and librettist Michael Stewart.

The original Broadway production starred Lilli Alberghetti as Lilli and Jerry Orbach as Paul, the puppeteer. The play was an instant success and spawned a couple of road shows. Ray Danton played Paul in one of the road shows that starred Ann Blyth as Lilli. Ray Danton's songs included, "I've Got to Find a Reason", "Everybody Likes You", "Her Face", its reprise as a counterpoint to Lilli's, "I Hate Him", and "She's My Love."

One of Ray Danton's last off-the-cuff live musical performances was a backhanded salute to his old boss, Jack Warner, a clever send-up and coy sendoff at the same time. Bill Orr was going to play his father-in-law in a spoof show called *My Fair Laddy*, a parody written and composed by Sid Kuller. The big guy persuaded his minion to bow out and Ray Danton stepped in to learn 90 speeches and several songs. It must have been a sequel to the party given by the Warner Brothers' actors for William Morris agent, By Marsh. This time there was only one ex-employee and he was about to depart for Europe to embark on a career as an actor-producer-director.

Starbuck (Ray Danton) and Lizzie (Inga Swenson) sing "Is It Really Me?" Gil Gravette, 1963.

Eurocines and Late 60's Americana

A Malaysian Pirate and Euro-Spies

As the 1960's progressed the American studio system was in a flux. The once dominant feudal style setup was threatened by the supremacy of television and the burgeoning revolution that was changing Hollywood. The old way of doing things was restrictive.

Those who were hit hardest by the new way of doing things were the B-movie actors and actresses of the old studio system. They belonged to a time when contract players were groomed for success and appeared in formula films hand-picked by the studios. Now, the concept of stardom had changed, along with the way films were being made. There was a slow meltdown and the new freedom posed the need for many to make career decisions.

Like so many actors of his generation, Ray Danton made the transition to Europe, where he could make movies with his name above the title. He could also pursue directing and producing, which he would do under the aegis of the production company that he would establish.

The promising Warner's career ended with the ensemble dud, *FBI Code 98* ('63). It was the swan song for a lot of the Warner actors and actresses. After that, it was dissemination into the television scene, re-packaging overseas, or retirement.

Ray Danton signed a six picture deal with the European producer, Ottavio Poggi. In the European exploitation film industry of the 60's, Danton became one of several American expatriates acting in an industry that was inspired by American genres of the past refined and reinterpreted through a Continental lens. Crime dramas, costume epics, spaghetti westerns, and horror flicks were the overseas offspring of the Hollywood that had just died.

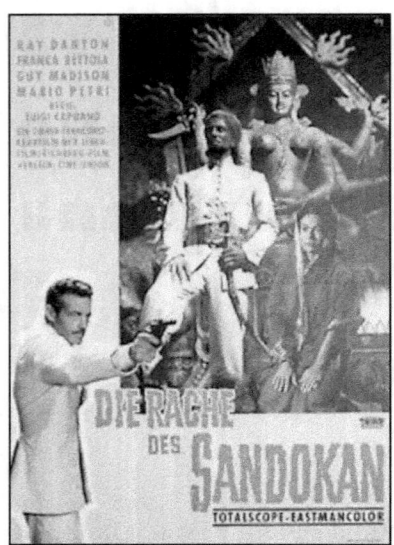

A poster for *Sandokan Strikes Back* under one of its many European titles. 1964, Eichberg Film-Liber Film.

Ray Danton's European career covers the gamut of exploitation genres. Swash-bucklers, Euro-spies, comic book heroes, and macho pulp busters are some of the roles from this period. Ironically, he did not star in a European genre that would have fitted him to a tee: the spaghetti western. This time around, his characters are on the right side of the law or, at least, standing in Machiavellian shadows.

Danton's romantic screen image will also take on a positive buoyancy when he makes the transition to Europe. As Euro-Spies and tough guys with integrity, he will get to romance a bevy of European beauties, among them Pascale Petit, Marissa Mell, Margaret Lee, Rosalba Neri and Pamela Tudor.

Ray Danton's future is a retrogressive leap into the costume adventures of a bygone Hollywood. He begins his European residence by playing a Malaysian pirate in *Sandokan Fights Back* and *Sandokan against the Leopard of Sarawak*, both made in 1964.

The plots of the films closely follow the legend created by Emilio Salgari in his novel, " The Tiger of Malaysia." The film series originated in1963 with *Sandokan the Great*, starring Steve Reeves. Yanez was played by Andrea Bosic. Reeves' Sandokan lives in another setting and time zone. His opponents are the forces of Queen Victoria. He followed that with *The Pirate of Malaysia* in 1964.

In the Ray Danton movies, Sandokan is a nobleman whose royal birthright has been usurped by the evil European, William Druk (Mario Petri). Forced by necessity to become a pirate, Sandokan gathers his followers to form a strong resistance in *Sandokan Fights Back*. The exiled prince is revered among the subjugated tribesmen, who rally to his cause. He is assisted by his blood brother, Yanez (Guy Madison).

Yanez and William Druk are the two faces of 18th Century Europe. Druk is a foreign conqueror who oppresses his subjects; Yanez is a freedom fighter. Druk has slaughtered Sandokan's family and rules through fear.

Sandokan is captured on the battlefield when he tries to regain his throne. 1964, Eichberg Film-Liber Film.

Yanez has aided Sandokan in past campaigns. The greatest benefit of the reclamation of the throne is the courtship of the Princess Somoa (Franca Bettoia). She gives the story its resonance and purpose. Without a queen to ascend the throne, a battle to reclaim it is useless.

The princess is a youthful beauty who is unhappy because she believes that Druk, her uncle, is an evil man and can't bear the brunt of his wickedness. The future will make her the queen of this oppressed kingdom because she is betrothed to Charles, Druk's nephew, who studies in India. He will inherit his uncle's lust for glory and become Sandokan's foe in the sequel, *Sandokan against the Leopard of Sarawak*.

The revolution ends with Sandokan and Yanez victorious. Sandokan and Somoa are united. Sandokan declares that he has become a man of peace as Yanez returns to his kingdom with his loyal troops.

In *Sandokan against the Leopard of Sarawak*, the onetime outcast and pirate rules over a peaceful kingdom, with his Queen Samoa. The idyllic court is upset when the queen is kidnapped by Charles Druk (Mario Petri), her cousin. He wishes to ascend the throne reclaimed by Sandokan. It is a role reversal of the original movie.

Charles uses the power of a psychic to hypnotize the queen into renouncing her love for Sandokan. She becomes a zombie robbed of passion and emotion, which disturbs Charles because he wants a natural love from her.

Aided again by his faithful European friend, Yanez, Sandokan mounts an effort to rescue Somoa. It is a mission fraught with peril. Along the way, he kills a tiger, thwarts double-crossers, bypasses deadly swamps and kills a python that embraces him with its powerful grip. He also dispatches the hypnotist, which breaks the spell on Somoa. In the film's climatic battle scene, Sandokan and Charles Druk fight each other in hand-to-hand combat as their troops wage war against each other. The film ends with Sandokan and Somoa standing on the balcony of their palace as adoring crowds cheer their victory.

Combined, *Sandokan Fights Back* and *Sandokan against the Leopard of Sarawak* form a single revenge saga. It is a blood feud between the bloodlines of the usurper and the vanquished. William Druk and his nephew battle the royal family of Sarawak from two vantage points. The father is the conqueror and the son is the claimant; both of them are fraudulent royals. Sandokan is outcast and prodigal son, a vanquished prince in both instances.

The poster for *Sandokan Against the Leopard of Sarawak*. 1964, Eichberg Film-Liber Film.

Luigi Capuano has created two fashionable exotic fantasy tales befitting a Saturday morning matinee. The look to the films is exotic and sumptuous and the action is non-stop. The pacing is fluid, as is the editing and the use of montages to convey action. The battle sequences on land and water are well staged, being reminiscent of the swashbuckler movies of the Forties and Fifties. The Eastern flavored musical score by Carlo Rusticelli is rousing.

Ray Danton makes an excellent pirate-prince. In the films, he fights the imperial army, has sword duels, battles tigers,

Sandokan battles an evil hypnotist to break the spell he has cast over Priness Somoa (Franca Bettoia). 1964, Eichberg Film-Liber Film.

and tangles with a python. Danton, wearing a turban and sporting a mustache and goatee, now uses his cunning manner to serve truth and justice. Against a background of the high seas and lavish kingdoms, he vanquishes the usurper of his family's kingdom and romances the fraudulent ruler's beautiful niece, the Princess Somoa.

Franca Bettoia is a ravishing princess. Her sensuality is enough to inspire any man to wage a revolution to reclaim a lost kingdom. There is an unspoken bond between Sandokan and Princess Somoa. It is the strength of her sense of justice that enables Sandokan to defeat her uncle and free her from a prearranged union.

Guy Madison-with dubbed voice-is a cool acting sidekick. He has a kingdom of his own, yet is glad to assist his brother in his quest for justice. He is a sophisticated European living the life of a ruler and adventurer. Being comfortable on land and sea is the perfect blend of nature and civilization. Mario Petri is commanding as the evil rajah and his nephew, two men with penetrating eyes that are devilish and a lust for power that is demonic.

The character of Sandokan was given a new incarnation in the 70's courtesy of Kabir Bedi. He has become the best known Sandokan because of two popular mini-series in 1975 and 1976. Bedi resumed the role twenty years later in *The Return of Sandokan* (1996) and *Son of Sandokan* (1998).

Ray Danton was in negotiations with Ottavio Poggi to star in *Richard the Lionhearted* with Stephen Boyd when he changed his mind to become one of the many James Bond-inspired Euro-agents played by American B-actors who made the trek across the ocean to star in a series of espionage spy thrillers.

The James Bond craze was a phenomenon that redefined the film industry. It created a genre that replicated the original until the market was saturated with suave secret agents. The proliferation of James Bond clones diluted the gene pool for original ideas. The further one got from the original premise, the more ludicrous the plots became, not to mention the contraptions that were supposed to delight audiences with their ingenious intent.

The spy genre as popularized by the James Bond movies produced scores of imitators. Some were honorable mentions, like Derek Flint (James Coburn); others were politely referred to as also-rans; Matt Helm (Dean Martin), for instance. The third type were European nods to American comics through a Carnaby Street kaleidoscope. Diabolik (John Philip Law) and Modesty Blaise (Monica Vitti) are examples of this offshoot of the spy phenomena.

The fourth kind belonged to the "Brand-X" variety: European or Asian movies that were unintentionally funny dramas. Often hampered by poor dubbing, choppy editing and outlandish plots, they served as camp delights on American 60's late-night television. That's what Ray Danton left his Sandokan role for.

In the James Bond tradition, he is one in a series of American expatriates making fast buck knockoffs of the real thing. Danton made five films that cast him as a secret agent extraordinaire. Some of them are noteworthy while others are perfect for late-night television schedules in remote regions of the world.

Danton's Sixties' European spy characterizations are urbane, cool, and cocky types. With these parts, he was able to extenuate his Fifties' image in Europe. The slick hair, sharp baritone, deadpan expression, and colorful turtlenecks fit in with the image of the suave Continental spy. The difference is-now-he was on the right side of law and order, plus his voice was occasionally dubbed.

Jeff Larson, Bryan Cooper, Mike Gold, Lucky the Inscrutable and Jimmy Logan are the names of Danton's spy contingent. They fight for justice and are protected by the unwritten bylaws of espionage campaigns.

In spy thrillers, five factors establish the secret agent's credibility: macho resolution in the face of danger, hair-raising action sequences, beautiful women, evil villains and imaginative gadgets. *Code Name "Jaguar"* conforms to these conventions; it's just the degree to which it does varies.

Spy footage winds up in a Washington conference room where military personal view it and are dismayed to learn that the Russians have equipment that is so sophisticated that they can transmit images from anywhere in the world to Moscow. The Chief tells them that the situation is so grave that he has dispatched a top-notch secret agent to send to Spain.

Corrida pour un espion was one of the European titles for *Code Name Jaguar*. 1965, Hans Oppenheimer Film (Ger), Midega Film (Es)-Trans-Atlantic Prod.-S.A.R.I. (Fr)

Enter the pugnacious secret agent, Jeff Larson (Ray Danton). Larson ultimately surmises that the Russian trawler docked in international waters has the transmission device hidden within it. It is an obvious deduction, yet one that eludes everyone's attention for a good part of the movie. It is because of their pigheadedness that Larson is obtuse and belligerent towards them.

Almost everyone dislikes him at one point or another in the movie. Throughout the movie, there is, at least, one person in a scene that has to contend with him, either verbally, violently, or romantically. Annoying and forceful, he is tolerated because he knows how to fight and he gets quick results.

The most effective action sequence is when the Russians send in a team of American ringers to infiltrate the military base. The shot of them running through an underground tunnel of golden bricks is breathtaking. The light from their torches reflects and bounces off the circular brick wall to create an impressive effect.

Jeff Larson (Ray Danton) shows off one of his high-tech toys to a non-plussed female conquest (Helga Sommerfield). 1965, Hans Oppenheimer Film (Ger), Midega Film (Es)-Trans-Atlantic Prod.-S.A.R.I. (Fr)

The same holds true of the retreat scene as the leaderless faction try to escape from their failed raid. Larson is prevented from following them because of their machine gun fire. He is aided by two soldiers who drive by and happen to have a flame thrower with them.

"Don't worry, sir", says one of the soldiers. "We'll roast them out."

The shot of the flame chasing the retreating spies is intriguing because of its cruelty. The spies are roasted alive and Larson croaks in his frog's voice: "Personally, I like mine well done."

This comment and the scene illustrate the mean-spirited accent to *Code Name "Jaguar"*.

With *Code Name "Jaguar"*('65), Ray Danton joins the ranks of American actors who played secret agents in European spy thrillers. Like most of the other screen spies, Jeff Larson is a poor man's James Bond. He is more lout than lover; outspoken than clever; and arrogant than smooth. He bullies most of the other characters, throwing around barbs as if they were clever jests.

Larson exasperates everyone that he meets because of his mercurial attitude. He is self-centered and is given *carte blanche* by the government to do as he pleases to accomplish the mission. The only thing that really makes him appear heroic is the level of buffoonery that surrounds him.

Little does it matter to Jeff Larson. He is a CIA operative and has to answer to no one. His mission is to neutralize the Communist spies who are tampering with his government's secrets. He accomplishes this without the aid of anyone, including four screenwriters without a clue, an editor with a slow eye and an unsteady hand, and a musical director who must have switched manuscripts with the score of a Flamenco movie.

The supporting characters are jokes. Commander Moreno is a feeble attempt at providing character conflict and the puzzle-Bob Stuart-is bland to the point of being wallpaper with a cane. They are played by Conrado San Martin and Roger Hanin.

The major villains in Code Name "Jaguar" would have been sidekicks and henchmen in the Nazi spy thrillers of previous generations. A loyal party puppet and his boss, plus a not-so-mysterious traitor round out the list of villains that challenge Jeff Larson's mission.

The alluring women are secret Agent Perez (Pascale Petit), Miss Calderon (Helga Somerfield), a club manager and a Russian scientist (Helga Lehner) on the trawler—all beautiful European women showing off their assets in a mid 60's way.

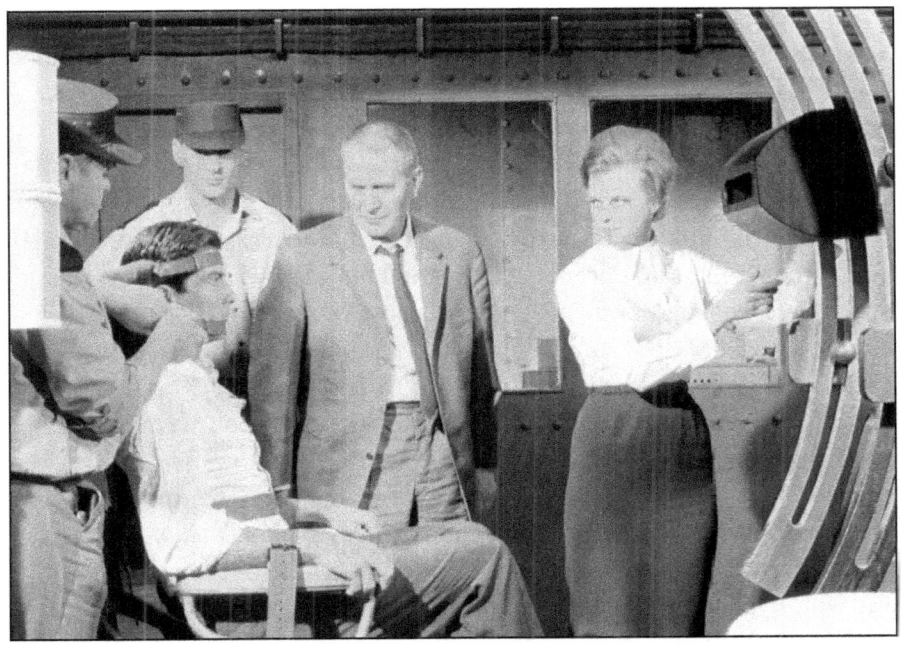

Enemy spies subject Jeff Larson (Ray Danton) to a mind-altering machine that will turn his brain into jelly. 1965, Hans Oppenheimer Film (Ger), Midega Film (Es)-Trans-Atlantic Prod.-S.A.R.I. (Fr)

The super spy's biggest challenge is disarming a bomb that will detonate if the top-secret camera it is attached to is touched. Larson also withstands a brainwashing technique that consists of flashing lights that bombard his eyes. It is a colorful light show that fails to achieve the intended purpose-to turn the secret agent's will into a "bowl of jelly."

He gets involved in a quarry demolition derby using derricks, uses ju-jitsu and acrobatics to beat up everyone in the hull of the Russian trawler and has an impressive rooftop fight early in the film.

Larson's best fight is an obligatory underwater confrontation that is strangely silent! Totally wasted is an impressive shot of Larson stabbing his opponent with a harpoon, releasing a torrent of blood that dissipates in the water.

True to the budget and imagination of the film, Jeff Larson only has one toy: the ring transmitter. It is the high-tech device that is supposed to set him apart from the other secret agents that were beginning to inundate the big and small screens across the world. The ring transmitter succeeds in distinguishing Larson as a low-rent James Bond because it is merely a gold-plated dime-store ring with an antenna attached to it.

Imagine how *Code Name "Jaguar"* must have been greeted in 1965. The secret agent craze reached its' zenith a year before with *Goldfinger*. The after effects stayed with *Thunderball*, the Bond entry that *Code Name "Jaguar"* had to compete with. The Bond film was filled with the usual imaginative gimmicks and won an Oscar for its special effects.

What audience would accept a dime-store transmitter ring after it had just been dazzled with a jet-propulsion backpack? And after the breath-taking underwater battle scenes in *Thunderball*, how could a one-on-one confrontation compete, dissipating blood flow non-withstanding?

The same year, Bond's most popular rival-Derek Flint-was introduced in *Our Man Flint*. Played with a devil-may-care surety by James Coburn, Flint outpaced all newcomers by a comfortable margin. *Our Man Flint* was a spoof that was dead on target. At the other end of the cash register was something like *Code Name "Jaguar."*

Not content with leaving well enough alone, Ray Danton planned to work for Maurice Labro once more in *Duel of Fauves (Duel of Beasts)*. He was to star with Peter Van Eyck but nothing became of the project. Labro and Van Eyck made their next stops on the Euro-exploitation market, as did Ray Danton with *Secret Agent Super Dragon*.

In 1966, there wasn't an official Bond release, which made it a year of attempts to replace, spoof, or compete with 007. A new competitor was unveiled-Matt Helm, played by Dean Martin. He was played in Martin's easygoing style and was not intended to be a serious rival.

In *The Silencers* and *Murderer's Row*, Helm battles with psychotic villains (Victor Buono and Karl Malden) and romances sexy women (Ann-Margaret, Camilla Sparv, Stella Stevens and Cyd Charisse). The movies were popular moneymakers that proved that exploiting the spy craze was still box-office gold.

The same year, trickle-down economics spread from Hollywood to Europe with films like, *That Man in Istanbul, Kill Panther Kill, Our Man*

Bryan Cooper (Ray Danton) assumes the Euro Spy's mandatory survival pose in a press release for *Secret Agent Super Dragon*. 1966, Fono-Roma.

in Jamaica and Attack of the Robots. There was also Secret Agent Super Dragon, starring Ray Danton.

It is the seriousness with which it takes itself that makes *Secret Agent Super Dragon* enjoyable. The movie is part Thirties' serial, Forties' *noir*, and Fifties' pulp filmed in the Sixties under the rubric of a Bond clone. The order of this spy film is beautiful women, international locales and close brushes with death. The music, with the exception of the shrill music box minuet, is highly effective, especially the xylophone refrain and the sad jazz trance piece.

Just as the gadgets became cheaper with the grade-Z budgets, so did the plots. Super Dragon's (Ray Danton) mission is to thwart a drug ring that has developed a lethal drug called Syncron. The nerve-shattering drug can destroy people's will power and even kill them—its effects vary with the dosage.

The drug distributor's first demonstration of Syncron's power is in Freemont, a small college town in Michigan. Unlucky college students have been ingesting the drug through spiked bubblegum given out *gratis* at Ross's Bowling Alley. It drives them insane. When Cooper's friend, also a secret agent, is killed investigating the case, he comes out of retirement to step in.

The ingenious Baby Face (Jess Hahn), released from Sing-Sing solely for this mission, aids the secret agent. Baby Face is an electronics wizard whose toy store inventions include a cigarette lighter/tape recorder, a synchronized watch that operates Morse Code, and a mini-sonar sub.

Super Dragon's challenges are out of the serials of the Thirties. His head is lashed to a factory track where an industrial machine on wheels will crush his face unless he gets loose. Suspended animation and inflatable bags help him survive a watery grave in a submerged coffin. And being trapped in an office building that is about to explode has him leaping through the air to a waiting rope ladder and helicopter flown by Baby Face.

Cooper is aided, abetted, and double-crossed by an assortment of beautiful women. His blonde sidekick is Cynthia Fulton (Margaret Lee). Charity Farrell (Marissa Mell) is the Amsterdam connection, Rembrandt 13. She is a sultry redheaded double agent whose will is controlled by Syncron. There are the secondary eyefuls: Verna (Adriana Ambesi), a woman emerging from the shower to do her scene in a towel and Elizabeth (Solvi Stubing), the nightclub manager who beds the secret agent in the film's closing moments.

Bryan Cooper (Ray Danton) has his own Miss Moneypenny, Charity Farrell, played by Margaret Lee, a popular actress in Euro-espionage movies. 1966, Fono-Roma.

The evil mastermind is Fernand Lamas (Carlo D'Angelo), a philanthropist who plans to hold a masked ball/high society auction as a way to spread the Syncron menace through specially treated Ming Vases.

Super Dragon and Fernand Lamas bluff each other into delusions of victory and possibilities of defeat. In the end, Secret Agent Super Dragon has defeated his scheme and spared the world from the Syncron menace until it later became known as LSD.

Ray Danton's hard-hitting tough-as-nails attitude matches the best of his early American roles. His two fisted qualities come alive in the fight scenes and he can still inflict pain and be so cool about it. As Super Dragon, he romances three of the women in the film with a chip-on-the shoulder that he borrows from Johnny Salvo.

Danton also handles the ridiculous secret agent stuff pretty well, too. Fighting the crooks with jujitsu on a barge, using his pec-

A lobby card set of *Secret Agent Super Dragon* highlights the movie's turning points in stills of a spiked masquerade ball, a college gymnasium in the Michigan town where the agent was killed, the mad scientists' headquarters and Mr. Big about to make a final withdrawal. 1966, Fono-Roma.

revolver to shoot a captor while raising his arms in surrender, and escaping an underwater coffin burial are done in matter-of-fact ways that make them hilarious because of their absurdity. The women are also sensual, chief among them Marissa Mell. Margaret Lee, the perennial spy film ingénue, is Bryan Cooper's version of Bond's Miss Moneypenny.

Secret Agent Super Dragon is definitely a step up from Code Name *"Jaguar."* It is coherent, has interesting characters, and the musical score is-for the most part-imaginative. Bryan Cooper aka Super Dragon has better toys, also. Among them are a cigarette lighter/tape recorder, a synchronized watch that operates Morse code, a bullet proof vest with a pec-revolver, and a couple of inflatable bags that enable his coffin prison to rise from the ocean floor in a literally breathtaking scene.

Experts on 60's Euro-spy movies may note that *Secret Agent Super Dragon* ('66) is one of the many spy film appearances by Margaret Lee. Danton will get his due mention as an exiled American B-actor. This film also has cult recognition status because of the *Mystery Science Fiction Theater 3000* lampoon of it. The movie has a strange charm that makes it a spoof in spite of itself.

MORE SPIES AND THE ABSURD SIDE OF THINGS

With the exception of *Lucky the Inscrutable*, Danton's espionage movies are weak tea spy flicks. That means that they are cheap and don't offer much in top-of-the line thrills! The best moment in the Italian-West German hybrid, *Man Only Dies Once* ('67), is it's explosive ending and a psychedelic imagination barely keeps the head of the Italian spy spoof, *Will Our Hero Find the World's Largest Diamond?* ('71), above water.

In the respective films, Ray Danton plays Mike Gold with a straight face and Jimmy Logan as a blatant fool. Pamela Tudor appears in both films.

Man Only Dies Once is more like a two part spy show than a movie. Mike Gold (Ray Danton) could be one of the heroes of *Danger Man*, *The Saint* or *The Persuaders* as they deal with espionage and drug smuggling. He is a lightweight compared to the big screen spies but fits in comfortably with the television heroes that are viewed from the comfort of an easy chair. One reason is that his mission is smaller; another reason is that so is the movie's budget. The amazing thing is the movie has two directors, Mino Guerrini and Giancarlo Romitelli. One is a *non-de-plume* for Ray Danton.

In *Man Only Dies Once*, Mike Gold is a secret agent sent to Beirut to investigate an arms smuggling operation after another agent, John Malsky (Marco Guglielmi) has been killed in the line of duty. It does not take long for him to get involved with the smugglers as he is made a target as soon as he lands at the airport.

Gold gets to show the audience his fighting prowess when he is trapped in a nightclub and has to fight his way out of the mess. It is one of the best scenes in the movie only because it is one of the more coherent scenes. Jane (Silvia Solar), the nightclub singer is victimized by a bunch of brutes and Gold cannot stand idly by. It does not take long for the club to clear out and for Gold to see that he is on his own or that he has been set up by the singer.

He follows a trail of spies that lead him to a charitable organization called the Kent

The poster for *Si Muore Solo Una Volta*, a spy melodrama set in the turbulent Middle East of the late sixties. 1967, Italcid.

Two blended shots of Mike Gold (Ray Danton) being set-up for a takedown in a restaurant after he comes to the aid of what he thought was a nightclub singer in peril. 1967, Italcid.

Foundation, run by Professor Ackerman (Julio Pena) and his assistant, Silvia (Dada Galloti). The foundation is really a front for the smuggling operation that houses a drugged out Malsky, who is not dead, after all. Throw in Ingrid (Pamela Tudor), the Interpol agent, and you have a round robin of spies, counter-spies and tricky villains.

The height of Mike Gold's heroics is preventing a band of terrorists from sabotaging a nuclear warhead at the end of the movie. One has to admire the props' department's creative use of handyman and construction site material to make the warhead. It is painted bright colors and passes for the real thing once you realize what it's supposed to be.

Aside from the junkyard nuclear warhead, the only effects occur in a scene where the villain releases poison gas through hidden portals in the garden that surrounds the wall to the foundation. The whole setup is meant to be intricate but it comes off cheap and is good for a laugh as the police are rendered useless.

A badly edited car chase that involves guns and rocket launchers is another point of interest as is a dummy (Malsky) falling off a bridge to a watery death in the movie's opening moments. Later in the movie, the dummy appears to be very much alive in a surprise plot twist. He gets to participate in the car chase and ultimately wish that he was the dummy that fell from the bridge because he is killed…this time for real.

Another twist is the crooked ally, played by Pamela Tudor. She and Gold find time for romance before the grand double cross. A crater is Tudor's grave in a flammable finale. Mike Gold walks away with his new girl friend, the woman who saved his life. She is played by Sylvia Solar. Other highlights are a couple of dance numbers in a Mid-Eastern nightclub where Gold is trapped in an ambush and the secret agent's one man raid on the crooks' hideout. The theme song is *"Che Cuome Sei"*, a Euro pop romantic dirge sung by Ammarita Spinaci.

For a thorough account of the making of the multi-national production of Euro-Spy dramas, read Matt Blake's excellent, *Eurospy Guide*. Not only does he do an amazing job of chronicling the phenomenon of the European spy film craze but he has managed to provide a brilliant road map to negotiate the terrain of international finance and co-productions, where actors and crews often use *non-de plumes* for their onscreen counterparts.

The spy franchise got a reprieve from a death sentence when Sean Connery returned to the James Bond role after George Lazenby's cruel rejection by the public. He would briefly play the role before relinquishing the part to Roger Moore, who was not reviled by the fans; anything but that!

Ray Danton returned to the spy fold with an international spy comedy-thriller, *Will Our Hero Find the World's Largest Diamond?*, made in 1968 and released a couple of years later. It is an Italian film directed by Guido Maletesta (and Ray Danton) and developed for a production company he formed, American Motion Pictures of Italy. The movie is a dubious addition to Danton's spy films and a light counterweight to *Lucky The Inscrutable,* it is an "in search of" type of movie, which gives it an excuse to be an eclectic mess. It is obvious that the movie had two directors, so distinct are the styles used to convey the story. One is post-60's psychedelic and the other is flat 20's slapstick.

Will Our Hero Find the Largest Diamond in the World? is a strange and interesting film. At times, it works as a wonderful spy spoof; at other moments, it is an amateurish mess stretching for cheap laughs. Jimmy Logan is

The poster for Ray Danton's last turn as a European secret agent. Jimmy Logan is a nerd whose spry imbecility enables him to evade danger, romance women and solve the case in spite of himself. 1971, American Motion Pictures Company of Italy.

pre-Austin Powers and post minstrel show, yet has elements of both. The look to the film is Sixties psychedelic and the style is hodgepodge and lack of harmony. Sometimes, the weirdness works; sometimes, it deflates. A staple of late night European television, it has its share of laughs and interesting routines along with tired slapstick gags and over-the-top performances.

The theme song to Ray Danton's last spy film is best thing about it. *Will Our Hero find the World's Largest Diamond?* is an adventure with Jimmy Logan (Ray Danton), a nerdish secret agent called in by the Italian prime minister to find the world's largest diamond. The gem was stolen from the Prime Minister in the film's introduction, an inept sequence of events that is supposed to be a daring heist. The minute Logan enters the picture it becomes an electric experience.

The spastic fool, Jimmy Logan, is Danton's last European secret agent. He wears glasses and has a nerdish manner to him. Despite his annoying gestures, he romances women and disposes of enemy agents with aplomb. Lanky and shrill, he is irresistible to women and able to defend himself in fights. On the pathetic end of things, Logan does a minstrel routine in blackface, has a labored fencing match with a group of asylum orderlies, and performs an old comedy bit in a suit of armor.

The hunt for the diamond is the best part of the movie because it gives the plot a chance to deviate into odd and strange segue ways. Strangely, it breaks down once the action settles on the insane asylum run by Dr. Froyd (Lewis Jordan). Instead of exploiting the comic possibilities of the asylum, the director resorts to lame reproductions of silent film laugh-getters that have neither the finesse nor the timing of the originals.

Jimmy Logan (Ray Danton) wonders whether or not anyone will confuse him with Legs Diamond. 1971, American Motion Pictures Company of Italy.

One thing is certain-the movie has a great theme song that is played in about every scene yet never suffers from overkill.

Ray Danton is spry and does his routines well. Omitting the tastelessness of the blackface routine, his bits are good. A water-ski sequence and a cheap, but cleverly edited, car chase scene are examples of successful comedy spots in the movie. For those who enjoy lame recreations of stale slapstick routines, there are tortured recreations of silent era classics.

Lewis Jordan is maddeningly over the top as the villain, Prof. Froyd. The spy under his command is Gladys, played by Pamela Tudor. Previously, she has been blown up and shot to death in two Danton spy fests; here, she falls through a trap door to nowhere after she has served her purpose to the evil doctor.

The other women in the movie are redolent of *Secret Agent Super Dragon* in that they are sexy in an Euro-trash sort of way. An airline hostess trained in jujitsu, an Asian seductress with earrings bigger than brass balls, a wide eyed blonde nymph named Lolita and the ill-fated Pamela Tudor are some of the women who ring Logan's chimes. They don't have a problem seducing him; to them, Logan is irresistible.

Comedy is not one of the things one normally associates with Ray Danton unless it is a dark sense of humor evoked by some of his sadistic characters. The notion of Danton doing comedy would seem comical to some yet he has played comedic roles on television and in the movies. The most notable example is the comedy, *A Majority of One* ('62). His nerdish character, Jerome Black, is more like a straight man and a foil than a jester.

Aside from *A Majority of One*, Ray Danton has played some funny characters. The trouble is how many people remember his light turns as Senor Velazquez, Harry Shayne, and Jere Fryer on *77 Sunset Strip: A Nice Social Evening* ('58), *The Roaring 20's: The Vamp* ('61) and *Death Valley Days: The Wooing of Perilous Pauline* ('64)? Even less would know of the Italian comedies whose original titles are *Lucky Intredpido, Ballata de miliardo* and *Riuscira il nostro eroe a ritovar piu grande diamante del mondo*? Translated, they are *Lucky the Inscrutable, How To Win a Billion and Get Away With It* and *Will Our Hero Find The World's Largest Diamond*?

It took a trip to Europe to bring out the comic actor in Ray Danton. His first European comedy was the screwball comedy-heist film! *How To Win A Billion...and Get Away With It!* It has gangsters from the 20's hatching casino heists while second story men try a double cross under the nose of Joe Martin nee Giuseppe Martino, son of an ailing American crime boss.

The son has to accomplish a noteworthy crime caper or else he will be officially considered a failure in the family. The ultimatum weighs heavy on Martino and it puts him in a series of comic situations that

The poster for the Italian made *Ballata Da Un Milaado*, shown on British television as *How to Win a Billion... and Get Away With It!* (It.) 1966, Augusta, (It.)

Danton deftly handles for laughs. He interacts well with the oddball characters of the plot because he is one of them. Actually, he is two because he also plays the wheelchair bound aging don, Big Smiley.

A charming movie that is muddled by sloppy editing, *How To Win A Billion... and Get Away With It!* ('67) is a cartoon replete with exaggerated characters and improbable circumstances. This casino robbery movie is an Italian screwball comedy done with a flair for broad wit mixed with bitter irony

The plot is simple: Big Smiley is an ailing crime boss who is distraught because Joe Martin, his popinjay son doesn't possess a talent for crime and cannot take his place as the head of the crime family. The *capo* makes a last ditch effort to make a success out of his son by sending him to Italy where he can discover his family's roots as Giuseppe Martino. Joe Martin leaves with his father's admonition not to return until he has done something big! It is a challenge that will haunt him throughout the movie.

Danton plays the roles of Big Smiley and his son, Little Joe. As the wheelchair bound Big Smiley, he is gray, gold-toothed and menacing. Speaking with an exaggerated Italian accent, the overwrought father condemns his son. The only thing that the two men share is a knockout smile. Big Smiley's menacing grimace is used to coerce associates into succumbing to his will. Joe Jr's smile conquers women, who faint when they look at his pearly whites. This is apparent in a scene at the airport, when he arrives in Italy. Two stewardesses faint, as does a counter woman. It is a funny gimmick that has ramifications when he finally meets a woman who is impervious to it.

Once he arrives in Italy, he is kidnapped by four of his father's former cronies. Kicked out of the United States at the height of their criminal expertise, they languish in Italy as remnants of a romanticized past. They tell little Joe that they have concocted a casino robbery inspired by John Dillinger's last heist. It even includes machine-guns and a getaway car, plus a cave near the casino where they can don their disguises.

Little Joe is perplexed by the insanity of their scheme yet is bothered by his father's admonition. He compliments the two when he decides to mastermind the casino robbery his way. It is his meeting with the mysterious Monica that changes his mind. She is incensed and engages him in a brief martial arts match that ends with a heated kiss. When it is over, he tries to dazzle her with his smile.

"Turn off that smile; it gives me the shudders", she tells him.

Joe, Jr. is astounded. With her by his side, he decides to headline their scheme. Once he commits himself to the job, Joe, Jr researches layouts, blueprints, and becomes ensnared in a comedy of errors. He learns his father's grimace and-after demonstrating it on one dissenting thug-asserts himself as the head of the gang. This delights the old-timers, who feel like they did in the old days-vital and respected.

The supporting characters are the four old gangsters who still have a pinch of larceny in them. They round up busloads of suckers to gamble at the casino the night of the robbery. Three con-artists are a team of experts who have ideas of their own on how to pull off a successful double cross involving counterfeit money. A geologist and his beautiful assistant are

Joe, Jr's (Ray Danton) good luck at the casino backfires because of its resounding success. Breaking the bank lands him in the pen but an escape clause in his contract will net him an underground getaway. 1966, Augusta, (It.).

A press book cover for *Jamaica Calling Mr. Ward*. 1967, Metheus Films-Orbita Films.

there to explore the caves beneath the casino and operate an elevator that can remove the safe from the vault.

The casino job and the traitorous sub-schemes are negated by Martin's good luck at the roulette wheel. A series of bizarre turns of luck make his rite of passage a gamble on fortune. A clever plot twist changes Martin's fate and complications lead to both good and bad luck before he rightfully makes his bones in the family business.

Mel Welles used the veteran director Julio Salvador's name for the credits of the stylish and lighthearted Spanish *Jamaica Calling, Mr. Ward* ('68), an entertaining crime caper. Glen Ward (Ray Danton) is introduced as an inept hotel house detective. His attempt to capture a jewel thief ends when a scantily clad blonde lures him into her apartment, where the thief knocks him unconscious. Ward awakes, wearing white boxer shorts and nothing else! He looks into the camera and explains his predicament to the audience. It is a device that is used throughout the movie.

A call from his friend, Pinky Pinkham (Carroll Brown), in Jamaica will be the start of an adventure that starts after he is fired for his ineptitude and his friend is murdered. Ward's Jamaican adventure involves tangling with a mob boss named Martnelli (Beni Deu), a local police chief named Rickers (Jorge Riguad), and a double-crosser named Liz Taylor (Pamela Tudor).

It takes Pinky's murder to turn Glen Ward into a dashing, if low rent, private detective. He is part spy because he shares some of the traits as Jaguar or Super Dragon. His foreign turf is Jamaica and it makes for a good locale for the film.

Allesandro Allesando's rhythmic score is one of the highlights of the movie and makes many of the scenes enjoyable as do the appearances of actresses like Pamela Tudor and Sylvia Solar.

An amusing highlight is the way Ward defeats his enemies in a chase scene that ends in a fire ball. He uses an aerosol can and a box of thumbtacks to side rail his pursuers in a high speed chase. They work for Martinelli, a crime lord who surrounds himself with beautiful women that tantalize Ward when he meets with the kingpin. Ward holds Martinelli responsible for Pinky's murder but the gangster maintains his innocence. The surprise enemy is played by Pamela Tudor. This time around, she is shot while party crashing dressed as a sniper in black.

Julio Salvador (Mel Welles) has directed a stylish comedy-drama. It has its good moments even though the private eye/secret agent challenges are laughable. The music is partially responsible for keeping a balance between the comedy and the drama.

One of the many press book covers and titles for *Jamaica Calling*, *Mr. Ward*. 1967, Metheus Films-Orbita Films.

Ray Danton plays it for laughs with Glen Ward. He is cool and romantic but finds himself in humorous situations. The people he deals with are apprehensive about him. Jorge Riguad plays the resourceful Inspector Rickers. He considers Ward a suspect and is distressed by his presence in the middle of the case. His meddling does not help matters, either.

Pamela Tudor is the dependable love interest until she is unmasked as the killer. She plays it in her usual sexy but firm blonde style. Benny Deu plays a seedy Martinelli, a mobster who commands two goons and is always surrounded by his gorgeous playmates. Pinky Pinkham may be the name of his murdered pal but it's not really *the* Pinky Pinkham although it is *the* Carroll Brown.

European Gold

The best films of Ray Danton's European period are Jesus Franco's inventive *Lucky the Inscrutable* and Mel Welles' brilliant elegy, *The Last Mercenary*. The movies make fine European counterparts to *The Rise and Fall of Legs Diamond* and *The George Raft Story*. They are similar because their main characters are strong individualists who make their surroundings conform to them until they lose control. The difference lies in their cultural sensibilities.

Lucky the Inscrutable stands out as a pleasant addition to Ray Danton's list of credits. He spoofs the erudite international spy by sending up the tough guy image that he popularized on American television a decade ago. 1967, Fono-Roma.

Legs Diamond and George Raft are from an American era between two world wars. Lucky the Inscrutable and Marc Anderson operate behind the Iron Curtain and in Brazil. They are Cold War operatives seen from the other side of the pond and south of the border.

By the late Sixties, celluloid spies were everywhere. It was if Bond imitators had overwhelmed the entertainment world. The movies and television were so glutted with spies that when the original big screen James Bond (Sean Connery) took a hiatus from active duty, it didn't matter.

Casino Royale, although an Ian Fleming novella, was a self-conscious Hollywood parody of the Bond films made in 1967. Not counting unintentionally bad movies, spoofs were becoming the only logical way to sustain the spy franchise. The same year as *Casino* Royale, Ray Danton starred in *Lucky The Inscrutable.*

Not only is *Lucky the Inscrutable* ('67) one of the best of Ray Danton's European movies, it ranks among the best of his work. It is directed and co-written by the eclectic and perverse Jesus Franco, versatile director, writer, producer, actor and cinematographer. Fast-paced and frenetic, inventive and bold, caustic and witty, the movie is a delight from start to finish.

The master spy is a conceited super hero who possesses a rapier wit that is used at everyone else's expense. Women swoon around him and men want to kill him. He is a Renaissance man who has an encyclopedic knowledge of languages that he speaks with the accent of other languages.

Punctuated and highlighted by clever sight gags, humorous dialogue and a brilliant score by Bruno Nicolai, the movie is Franco's good-natured homage to the spy genre and uses Danton to the best of his abilities. It ranks among the director's best films and ensures Danton a spot of recognition with a special segment of spy genre lovers. For all they know, the character's dubbed cartoon voice really belongs to Ray Danton.

A secret society of financiers called Archangel hires Lucky the Inscrutable (Ray Danton) to foil an ingenious counterfeiter named Goldglasses (Marcelo Arroita-Jauregui), a former bio-chemical specialist who is flooding the world market with phony hundred dollar bills. The future of the free world's monetary strength depends on the efficiency of a buffoonish super hero.

Some of the antagonists Lucky encounters during his mission are Cleopatra, a master spy, a deadly blonde spy in red, a dominatrix-styled captain of the Albanian secret police, a go-go dancer in disguise and a

The CD cover of Bruno Nikolai's excellent score features Lucky (Ray Danton) and Mikail (Danto Possani) battling the Albanian police. 1967, Fono-Roma

mysterious assassin with a bad cough. The anarchy leads to the classic showdown with the villain at his high-tech headquarters.

Goldglasses gives the secret agent the traditional tour of the facilities before the film's fiery climax, which ends with his elimination and a finish with a twist. *Lucky the Inscrutable*, as a character and a movie, is an oddity and a treasure.

Although he is heroic, Lucky is also part clown. That is what makes the premise so ludicrous: the well-ordered balance of Western civilization depends on the antics of a jester in a super hero's costume. Not to worry- at the behest of Archangel's Guardian-Lucky will operate undercover as a pedestrian who just so happens to look like a suave continental spy.

The trouble with Lucky's disguises is that everyone recognizes him. Whether he is a hipster in turtleneck racing across the terraced rooftops or an Inspector Clouseau look-alike with wraparound bug-eyed sunglasses, he is always greeted as" Lucky." This exasperates him. He can't believe that mere mortals can penetrate his disguises and identify him by his real moniker.

Lucky's gargantuan ego makes him take his greatness for granted. He is unmoved by compliments because they are an accepted part of

Lucky (Ray Danton) is once again recognized despite his debonair disguise and flip French accent. 1967, Fono-Roma

his myth. He thinks that he is perfect because he is a comic book super hero with five adventures left on his contract. Such surety has made him *blasé* about the spy business.

From the beginning to the end of his mission, Lucky faces anyone and anything with a casual manner. He is bored because he knows that he will triumph in every encounter. Even when he is subdued by the villain's henchmen and tossed into a furnace, he doesn't acknowledge being saved by his sidekick, Mikhail (Dante Posani). Lucky climbs to safety without missing a beat. A thank you is preposterous because his survival is taken for granted.

Lucky is knowledgeable about running any machine, translating any code and solving all problems. His cavalier attitude makes him unfazed by the magnitude of his mission. He effortlessly moves from one point to another, connecting the dots as he goes along. In the end, Lucky has an answer to his puzzle. That's why he is a super hero.

Like all super heroes, Lucky is a magnet for beautiful, but deadly, women. There is Cleopatra (Teresa Gimpera), one of his doomed contacts at a masquerade ball.

The blonde spy (Beba Loncar) in a red bathrobe tries to kill him. First, she tries to poison the super hero but he declares that the drink was the "best glass of poison I ever drank." Her attempts to shoot him fail because of the inaccurate sites of her Yugoslavian pistol, a fact that Lucky casually points out as the rounds ricochet around him.

Lucky's hottest encounter is with Yaka (Rosalba Neri), a sergeant-in-whips dominatrix of the Albanian secret police. She flogs him with her whip when he refuses to answer her questions. At first, she is repressed until Lucky provokes her with challenges to her sexuality. Their consummation is humorously depicted in cartoon panels.

His deadliest rendezvous is with a trusted go-go dancer (Barbara Bold) with a treacherous secret. Her continual aid to Lucky is a way to be led to Goldglasses' counterfeit fortune. The printing plates are her lure and she uses her dance charms to befuddle Lucky.

Lucky the Inscrutable is a superior spy spoof because it denies all of the conventions that make its' model a success. It is directed and edited in a frenzied cartoon fashion that ridicules the finesse, charm, and sophistication of the "legitimate" secret agent films, namely the James Bond franchise. The score by Bruno Nicolai offers an extraordinary accent and spice to the movie. Each scene is enhanced by his eclectic arrangements, which add to the film's brilliance because the music is a perfect fit!

As Lucky, Ray Danton spoofs the bare-knuckled qualities of his early Hollywood pulp roles. Danton's deadpan manner adds to the character's charm, as does the badly chosen voice used to dub his voice. The timbre is an octave above his baritone and it sounds the way you'd imagine a jack-in-the box would if it could speak. The effect adds to the hilarity of this Franco jewel.

Lucky the Inscrutable may have been considered a European Z-flick special at one time, but now it's absurdity exposes the pretentiousness of the box-office smash spy flicks. Let *cineastes* gloat and agonize over the best films in the "constipated classics" category. It is time to enjoy what was once a guilty pleasure of insomniacs and connoisseurs of offbeat movies. Hats off to *Lucky the Inscrutable*!

The Last Mercenary contains what may be Ray Danton's finest role. He gives a blistering performance as a mercenary who enters a dream world where quick-cuts fool the eye and sound effects dazzle the ear to tell a fairy tale drenched in perfume and blood. Mel Welles' delirious vision

Lucky (Ray Danton) and Yaka (Rosalba Neri) ignore the Cold War in a cartoon interlude, a comic book technique used throughout the movie. 1967, Fono-Roma

Le' Ultimo Mercenario is about an over-the-hill mercenary who defends a small village's mining operation against the hostile takeover mentality of an underground syndicate. 1968, Orbita Films.

is supported by the intense performance of his star and a hauntingly beautiful score by Bruno Nicolai.

Marc Anderson (Ray Danton) is a fading soldier of fortune who is hired to protect a Brazilian mine from being overtaken by a rival concern. His main battle is facing the challenge of making a decision about the direction his life will take for its twilight season.

At the beginning of the movie, Christ the Redeemer (*Cristo Redentor*) stands on Hunchback Mountain (*Corcovado*) in Rio and offers outstretched arms that proffer different choices for Marc Anderson to make. One is a road guide, showing him two paths to choose between; the other is a holy embrace of support. By the end of the movie, Anderson will have made a choice and shared an embrace and the choice will be the result of an ill-fated embrace.

The scenario is Anderson's private dream, a cruel fairy tale whose ethereal atmosphere is enhanced by Bruno Nicolai's stirring motifs. The mercenary's personality is split into three supporting characters: a golden haired girl, a crippled mine owner and his Gorgon wife.

Isabel (Inma de Santis), the golden child, is Anderson's guardian angel, the way out of his blood-silver way of life. Her aura is the rhythm of the calliope music from a merry-go-round that is the central charm of *The Last Mercenary*. It is a variation of the kiddie-car ride theme in *Ride a Pink Horse*. The carousel is the first thing Anderson sees when he arrives in the Brazilian mining village. An organ and nylon-stringed guitar play a beautiful waltz while the carousel revolves. Anderson sees the golden haired girl standing on a hill. She has the face of an adult and is dressed like the old women of the village.

Manuel de Largos (Georges Regaud), the wheelchair-bound mine owner, is the corrupt hunger that fits the bill for Anderson's services. He is need of Anderson's services because his mine is under siege by corporate predators. His handicap is also his masquerade. His confinement to a wheelchair give the impression of helplessness but the firmness of his voice and the gleam in his eyes suggest that he has a quiet reservoir of strength.

Maria (Pascale Petit), his wife, is deception whetted by subsistence. She is a stone-faced Gorgon who rises out of the little girl. Maria wants to help Anderson betray her husband and let the mining operation be taken over by his rival. She needs the mercenary to liberate her from her miserable life. He is only interested in keeping his word. Towards the end of the film, after Anderson has given the miners hope of defending their mine, Maria asks him if he accepts the bleak way a mercenary dies.

"What else is there?, he answers in a bitingly stark tone.

The choice for Marc Anderson is the redemptive way shown by the little girl or the way of the mercenary as exemplified by Maria. He chooses Maria by rejecting her and rejects the little girl by embracing her. His choice is deliberate because he believes in the nihilistic climax of a mercenary's life.

Throughout his mission in Rio, three assassins dog Anderson. The killers are the mercenary's evil familiars: a Nordic man in black (Gunther Stoll), a Hispanic man in white, and an impeccably dressed bald ogre. They harass, torture and beat him to make their boss's point: Anderson is resilient and gets a revenge that is twice as brutal.

The trio is led by Steinman (Carl Mohner), Anderson's alter ego. They fought together in Africa and other campaigns; in Brazil, they are on opposite sides of the mining operation. Unlike Anderson, Steinman won't let sentiment stand in his way. He double-crosses Anderson in a gunrunning sale turned sour because he has accepted a larger offer from the industrialist's opposition. Before the double-cross, Steinman accuses Anderson of slowing down and sounding like an antique because he speaks of their profession in obsolete jargon.

"Nobody uses revolution anymore", says Steinman. "They're insurrections, people's fronts, popular liberation movements…"

Updating his comrade on the euphemisms for revolution, Steinman's discourse on the new cautionary terminology of their profession

Ray Danton's stark portrayal of a faded mercenary holding on to a past that is slipping away makes Marc Anderson the actor's most compelling character. 1968, Orbita Films.

defines Anderson and himself as fighting a battle waged "in the fading pages of history." Anderson knows what Steinman says is true but he won't admit it.

The battle of the mine should be Anderson's last contract. It is a smalltime operation with blurred intentions and tentative results. The terms of his services are antithetical to the mercenary's code. The opposition has offered him more money yet he stubbornly sticks to his nominal fee. A fee tempered by altruism is self-neutralization for a soldier of fortune. It is a fact that he denies and ignores even though the source of change is before him.

Marc Anderson will pretend that he fought and won the battle according to the monetary code of his profession. Unable to accept the role that fate and altruism had to play in it, he will head to Haiti with Steinman to play out a drama on his own fading page of history.

Marc Anderson is Ray Danton's rawest characterization, a crystallization of all the hard-edged attitudes of his past roles. There is nothing phony about Anderson's vitriolic stares or spitfire comments. His fighting is also at its most intense: he is beaten, knifed, and shot, not to mention the amount of shooting and pulverizing he does, himself.

He plays the one-man army for hire as a ferocious jungle beast with a soft underbelly.

Marc Anderson (Ray Danton) pays Steinman (Carl Mohner) for running guns to him only to be betrayed and robbed by his cohort in past revolutions. 1968, Orbita Films.

Marc Anderson (Ray Danton) returns a beating given to him by one of his dark angels. His comrade Steinman (Carl Mohner) and the Silent Man in Black (Gunther Stoll) watch. 1968, Orbita Films.

You can find *El Mercenario* on the list of a Spanish language library for television rentals or on a commercially released PAL version in German-*Die Grosse Treibjagd*. Sometimes, a slow wind from China will blow one in that has an English soundtrack to provide a great viewing experience.

Just as *Lucky the Inscrutable* is a timepiece of the psychedelic-secret agent era *The Last Mercenary* is a child of the post-flower power age when real power was seen as something that was wielded with a lock and load attitude.

Legal authorities were scrutinizing films on both sides of the ocean as the obscenity and freedom of speech laws were being challenged on all fronts. *The Last Mercenary*, because of brief nudity, was classified as "adults only", along with other European films like *Wild Cat*, *To Save Face* and *There*.

Scenes were also left on the cutting room floor. It was a sign of the times and *The Last Mercenary* was deemed Adults Only for this; never mind the slaughter and carnage that defined the lives of the mercenaries. It was a brief nude scene that prompted the courts to seize the films and make the suitable changes for the desired ratings.

After *The Last Mercenary* was completed Ray Danton readied his next project for Orbita Films of Barcelona. He was to direct an original comedy by Stanley Ralph Ross called, *Tom Scott and His Electric Thing*. It was about an eighteen year old's picturesque adventures in several European venues, a very 60's-ish in-search-of-self odyssey. Ross previously worked on Rowan and Martin's, *The Maltese Bippy* and Cinerama's *Follow Me*. Funding for the movie never materialized and the project, to have been co-produced with Arrow of Hollywood, was scrapped.

NETWORK RELEVANCE: THE NEW AMERICAN TV DEMOGRAPHICS

When the Sixties found its personality in the United States, it had an arrogant contempt for all that passed before it. The remnants of the Fifties were challenged according to a relevancy quotient. A chosen few passed and made the successful transition. Those that failed the test were subject to pitiless ridicule; marginal apologists were allowed to be assimilated on a second-tier basis; and others became symbols of evil.

Overseas, Ray Danton's Fifties persona was the stuff that his heroes were made of. Secret agents Jeff Larson of *Code Name, Jaguar* and Brian Cooper of *Secret Agent Super Dragon* looked the same as their stateside counterparts. The difference was in Europe the continental look was adjustable to Sixties relevance.

Ray Danton may have been able to parlay his look into a European success for the rest of the decade but in the States the grease top hairstyle and sharp-voiced intimidation equaled pure evil. Danton played the villain in stateside spy shows around the same time he was a heroic secret agent overseas.

The first two stateside counterparts of Ray Danton's European heroes are Sonny, the grifter in *Honey West: The Swingin' Mrs. Jones* ('65) and Vincent Carver, the Thrush spy, in *The Man From U.N.C.L.E: The Discotheque Affair* ('65). The last will be Ortega, the seditious Secretary of State in *Its Takes A Thief: The Baranoff Timetable* ('69). Ortega is Danton's swan song to the Fifties dark hard-boiled bandit Romeo.

Cocktail horns, bongos, honeycombs, a beauty mark, and full lips introduce us to Honey West (Anne Francis). A collection of stills shows an attacker lose his edge and become prone when he tangles with the black clad blonde private investigator. Leather turns to lace and the horns turn sly as she poses in a curvy white gown. Her ferocious presence morphs into Bruce the ocelot.

Honey West is a true rarity in Sixties television. She is independent and resourceful, able to protect herself with martial-arts and possessing a keen mind and sharp wit. These traits add up to a fiercely independent and sarcastic private investigator-not to mention—a sexy one, too.

In *The Swingin' Mrs. Jones*, a lonely hearts scam has Honey in disguise as Mrs. Jones at an exclusive vacation resort where poolside hustlers bait single women. Catcalls and wolfish eyes bombard her as she walks poolside in her leopard outfit. Among the cheap hustlers is Sam (John Ericson), her partner, who is posing as Touch Carstairs.

Sonny (Ray Danton) can't believe his luck when he encounters Mrs. Jones. He just does not realize that his serendipity is really retribution. 1965, Four Star Productions.

The other bloodhound is Sonny (Ray Danton), a deadpan mama's boy who runs a sting operation headed by his mother. Sonny is the prince of gigolos, an oily and loathsome parasite who struts a low-rent charisma to lonely, vulnerable and well-heeled socialites. Sonny and Touch make a 80/20 split on taking Mrs. Jones. Carstairs will wine her, dine her, bed her and photograph it all with a hidden camera. It falls apart when Honey and Sam are exposed yet still able to turn the tables on Ma and Sonny.

The role of Sonny is the beginning of the end of Ray Danton's undaunted cool and sleek persona. The cruel player with the gift of graft had played its course. It was the changing mores of the times. The Sixties revolution was taking shape and, at this point, a new hip was being defined. Anything from the Fifties was declared null and void. Ray Danton had an old look in progressive times. That is why Sonny is left to choke on his pride and lose sight of the big picture. Ray Danton's next role is a case in point.

The Man from U.N.C.L.E was inspired by the success of the James Bond films and the spy franchise that it created. It starred Robert Vaughn as Napoleon Solo and David McCallum as Ilya Kuryakin. It was a rare to have an American and a Russian as partners during the Cold War and that is what gave the show its unique edge. The program ranged from the ridiculous to the sublime and lasted for four years. It also produced a short-lived spin off, *The Girl from U.N.C.L.E.*, starring Stephanie Powers.

In *The Discotheque Affair*, Vincent Carver (Ray Danton) runs a disco named The Bealors. The logo on the disco's awning resembles the Beatles signature bass drum sign and is a reminder of the show's Sixties' self-conscious sensibility. Complete with cages for go-go dancers and cardboard college-types to fill the dance floor, the club is a front for THRUSH, a totalitarian organization bent on ruling the world.

Aided by Tiger Ed (Harvey Lembeck), a rotund dancing fool with a penchant for partying and eliminating liabilities, Carver commands a crew of go-go girls who act as adoring slaves. Their enemies are U.N.C.L.E. agents Napoleon Solo and Ilya Kuryakin.

The Discotheque Affair is a case of the new hip versus the old cool. The beat generation is now on the opposite side of Cold War politics. It is the enemy of the mods and rockers who have taken over. Vincent Carver is the slick continental type in a hip Sixties' disco setting. His assistant, Tiger Ed, has undergone the Sixties modification process: he sports Beatlesque bangs and loud turtlenecks. A decade earlier, Danton and Lembeck were the leads in Jack Arnold's *Outside the Law* ('56) and *Girls In The Night* ('53), respectively. Now, they are old-age hipsters about to be conquered by the heroes of the swinging Sixties-the ultra-cool secret agents.

Napoleon Solo and Illya Kuryakin represent the adventurous spirit of the early Sixties. It is a period when the vestiges of the previous decade have finally fizzled out and a new one has developed its own attitude. Danton still has the raw edge of his Legs Diamond persona but now the slick hair, silk ascots, and rakish cruelty are cartoonish.

It is ironic because the same look and attitude made Danton successful in his overseas Euro-Spy movies. Harvey Lembeck's Tiger Ed is a cartoon twice removed. Lembeck already lampooned the over-the-hill greaser with his Eric Von Zipper character in the popular Beach Party movies. In the role of Tiger Ed, he is a middle-aged Fifties' hipster trying to be reborn as a Sixties party hound.

In *The Man From U.N.C.L.E.*, Ray Danton and Harvey Lembeck still delivered what they promised their audiences in their heyday; it's just that the times were changing and, pretty soon, they would have to change, too, if they planned to continue working. The following year, Danton was still doing his slick haired suave rake in Europe; only he was on the right side

Vincent Carver (Ray Danton) and Tiger Ed (Harvey Lembeck) adapt their 50's personas to 60's discothèque cool. 1965, MGM Television.

Vincent Carver (Ray Danton) is immune to the barbs of one of his female subordinates. He is a Bolshevik automation in the employment of THRUSH. 1965, MGM Television.

of the law. He kept his look but reinvented his image by playing secret agents. Ironically, a decade later, Ray Danton would become a Seventies version of the Sixties disco king.

Before he did that, Ray Danton returned to Europe to star, direct and produce a string of movies. He completed the unique *Lucky the Inscrutable* before he came back to the States to star in a format that he was familiar with: the western. The popularity of American westerns had declined considerably by the mid-sixties. There were the tried-and-true standbys like *Gunsmoke* and *Bonanza* but, by and large, the genre had faded away, a casualty of the sudden shifts in American sensibilities.

The Big Valley was a rare exception and its popularity was due to its star power and the comfort it provided a segment of the American demographics that were uncomfortable with the social changes going on around them. The show lasted from 1965 to 1969, the core years of the 60's revolution.

Barbara Stanwyck starred as Victoria Barkley, the steel willed widow who headed a wealthy family in 19th century Stockton, California. Her eldest son was Jarrod Barkley (Richard Long), a refined lawyer who was the voice of reason that served as a bulwark between his brothers, the mercurial Nick (Peter Breck) and sensitive but tough Heath (Lee Majors), who was actually the illegitimate son of Thomas Barkley, Victoria's late husband. Audra (Linda Evans) was the only daughter and she was just as tough as her brothers and yet possessed the ladylike charm of a western ingénue.

In *The Devil's Masquerade*, Heath is the only character not impressed with Jim North's (John Doucette) impending marriage to a mail order bride. His suspicions are legitimate but he does not voice his opinion until he can prove his point. There is something familiar and unsettling about Nancy (Ann Helm), the bride-to-be. The same goes for the new stranger in town, Reed Clayton (Ray Danton) an overly charming gambler.

Reed Clayton is an addend to the Vince Jackson character. He is sharp, confident and aggressive, which is nothing new for a Ray Danton scoundrel. He handles the cards well, smokes his cigars with sophistication and is quick on the draw with his derringer until he tries to shoot the wrong man.

Clayton is really the disgraced son of a successful businessman. Clayton Industries may be a burgeoning industrial power in the expanding West but Reed will not be a part of it because his father has disowned him and this makes him the black sheep of the family. That leaves him with the unprofitable life of an itinerant gambler. He is no charmer like *Maverick*, the resident gambler at Warner Brothers' Burbank Studios. Clayton is a hustler and a murderer and he will do anything to lay that big stake that will redeem him in his father's eyes.

Taking a lesson from Vince Jackson of *Laramie: The Fortune Hunter*, Clayton has bogus marriage plans all right; however, he is not the one who will be exchanging vows and rings. His lure is Nancy (Ann Helm), his lover and former dance hall queen, who assumes the guise of a mail order bride for the rancher.

North is an aging widower who owns a large ranch and his loneliness has been eased by correspondence with the prospective mail order bride. The real Nancy was a teacher and she looked forward to marrying North and becoming the town's schoolmarm. The only problem is that she is killed in an apparent stagecoach holdup, along with the driver. Clayton and the bogus Nancy were the only survivors and that is how they get their con off to a start.

Heath suspects fraud because the ersatz Nancy reminds him of someone he once encountered in Copper Creek. If that is not enough to arouse his suspicions, Nancy's inability to recall certain facts that would

Reed Clayton (Ray Danton) compensates for his lost inheritance by swindling lonely but rich widowers into marrying his girlfriend, Nancy (Ann Helm). 1968, Four Star Productions.

have been mentioned in Jim's letters lead him to mistrust the woman. This bothers Nancy and she complains to Jim that Heath does not like her.

Nancy is getting nervous over the prospect of Heath discovering the fraudulent setup and wants to back out of the arrangement but Reed Clayton forces her to go through with it. His plan is to have her marry North and leave him after a few months, claiming a nice settlement for her lost honor. This is the money that Clayton plans to use to finance his resurrection.

Heath travels to Copper Creek and goes to the local saloon to ask some questions but gets an immediate answer when he finds Nancy in her dancehall regalia hustling a cowboy for drinks. She tells Heath the reason for her change in plans and beneath her cynical exterior is a touch of honesty that impresses him. Heath has a change in heart and convinces her to return to face Jim with the truth. On the way out, she spots someone aiming a gun at Heath from a barn hayloft. It is Clayton, who plans on finishing the job himself; he, too, is no match for Heath and bites the dust Nancy returns with Heath and all is well in a happy ending that has Jim and Nancy asking Heath to be the best man at their wedding.

The media characterized 1967 as The Summer of Love but it was year the weirdness settled into mainstream consciousness. The counterculture had challenged the Old Guard and won. A hard edge crept into the primetime lineup. By 1969, it had a warped attitude, the politics of violence having replaced flower power.

Truth, Justice and the American Way was the Fourth Estate's bromide during the political upheavals of the time. It was the basis of the Tele-Film, *Fame is the Name of the Game,* which inspired *The Name of the Game,* a ninety minute show that revolved around the three power players of Howard Publications. Gene Barry played Glenn Howard, the publishing dynamo who started his empire from nothing. Robert Stack was Dan Farrell, the hardnosed editor and Tony Franciosa played Jeff Dillon, investigative reporter without peer. Each star highlighted a weekly episode.

In *The Inquiry,* Glen Howard's sterling reputation is being smeared in a Senate investigation led by the pernicious Sen. Creston Collins (Barry Sullivan). He accuses Howard of stealing government funds during a covert OSS guerilla operation in WW II Italy. Collins' principal witness is Sgt. Ernest Maxwell (Gene Evans), an embittered veteran whose animosity against Howard colors his testimony against his former commanding officer.

Howard has to relive the reconnaissance mission and encounter all of the principals to clear his name. That means traveling to Europe and rekindling tenuous acquaintances. Two of them are Cesare Moreno (Edward Asner) and Pietro Bertelli (Ray Danton).

The flashbacks portray Bertelli as a battle hardened partisan fighter and Moreno as a meditative and philosophical freedom fighter. The OSS had to decide what partisan group to back, one led by Bertelli or the other led by Moreno. The decision was difficult and was based on their actions regarding a German supply train.

Bertelli blew it up while Moreno did nothing to prevent its passage. When pressed for a reason for his inactivity, Moreno told Howard that five important members of the resistance were being held hostage on the train. They were to hold important government posts after the war. Moreno weighed the importance of their lives against the train reaching the German supply lines.

Howard asks Bertelli if he was aware of the hostages and he replies that he was; that is the why he blew up the train-the Germans didn't think that the resistance would do it. Howard realizes that Bertelli is firm but he cannot be trusted. Moreno seemed more trustworthy and that is why the OSS backed his partisan group.

The present sees Pietro Bertelli as a man fallen on hard times. He is jailed and tubercular, living off the money earned by Lisa (Carla Borelli), his streetwise daughter. Bertelli is bitter and angry, his face twisted by rage and his hair grey from an unhappy old age. He is no help to Howard, who refuses to pay him for any assistance he may offer.

The part is an interesting parallel to Marc Anderson, a role Danton played in *The Last Mercenary*, made in Europe the same year. The resistance fighter is a match for the mercenary during his years fighting with the underground. The battle scenes show Bertelli as a fierce fighter and are reminiscent of Marc Anderson in combat mode. For Bertelli, the glory days were a quarter of a century ago. His last days are hollow, probably like the way Anderson will spend his last days if he lives to a ripe old age. Both men's ultimatums are empty gestures to their fate.

Moreno is now happily married to Renata (Gia Scala), a woman with romantic links to Howard during the Resistance. He, too, is apprehensive about aiding Howard because of insecurities that have resurfaced with the appearance of his wartime ally and romantic foe. He eventually relents

A flashback of Bertelli (Ray Danton) and Moreno (Edward Asner) during their resistance days. 1969, Universal Television.

and gives Howard some information that may clear his name and save his reputation.

The Inquiry uses flashbacks to cut back and forth from the past and the present and makes effective use of the effect, especially when portraying the principal characters under different circumstances and at various points of their lives. It also has a *Roshomon*-like effect because of differing versions of the operations told by spectators with dissimilar agendas. The episode also features Fritz Weaver as a fellow OSS officer and Jack Kelly as Fowler, a team member who is captured and tortured by the Nazis. He holds the clue to the mystery and it proves to be his embarrassment and reveals a shame that he has harbored for decades.

As the 60's was about to pull the rug out from underneath itself, Ray Danton kept his continental look and flip flair for intimidation for two more roles. *Ironside* was Raymond Burr's successful follow up to *Perry Mason*. The show originally aired from 1967 to 1975, the height and aftermath of the social upheaval in the United States. It's sensibilities are reflections of the era and it is very much a timepiece, much like *Perry Mason* was of the 50's. Like his previous show, Burr's new character had a great theme song, this one composed by Quincy Jones.

In *Ironside*, Burr played Robert T. Ironside, a police commissioner confined to a wheelchair because of a failed assassination attempt. He is aided by two square detectives, Ed Brown (Don Galloway) and Eve Whitson (Barbara Anderson). His wheel chair attendant is Mark Sanger (Don Mitchell), the hip (in a T.V. sense) streetwise ghetto survivor.

In *A Drug on the Market*, Karin Martin (Betsy-Jones Moreland), a pharmaceuticals heiress, is being driven insane by a stalker who is playing morbid practical jokes on her. He claims that she has four days until she will die and the tension is slowly killing her. Strange voices, menacing strangers, mind altering drugs and eerie death threats impel Ironside to help out his old friend, even if she does not welcome his assistance.

There are the usual suspects, chief among them Avery Corman (Ray Danton), her blustery brother. He is now running Martin Labs, the pharmaceutical company founded by her late husband. Corman stands to make a substantial profit if the company merges with Abrex, a Swiss company. The only thing that may hold up or even cancel the merger is the chief chemist Dr. Braven's (Fred Beir) claim that the developmental drug being prepped for the market has lethal side effects.

Much of the investigation focuses on Corman, whose strained relationship with his sibling gives the police reason to suspect him because of his less-than-flattering assessment of her state of mind. He also browbeats Dr. Beir and reminds the scientist that he is merely an employee of the company, albeit a brilliant one whose revolutionary discoveries are patented by his new boss.

Dr. Braven has given Karin a dossier on the drug and she threatens to expose her brother if he continues with the merger. Avery Corman is portrayed as an avaricious power-hungry neophyte who lacks scruples and ethics. He is the obvious suspect because all clues point to him which, in most cases, turns out to be a misjudgment that leads to clearance.

In this case, clearance starts with Ironside's investigation into the matter which proves that these claims are false because all of the test subjects of the drug have received new leases on life. Chief among these is the exuberant George Zuppas (Nick Dennis), a Greek fisherman who can still drink, arm wrestle and share tall tales with his buddies.

In the episode's climatic scene, Karin is about to lose her mind in her mansion because of the slurred, demonic voices that encourage her to commit suicide. It comes to a head when her brother crashes through the window, seemingly to attack her. He is knocked unconscious by the hysterical woman and falls down a flight of stairs. His concussion does not end Karin's torment because it turns out that her assailants are the vengeful Dr. Braven and Judith (Victoria Shaw), her envious best friend and Avery's bitter wife.

They mock Karin as she pleads with them and try to push her over the edge but it is of no avail because Chief Ironside has been monitoring the situation from a hiding place in the yard. He and his crack crew show up in time to bust the criminals in a case that even Jimmy Logan (the papier-mâché European secret agent Ray Danton had played the same year) could have unraveled the scam to drive the heiress insane. This time, it was not all in the mind.

The last time that Ray Danton acted with Raymond Burr was in *Lux Video Theatre: The Web* in 1957. Betsy Jones-Moreland was a little known television actress who fans of Chiller Theater will remember as the star of *The Creature from the Haunted Sea* and *The Last Woman on Earth*. Nick Dennis was a diminutive actor who carved out a career playing jovial and bellicose Greek working men. His best roles were in *Slaughter on Tenth Avenue* and *Kiss Me Deadly*.

The last role to feature Danton as his Fifties persona is Ortega in *It Takes A Thief: The Baranoff Timetable*. The star of the show is Robert Wagner, one of the Fifties actors who remained a star through the subsequent decades. During the height of the 60's he played Alexander Mundy, an international thief employed by Uncle Sam. His boss was Noah Bain (Malachi Throne), a sarcastic and flabbergasted man who often engaged in verbal repartee with his underling before becoming the punch line to Mundy's joke.

Mundy's latest mission is in South America and involves stealing the Baranoff Timetable, a plan for the Communist takeover of Latin America. His aid is Laurie (Jessica Walters), a jet-setter who secretly has ties with Ramon Ortega (Ray Danton), a corrupt government official with dreams of power driven home by the hammer and sickle.

His contacts lead Mundy to believe that the president's pro-American sentiments are a sham and the Baranoff Timetable is his unification plan for communist autonomy in Latin America. These leads turn out to be false when Mundy is betrayed by Laurie and Ortega, who plan to overthrow the pro-democratic government and install themselves as rulers. The Baranoff Timetable turns out to be a forged document discrediting President Gutierrez's (Renzo Cesana) cooperation with the

Vice-President Ortega (Ray Danton) keeps Mundy (Robert Wagner) under wraps so the jewel thief turned secret agent cannot impair his televised presidential coup. 1969, Universal Television.

United States. It is meant to link him with the Soviet Union and lay the groundwork for a takeover by Ramon Ortega.

The revolution will be televised as it happens during the president's presentation. He will be forced to make a concession speech because Ortega has kidnapped the president's daughter, Maria (Kay Cole), and is holding her hostage. Ortega will make the change in power when he gives his inaugural speech directly after President Gutierrez has abdicated power. Mundy, through electronic sabotage, interferes with the broadcast. The plot is foiled and Ortega becomes as defenseless as the Baranoff Timetable.

The episode is a time capsule of the 60's, not only in a political sense because of the fashion and dance crazes of the time. Among Mundy's formal wear is the Nehru jacket and El Presidente's scatterbrained daughter is hung up on American dances and this figures big at the dance ball where her gyrations unintentionally distract the guests so Mundy can steal the Baranoff Timetable.

Until then, it is the usual cat and mouse espionage antics that were endemic of the anti-Communist themes of the era and given the television treatment for the umpteenth time: a conniving Vice President who plans a coup that will make him the Socialist usurper of the Yankee installed throne; a beautiful and duplicitous sidekick who turns out to be playing both sides against the middle; an inept conniving underling such as Achille Morales (Larry D. Mann), a useless assassin who winds up being murdered; and the true blue leanings of the democracy loving C.I.A.

Vice President Ortega is the South American counterpart to Vincent Carver, the Thrush agent from *The Man from Uncle*. He is made of marble and often hides behind sunglasses. Ortega is a smooth, charming, and calculating. He speaks in a cultured and serious tone but appears to be sizing up whomever he is having a conversation with. Stylish and well-mannered to a fault, Ortega is a cobra ready for its moment to strike.

One senses that his bedside manner has seduced Laurie into believing that she will make a magnificent First Lady. She dotes on redecorating the presidential palace while he relishes the thought of pocketing vast sums of American aid to his country. He plans a bloodless coup that will be televised. Alexander Mundy foils his attempts and the would-be dictator is shot and killed when the President's troops over run the television station.

Ortega will be the last character that has the hallmarks of Danton's trademark look. The greased back hair and continental look were about to become remnants of the past. In their place would be a Caesar cut, garish clothes, medallions and just a hint of the old treachery.

The Disco Era

70's Overview

From 1964 to 1970, Ray Danton enjoyed star billing in Europe. When Danton returned to the United States, he left his star status overseas. In America, he found himself at the other end of the rainbow. The slim and grim pickings of the Seventies were a stark contrast to the bountiful offerings of the Fifties and early Sixties. Many of the promising newcomers of the Eisenhower era were now rounding out the casts of independent drive-in films and making regular appearances on prime time television.

The returning expatriates may have enjoyed the good life during their European stay but their estrangement from Hollywood resulted in an exclusion from popular main stream market films, unless it was a bit part in a major studio release. The stars that had left the dying dynasty of the studio years returned to a Hollywood that was alien to them.

The social upheaval in the late 1960's expanded the 1970's judicial interpretation of censorship and freedom of expression. This resulted in a bold revolution in the arts, especially the movies where new attitudes tested old traditions and confrontational politics became the new American norm. New trends pushed the envelope in creative expression by stretching old themes into current socio-political setups.

It was an attitude that spread from books and the big screen to television shows and movies of the week; pretty soon, themes about Black Power, Women's Liberation, The Pill and other viewpoints that had traditionally been considered taboo took center stage to show other perspectives of American life. It was a fertile time for Hollywood, in the movies and on television.

CESARÉ DANOVA

William Morris Agency, Inc.
CR-4-7451   BR-2-4111

MICHAEL DANTE

Lew Sherrell Agency, Ltd.
Associate
Chan Gross
271-5236

RAY DANTON

Stephen Yates Associates, Ltd.
657-4380

SEVERN DARDEN

Phil Gersh Agency, Inc.
274-6611

JAMES DARIS

The Sackheim Agency
276-3151

TV Commercials
Dorothy Day Otis Agency
461-4911

A page from the actor's registry lists Ray Danton in his new 70's incarnation. 1970.

For once, the resistance was the once dominant audience that still enjoyed the wholesome traditions of yesteryear. They were the new counterculture and were granted a charmed existence with the nostalgia rebirth of a wave of television shows that featured the stars of their youth whose heyday was still alive on late night television.

The mainstream movies of the Seventies belonged to a new generation of filmmakers who, because of the easing of the censorship laws, had a creative freedom unavailable since the pre-Production Code Hollywood. Filmmakers were preoccupied with reinventing the medium in the names of creative expression, technical innovation, and windfall profits.

Four genres were invigorated and a new trend was created by a series of powerful films that set the tone for the rest of the decade. Robert Altman's *M*A*S*H* was a powerful anti-war black comedy that toppled sacred cows and paved the way for social protest movies. William Friedkin's, *The Exorcist* revived the horror genre and inspired a legion of imitations. Francis Ford Coppola's, *The Godfather* redefined the gangster romance and a new cycle was created, one that also turned television programming on its ear.

The last genre was unique in that it was one of its kind and it was labeled as the blaxploitation film, which was basically a Black Power themed film. Ossie Davis' *Cotton Comes to Harlem* created a tidal wave that not only included original characters and themes but the reframing of horror classics like *Frankenstein, Dracula* and *Dr. Jekyll and Mr. Hyde*.

Anything outside of the orbit of the big time players was considered independent, which did not have the respect and consideration that it has today. Anything that did not have the slick Hollywood gloss was considered cheap and tawdry. Low budget was considered beneath contempt and the independent market meant exploitation dreck, drive-in quickies, grind house specials and overseas exclusives.

Ivory tower critics and the video stream mentality may cringe at anything less than slick and seamless but lovers of *pyschotronic* cinema understand that low budgets, poor production values, and erratic acting patterns can be cinematic virtues. These traits filled the films that Ray Danton ended his Hollywood acting career with.

Ray Danton's 70's big screen efforts are obscure oddities: *Triangle* ('71), *The Ballad of Billie Blue* ('72), *Blood, Black and White* ('74), *The Centerfold Girls* ('74), *Apache Blood* ('75), and *Six-Pack Annie* ('76). To locate these rarities is a matter of waiting for them to cross your path.

They will come out of nowhere and surprise you because they have Ray Danton in inconsequential roles.

During the Seventies, Danton starred in only two films, *Apache Blood* ('75) and *Our Man Flint: Dead On Target* ('76-TVM). The rest of his appearances were supporting roles and cameos. Outside of the made-for-TV movies, they were all drive-in cheapies and a couple of never-to-be released films. Other than that, it was stock heavies on prime time crime dramas. That was usually the third phase of the 50's contract player and 60's European marquee name.

A candid snapshot of Julie Adams and Ray Danton at a film industry convention. 1970's, Fan Collection.

Clint Eastwood was the only actor who enjoyed European stardom to establish himself in 1970's Hollywood after having been deemed unemployable almost a decade earlier when *Rawhide* ran out of stampedes. He became a successful actor and director and has maintained that status ever since.

There was also success for actors and directors who were establishing themselves around the time when Ray Danton was a star and who remained to take advantage of the collapse of old Hollywood while others went to Europe to enjoy star billing in cut rate productions. Two actors who shared Ray Danton's bold faced and assertive acting style were Lee Marvin and James Coburn. Lee Marvin had several small roles as sadistic malcontents and played a hard-nosed police detective on *M Squad* during the 1950's.

During the same period, James Coburn was a bit player on television until he became one of *The Magnificent Seven*. Both actors hit it big in the new Hollywood of the late-60's and early 70's. Ray Danton had an advantage over them because he could also turn on the charm and play polished dreamy types. His dissatisfaction with being a bit player led to his migration to Europe but it was Marvin and Coburn's similar stints that led to stardom when the following decades began to celebrate their offbeat types as anti-heroes.

Ray Danton could made the same counter culture movies that some of his 50's and 60's associates were starring in. Clint Eastwood, Lee Marvin and James Coburn were the obvious examples. Even Tony Curtis—former star at Universal-International and one of the few B actors who made it to the A level—was able to ride the tide of the 60's new reality-themed movies with a couple of pictures before joining Ray Danton and other former contemporaries on the cheapie circuit during the 1970's. Warren Oates, who played Ray Danton's brother in *The Rise and Fall of Legs Diamond*, also found well-deserved success in the 70's.

The anti-hero theme was also one that made Robert Altman a successful director during the 1970's. He worked with Ray Danton on *The Roaring 20's* and *The Gallant Men*. The men often shared opinions and ideas and Altman was said to be the only one who picked up on Ray Danton's interpretation of Legs Diamond as a walking dead man. Yet there was no connection between them in the 70's; in fact, there was hardly a connection to anyone anymore.

The producer Quinn Martin was the only link to the past who offered any opportunities to the actor. Martin was a successful television producer and responsible for many of the 1970's best crime shows. Ray Danton made the rounds of the Quinn Martin shows with the same frequency that he did the circuit during his Warner Brothers era.

Still, if industry jokes were the writing on the wall, it would be an uphill battle for Ray Danton. The Writers Guild presented its' mini-show in March, 1970. It was a mixed affair with x-rated spoofs of movie themes and a rhythm and blues group called The Master's Children. The highlight was a spoof of MGM's upcoming auction of classic props.

The writer Artie Julian played the M.C. and the articles he offered "included films taken of Fred MacMurray once picking up a tab; the pix taken by Rudy Vallee with a borrowed camera; a vial of poison taken from the hand of George Stevens when he was told he had a Ray Danton commitment; shoulder pads worn by Jack Oakie and Joan Crawford in all their pix; a gun taken from a stockholder after MGM announced it was going to remake Four Horsemen of the Apocalypse; a stag film starring Lassie and Asta; and a toupee worn by Gene Kelly."

Not exactly a one-in-a-cast-of-thousands billing like *The Longest Day* but still a not-so-honorable mention and not so auspicious way to jumpstart a Hollywood career. Things were so rough that, for a time, Ray Danton retired from acting to coach his son's high school football team in Arizona. His ace-in-the hole was being an independent producer and this enabled him to negotiate the 70's from another perspective.

The Return to Hollywood

Ray Danton hoped his return to the United States would enable him to establish a movie career as an actor-director-producer. Before he could do that, he had to change his image to fit the new kaleidoscopic party-hardy look of the new decade. In order to adapt to the drastic changes in television brought on by the 60's, many actors and actresses from the 50's entered a time machine to undergo the cookie-cutter image-enhancing process. This was an identity alteration procedure that redressed the past and created a fresh personage with a familiar name in accordance with the rules of Seventies self-conscious cool.

The return to the Western Hemisphere signaled the farewell of the suave Continental player and the introduction of the Seventies' bunco artist. Ray Danton was reincarnated as a middle-aged swinger who tried to remain relevant in a cartoon kitsch world of sunglasses, suntans,

Carlo di Fermi set the style for the gaudy and obnoxious 70's disco hipster. He is too cool for his own good but it was the sign of the times to let it all hang out and get in your neighbor's face. 1971, Commonwealth Entertainment, Inc.-Federal Film Group.

loud colors, pinky rings, garish medallions, leisure suits, and outlandish hairstyles. The times had changed and it was hard to equate the 70's Danton with his 50's and 60's personas. However, his two different appearances with the slicked back hair and the retro Beatle mop top style exemplified their respective times.

Although Ray Danton did not have any problems in finding work on television, he did not appear in an American movie until a year after his return to the United States. That would be *Banyon*, a television film for his old studio, Warner Brothers. His first post-European Seventies' movie was the Canadian-made *Triangle*.

The original title was *The Fire Within* and that was changed to *Façade* and then to *Crossroads*. The three titles were appropriate names for the film; so is *Triangle*, which benefits from "the participation of Ray Danton." This was a European method of billing for a performer who could not get top billing and who refused to be relegated to a secondary credit. "With the participation of Ray Danton" offers the New Age Carlo di Fermi, a bi-

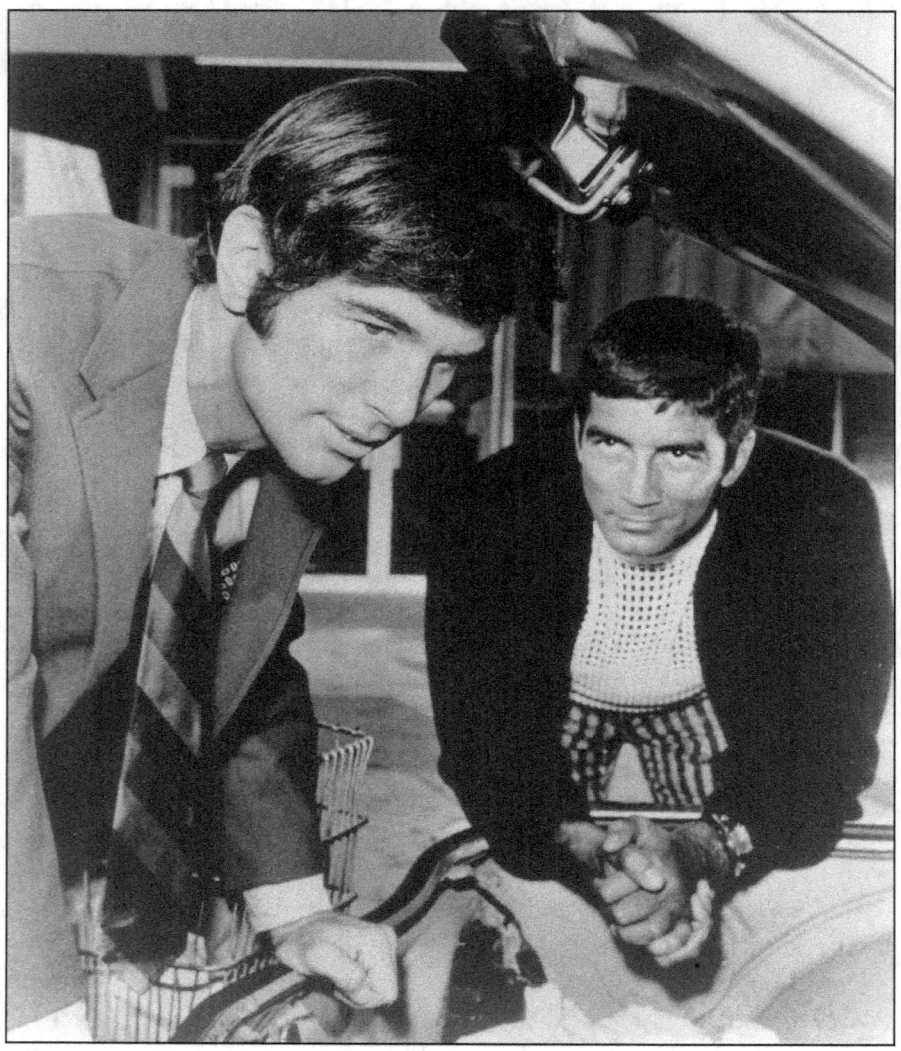

Carlo (Ray Danton) has a hidden agenda to bolster the ego of fledgling English literature professor, Todd (Chris Robinson). 1971, Commonwealth Entertainment, Inc.-Federal Film Group.

sexual sculptor teaching art at a private college for women. He competes with a disturbed student for the attention of the new English teacher. The role-and the look-is a clear departure from his Hollywood and European images.

A Caesar-styled haircut complimented neckerchiefs, sunglasses and mystic medallions. All that remained of the old Ray Danton were the attitude an occasional turtleneck sweater. Carlo di Fermi is the start of the pendant wearing Seventies disco creep: arrogant, personable, colorful and in-your-face. It is a role that Danton played to the hilt on the gaudy disco influenced television shows of the Seventies.

Identity crisis-a hangover from the Sixties—was a popular subject for movies of the early Seventies. In *Triangle*, Todd (Charles Robinson) is a confused young writer who is hired to teach literature at his Aunt Olive's (Dana Wynter) all girl's college, where sexual politics and intrigue are part of the curriculum. At the school, he becomes acquainted with two people that will help him to re-define himself: Sharon McClure (Tiffany Bolling) and Carlo di Fermi (Ray Danton.)

Sharon McClure is a disturbed Seventies child. She is a neo-hippie without the flowers and love beads. Instead, she has an inheritance and the burdensome memories of parents killed in a car accident, plus a life of emptiness and nymphomania. Sharon is obstinate, obdurate, and cold.

In the gym, Todd meets Carlo Di Fermi. The art teacher is working out as he sizes up the new teacher in a predatory fashion. He gives Todd the lowdown on the school and caps it with a prissy impression of Todd's aunt. The sculptor adoringly looks at Todd laughing at his effeminate performance.

Throughout the film, Carlo and Sharon bare their claws at each other, ready for attack or retreat. Carlo feels threatened by Sharon's inroads with Todd and turns spiteful when a stern warning to stay away goes unheeded.

Carlo takes advantage of the younger man's insecurities. Explaining one of his sculptures, sharing tips on selecting ripe honeydews, and pep talks about being there when one of them stumbles are some of the lures Carlo uses to soften Todd up.

All is in vain because Sharon's lure is stronger than Carlo's attraction. Things come to a boil when they clash at Carlo's testimonial dinner to himself. It is a collision that redefines the triangle and makes it a straight line.

Despite Carlo's unmasking of Sharon's promiscuous history, his grip on Todd is loosened by his cruel behavior at the party. Sharon's near-fatal

Sharon McClure (Tiffany Bolling) has a sensual charm that upsets the balance of power at Carlo's farewell dinner to himself...but not without dire consequences. 1971, Commonwealth Entertainment, Inc.-Federal Film Group.

car wreck bonds her to Todd in the film's dramatic climax as Carlo is left alone after his farewell party crashes and burns.

Triangle is preachy and stereotypical at times, although there are some fine bits. It is a bold movie for its time considering that it was the beginning of the 1970's and conservative influence was the still dominant. Chris Robinson is vapid and lachrymose. A clothes' hanger in a turtleneck could have played his part and no one would have noticed anything wrong. One might even have had sympathy for the character.

Tiffany Bolling is sensuous as Sharon McClure. She is coquettish and self-destructive, a lady bobcat in a schoolgirl's uniform. Sharon lives on the edge of her fears and desires , a temptress driven by her own temptations. Ray Danton is effectively bitchy as the possessive and manipulative Carlo Di Fermi. He is an Iago type of character, a conniver who is a frustrated sculptor with dreams of making it big in New York. His torment is masked by a pretense of sophistication.

The minor characters are nondescript and are merely there to convey character exposition and chorus like perspectives. Paul Richards, as the school shrink, gives a churlish performance. Dana Wynter-smug and repressed-is the head school mistress who also happens to be Paul's aunt and the lover of the shrink.

The score is basically one song redone in various moods and tempos. It's a bad song from the start, so using it to convey mood is a lost cause because it only adds to the drab pace of the film. It is by veteran composer Raoul Krasshaur, who wrote the music for *Invaders from Mars* and the two Abbott and Costello television theme songs among other fine film scores. There is no trace of the old inventiveness in his score for *Triangle*.

Luckily, for stars of Ray Danton's generation, there was an offshoot of the Seventies auxiliary wing of nostalgia: Made-for-TV Movies. They were filmed on videotape and often starred former screen heavyweights and exciting newcomers. They were also a safe haven and welcome reprise for bygone stars and second bananas.

Ray Danton's television movies, for the most part, are farcical, the exception being *Banyon* ('71). *Banyon* was an excellent homage to the hard boiled and West Coast detective genres. Most made-for-television nods to the past were clichéd, derivative, and formulaic. Was *Banyon* clichéd? To a certain degree, it was. Did it appear derivative? At times, it did. Did it seem formulaic? In the sense that you knew what was coming. Was it a bomb? No-in fact, *Banyon* is a well-made and entertaining period piece.

Miles Banyon (Robert Banyon) is a laconic private eye framed for the murder of Irene Fortolla (Deidre Daniels), a mobster's ex-paramour, after

As Victor Pappas, a vengeful mobster recently released from prison, Ray Danton has a brief scene making a phone call to Banyon His presence is felt throughout the film until his reappearance as a still life at the end of the film. 1971, Warner Bros. Television.

the woman's corpse is found in his office. The mobster is Victor Pappas (Ray Danton), recently released from prison. Although seldom seen, he is the topic of the first half of the movie. Several characters fear retribution for helping to send him to prison. In the end, the assumption is a false one and the much-feared gangster turns out to be a dupe.

Irene Fortolla was led to believe that she was to be reunited with Pappas by Lou Moran (Ned Glass), a kindly older man who treats the woman like his niece until it is apparent that he has set her up for a mob hit. He drives her to the office building and gives her an office number. Irene rides the elevator and enters the office where a creepy looking man (Carl Horner [Joseph Ruskin]) looks at her from behind a desk and says, "You must be the one." He takes a revolver hidden by a newspaper and shoots the woman. Leaving the office, he strips the phony address that hid Banyon's name and office number on the frosted glass.

The detective on the scene is Lt. Pete Cordova (Darren McGavin), Banyon's ex-partner on the force and current nemesis. Cordova knows that Banyon was framed and believes that it is retribution and payback on behalf of Victor Pappas because the victim and the private eye were instrumental in providing incriminating evidence during his trial.

Banyon is drawn into a dark labyrinth of betrayal and misinformation. One of his benefactors in the case is Lee Jennings (Jose Ferrer), a bellicose radio commentator fashioned after Walter Winchell. Jennings hated Pappas and used his radio broadcasts to crucify the mobster. Now, he is prepared to aid Banyon in his quest for justice. Little does the detective know that Jennings is not on the level or that payback is the price for having a beautiful and coquettish wife, Diane (Anjanette Comer). It takes courage and perseverance for Banyon to scoop Lee Jennings on his own story before he turns the broadcaster into the mourning headlines.

What makes *Banyon* work so well is that it is a movie-of-the week that has the spit and polish of the original genre films that it emulates. Robert Day's direction is tight and so is the editing. The cinematography successfully translates the harsh black and white reality of *noir* to color. The music is topical; so are a few references that may be self-conscious but that adds flavor to this timepiece. The script is rehashed clichés but they are refreshed by the professionalism of the actors and the technical crew.

Miles Banyon is one the many descendants of Sam Spade. He may be retrograde but he can pull his own weight. The facial resemblance between Robert Forster and John Garfield is apparent from the start. The resemblance ends once Forster begins to act because he has a style all his own.

Sardonic and straight to the point with a touch of humor to lighten the load, Forster's detective is a survivor with the strength to carry the weight of his past. Banyon is the innocent outsider drawn into a web of deceit. It is his task to find the truth in a lake of red herrings. He is constantly being led into the wrong direction but a series of false trails ultimately leads him to an honest conclusion.

Robert Forster shines as Miles Banyon, the sullen private investigator framed for murder. Darren MacGavin, Jose Ferrer and Anjanette Comer give solid performances as an intrepid detective, a blustery radio commentator and his flirtatious wife. Banyon and MacGavin are former partners with an uneasy alliance, one based on mutual feelings of betrayal. They are nemeses' because of past departmental discipline.

Jose Ferrer adds spit and polish to his arrogant and aggressive radio commentator. He has the power to make and break men but one man who cannot even bend is Banyon. He can't even frame him or have him erased from the case.

Anjanette Comer is everything that you would expect the femme fatale to be in a murder-mystery. She is the cause of it all which is a labyrinthine who-done-it? not planned and carried out in the name of honor and chivalry but as a cover-up for the price of infidelity.

Banyon (Robert Forster) is caught in a maze of frozen ice as a jealous gigolo targets the detective for imagined indiscretions.
1971, Warner Bros. Television.

Herb Edelman and Leslie Parrish add touches of vulnerability and loss as Ruth and Harry Sprague, an unhappy couple with close ties to Banyon. He is Banyon's reluctant leg man and she still wishes that it was the private eye's yellow band that she was wearing. Hermoine Gingold has a charming minor role as Peggy Revere, the owner of a temporary secretary agency where Banyon recruits his interns and Ned Glass has a sinister bit part as Lou Moran, a sweet admirer of the woman he sets up for the hit that opens the movie. Stanley Adams also has a part as a gruff voiced auctioneer.

Ray Danton has a small role as Victor Pappas, a mobster recently released from prison and the subject of paranoid concern involving the people who help to send him up the river. He is subject to be feared but a red herring in the end. Pappas is only shown in two scenes; he is breathing in one of them. This fleeting appearance was Ray Danton's return to Warner Brothers and American television.

Danton's role as Victor Pappas in *Banyon* is minimal but the film is so good that it's a plus among his work. As Victor Pappas, Danton has two brief scenes: in a short but threatening phone call to Banyon and doing a lifeless facedown recline in a drained indoor swimming pool at an upstate mansion hideaway. Danton's character is the victim of Carl Horner, a hit man played by Joseph Ruskin. Tens years earlier, Ruskin played Matt Moran, Arnold Rothstein's bodyguard in *The Rise and Fall of Legs Diamond*. His services were terminated by Ray Danton's star turn. Now, Joseph Ruskin returned the favor.

The next television movie was a transition from the hard-boiled West coast shamus to the tenacious spinster sleuth in a revival of the Hildegarde Withers character created by Stuart Palmer. Hildegarde Withers is an inquisitive battle ax who fancies herself an amateur detective. Not content to intrude on the mundane affairs of her friends and neighbors, she spends her time annoying the local police captain, Oscar Piper for clues and information about odd cases that interest her.

The character originated in novels but was the basis for six movies during the 1930's with Edna May Oliver, Helen Broderick and Zasu Pitts taking turns as the sleuth and James Gleason as the raspy inspector. ABC had visions of re-launching the character for a television series and they tested the waters with a television movie with Eve Arden as the amateur detective and James Gregory as Piper.

This time around, it's a missing person case that emerges in the middle of a seemingly unrelated murder case. It appears that the missing

Eve Arden took her bow as one of the actresses to play Hildegarde Withers, Stuart Palmer's inquisitive amateur sleuth. 1972, Universal Television Prod.

person knew the murder victim, Captain Westering (Ray Danton). The captain is a guru without the long beard, clinking love beads and flowing robes. Instead, he is dressed like a traditional yachtsman with cap, Navy blue blazer and gray knit turtleneck sweater.

He is the captain of a yacht named *Karma* and is spearheading an ocean pilgrimage to a new age Eden. Before his dream is realized, Captain Westering is poisoned by one of his groupies. Hildegarde Withers badgers the suspects and Captain Piper until she gets the right pieces to solve her puzzle.

A Very Missing Person is like a lot of the television movies of the early 70's: full of stereotypical roles played by familiar faces. Eve Arden is persistent and James Gregory acts irritated as Hildegarde Withers and Captain Piper, respectively. Julie Newmar is beautiful and mercurial as Althea, the murder victim's wife. She is the one who wears the robes in the family when she is not busy working as a *maitre de* at a local restaurant. Ray Danton is the charming rogue, Captain Westering, and Pat Morita plays one of the mindless hippies that comprise his entourage.

Captain Westering has a few scenes in *A Very Missing Person* before he drinks poisoned wine in the Hildegarde Withers mystery. He is a yachtsman with a utopian bent and a crew of hippies at his command. They are ready to embark on a voyage that will establish a tropical Utopia. It is an interesting, if brief, role because it is so odd.

Westering is dressed in the traditional yachtsman's outfit and has a combative attitude yet he is a guru to a group of peace loving droids blindly following his terse commands. He is poisoned because of love, not animosity.

A Very Missing Person was part of a proposed rotating series of popular detectives that included Sherlock Holmes (Stewart Granger),

Captain Westering may dress like a traditional yachtsman but he commands a Utopian bound hippie commune. 1972, Universal Television Prod.

Nick Carter (Robert Conrad) and Charlie Chan (Ross Martin) but the TV movies did not garner satisfactory ratings.

Runaway is a modest thriller about a trainload of collegiate and faculty returning from a ski holiday. Their train has lost control and careens through the snowy mountainscape. The movie consists of the actors dealing with the crisis as rescuers try to save them.

Holly Gibson (Ben Johnson) is on his last run and he starts it by lovingly admiring the train's path through the snow covered mountains. The tracks have taken him to places that make up the stories of his life. He would stay five more years if he wouldn't lose the benefits that come with retiring now. The crisis makes him love his job more because it gives him the makings of the final story of his lore. The other stories belong to the generic characters that comprise the passengers on the doomsday train.

Macho Pop (Martin Milner) and his son face their final moments in heated confrontation. Pop can't accept his boy's disinterest in the manly arts, especially hunting and rejects the child's claim that it takes a different kind of courage to act on stage, which is something he enjoys doing. The stage is not an option for Macho Pop.

A middle age couple (Ed Nelson and Vera Miles) face a crisis for people of their generation: impending divorce. It was the beginning in

The philandering Professor Dunn (Ray Danton) confronts his mortality as the runaway train gains speed on icy tracks that lead through a mountain canyon. 1972, Universal Television Prod.

Holly Gibson (Ben Johnson) ends his last run on a heroic note, ensuring that a steel rail legend will grow up around him. 1972, Universal Television Prod.

the tearing of the marriage vows and such a decision required deep soul searching. They try to formulate a way to break the news to their daughter. The train ride is time spent reflecting the ups and downs of their marriage.

A young Romeo (Ben Murphy) rides for free and has his confident façade shatter as the drama intensifies. He refuses to help the others fortify the train for a possible collision; instead, he hides in rack full of luggage that he hopes will cushion the impact.

A co-ed (Darleen Carr) is suicidal because she was the holiday conquest of Professor Dunn (Ray Danton, who no longer wants any contact with her. Impending doom makes everyone re-consider their lives and the heroes and cowards emerge.

The movie clearly belongs to Ben Johnson, the conductor whose task it is to tame the runaway train. He walks away with the honor of giving an excellent performance. He keeps the train on track as an old buddy (Judson Pratt) prepares to catch up with the train at the intersection and couple with it to bring it to a halt.

The young stars of the time played the college students, the main players being Ben Murphy, Darleen Karr and Kip Niven. Stars from better times are Martin Milner, Vera Miles, Ed Nelson and Judson Pratt, whose small part is vital in the heroic rescue effort. Ray Danton plays a philandering professor whose icy rebuff makes his student conquest consider suicide by railway. It is a brief and thankless part, one that is buried beneath the psycho-drama of the other characters.

THE NEW AGE TECHNICOLOR HIPSTER

One of the escape clauses of the 70's television entertainment industry was its tendency to recycle the Late Show universe for television shows with traditional tried-and-true plots and syndromes. The motion picture industry of the 1970's may have had contempt for the Old Guard but the era's television schedule is where the familiar faces from the past appeared in shows that were cotton candy versions of a bygone cinema.

Ray Danton continued to appear in American living rooms via television appearances. He started the decade in earnest, giving well-rounded performances in popular shows like *The F.B.I., Hawaii 5-0, Nichols, McCloud* and *Night Gallery*. By mid-decade, he had become typecast as a stock mob heavy who snarled, made faces and swore oaths of vengeance on shows like *Police Story, Switch, The Rockford Files,* and *Barnaby Jones*.

Kane Walker and Joe Melchior are the *alpha* and *omega* of Ray Danton's 70s' bunco artist. Walker is the new age Narcissus whose mirror is his source of delusion. Joe Melchior is the *macho* man as Prometheus-a bringer of fire and prisoner of conceit.

The stories and blackouts of *Love American Style* were usually lighthearted and hardly taxing to the mind and nervous system; not so with *Love and Mr. Nice Guy* ('70).

The skit, although punctuated with generous spurts of canned laughter, is mean-spirited and depressing. This strange episode seems dramatic today. The most disconcerting thing about the playlet is the abundance of laughter. It is a mix of mirth and de Sade.

Erica (Alexandra Hay) is an insecure, self-hating woman who is irresistibly attracted to abusive men. It is nerve-wrenching to listen to her self-loathing monologues that find approval with a boisterous laugh track.

Kane Walker is the swaggering hipster at the dawn of the Seventies: Caesar-style haircut, California tan, bare chest and medallion, crushed blue velvet bathrobe and peach-colored bell-bottomed pants. He is trained in martial arts and is the classic playboy, replete with a philosophy that

Kane Walker (Ray Danton) assumes a martial arts stance to intimidate the mild-mannered Peter (Wally Cox), who becomes an Alpha male when he heeds the hipster's sage advice. 1970, ABC (American Broadcasting System).

has guided his successful life.

Peter (Wally Cox) is a milquetoast who believes that kindness and restraint will make a favorable impression on the scatterbrained Erica. Kane regards Peter's concern as a total misunderstanding of Erica's personality. He believes that she, too, has a sickness because she likes mean guys. Kane disassembles Peter's conceit with a simple question: "Who would you rather be: me or you?"

It is a question that transforms Peter into a low-rent Kane Walker. Surprisingly, this works because Erica has an epiphany and becomes enflamed with passion for the transformed Peter. She explains this to him and Peter reacts with the cool, detached manner of the playboy who has heard it all before.

As feminist perspectives began to change sexual perceptions, the mean-spirited *macho* man was now seen as a buffoon who deserved to pay a price for his arrogance. Ray Danton continued to play aggressive lover boys, only now they paid a price for their indiscretions. A case in point is Joe Melchior in *Night Gallery: Miracle at Camafeo* ('72).

Night Gallery is a supernatural anthology series hosted by Rod Serling, who occasionally wrote scipts for the show. Unfortunately, it never got the full credit it deserved because it had to immediately live up to the reputations of *The Twilight Zone* and Serling's classics from the live-TV era of the 50's. That's two generation of critics that probably didn't have warm feelings for anything beyond *Your Hit Parade* and black and white Philcos. Fortunately, new generations of fans were created by cable television runs and DVD availability of this well made thriller anthology.

In *The Miracle at Camafeo* ('72), an insurance investigator (Harry Guardino) suspects fraud in the paralysis case of Joe Melchior (Ray Danton). Melchior had successfully collected an insurance reward and has come to Camafeo to seek a cure for his burden.

The investigator questions his wife Gay Melchior (Julie Adams) in the bar downstairs. He refers to the throng of penitents who crawl or are brought to the chapel to pray for Blessed Mother's grace. One of them is a

Joe Melchior has finally made it to a shrine of his own making in a remote Mexican villa. The Sun King will bless him with riches that will blind him. 1972, Universal Television.

mother who has brought her blind son. He tries to make Mrs. Melchior feel guilty, something that she is afraid to express because of her husband's explosive anger.

Joe Melchior is mean-spirited because of his cockiness. His notion cannot go wrong because his arrogance is supposed to be a fuel for his desire to have it all. He plans to use the annual pilgrimage to the healing site of Camafeo to end his confinement. Fate has other ideas for him and his cure will also be his curse.

He is going up against a power he doesn't believe exists. His fate is one of the best comeuppances for a Danton conniver. To mock the spirits is one thing; to trivialize the faith of his fellow penitents is another.

The shot of a panic stricken blank-eyed Melchior is the perfect publicity shot of the disco hustler's exchange rate for pain. He is bewildered and doesn't have a clue to the enormity of his curse. He is not even able to see the miracle of the blind child who has regained his sight.

Before settling into the new disco cool attitude of the decade, Ray Danton essayed one more thoughtful western role as an Apache at the dawn of industrial America. *Nichols: Deer Crossing* ('71), takes place in the turn-of-the century West. Ray Danton plays Juan Garcia, an Apache who challenges federal hunting ordinances. Juan Garcia is an Apache ostracized from his tribe because his wife is not an Indian. He matches wits with a spoiled town braggart in hunting a buck they believe they have the rights to bag. Juan Garcia trumps the conventions of two worlds by remaining steadfast to the law of his soul.

Nichols was a unique western starring James Garner in the title role. He plays a war-weary veteran soldier who refuses to re-up. Anxious to start life over again, he returns to his home place, the town that bears his birth name because it was founded by his father. Nichols is an unwanted stranger in the town that bears his name. It is now owned by Ma Ketchum (Neva Patterson), an ornery cuss of a woman with a strong sense of fair play.

It is her soft spot for her only son, Ketchum (John Beck), that allows him to run wild like a spoiled brat. He makes many enemies that are powerless to do anything about it. The only person who is not intimidated is Nichols, who has to prove his mettle when he raise everyone's ire with his individualistic independent personality.

It does not matter because Nichols is an honest maverick who earns Ma Ketchum's approval and that is why she makes him sheriff. He accepts the job on his own terms and they are that he does not uses a side arm and he can leave anytime he wants to.

These conditions are one reason why Nichols was so unique. Another reason is that it was played out in 1914, when the Old West was dying and being transformed by the Industrial Revolution. That is one reason why Nichols rides a newfangled motorbike instead of a horse. There were other reasons that made this show unique and that was its grim tone and unusual lack of close-ups and traditional mood music.

Juan Garcia is an outcaste of two worlds as he tries to find a place in the world for his family in *Nichols: Deer Crossing*. 1971, Cherokee Productions, Warner Brothers Television.

The show only lasted one season, which had nothing to do with lack of quality. It was just the opposite because the show was unique. It still featured a charming leading character by James Garner but it was fine tuned to an eccentric perspective, possibly due to the anti-authoritarian and contra-traditionalist moods fostered by the unpopular Vietnam War.

Ray Danton starred as Juan Garcia in *Deer Crossing*, one of his rare full-bodied characters during the 1970's. Other than the *Nichols* role, Ray Danton's other 70's parts were heavies. His occasional leading role always guaranteed an excellent portrayal of the character. Juan Garcia is a loner who still lives by Apache law even though the Apache nation no longer exists. He is a man caught between two worlds: he has taken a non-Indian for a wife and he lives with his family on the outskirts of town. This does not bode well with the white man's law nor does it sit well with the Apache way of life.

Juan Garcia's only ally is Nichols, another anachronism. The new breed of western lawman belongs to the old West because of his character and gumption and his sympathy for Garcia inspires a plan that indicts Ketchum for violating hunting laws and paves the way for the Apache to lay claim to the buck when he has the hunting grounds all to himself.

Nichols tries to dissuade Juan Garcia from hunting until the season begins. He will arrest him, if only to protect him from the newly arrived Marshal Durand (Gene Evans). Juan's Apache pride bolsters his determination to bag the deer.

A battle of wits follows. Mitch (Stuart Margolin), Nichols' dim-witted and treacherous deputy, deputizes Ketchum's debtors and turns them into a drunken mob of blood thirsty louts. They aim to patrol the forest and prevent Juan Garcia from hunting out of season. Marshal Durand disapproves of Ketchum's and Mitch's ill intentions but is powerless to stop the mob because they are now legal game wardens. The marshal warns the mob that they better stay within the law.

The lynch mob's hysteria is cooled when Ketchum becomes entranced by the deer sighting. He loses his composure and fires, narrowly missing the buck, who stalks off into the forest. Marshal Durand rescinds his deputy commission and arrests him. The mob loses its enthusiasm and disperses, electing to go into town and continue their imbibing.

In the end, Juan Garcia will win the battle for the buck. None of the townsfolk will hunt the deer out of fear of Ketchum and no reservation Indian will stalk the buck out of fear of Juan Garcia. Marshal Durand has suspended Ketchum's hunting license and Juan will have the hunting ground all to himself.

Three television performances set the tone for Ray Danton's career for the rest of the 70's. He has a supporting role in *Dan August: The Color of Fury*, a lead role in *F.B.I.: The Inheritors* and a small part in *The Young Lawyers: And the Walls Came Tumbling Down*.

Burt Reynolds was an established television star before he became a screen sensation in the 70's. He first appeared on *Riverboat* with Darren MacGavin and starred in *Hawk*, a cop drama. *Dan August* was another cop drama produced by Quinn Martin. The opening credits were indicative of 70's television, full of shots of the star jumping over cars, sliding across floors and chasing criminals. All that was missing were the freeze-frames that became popular later in the decade.

Dan August: The Color of Fury dramatizes the antagonism between the Italian-American community and African-American community. Each claims that the other is encroaching on their rights and are taking what does not belong to them. Simmering tension reaches a rolling boil when an Italian councilman's sister is murdered and the prime suspect is a strident black activist.

The Color of Fury is a heated melodrama that succeeds as a period piece on race politics. It was made in 1970 when the effects of the 60's revolution was still in full swing. This episode is an example of television's rare honesty at the time in dealing with the race dilemma, something it ignored before and soft-peddled afterwards.

It was not unusual to see characters based on the Black Panthers and other revolutionary types anxious to break away from docile subservient stereotypes. Raymond St. Jacques plays Jimmy Barlow as a man against the system. He looks at black cops, lawyers and reporters as being Uncle Toms even though they would not be considered so today. Still, this was 1970 and things were still raw so everything outside of the ghetto was enemy territory for Barlow and to his supporters.

That is why Dan August is considered a white honky pig, along with his sidekicks, Sgt. Charles Wilentz (Norman Fell) and Sgt. Joe Rivera (Ned Romano). The only sympathetic white face in the crowd is Chief George Untermeyer (Richard Anderson) and that is only because he doesn't want to start a riot in the ghetto.

The Italian-American community is portrayed as working class thugs. Are they racist louts or independent-minded people who refuse to pay for America's racist policies? Nehemiah Persoff plays a tolerant councilman who turns into a militant himself when his district becomes a crime zone. He is viewed with suspicion because he has trained his community to fight back.

Ray Danton plays Andriotti, a scheming aide who despises the "black commandoes." He once served time for trying to bribe Barlow to take a dive. He is hounded by the cops but they relent when they realize he is not the murderer. They don't know if he is a racist or just unafraid of threats to his community.

There appears to be no right or wrong as both groups struggle to survive. One group wants to maintain its independence; the other group is trying to gain a stronghold long since denied them by an exclusionary system.

The system that was at fault works when it exonerates Barlow and incarcerates Cassoni. The militant gains legitimacy and the community icon is disgraced. It does not matter to Barlow, he still refuses to drop to his knees in appreciation to the man. Nothing has changed as far as he is concerned and that just burns up Dan August and his boys.

Ray Danton next role is one of his best 70's characters, one of the leads in *The F.B.I.: The Inheritors*, a tale of two grifters who cancel out each other. *The F.B.I.* was a hit show produced by Quinn Martin and it ran from 1965 to 1974. It starred Efrem Zimbalist, Jr as Inspector Erskine.

Glen Frye (Ray Danton) and Temple Alexander (Suzanne Pleschette) are a pair of con artists who parted on bad terms many years earlier. On the lam for a con turned bad, Frye catches up to Alexander when she is about to marry Harlan Franciscus (Gene Raymond), a wealthy winery magnate. It is a May-December romance, something that concerns the son (Larry Linville). They make a pleasant couple and it seems that they can be happy with each other. It all unravels when Frye shows up and demands a piece of the action.

The episode opens with Frye and his partner busted in the middle of a stocks scam. They exit the premises through a window and drive away. Frey leaves his partner stranded in the middle of an inter-state highway when he asks him to check out a possible defective tire.

He re-enters Alexander's life and tries to cut himself in on the deal. Her love for her prospective husband prevents Frye from doing much damage outside of exposing her.

The more Temple tries to assuage Frey's hunger, the more she implicates herself through association. The F.B.I. men catch up to Frye as he is trying to squeeze Temple for the last time and she is arrested only because she was at the wrong place at the wrong time. Frye is shot in a confrontation with Inspector Erskine, who does not want to hear Franciscus' starry-eyed dissertation on Temple's genuine need for him.

Temple Alexander (Suzanne Pleschette) sees her future disappear when Glenn Frye (Ray Danton) outlines how he will take a percentage of her impending marriage to a wealthy wine grower. 1970, Quinn Martin Productions.

Glenn Frye is one of Danton's best defined 70's roles, mainly because he is still connected to the suave and urbane hustler that he originated in the 50's. He is sharp and lethal as a high stakes con man. Frye is a sophisticated smoothie who becomes too bold when he raises the stakes to settle an old time betrayal.

He is notorious for double crossing partners and it is rare that someone gets the upper hand on him. That someone was Temple Alexander, who got Frye to front her $10,000 for a scheme that ended with him left holding an empty bag. Frye is willing to forgive so long as he can ride the new gravy train. He shows up unexpectedly but intrudes when he passes himself off as Temple's brother at her engagement announcement.

Ray Danton's appearance on *The Young Lawyers* is the first of a series of thankless parts he played on television and in low-budget films: the murder victim. *The Young Lawyers* was another show that reflected the social sensitivities of the 70's generation. Equal justice for all was a theme that carried over from the turbulent 60's. David Barrett (Lee J. Cobb) is a wizened vet who set up a law firm in Boston to help the indigent and the helpless. He is assisted by two young lawyers played by Zalman King and Judy Pace.

In *And the Walls Came Tumbling Down*, Ray Danton plays Josh Ferris an over-the-hill singer who speaks like a 50's beatnik. He is annoying and grates on the nerves, especially when he tries to dominate a young woman who eventually is accused of murdering him. Danton appears at the beginning of the episode and is also represented by a pair of plaid legs stretched out on the floor behind a chair after his demise. That is the extent of his appearance. Julie Adams also appeared in the episode in a larger part.

The counterpoint of the 50's and 60's continental hipster was the 70's disco king. Ray Danton's 70's characters still had that razor sharp ruthlessness and grating persistence when it came to business. Three characters that are the perfect cross section of his new style appeared in three episodes of *Hawaii Five-0*.

Jimmy Nuanu in *The Last Eden*, Fred Akaimi Loy in *Cloth of Gold*, and Ron Colby in *Steal Now...Pay Later*, exemplify the disco king on different power trips. Two of the parts, Jimmy Nuanu and Ron Colby, are lead roles divided between heroics and villainy. The third, Fred Akaimi Loy, is a loathsome supporting character with a built-in demise.

Hawaii Five-0 was a very successful police drama that ran for twelve years. The colorful Hawaiian scenery and the excellent stories and guest stars were big factors in the show's success but it was the stoical personality of the show's star, Jack Lord as Steve McGarrett, that gave the show its unique dimension.

His sidekick was played by James MacArthur as Danny Williams, often referred to as Danno. The show also had a dynamic nemesis, the noxious Wo-Fat (Khigh Dhiegh), a Red Chinese operative, who periodically popped up from time to time to make things difficult for McGarrett.

In *The Last Eden*, Jimmy Nuanu is a popular nightclub entertainer who lectures his audiences about environmental issues. His lament is that the Hawaiian Islands are a paradise endangered by land developers. The management of the Canoe House at the Ilikai Hotel doesn't appreciate Nuanu's heavy-handed philosophy; neither does land developer Walter Colfax (Paul Stevens).

Colfax plans to take over the island's waste management business, which doesn't sit too well with the outspoken nightclub entertainer. Nuanu uses the spots between his songs to zing Colfax, which makes him the perfect fall guy for a Colfax scheme. The industrial plant is blown up by a saboteur. Nuanu is arrested at the scene of his crime. The detonating caps found in the trunk of his Rolls Roycer incriminate him, as does his war time demolitions record.

Jimmy Nuanu (Ray Danton) is an ecology-minded nightclub entertainer who is framed for murder and industrial sabotage. 1970, Quinn Martin Productions.

Jimmy Nuanu is behind bars and even Steve McGarrett doesn't know how to read him. Nuanu tries to assuage the cop's anger with schoolboy humor but the detective is unmoved, even when he finds out about the mangled corpse in the wreckage.

McGarrett's scrutiny uncovers a setup and a double cross.

The role of Jimmy Nuanu is one of Ray Danton's last good parts. It retains all of his old flair. The only difference is the 70's look. The caliber of his performance prevents the look from being comical. Jimmy Nuanu is a credible Seventies Hawaiian performer and the new look is perfect for the part.

Nuanu's anti-establishment attitude makes him topical. It was a time when social relevance meant that being a saloon singer wasn't enough. An entertainer had to be a social philosopher as well. Ray Danton varies his performance, from loving father and loyal friend to vicious brawler and angry revenge seeker.

His next character-Fred Akaimi Loy-is anything but loving and loyal. His disguise is a deadpan expression, dry humor and masked shades. The abrasive Loy is one of a trio of doomed swingers in *Cloth of Gold* ('71), a pointed commentary on the Seventies' lascivious side. It is a horror story whose mood is enhanced by eerie underwater photography and weird sound effects.

Ralph Mingo (Jay Robinson), Fred Akaimi Loy, and Wallis (Jason Evers) are a trio of sleaze merchants. They peddle cheap thrills and accept total subservience as payment for their services. Their daylight cover is a real estate outfit that sells worthless island real estate based on impressive but misleading videos and sales pitches. They are bunco artists whose success has led to excess and arrogant hedonism.

Their island empire begins to crumble at Mingo's birthday party. A pall is cast on the festive mood, which turns to terror when Mingo suffers convulsions. The crowd is helpless to assist the old man, whose grimaces and death chortles seem amusing compared with his brash behavior moments earlier. Everyone is stunned by Ralph Mingo's sudden death.

5-0 is mystified by his strange death. They don't get much cooperation from the dead man's partners, Loy and Wallis. Loy is openly hostile to the police, as he is with everyone else, except his bimbos. He is cold and hides his eyes behind island shades.

Loy is contemptuous of Wallis, who believes that one of them is next to die. His fear is tantamount to cowardice in Loy's eyes. Splitting

Fred Akaimi Loy shows his contempt for the "fuzz" by ridiculing them in front of his sycophants. He didn't count on the Cloth of Gold. 1972, Quinn Martin Productions.

up Mingo's share doesn't appear to be a hardship to him. To celebrate his increase in wealth, Loy takes dip in the ocean with two lovelies. The next morning, he is found dead and sitting up in bed with his hands around his own throat.

Fred Akaimi Loy belongs to Danton's list of doomed swingers. Loy acts like he is invincible. Nothing will stand in the way of enjoying the good life. He didn't count on the Cloth of Gold, a poisonous gastropod used by the butler to polish off the business associates.

The butler holds them responsible for corrupting his daughter and driving her to commit suicide. That is his way out when he uses the mollusk on himself as McGarrett closes in on him after a sea chase that follows the murder of Wallis. The butler, having exacted his revenge on the trio, tumbles and sinks in the ocean as he is caught in a dreamy prismatic blue freeze frame.

Ray Danton's last meaty role of the 70's lacks any positive character traits, too; that's why grand larceny and murder are Ron Colby's specialties in *Steal Now...Pay Later* ('73).

Colby is a shark in the wholesale business. His bootlegging operation leaves no trails and evidence is something that is impossible to find. Tax free profits provide the thrill that energizes him. He runs his company from his poolside, using a mechanized punch-card phone that can't be traced.

Hijacking made-to-order is his business style and no questions asked is the no return policy his buyers agree to. It is an operation micro-managed by Colby and made to be as real as an invoice but untraceable due to multiple storage spots leased under different names.

The murder of a federal agent and the use of one of Colby's hot refrigerators as a deep sea coffin provide leads for McGarrett and 5-0. A small fish about to be fried will be the lure that brings Colby in. It wouldn't be a classic Ray Danton role if there wasn't a small fish at the end of his hook.

In this case, it is Mr. Swift (Casey Kasem), a jobber excited by the low prices and high quality of Colby's merchandise. After Swift brings his uncle into the scam, everything turns sour when 5-0 traces a lot of stolen swimwear to the uncle, who is killed in a guilt-induced panic attack. In a sting operation orchestrated by McGarrett and the 5-0 team, the small fish reels in Colby.

Ron Colby is slicker than his loud colored clothes, one of the garish aspects of Seventies' style. An amusing thing about this episode is the

Ron Colby's phantom factory vanishes when he gets busted in the electronics section of a real time department store. 1974, Quinn Martin Productions.

parties Colby throws for his jobbers. They are a kaleidoscope of paisley prints, polyester leisure suits and blow-dried toupees. In Colby, Danton finds a balance of the decade's traits. He is a hustler, a profiteer, a player and a crook.

This episode has unintentional references to Danton's previous work. The hijacking-fence operation is as slippery as the counterfeiting ring in *Outside the Law* ('56). Colby surrounds himself with sexy young women like Martinelli in *Jamaica Calling, Mr. Ward* ('68). He assumes Magnus Repp's deadpan expression, dry humor and masked shades in the interrogation scene with McGarrett. The only thing missing is Collin Maese's attitude and a half. McGarrett's style is soft and easy but heavy on the justice.

Indies, Vampires, Radio and the Stage

The Seventies was a time to step outside of the box because of necessity. There was a resistance from the industry to Ray Danton's attempt to resume his acting career on the same professional level that he left it when he made the switch to the European film industry. He had co-directed and co-produced some of his European movies so it was not a stretch or him to broaden his behind the scenes talent.

Ray Danton directed a couple of movies stateside and in Europe during the early 1970's. The most widely distributed European film directed by him is the sociopath-kidnap melodrama, *Senza Via D'Uscita*. It was produced by Pierluigi Torri for his wife, Marisa Mell and distributed by Ray Danton's film company, American Motion Pictures of Italy. Marisa Mell recommended Ray Danton as the director because she remembered the actor's aspiration to become one when they filmed *Secret Agent Super Dragon*.

The *giallo* was an Italio-Franco-Spanish production and Ray Danton received director's credit under the actor Piero Sciume's name because Italian film unions forbade foreigners from working on films made in the country. As was the case with many multi-national films, the movie was released under a variety of titles. It was called *Las Fotos De Una Mujer Decente* in Spain, *La Machination* in France, *Terrari* in Finland and *No Way Out* in England. The movie was released in the United States under two different titles, *Homicidal* and *The Devil's Ransom*.

Gilbert (Phillipe Leroy) and Michele (Marisa Mell) are a married couple whose staid and boring life is interrupted by the abduction of their son. The first odd twist to the plot is that the kidnappers are the illicit lovers of the couple. Kurt (Roger Hanin) is a down-on-his luck photographer who is too bold for his own good. He is a psycho who once romanced the wife on a summer vacation. Britt (Lea Massari) is his girlfriend while not being the paramour of Gilbert, a stone-faced man who works as a courier for a prestigious banking firm managed by a stern mannered man named Bergman (George Rigaud).

In the long run, they are not what they appear to be and that is what gives the movie its demented perspective. The movie, for the most part, is anti-septic like the couple's life and the atmosphere of the bank. The plot development is low-key with the usual ransom demands and scurrying for the payoff money. In between, there is the character exposition. The couple's conservative home life is contrasted with their kinky secret rendezvous'.

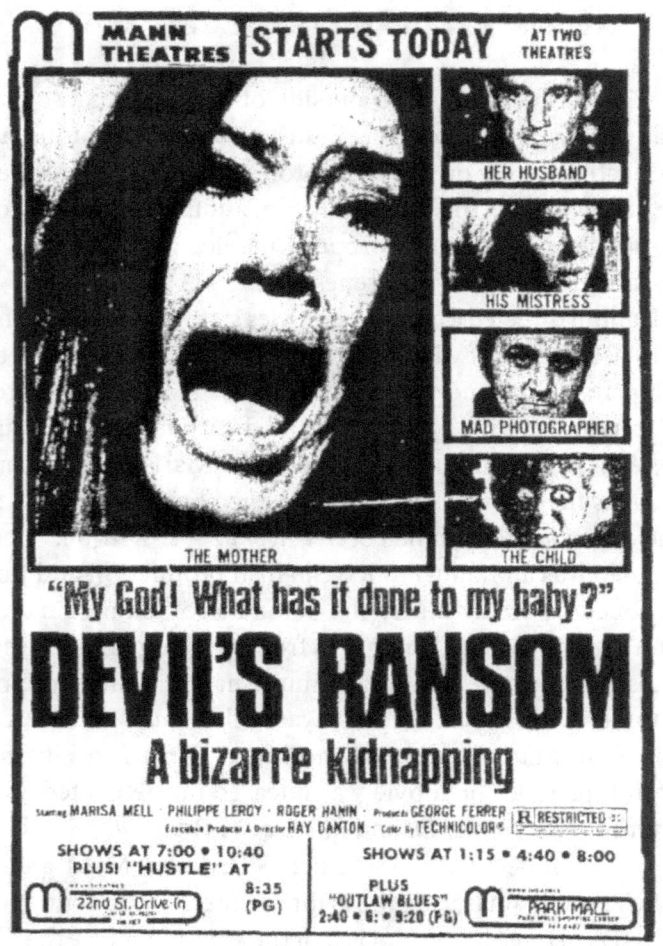

A poster for *The Devil's Ransom*, the United States version of *Senza Via D'Uscita*. 1970, American Motion Pictures of Italy.

The metallic ambience of the bank gives it a bunker quality as a militaristic sense of efficiency makes it an impenetrable defense. The same military tidiness disinfects the banker's home life and this creates an underworld for Michele to unleash her repressed desires. The movie has a chilling climax where Michele becomes a victim two times over and Kurt does not live to spend the ransom money. Only Gilbert and Britt get to share a train ride through flashbacks of the movie.

Senza Via D'Uscita is a delirious kidnap melodrama with wicked touches to it. It has some odd moments that elevate it from the usual Euro-crime dramas of the 70's.

Gilbert (Phillipe Leroy) and Michele (Marisa Mell) explain their problem to the boss, Mr. Bergman (George Rigaud). 1970, American Motion Pictures of Italy.

There are creepy touches to the movie, such as Michele's dreamy flashback sequence of her and her child at the beach. The shots are overexposed and set to a quiet music-box type of music. It is sad and poignant but not given a full gravitational effect until the ending, which adds a different and horrific meaning to the pounding surf.

Michele's unstable frame of mind is expressed through an interlude at the Kurt's studio. She is lured there by the photographer, who promises to reunite her with her boy. She is trapped by the glare of floodlights held by nude men before she is surrounded by a group of female mannequins. They trap the missus in their sights before they come to life to smother her with sweet regrets.

There is also an alluring S&M photography session with some breathtaking shots of Michele that are later used to bombard Gilbert with huge expectations of remorse in a showdown between him and Kurt. He enters her apartment after she has taken a sleeping pill and takes advantage of her lightheadedness by molesting her with his camera.

Gilbert has a mild breakdown of his own during a session at the bank's indoor firing range. He has to keep his shooting prowess up to par to deal with the dangers of his job as a courier. He is tense as he fires at filmed images of assailants trying to attack him. He starts the session with several bull's eye hits that eventually turn to misses as he thinks about

Only two of the players in an ill-fated triangle will survive to form a basis for an illicit union. 1970, American Motion Pictures of Italy.

his dilemma. He begins to unravel and his final shots are cancelled out by Michele's S 'n' M photos super-imposed over the images of his assailants.

Senza Via D'Uscita turns out to be a Chinese Puzzle Box of misinformation. It is not until the film's climax that the viewer realizes that every impression is false and that the movie is not really a kidnap melodrama, after all. To reveal more would be to spoil the stunning effect achieved by the denouement. The last two scenes redefine the characters and Gilbert's dream-flashback sequence offer the opportunity to relive the movie from another perspective.

The viewers' hatred for Kurt and sympathy for Gilbert will be transferred from one man to the other. Michele will be seen as fragile and delusional instead of nervous and distraught. Britt will no longer be a nondescript footnote to the men in her life because she is the underlying influence that defines them. The kidnapped child will become a phantasm flashback in every sense of the phrase.

Kurt is really an inept dupe and fits the puzzle as a kidnapper-lover-fall guy. He has taken S&M photos of Michele and blown them up in his studio. They are a conceit used against him. A bullet to the forehead is the basis for the final irony of having police photographer's shoot his corpse from several different angles.

The cross-cutting from his shooting death to the crime scene is agile and increases the tempo of his unexpected murder to a frenzied pace. Gilbert's false explanation of the blown-up photos to his boss indict his doomed wife as a co-conspirator to the final crime, which is viewed as a murder-suicide, the presumptive evidence of Michele's fall from grace.

This leaves Britt, who-until the ending-is a minor player. She seems to be a mindless plaything because she is the quiet lover of both men. This connection also links the men, enabling them to exchange destinies. Her brilliant deception enables her to disguise her fidelity and betrayal. She is the one who has been playing bait and switch all along, enabling her and Gilbert to rid themselves of their excess baggage, namely Michele and Kurt.

In 1970, Ray Danton directed his first film in America, *Deathmaster*, an A.I.P. horror film. Robert Quarry was the mastermind behind the movie and he served as the executive producer. He had starred in the wildly successful *Count Yorga*, a low budget film that made an astronomical amount of money during the first weekend of its release. It was his intention to make a vampire movie influenced by the sign of the times, namely Indian mysticism and the Charles Manson murder cult. The working title was *Vampire Guru* and he received the seed money from his business partner, Bill Sadroff.

Deathmaster is noteworthy because it is a product of its times, not only in sociological terms; it also serves as a primer for the 70's independent drive-in and grind house circuits. The movie was made in 17 days on a shoestring budget and includes stock elements of other drive-in genres, notably bikers and a mockery of kung-fu heroics.

Ray Danton was a friend of Robert Quarry and was engaged to direct the film, which was made in 1970 and sold to A.I.P. as a tax write-off for Sam Z. Arkoff, chief executive at American-International. Danton had just finished his European sojourn and was well-versed in the short schedule and grueling hours of making such exploitation films in Europe. Robert Quarry credits Jesus Franco (*Lucky the Inscrutable*) as being an inspiration for Ray Danton's workmanship.

Check out the deluxe DVD edition of *Deathmaster* if you would like to hear Robert Quarry's excellent recollections of the making the movie, including the daunting experience of signing a contract with Samuel Z. Arkoff, the controlling A.I.P. executive with the one-track mind. Arkoff was such a control freak that his contract with Quarry stipulated that he could not act as a vampire outside of the aegis of A.I.P. That quashed an offer to play the role of the vampire in the first *Night Stalker* movie, starring Darren MacGavin as Carl Kolchak. It was Arkoff's intention to groom Robert Quarry as the successor to Vincent Price's reign as A.I.P.'s horror maven. Unfortunately, the horror genre was about to go into one of its periodic slumber modes and this vision never materialized.

Taking place chiefly in a manor by the sea, *Deathmaster* is an atmospheric and claustrophobic period piece where 60's leftover space cadets become slaves to a vampire's curse. Robert Quarry plays Khorda, a charismatic vampire-guru who recruits the members of his coven from a

The DVD cover for *Deathmaster*. 1971, AIP.

small town's hippie community. He wears his hair long, sports a beard and goatee and dresses in flowing robes and custom-made sandals.

Robert Quarry hams it up in a mock-Shakespearean style calculated to impress his amateur co-stars. As a self-styled guru, he recites philosophical passages in a cultured voice. Because his coven consists of burnt out hippies, it doesn't take much to dumbfound them. Even a scene of him departing the room and vanishing into thin air isn't enough to alarm them. They are merely stunned as if they were experiencing an intriguing hallucination. Monk Reynolds (William Jordan) is a biker who is the only challenge to the vampire's game and he is summarily removed from the movie on a dark night.

Robert Quarry's portrayal of Khorda is, of course, the main attraction of the movie. His character is the most developed personality in the film, which is not surprising considering that he has been alive for centuries. Quarry's most effective scene is when Khorda relates the torture of being an nocturnal immortal after Pico (Bill Ewing), the film's protagonist, complains about the zeitgeist of being a mere human being.

Khorda replies that he measures time in centuries, not years and recounts the succession of tyrants and the mayhem they have caused around the globe. From Caesar and Attila the Hun to Hitler and Stalin, he has witnessed the vainglorious follies of human nature. Ray Danton focuses on a dimly lit profile of Khorda and Robert Quarry's acting does the rest.

The only question is why a world-weary traveler like Khorda would waste his time with a bunch of burnt-out airheads; but, then, that would take all of the fun out of the movie which, from a certain perspective, is an effective send-up of hippie culture. It parodies the parasitic nature of the flower power movement and exposes the sub-culture as the antitheses of what it purported to be.

Ray Danton directs his lead, Pico (Bill Ewing), in the party sequence when Khorda introduces himself and casts a spell over the hippies.
1971, AIP.

Count Khorda (Robert Quarry) loses a grip on the night life in the requisite death scene. 1971, AIP.

Deathmaster has all of the traits of a 70's low budget horror film: a novice director, amateur actors crowned by a lead who deserved better projects, and interesting bits that make the movie worth watching. In *Deathmaster*, the interesting bits are a zombie named Barbado (LeSesne Hilton), tribal dancing by the vampire's children, Grade Z transformation-to-ashes effects, and occasional mood shots of the beach, the manor and an underground cavern that give the movie a certain humor.

Barbado is a towering giant with an unkempt Afro and unsettling blank eyes almost reminiscent of the zombie movies of the 40's. He never speaks and always has a blank stare but his fellow hippies have no inkling of his weirdness. Khorda makes him his keeper and the flute-playing lackey keeps everyone in check because of his super-human strength. Outside of Khorda, he is the most interesting character in the film. One wished that he became the subject of his own series of films.

The coven dances in a free-form tribal style to mystical primal music played with flutes, cymbals and drums. It is one of their releases and they are in the middle of a number when they are transformed into ashes off screen. That is how the film's hero, Pico finds them after he kills Barbado and Korda in the movie's climatic confrontation.

The cinematography includes stunning shots of the beach, sunsets and an underground cavern where some of the action takes place. The movie begins with Barbado performing a ritual that guides Khorda's coffin ashore from a waterlogged journey before an ill-fated surfer finds it. There are many other fine shots of the beach at various times of the day. One of the most impressive shots is Barbado performing an arcane ceremony at sunset. According to Robert Quarry, the cavern was an underground escape hatch of a 1920's bootlegger. The star's account of camera placement to expand the depth of the cavern is an example of movie-making magic.

Extra attractions are leeches in a punch bowl, a desultory melodic score, a tough beer swilling biker and his sexy moll, plus a final-if brutal-remedy to John Fieldler. Also included are artsy pans, rotating effects and dissolves, and an odd folk song written by Ray Coniff.

The leeches are added for their blood lust and serve a purpose in annoying the hero and the villain. William Jordan gives a great performance as Monk Reynolds, a rough and tumble biker who embodies everything that is the polar opposite of the 60's. Betty Ann Rees is Esslin, his sexy and earthy biker chick. Rees had a respectable career during the 70's, including the cult classic *Sugar Hill*, and she is alluring as Khorda's first victim.

John Fielder is an anachronism as Pop, an oddball oldster who dresses in the shaggy style of the hippies. He runs the local arts and crafts shop with his beloved pooch, who later becomes a victim of the vampires. Although the credo of the 60's was not to trust anyone over 30, Pop gets the seal of approval from the kids. It's too bad, because he and his dog pay a dear price.

One of the hippies is Bobby 'Boris' Pickett, famous for his novelty record, "Monster Mash" in the early 60's. He sings the solemn "A Man Without a Vision", as he strums his guitar. The musical score was composed by Bill Marx, Harpo's son. It is a fine score and adds atmosphere

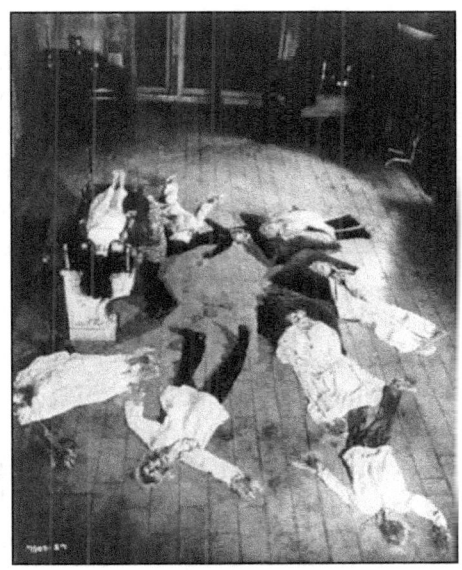

The count's coven of burnt out hippies become ashes and dust after their master is destroyed. 1971, AIP.

to the movie. He also scored the two Count Yorga flicks, among other 70's horror oddities.

This leaves the movie's antagonists, Pico (Bill Ewing) and Rona (Brenda Dickson), a young couple trying to figure out the meaning of life. He is overwhelmed by his existentialist dilemma but Rona is happy to be in love with him. He survives the carnage but not without getting the life's lessons that he yearned for. She is recruited into the coven of vampires and turns to ashes on a sacrificial altar after Khorda-her master- is destroyed by Pico, her lover. The movie ends on this downer.

In the film's commentary, Robert Quarry has high praise for Ray Danton, whom he calls "difficult, at times." That was nothing new, as just about everyone who worked with Ray Danton voiced the same sentiment. He had respect for his director, whom he called, "highly intelligent." He acknowledges that many people called him egotistical and claimed that this worked against him in the business. That was one reason why trying to reestablish himself in Hollywood during the 70's proved to be a dead end. It was industry payback for his aggressive personality during his heyday.

A year after the release of *Deathmaster,* Ray Danton directed another vampire movie, *Hannah, Queen of Vampires*, a peasant folk tale with a somber composition, bleak mood, and meditative style. It is also an international horror film because it is pieced together from Julio Salvador's *Tomb of the Cursed Island* (*La tumba de la isla maltida*) and Danton-directed footage added by American distributors.

Young Hannah, Queen of Vampires is a hybrid movie. Ray Danton was recruited to augment the original European version for American release. Hybrid is the perfect description of a movie whose elements are a combination of opposites. It is meditative and boring; intriguing and predictable; exquisitely shot but also poorly lit; well-acted with bursts of histrionics.

Chris Bolton (Andrew Prine) travels to Vampire Island to retrieve the remains of his father, Prof. Bolton (Mariano Rey), who was killed conducting archeological excavation at an ancient tomb. His violent death was caused by the three ton tomb crushing him to death. It is deemed an accident by his son but the islanders know that it was murder because he had stumbled upon the tomb of a dormant vampire.

She is Hannah (Teresa Gimpera), the young betrothed of King Louis VII, who brought her along on one of his Crusades so he could marry her on the island. The only problem was that while he was away in combat she and most of his army had become vampires, although how and why is never explained. The army of vampires was destroyed but the king commands that his wife-to-be was to be buried alive, easing a guilty conscience about having to destroy the woman he loved.

Hannah has been at rest in the tomb when the professor discovers the tomb while conducting his research. It seems that he was not the first person outside of the islanders to know about her presence. Peter, the local jack-of-all trades and sister of Mary, the local school teacher, is also cognizant of Hannah's existence. He should be because he has become a devil worshipping devotee who has pledged himself to resurrecting the female vampire.

Poster for *Hannah, Queen of Vampires*, another co-international production with two directors and different versions available in various formats. 1973, Orbita Films.

Peter was on the island to conduct research for a book he was writing on the Crusades when he learned about Hannah. He is revealed to be a force of evil in the opening sequence because he was the one who killed the professor. Peter is aided by the Wild Man, a feral human who looks and dresses like an unkempt Sonny Bono from his Sonny and Cher days. The Wild Man kills without discrimination and is actually one of the highlights of the movie.

When Chris arrives, he scoffs at the vampire legend and dismisses the islanders as a bunch of anti-social illiterates. As the movie progresses they take a liking to each other as they need each other to combat Hannah once it becomes obvious that she is real.

Hannah makes her appearance more than an hour into the movie, after being awakened by the son of the murdered archeologist. The vampire terrorizes the dreary Turkish island, first as an invisible force, then as a wolf and finally as herself. The stark, almost numb, atmosphere of the island makes a nice contrast to the baroque style of the crypt, where most of the mystical plot elements unfold. The polarities represent the clash of cultures.

The islanders are initially presented as stoical weather-beaten peasants. The only one who is interesting is the blind concertina player.

He plays a depressing tune while his dog languishes at his feet. Character exposition reveals them to be superstitious fools and they are dispatched by either the vampire or a hirsute maniac in furs who haunts the forest.

It is unfortunate that the beautiful Teresa Gimpera is totally wasted in the role. She does not have much to do except open her eyes and breathe heavily during her introductory scenes, which occur well into the movie. Other than that, she moves in slow motion and it is a wonder that nobody can outrun her.

She also has the ability to turn into a werewolf that bears a remarkable resemblance to a Siberian Husky and also has the power to turn into a mist. This enables her to escape peril. Her most animated scene is during the film's climax when she is immolated and turns into a fire scarred hag screaming in agony as she tries to escape a circle of angry islanders brandishing torches.

The gruesome touches include a hanging black goat's bloody carcass, a marble tomb collapsing on an archeologist, a half-witted, half-faced feral man mutilating the curious, and the beautiful vampire turning into a flaming piece of French Toast at the film's climax.

Andrew Prine is droll as the archeologist's son. He had appeared with Ray Danton in his television show, *Wide Country* and would star in *The Centerfold Girls*, a slasher movie that featured Ray Danton. Prine was ubiquitous during the 70's and starred in many drive-in and grind house cheapies. In fact, *Young Hannah, Queen of Vampires* was exhibited on a double bill with *Simon, King of Witches*, also starring Andrew Prine.

Teresa Gimpera is silent and mysterious as the damned angel. She does not have much to do and is totally wasted in the role. She has long, blonde hair topped by a tiara. Occasionally, she grimaces to reveal plastic fangs. Other than that, she strolls around the island at a languished pace. Gimpera played Cleopatra in *Lucky the Inscrutable*, the inventive spy-comedy that starred Ray Danton in the title role.

She was also a formidable presence in European films, as was Patty Shepherd, who is dark and sensual as Mary, the school teacher who warns Chris about the island's evil secret and eventually falls in love with him. Sheppard also had a small role in *Lucky the Inscrutable* and displays her hysterical histrionics in this endeavor, especially after she is kidnapped by the Wild Man.

Her brother is Peter, a devil worshipper played by Mark Damon. His demonic deception is revealed at the outset of the movie, ruining any hint of suspense or twisted character development. It is a shame because he is

Chris (Andrew Prine) and Mary (Patty Shepherd) are caught in a beautiful dissolve. 1973, Orbita Films.

a likeable person and aids Chris in his quest to free his dead father from the rubble so he can have a decent burial. When not being sociable, Peter conducts a Black Mass in Hannah's tomb and gives orders to the Wild Man to strangle people.

Noted European actor, Frank Bana, plays the blind concertina player. He has one of the best parts in the movie because he gets to speak ridiculous dialogue warning everyone about Hannah's evil and alluring power. The best thing in the movie is the trick ending, which is eerie and foreboding. Hannah may have been killed but the island is not rid of its resident vampire. The clever point is driven home by shots of a statue that once had Hannah's likeness. Perhaps, the most unsettling point is the still photos of the new vampire's first victim playing as children do as the final credits roll.

Ray Danton returned to radio for Rod Serling's *Zero Hour: The Princess Stakes Murder Case* ('73) with Howard Duff and Julie Adams. *The Zero Hour* was an Eliot Lewis production narrated by Rod Serling. It was broadcast over The Mutual Network with an over-the-top theme composed and played by Ferrante and Teischer. Its original premise was presenting a five part story arc for its weekly broadcasts until its last season when daily stories were used.

In *The Princess Stakes Murder Case*, Howard Duff gets to resurrect his Sam Spade radio character under the name, Max Roper. He is a visceral man who protects himself with ju-jitsu and mordant one-liners. He'll need plenty of sarcasm during a week that will involve him in danger,

Hannah (Teresa Gimpera) does the old levitation trick before going up in flames. 1973, Orbita Films.

deceit and an assortment of oddballs as he tries to solve the murder of his jockey friend, Willie Rich.

Julie Adams is Monica Clayton, the former Monica Moore, once-upon-a time successful B-Movie actress. She is peripherally involved in the murder and turns out to be the catalyst for an old murder that led to her being blackmailed for it. The blackmail ultimately results in the killing of the jockey, who stumbled onto the diary of the original murder victim, who was also Monica's first husband.

It seems that Monica is the benefactor of Lewis Charnak, an effete metaphysical quack who believes that he does possess psychic powers. Charnak is played by Ray Danton, who uses a cultured and controlled voice to project an air of superiority, sophistication, and detachment. At first, the listener is led to believe that he is the dupe of Wesley Dorn, his partner. He tells Roper that Dorn is blackmailing him for a past indiscretion and that his success is merely a front for Dorn.

It turns out that Charnak is the murderer but we don't find out until the closing moments of the last chapter. Being spurned in favor of another man by Monica is the motive for Charnak's killer instinct, although he insists that he didn't poison the first victim. He claims to have used his supernatural powers to kill his rival.

"After all, I am a psychic", he intones before being stomped to death by a horse who loses control at the sight of a lit match.

The radio drama is effective and has all of the characters you would find in a racetrack murder mystery. The motley crew ranges from a washed-up jockey who was aided by Willie Rich to a gun happy Texas millionaire who is the latest husband of the ex-actress. Along the way, there is a trail of bodies, from an innocent receptionist to a scheming health spa director; even Dorn is scratched from the action once he has served his purpose. There is also the Isotron, a massage machine that is so powerful that it can tear a man in half. Just ask Max Roper; it almost happened to him.

Ray Danton took his first step behind the television camera when his stories were used for three *McCloud* episodes: *Top of the World, Ma*, *The New Mexican Connection* and *This Must be the Alamo*. He had parts in the last two productions, first as a suave hit man and then as unlucky sidekick to Van Johnson, someone who didn't learn the lesson of the real Alamo.

Ray Danton also delved into directing theater with a dinner theatre version of *South Pacific* on Dec. 20, 1974. It was originally scheduled to open in a Waikiki hotel but was moved to the House of Janus, a catering-banquet firm's Away-From-Kaikiki facility. Producer-promoter Don Over opted for the House of Janus because it could be transformed into a 500 seat facility, whereas the original venue could only seat half of that. The production was a lure for tourist package bookings and was scheduled to run seven nights a week.

The production boasted a technical crew of 50 and 36 performers, including Varoa Tiki as Bloody Mary, Jocelyn Suan as Liat and Les Freed playing Lt. Cable. Scott Michaels was the choreographer and Donald Yap served as the musical director and conductor. Five years later, Ray Danton would helm another Don Over production in Honolulu called, *Return to Paradise*.

The 70's Nostalgia Bust

BOTTOM OF THE BARREL

Ray Danton's luck on the big screen was beginning to thin as he signed on to star in two never-to-be released films. In 1971, producer-director Byron Mabe signed Ray Danton, Wanda Hendrix, Ron Foster, Clare Brennan and Shirley Ballard to star in *Mystic Mountain Massacre*. It was an Adonic Productions feature that started filming in Arizona during the summer of 1971. Not much has been heard of it since then. *The Sagittarius Mine* was to be made the next year with Richard Basehart, Steve Forrest and Diane Baker. That never made it beyond the casting.

Blood, Black and White fared a little better, having been made and marketed with a limited distribution. Ray Danton starred with Norman Alden in a blaxploitation flick about the Mob muscling in on the Harlem numbers racket. For Danton and Alden, it was an update of their turns as thugs on old time network television and early 60's retro-gangster film cycle. It was also a long way from the glory days of Legs Diamond and Dutch Shultz.

One of the hazards of being an actor from a bygone era was that if you lost your footing you could coast awhile as a non-entity. Non-entity status included irrelevant cameos and the *corpus delecti* sideline. Ray Danton put in his time as both with various degrees of dialogue on television and in independent movies.

In *The Ballad of Billie Blue* and *The Centerfold Girls*, Carl, Blue's scheming manager, and Perry Sutton, an over-the-hill *fashionista*, earn their paychecks with violent demises. It was the same course of action for Victor Pappas and Captain Westerling in the television movies, *Banyon* and *A Very Missing Person*.

During a time when there were still small theaters and a drive-in circuit, many independent producers made low budget potboilers and out-of-the way movies for a regional market. The best thing about these obscure productions was that they often featured once well-known names from the Late Show reruns.

The Ballad of Billie Blue is a country western-chain gang epic starring Jason Ledger as a self-destructive country-music singer who fizzles before he explodes. His rise to the top ends when Blue is convicted of killing his manager in a fight where Carl (Ray Danton) is brained by Billie's wife with a whiskey bottle during a fight. An intrepid reporter tries to clear the singer's name.

The movie does not waste any time in trying to establish Billie Blue's (Jason Ledger) huge stature as a pop singer. Concert footage shows a maudlin performance inter cut with shots of an arena crowd going wild over him. The fluted curtains and the flat wood stage are out of a high school auditorium but we are to believe that he is singing to a sellout crowd.

The next scene continues the cheapness passing off as success. Backstage, in a drab and dreary dressing room, his smooth talking manager tells Blue of an impending three picture deal and opportunity to start his own record company. It will be discussed at a party thrown in his honor. The superstar tells his manager that he isn't interested in going to the party and all he wants to do is to enjoy some take-out food in his apartment.

His brassy wife (Sherry Bain) has other ideas. She did not stick with him through the lean years so he could nonchalantly turn down big money negotiations at a party thrown by a powerful producer. She is crude in telling Blue what the equation of their relationship is.

Anxious to go to the party, she asks Carl to take

Billie Blue (Jason Ledger) sings to capacity crowds and is on the verge of the fame that he seeks but will ultimately reject. 1972, B.E. Productions.

her. The opportunistic manager, dressed in white turtleneck and black blazer, downplays the invitation. He is really a sharpie who can't wait to be alone with Mrs. Blue.

Billie Blue's frenzied and successful tour hits a major snag when he appears drunk at several of his concerts. At an arena that looks like a skating rink, his obnoxious behavior alienates the crowd. The fans boo and desert the singer, outraged that he is unable to perform. A worrisome Carl tells Blue's wife that their success is being jeopardized by his self-destructive descent.

The volatile triangle explodes when Blue discovers a bath-robed Carl and his bedded wife in consensual betrayal. Carl is killed when he is hit over the head with a whiskey bottle wielded by Blue's wife while the two men fought.

Blue takes the blame, is charged, tried and convicted of murder. Arty Tripp (Marty Allen), a short, squat, obscene blob of a reporter believes that Blue is innocent and sets out to prove his case. The film follows his attempts to prove that the performer took the rap for his wife. The subplot deals with incarceration and liberation and is told as a chain gang cum salvation story. In an interesting parable, a preacher testifies to the chain gang. He is personable and gives sage advice to the men in the heat.

The preacher selects a twenty year man named Justin as an example of how God can help a man break his chains. After a sarcastic verbal exchange with the preacher, Justin drags him down to the river and submerges him in a baptism of hate

The movie ends when Blue is attracted to a church by the singing of a gospel choir. In a trance, he walks up the stairs and stops in a vestibule to watch a crucifix's light create a star pattern. The cross's redemption brings a dissolute Blue to his knees and he finds salvation with outstretched arms in freeze framed supplication. An ornately inscribed "The Beginning" ends the movie.

It is possible that the budget for this movie was close to non-existent judging by its amateurish look and feel. Cheap sets, forced acting, listless directing and clumsy editing combine in textured layers of blandness. It is absurd to try to convey superstardom with this sort of cheapness. It would have been better to show the underbelly of show business because that's the only place these characters would occupy.

It is a place of desperation where persistent no-talents forge careers of being a never-was. Billie Blue belongs in that category of entertainer It's not that he's without talent; he doesn't have enough of it to command

Carl (Ray Danton), Blue's manager and his wife Reba (Sherrie Bain) watch their meal ticket wither as Billie Blue performs drunk once again at another venue. 1972, B.E. Productions.

arena crowds and make three picture deals. Blue's venue is a motel lounge or a street corner.

The acting is broad and heavy and, because of a tinny soundtrack, the voices are strident. Chief among the irritants is Marty Allen as Arty Tripp. One would rather have seen Allen and Rossi stay together if it meant that Marty Allen wouldn't co-star in this movie.

He delivers his lines with a delayed reaction effect. It's as if he is reviewing them before he speaks. The funny thing is most of his lines are monosyllabic! He may not do his pop-eyed look but he still grates on the nerves. His sense of tough righteousness is laughable although compared with the other sleazebags of the movies, Tripp is laudable.

The alleged star of the movie is Jason Ledger as Billie Blue. He is listless and lacking in star power and acting ability. Even after his soul is saved, he seems zombified. The closing scene of him on his knees in a Baptist church makes him look more like a drunk doing Jolson than a lost soul finding salvation.

Although he gets top billing in some versions of this oft-retitled film, Ray Danton's character, a scheming manager caught cheating with his star's wife, is beaten to death at the beginning of the movie. Maybe the scriptwriters did him a favor when they put his character on ice early in the film.

Sherry Bain is the cheap beehive haired vixen personified. She disappears from the movie after Carl's murder and reappears near the end. She is employed in a brothel and Blue has to pay her twenty dollars just to talk to her. She shouts her lines and is so hostile that her vitriol drives him from the house and her over the railing because of her uncontrollable tirade.

Poster for *The Centerfold Girls*, a nasty slasher film, even by the genre's brutal standards. 1973, General Films Corp.

The Ballad of Billie Blue is a low rent redemption drama and is noteworthy only because it has Marty Allen in a lead role, Erik Estrada in an early performance, and Ray Danton as a smooth-talking manager turned Exhibit A. The only thing to come out of the movie was the formation of Fresh Air Records by Basic Empire Productions. Their first release was the soundtrack to *The Ballad of Billie Blue*.

Ray Danton's next non-entity coast-a-long is a whistle stop at the graveyard of late-show stars: 70's slasher flicks! In 1955, Universal-International suspended Ray Danton for refusing to appear in *Cult of the Cobra*. He was one of the studio's new arrivals and he risked disciplinary action over a creative difference. Nearly twenty years later, it was almost obligatory for yesterday's new arrivals to appear in, at least, one Seventies horror film.

In *The Centerfold Girls*, Ray Danton's Perry Sutton is an over-the-hill fashion maven turned pimp hanging on to whatever vestiges of polyester youth that is left. He arranges for willing models to work as escorts to wealthy patrons for 20% of their earnings. Aware of his vanishing stud powers after a model rebuffs his advances, Sutton finds solace in midnight drinking.

A shadow within an alcove turns into a knife in the chest followed by a tumble over the balcony. Confusion reigns as the body count mounts. The next morning, six covered corpses lie on the beach while a cop interrogates the confused caretaker.

The Centerfold Girls is an unpleasant, low-rent slasher movie made to exploit the easing of censorship laws in the early Seventies. The gratuitous 'T&A' and liberal bloodletting is a hook for a plot that deals with the shopworn character of the self-righteous pervert who absolves guilty nude models of their sins by murdering them. The cast and the setting changes with each victim. The only constant is Clement Dunne (Andrew Prine), the bespectacled twit with a knife.

The film is a three-in-one slasher movie. The first segment is terror by Mansonesque hippies, the second is terror on the secluded island in a house without electricity, and the last is the terror of hitchhiking alone.

The common thread to the segments is the psycho killer. Dunne is an unappealing spindly runt who has unkempt long hair and wears running shoes with suits. You can spot his weirdness at a glance yet the characters in this movie aren't so observant.

He lives in an oblong room where everything is white and his obsession is centerfold models. Dunne toys with his victims by making obscene phone calls and stalking them. After each murder, he concludes

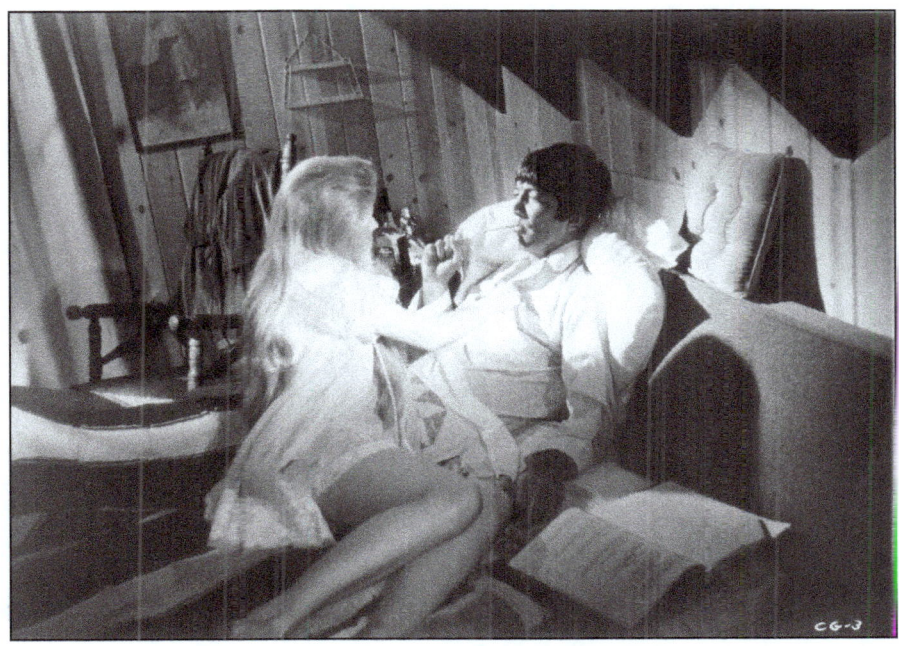

Perry Sutton (Ray Danton) outlines his managerial services to aspiring model, Charley (Alexandra Hay). 1973, General Films Corp.

the rampage by mutilating a photo of his victim. His intended victims are Jackie, Charley and Vera.

Jackie (Jaime Lyn Bauer) is now a nurse who believes that she has to get away from it all so she applies for a position in a small town. The doctor isn't in for the interview so Jackie decides to stay at her parents' summer home. Out of kindness, she gives life to a hippy waif. Little does she realize that they are being observed by three Mansonesque characters. They are ecstatic because the waif is their lure and Jackie is the catch of the day. Her humiliation is tripled by an unsympathetic motel manager (Aldo Ray) and a final meeting with Clement Dunne.

The next segment stars Charley (Alexandra Hay) in an interlude in a house without electricity on a secluded island. A cranky caretaker (Mike Mazurki) takes the crew for a nudie shoot to the island. Melissa (Francine York) is the coordinator and her assistant is Perry Sutton (Ray Danton). They are accompanied by a photographer and three models.

Former lovers, friction is an emasculating Melissa accusing Perry of being a pimp because of his procurement of model's services, including Charley. After his prize blonde is found dead at the foot of the cliff, a night

Ray Danton and Francine York (center) are two fallen stars in the second segment of *The Centerfold Girls*, a trilogy about a deranged stalker of models. 1973, General Films Corp.

of grisly slaughter begins. The next morning, six corpses covered with sheets lie on the beach while a surly detective (Jeremy Slate) interviews the cranky caretaker. Apparently, the killer appropriated one of his boats to get to the island.

The last bit concerns Vera (Tiffany Bolling), who is the heroine of the movie because she kills Clement Dunne, not before she suffers the requisite degradation typical of this type of trash. Vera's bad luck culminates in her being given a lift to the wilderness by Dunne. She escapes from the car and flees into a wilderness of dead trees and gnarled branches. A struggle with the killer ends when he is pinned to a branch and Vera sobs as the credits roll.

Typical of the low-budget 70's drive-in independents, *The Centerfold Girls* is cheaply made and stocked with nubile actresses plus actors and actresses who had seen better times in previous decades. Jaime Lyn Bauer, Jennifer Ashley and Tiffany Bolling star as the centerfold girls. They were part of the contingent of young actresses working the exploitation circuit, each having series of credits to their names.

The oldest veteran in this travesty is Mike Mazurki. Once, he was made of granite but now suffers from phlegm deposits. He plays it irritating, instead of tough, as does Aldo Ray. Ray had a successful career as a belligerent tough guy, appearing in *The Naked and the Dead* ('58) and *The Green Berets* ('68), with John Wayne. He appears in the first segment as a vile motel manager. Just as badly off, although for different reasons, are Francine York and Ray Danton as bickering *fashionistas* reduced to "nudie shoots." Screen veteran Dan Seymour is somewhere among the oldies in the cast.

THE TWILIGHT MOB: CRIME BOSSES, CON MEN AND ASSASSINS

70's television followed the trends and styles of Hollywood. One of the biggest influences was Francis Ford Coppola's *The Godfather* ('72). It swept over the entertainment industry like a tidal wave and, in its wake, created a huge demand for mob bosses, hit men, stoolies, and hard-nosed cops, plus molls, police women, and shady dames.

Ray Danton's credentials easily landed him spots on television crime shows. For the duration of the 70's, he mostly played three types of stock heavies on television. There was the top-level crime boss who sometimes did the job himself to make sure it was done right; the mobster who is caught in a sting operation by shady types with a sense of justice; and the mob-connected stooge who used to be somebody before he became a shill.

The prototype of Ray Danton's stock heavy is Stokes, the stylish and methodical hit man, in *McCloud: The New Mexican Connection*. *McCloud* premiered in 1970 as part of a revolving mini-series called *Four-In-One*. *McCloud* alternated with *San Francisco International Airport*, *Night Gallery*, and *The Psychiatrist*. Only *McCloud* and *Night Gallery* were successes.

Rod Serling's *Night Gallery* became a weekly hour-long show and *McCloud* became part of another idea, the wildly successful NBC Mystery Movie. *McCloud* rotated with *McMillian and Wife*, starring Rock Hudson and Susan St. James and *Columbo*, with Peter Falk. All three shows were ratings winners and *McCloud* stayed on the air until 1977.

McCloud was a legitimate detective show but its premise had a twinkle in its eye because Sam McCloud was a western deputy from

Taos, New Mexico sent to work in the Big Apple. His homespun ways contrasted sharply with the brusque and cynical attitudes of his New York counterparts. Nevertheless, he gets the job done without losing any of his small town charm and he always collared the criminal, much to the exasperation of his superior, Inspector Clifford (J.D.Cannon).

In *The New Mexican Connection*, McCloud is on a stakeout when he recognizes Wilks (Gary Vinson), a suspect in a bank bombing that killed three people three years earlier in Taos. He chases, wounds and apprehends the man but is forced to release the suspect when he receives an anonymous call threatening the life of his girlfriend, Chris Coughlin (Diana Muldaur) if he fails to do so.

Wilks is put under surveillance by Marshal Ben Melendez (Gilbert Roland) in Taos after he is extradited and released. The anonymous caller is aware of the tail and reiterates his threat to McCloud. The resolute detective works around the threats and pieces together a puzzle that began with the bank robbery and winds up in a horse drawn coach riding through Times Square. He even manages to withstand the haranguing criticisms of a media watchdog named Adrian Becker (Murray Hamilton), who claims that the New York police force are a gang of vigilantes.

It is discovered that Wilks is blackmailing another gang member who turns out to be the popular singing sensation, Jimmy Roy Taylor (Rick Nelson [who sings his hit, Garden Party]). Winn Hollis (Jackie Cooper) is the singer's manager and the mastermind behind hiring the anonymous hit man, a former Army operative named Stokes (Ray Danton).

Stokes has an executive look to him and carries himself in a perfunctory businesslike way. The professional killer has a brutal style that places him in the same league as Oscar Wetzel. He is assured that spot when he uses a suitcase bomb to rid his employer of Wilks, the blackmailing liability.

One man Stokes cannot liquidate is McCloud (Dennis Weaver). The cowboy detective is too clever for him in a scene where he outwits the hit man by luring him into a trap that ends up as a downward ride on an ascending escalator.

Ray Danton gives a chilling performance as the stone faced professional killer who backs up his monotone pledges with boldfaced efficiency. It is a first rate portrayal that became watered down with subsequent renewals.

Ray Danton's next hit man is actually a syndicate boss who decides to do the job himself in *Cannon: The Hit Man*. *Cannon* was another successful

Stokes is a fastidious former special service operative who makes a living as a methodical hired killer. He zeroes in on McCloud but gets erased from the equation when the plan escalates with his demise. 1972, Glen A. Larson Productions, Universal Television.

show produced by Quinn Martin. William Conrad starred as the portly balding private detective who poses as a hit man whose assignment is to assassinate Bishop Michael Harrigan (Richard Kiley). The cleric has been asked by a member of his parish to spearhead an anti-crime committee to stem the criminal infiltration of the neighborhood. Drugs, prostitution, policy rackets and forced protection plans have ruined the once serene community.

Cannon gets the assignment from Leo Crothers (Val Avery), a hired killer who gets cold feet because he is a Catholic and does not want to insure a definite space in Hell for killing a cleric. The raspy voiced detective accepts the job so he can trap Alex Brennan (Ray Danton), a crime boss, who ordered the hit on behest of his backer, Lester Cain (Paul Stewart.)

Alex Brennan senses something strange about the extra large hit man and tries to entrap him with a series of misleading questions and an important phone call to Mr. Big. Cannon earns his credentials as Leo Crothers, although Alex Brennan still does not have confidence in him The mobster quickly becomes dissatisfied with Crothers nee Cannon's lack of progress so he decides to perform the job himself. He warms up

Alex Brennan (Ray Danton) is a crime boss who returns to his roots as a hit man when he completes a contract taken out on the crime fighting Bishop Harrigan (Richard Kiley). 1974, Quinn Martin Productions.

by beating up Father Joseph (Christopher Connelly), the bishop's deacon, and ends his enterprise by bringing the bishop to his knees in church before being knocked out by a brass bell that shakes up his world.

Alex Brennan is Stokes cranked up a couple of notches. He is a mid-level manager who still has the finesse to do the job himself. This time around, the church's brass bells were more powerful than his brass nuts and bolts way of doing things.He has lost his fight against the bishop, whose campaign of law and order stamped out his chapter of the mob activity. That includes razing Cain.

The most satisfying parody of Stokes is Johnny Landros in *Police Story: Countdown (1&2* ['72]). Sgt. Joe La Frieda (Vic Morrow) becomes a man against the mob after he shoots the younger brother of Chicago mob bosses in a warehouse robbery gone awry. The hot-headed mobsters, Johnny and Martin Landros (Ray Danton and Anthony Caruso), take umbrage with their baby brother's death. They consider it murder because of the animosity that existed between the cop and their sibling. Vengeance is a contract put out on La Frieda's life.

The 70's Nostalgia Bust | 347

Johnny and Martin Landros are like a two-headed monster and it is fitting that Danton and Caruso should play the brothers. All they had to do was dust off the old scowls and brush up on their snarls. The brothers balance each other while weighing plans to kill La Frieda. Their hot-headed

Top and Bottom: Johnny and Martin Landros (Ray Danton and Anthony Caruso) are crime bosses intent on avenging the death of their younger brother. Constantina (Anjenette Comer) is the avenging angel of the family, the doting daughter and baby sister with the sting of a cobra. Paul Stevens is the handyman whose task it is to see that things are done. 1974, Columbia Pictures Television, David Gerber Productions, Screen Gems Television.

Mediterranean passion is kept in check by a cool and collected Madonna figure, sister Constantina (Anjanette Comer). She is more deadly their her brothers but disguises it with a hypnotic voice and helpless eyes.

Countdown is a two-parter that is an old-fashioned crime drama with enough familiar faces to make a comparison with the Fifties originals a comfortable fit. Vic Morrow, Tige Andrews, Ray Danton, Anthony Caruso, Paul Stevens and Ina Balin have all done time on the old school crime drama circuit. They bring their old magic to this episode, mixing it up with the new faces of Larraine Stephens, Anjanette Comer, Jennifer Billingsly, Lana Wood and Joe Santos.

Johnny Landros is a substantial role but it set the dye for Danton's crime bosses for the remainder of the decade. By the mid-Seventies, Ray Danton had settled in to being typecast as stock heavies and mob bosses. It was just a matter of job title and ethnicity, sunglasses or none, pounding fists or snarling death threats.

Al Royce and Al Dancer are two crime kingpins who are hunted by top cops. Royce is literally hunted by a dying cop and Dancer is hounded by an honest detective trying to clean up the old neighborhood. Royce wears the sunglasses and Dancer dons the turtleneck sweater and mystic pendant. Both thankless parts occur on *The Streets of San Francisco* and *Toma*.

The Streets of San Francisco was another hit cop show by executive producer Quinn Martin. It was shot on location and exemplified the gritty beat that Quinn helped to popularize. Karl Malden starred as veteran detective Mike Stone and his young partner was played by a neophyte actor named Michael Douglas. Kirk Douglas once remarked in an interview that he wanted his son to play the role so he could get top-notch acting training from a veteran like Malden. The two worked well together and it proves that expert acting can take perfunctory scripts and themes and elevate them above mediocrity.

In *Before I Die*, the two cops try to prevent a career cop named John T. Connor (Leslie Nielson) from executing a mobster named Al Royce (Ray Danton) in cold blood. Connor is diagnosed with an incurable disease and given a short term lease on life. This gives him the excuse to murder Royce, the original Teflon Don because of his ability to prevent any investigation or indictment from sticking to him. Justice prevails and Connor is shot by his partner as he targets Royce at the race track.

In *Toma: Pound of Flesh*, he plays Al Dancer, a crime boss without the outer trappings and expensive tastes of Al Royce. This Al is an old

Al Royce (Ray Danton) and John T. Connor (Leslie Nielson) square off for a life and death battle royale. 1973, Quinn Martin Productions, Warner Bros. Television.

neighborhood crime czar and his rackets are street hustles that involve loan sharking and shaking down local restaurants for protection money.

This does not sit well with Toma (Tony Musante), one of the many maverick good guy detectives of 70's crime dramas. Like many of his 70's contemporaries, Toma had relatively short time to do his thing because his series did not last long. However, during his tenure he did get to bring down mobsters like Al Dancer.

Al Dancer is another thankless part; however, it stands out from Danton's second tier crime bosses because of his shady appearance. Dancer is sleazy even by 70's standards. He wears a strange pendant that he occasionally wore for other roles, notably Carlo De Fermi in *Triangle*, his first 70's movie. It is not unusual, considering that Ray Danton was one of the modern descendants of the 17th century Cabbalist, Vilna Gaon.

Before Ken Howard, the former basketball star, scored in a couple of years with *The White Shadow*, he played Dave Barrett, *The Manhunter*, a citizen turned crime buster after his parents were brutally murdered by thugs. It was a short-lived series set during the 30's Great Depression and based on a Tele-Movie of the same name.

Ray Danton plays Homer, a stock crime show figure in *The Man Who Thought He was Dillinger*. He is the sidekick to the crime pin, the gang member who is making out with the boss' girl. The only thing that makes this role stand out is that Ray Danton wears his trademark hairstyle from his salad days because the show was set in the 30's. Aficionados of Ray Danton's persona from the 50's and 60's will be delighted because it's almost like seeing Legs Diamond again except that he is a second banana when he should be playing the lead.

That honor goes to Mitch Ryan, who plays Tom Bailey, a noxious bank-robbing gangster. He and his gang open the show by taking out a gang of feds who descend on their farmhouse hideaway. Machine gun fire and tear gas because the gang has escaped through a trap door and detonate explosives.

Jeffrey Donenfield (David Hedison) is the head fed and only survivor, though he has been blinded by the explosion. This does not deter him from settling his score with Bailey. All he needs is a set of eyes and he finds them in Dave Barrett.

They track him down on the information provided by Marco (Eddie Firestone), an ill-fated double crossing informer who leads them to Blueprint Kelley (Robert Emhardt), the man who finds the opportunities for Bailey to exploit. This time, it is a fortune in uncut diamonds to be transported by armored car. Barrett and Donenfield disrupts the plan in a shopworn scenario that has the gang impersonating the guards.

Homer has designs on Kelly (a pasty-faced Alexandra Hay), the boss' Moll and they plan to murder Bailey and front the gang themselves. It is not meant to be as Bailey forces Homer to drive the armored car into the Kelly's car, pushing it over a cliff. Afterwards, Homer is killed when the armored car is forced off the road by one of the man hunter's clever tricks. Bailey is shot dead in a final confrontation with Barrett.

The Man Who Would be Dillinger is standard and predictable, strictly on the other end of the scale for producer Quinn Martin. Its main interest is seeing Ray Danton looking like Legs Diamond. It is a shame that Danton did not play the lead role considering his brilliance as the title character of *The Rise and Fall of Legs Diamond*. He is somewhat timid in this, a queasy right hand man to a boss who knows that he has been cuckolded by the two people closest to him.

Bailey has to play two strategies: one to out maneuver Barrett and the Fed and the other to exact revenge on Homer and Kelly. He gets more than he bargained for when he becomes the third body in a three car pile-up.

Ray Danton scored like he did during his heyday at Warner Bros. television when he appeared in back to back episodes of *Cannon* and *The Manhunter*. Sept. 18, 1974, TV Guide.

David Hedison is effective as the sightless federal agent who helps Barrett bring down Bailey and his gang. Robert Emhardt was the same manipulating sleaze merchant that he played on old time shows like *The Untouchables*. He is the contact man and event planner who has to take to the field.

Eddie Firestone-an original Untouchable in the two-part pilot-was a familiar character actor for viewers of 50's and 60's television. He plays a two-faced informer with no way out of his fatal dilemma. Ray Danton had starred with Alexandra Hay on *Love, American Style: The Nice Guy* and would appear with her again in the brutal slasher flick, *The Centerfold Girls*, made after *The Manhunter*.

Ray Danton was able to briefly return to his halcyon days with his next role. Not only does he wear old hairstyle again but gets to play the boss this time around. He's the ruthless crime king on *Nakia*, an excellent, if short-lived, show starring Robert Forster as a Native American law enforcement officer. Like his previous show, *Banyon*, *Nakia* was based on a first-rate television movie.

The brandy snifter shot of retro boss Norm Rodale is a nod to Ray Danton's original suave continental player persona. 1974, David Gerber Productions, Columbia Pictures, Television.

In *No Place to Hide*, Archie MacIntosh (Gabe Dell) is a man trying to escape his past as the adopted son of a mobster and an accountant for the mob. His family and former business associates are now his enemies and they feel that he is a liability as he leads a peaceful life in small New Mexican town where Nakia presides over the law and order.

Nakia and his nephew, Bear Cub (John Tenorio, Jr.), befriend Archie but Sheriff Jericho (Arthur Kennedy) is wary of his presence after a hit man (George Loros) puts the fear of God in the mob renegade when he booby-traps his apartment with a bomb detonated by a light switch.

Norm Rodale (Ray Danton) is a suspicious and ruthless mobster who can sit behind a desk and give orders besides working the field when he has to. To make a point, he visits Archie at a tram ride to give him an ultimatum. The hard-headed *capo* does not consider retirement an option. It's either conciliation or elimination. When it is the latter, Norm hires a cold-blooded Texas hit man played by Marc Singer. It takes more than that to defeat Nakia.

Ray Danton's performance is curious because of its retrogressive nature. This time around, he was the boss and it is a reminder of the power he projected when he had a strong role. The shot of him drinking from the brandy snifter after giving orders on Archie's hit, plus the death sentence glare on the tram, are two instances that come to mind. The brandy snifter shot, alone, is worth more than most of Ray Danton's Seventies' roles combined.

Of all of his parts during the 70's, only two of Ray Danton's characters were ordinary people. He played a brother of a murder victim in *Cannon: Trial by Terror* and an assistant to crooked businessman Van Johnson in *McCloud: This Must be the Alamo*.

In the *Cannon* episode, he plays Earl Dakin, a used car dealer whose brother, Charlie (Joey Aresco), is the kidnapper who abducted the daughter of Judge Sumner Haynes (Simon Scott), a judge presiding over a trial of the vicious mobster Len Francisco (Keith Andes). The mobster's behind-the-scenes intention is to force the judge to declare a mistrial. Cannon is secretly hired by the judge, an old friend who beseeches him to find his daughter before he has to resort to this miscarriage of justice.

Ray Danton has three brief scenes as Earl Dakin: being questioned by Cannon on the whereabouts of his brother, the suspected kidnapper; being taken to the roadside crime scene where his brother's body bag is being loaded into an ambulance; and sitting at his office desk, drinking away his remorse while Cannon conducts a follow-up interrogation.

Cannon gets the information that he needs to rescue the judge's daughter after the required loud shootout with the kidnapper-murderers. The hostage becomes the returning princess and the trial concludes with the conviction of Francisco.

In the *McCloud* episode, a sports betting ring that uses inside information based on injuries is jeopardized when a little black book with

Earl Dakin (Ray Danton) surveys the crime investigation scene that centers on the corpse of his younger brother. 1973, Quinn Martin Productions.

vital information disappears. Dan Kily (Van Johnson) is the leader of the ring and panics at the loss of a small book that can mean big trouble for him. It happens after Manny Donner (Jack Kelly), a small time minion, is cuckolded by Shannon Taylor (Laraine Stephens), one of his bimbos, who has recorded all of the secret information for her leverage.

She shoots Donner to death after he tells her to pack her bags when he finds her with Elton Packer (Marc Hannibal), her grid iron lover. He is a star player who sells information to the gang and she has been cheating on Donner. Shannon wounds Packer and flees the crime scene, only to be arrested by the police as she runs along 2nd Avenue in her blood-covered dress.

Shannon is arrested and stashes the book in the station latrine before she is killed by the mob's mechanic, Rockford (Eugene Roche), who poses as her lawyer so he can get access to her in her cell. He later kills Packer with the same cool, calm and collected manner as the football player recuperates in the hospital.

Ray Danton plays Chet Mason, Kily's assistant and hands-on man. If anything needs to be done, Chet is the man to do it, including locating missing persons or getting air conditioners to stave off a heat wave that is crippling the city.

Mason okays the death of Shannon Taylor but pleads for the life of the football player because "he is such a nice guy." Kiley agrees but points out that he is the last link to them. Donner and Shannon are dead and Packer has to be added to the hit list. Mason becomes a gangster is when he goes along with the hit; later, he reluctantly trains two guns on the cops is that are commanded by Rockford to hit the ground. Their identities will be useful when he forced by circumstance to raid a police station to retrieve the book. Chet Mason and a phony reporter have to cover his bank in a job that is beyond their expertise.

A blackout has crippled the city and diminished the police force and Kily uses Rockford, the cold-blooded killer, to mastermind a scheme that will retrieve the book for him. Rockford, along with Mason and a phony cub reporter named Scoop Henderson (Robby Weaver)wear stocking masks and stage a takeover that ends in a wild shootout with McCloud, who arrives and shakes things up with Rockford's shooting death and the meek surrender of Chet and Scoop.

"Don't shoot! We give up!", Chet cries as he raises his hands in surrender just as the power comes on and light is restored to the plundered stationhouse. McCloud puts an end to the siege but gets blamed for the

Dan Kiley (Van Johnson) listens to information about the layout of a police station that he plans to raid for an incriminating black book. Chet Mason (Ray Danton), Kiley's assistant, listens to the details of a plan he will have to execute. 1974, Glen A. Larson Productions, Universal Television.

destruction of police headquarters even though he was the one who showed up to save the night from itself.

1975: SPIN OF THE COIN

1975 was like a coin flip for Ray Danton's career. Either way, it could be heads or tails. It didn't matter! He was at a crossroads. A starring role in *Apache Blood* and a small role in *Six-Pack* Annie were dubious necessities that showed the shape of his acting career after being in the movie business for twenty years. They were also ways of successful solutions to dealing with personal and professional financial woe-be-gones!

Being the co-writer and director of *Psychic Killer* and executive producer of *The Manchu Eagle Murder Mystery Caper* were the signposts to the future. A career behind the camera was where Ray Danton would find a way to express his creative inspiration. He signed a contract with the William Felber Agency to represent him as a director in films and theater. Along the way there were the atypical gangster portrayals for run-

The poster for *Pursuit* (*Apache Blood*), a low budget Western chase movie featuring a silent Ray Danton as an avenging Mescalero warrior. 1975, Lighthouse Productions.

of-the-mill cop shows like *Caribe, Joe Forrester, Matt Helm* and a Hall of Fame classic like *The Rockford Files*.

In Ray Danton's last starring role on the big screen, he gives a curious performance as a revenge seeking Mescalero Indian in a bare bones Western called *Apache Blood* ('75), a dull desert trek movie. What could have been an excellent western turns out to be an exercise in boredom where patience is sustained by anticipation.

If only the mechanics of filmmaking had been learned before the movie was made, then, perhaps, there would have been a semblance of cohesion and coherence. To say that *Apache Blood* is inept is to use polite understatement. The movie has a theme but no plot, invisible acting, insipid direction, dull cinematography, out-of-synced sound and an inappropriate score.

The opening scene is encouraging: Yellow Shirt stalks a wounded Cavalry soldier and scalps him. The freeze frame of Yellow Shirt raising his knife is impressive. It is a backdrop for the opening credits. Once the movie gets underway, it is all downhill. The rest of the movie is a series of shots of the chase-over and over again! In a movie that is basically a silent movie, this can be deadly.

Revenge via the hunt is the theme for this quasi-silent movie. It begins with Danton narrating the genocide of the Mescaleros. That will be the last time we hear his voice. The character of Yellow Shirt is silent, which befits a movie that borders on the somnolent. According to the narrator (Ray Danton), Yellow Shirt and his wife are among a small band of Mescaleros that have survived a Cavalry massacre. Seeking vengeance, Yellow Shirt masterminds a war on the white man.

The alternate story is the challenge of a scout (Troy Nabors) to stay alive after he's been mauled by a grizzly bear. As he drags himself towards a Cavalry outpost, he faces obstacles that test his strength and perseverance. The two men cross paths and Yellow Shirt becomes the leader of a hunting party that stalks the wounded guide. Although alone, the scout proves more trouble than they can handle. Using his keen wit and old-fashioned ingenuity, he devises a series of traps that kill the Indians, one at a time. All die, except Yellow Shirt. *Apache Blood* is a sad waste of time and money for both the producers and the audience.

The biggest waste of the movie is Ray Danton. It is hard to believe that this is the same Ray Danton who gave many excellent portrayals on the best of Warner Brothers' television westerns. As Yellow Shirt, he should have been able to deliver a tour-de-force performance. What we get is a

Yellow Shirt (Ray Danton) is ready to kill any intruder into his territory, a desolate wasteland made that way by the avaricious Westerners. 1975, Lighthouse Productions.

mute portrayal of a sallow Indian riding around or swinging his machete.

I don't know what the reason could be for Ray Danton remaining silent throughout the movie. Maybe, the filmmakers didn't pay him enough money to speak lines so he just lent his presence for a fast buck. It is still inconceivable that someone with such a powerful voice and imposing attitude would retract these details when interpreting a role like Yellow Shirt.

Through default, Troy Nabors steals the movie. He has two compelling scenes that show his range of acting expertise. In the first scene, the sun has finally baked the scout's brain to point where he begins to hallucinate and sees phantom images of the Cavalry troopers who were ordered to keep his death vigil.

He writhes and twists in the air, acting out the movements of madness via elementary acting. Screaming, "We ain't friends no more. You can count on that!", he rolls down a hill. It is topped by the next acting *tour-de-force.*

The scout, crawling on all fours, spots a lizard and zeroes in on it. Grabbing hold of dinner, he sticks its rubber head in his mouth and begins chomping on it. The alleged horror of the scene is offset by a rapid cut to a shot of the invigorated scout hopping from boulder to boulder.

The only impressive scenes are the beginning and end of the film: a freeze frame of Yellow Shirt scalping a Cavalry soldier and a solarized scene of Yellow Shirt sitting by a campfire with his wife.

At the film's climax, there is a powerful montage that recapitulates the plot in a contorted, tortured way as part of the twist ending. The filmmaker scores with a surreal scene that is the best thing in the movie by using special effects and voice distorters.

Maybe if the producers edited the scalping at the beginning to the montage and the ending with Yellow Shirt by the campfire, they could have palmed *Apache Blood* off as a short silent foreign film and it would have garnered its share of prestige and mystic awe. As it stands, it's not even a rough sketch of what could have been a compelling movie.

Apache Blood was reissued as *Pursuit*. Its original shooting title was *A Man Called She*. The only notes of interest to the movie besides it being Ray Danton's last starring role is that the proceeds of its preview going to AMVETS and the location of the movie's filming, Carefree, Arizona is where *Zabriskie Point* ('70), *Electra Glide in Blue* ('73), and Orson Welles' *The Other Side of the Wind* ('70's) were made.

Five years after the manipulative Carlo Di Fermi was introduced in *Triangle*, the Disco age creep would run his course in the drive-in circuit's *Six Pack Annie*. Billed as Raymond Danton, he has a small part as

Yellow Shirt (Ray Danton) ends the movie by pondering the fate of his faith. 1975, Lighthouse Productions.

Mr. O'Meyer, a hotel bar Lothario playing it for ugly laughs in a bucolic risqué comedy of errors.

Like Carlo di Fermi, Mr. O'Meyer is a shaggy browed hustler who cruises with an aim to manipulate and outwit their conquests. He succeeds where the prototype failed; neither escapes the bottom of the barrel. Neither did the other disco kings played by Ray Danton during the closing years of his acting career.

Six Pack Annie is a risqué version of Ma and Pa Kettle and Hee-Haw country western humor revue. The movie is a rural sex comedy, a collection of skits, scenes, vignettes, and blackouts strung together to make a movie. It has a raucous country-western score by none other than Raoul Krasshaur, who seems to have awakened from his *Triangle*-induced torpor. His soundtrack keeps things moving along. There are a couple of original songs thrown in, with the title tune being one of them.

Poster for *Six Pack Annie*, a typical teen exploitation movie made for the drive-in and grind house market. 1975, American-International.

The movie has all of the elements of Danton's 70's big screen efforts: a low budget, strained writing, stereotypical characters, and broad performances. What makes it works is this movie's creators knew the fundamentals of filmmaking. Because of this, the movie is interesting and funny, at times. *Six Pack Annie* is a regional release with a charm that goes beyond its demographics.

Naïve vixen and elective promiscuity seem like oxymoron's but they're not when they come to the titular character of Annie Bodine (Lindsay Bloom). Packed with enough dynamite to bore a hole in any libido, Annie is a country nymphet who likes to drink beer, skinny dip and help her Aunt Tess (Danna Hansen) out at her diner. She may be an air head but she has verve and spunk, possessing an energy that dominates every scene she is in.

The crisis is a foreclosure by the bank on the diner and Annie's attempt to solve it by landing a sugar daddy in Miami. Like most picaresque adventures, it is the characters that make the story work. *Six Pack Annie* is not short on eccentric characters. Besides redneck staples that include

The sisters hit on a rich Texan (Richard Kennedy) in an attempt to raise the money needed to save their aunt's diner. 1975, American-International.

a dumb hometown sheriff there are the prospective sugar daddies she meets in Miami, among them a drunken Texas oil man and a perverted, emaciated Napoleon named Louis Danton (!).

Lindsay Bloom is fine as an R-Rated Daisy Mae. Determined, with an odd hybrid style of passion and pure mindedness, her reactions to big city corruption are funny and poignant. Her sister is played by Janna Bellin and Bruce Boxleitner plays her boyfriend. Joe Higgins puts in a funny performance as the sheriff and Doodles Weaver plays a checker playing font of country wisdom.

The Miami hucksters range from pathetic to oily. A cadaverous Oscar Carthier plays an overheated Napoleon named Louis Danton. What is supposed to be humorous becomes harrowing because of the actor's dreadful physical state. Richard Kennedy gives great performance as a Texas oil man stewed to the gills on Coco Locos. While drinking his brew from halved coconut shells, he trades barbs with the bartender, played by Pedro Gonzalez-Gonzalez.

Ray Danton plays O'Meyer in a twist on the country bumpkin fleeced by the city slicker. At the tail end of the movie, a wide-eyed Annie asks the bartender about the prospects of finding a sugar daddy in the airport bar. This is Mr. O'Meyer's cue to slither up to her on a bar stool. In cheap hustler's fashion, he cons the desk clerk into giving him

Mr. O'Meyer (Ray Danton) shows Annie (Lindsay Bloom) the dime store ring he bought her as a token of his esteem. 1975, American-International.

a room and buys a five and dime ring from the gift shop. The ring, the room and O'Meyer's claim of riches are enough to get Annie to share her earthly delights with him. The next morning, she is awakened by a call from the desk clerk wanting to know about the arrival time of her luggage. The confused woman finds a note on the pillow from her sugar daddy. Danton's voice in echo mocks: "Better luck next time-city slicker."

In *Six Pack Annie*, Stubby Kaye and Sid Melton are other old-timers on the skids. Stubby Kaye had lost his infectious enthusiasm to desperate times and, in this movie, *Shenanigans* meant something totally different from what it did on his 60's kid show. However, his routine as a traveling salesman is one of the highlights of the movie. Sid Melton no longer had that hapless but funny look in a role that was a lifetime away from *Captain Midnight* and The *Danny Thomas Show*. In *Six Pack Annie*, the venerable Sid was sick, pale, and seedy as a john dealing with a whore's flatulence in a wicker basket.

Ray Danton fared a little better with his television roles. They may have been stock mobster types but, at least, they were on shows with credible stars. *Caribe* and *Joe Forrester* were two crime shows that came and went without anyone noticing. The only thing of note is that television legend Lloyd Bridges had the thankless part of *Joe Forrester* and future Mike Hammer Stacey Keach played the lead in *Caribe*.

Caribe was a detective show that derived its atmosphere from its Miami and Caribbean locales. Lt. Ben Logan (Stacey Keach) and Sgt. Mark Walters (Carl Franklin) are two members of the Caribbean Force assigned to the Miami police department. In *The Plastic Connection*, Logan infiltrates a crime ring that uses plastic surgery to alter the faces of undesirables so they can be smuggled into the United States.

He pretends to need their services and this puts him in personal contact with the operation headed by Ray Danton, Jack Ging, Ellen W. Weston as the "shrink" and Mr. Big. *The Plastic Connection* is another episode where Ray Danton starred with Julie Adams. Ray Danton would later become one of the resident directors for Stacy Keach's version of *Mickey Spillane's Mike Hammer* in the 80's.

Lloyd Bridges achieved television immortality with his portrayal of Mike Nelson in *Sea Hunt*, a very popular show from the late 50's and early 60's. He also starred in *The Loner*, a western created by Rod Serling. *Joe Forrester* was his entrance into the cop show genre that gutted the tube during the 70's. He was the veteran cop who still walked a beat because he bucked the system. *Target: Mexican Connection* dealt with drug dealing-a television staple because of the success of *The French Connection.*

Chester Sierra in *The Rockford Files: Chicken Little is a Little Chicken* ('75), is a good role, a funny parody on the stock characters Ray Danton played with frequency. He is the opposite to the perfunctory sad sack, mob front Frank Saxon in *Matt Helm: Game of the Century* ('75).

The Rockford Files was a classic variation on the laid back West Coast private eye. A lion's share of the show's credits goes to James Garner for his portrayal of the dogged and beleaguered gumshoe. The show benefited from excellent writing, a catchy theme song and interesting supporting characters, chief among Angel Martin, played by Stuart Margolin.

Angel Martin is a seedy low level con artist who serves as eyes on the street and a player in some of private eye Jim Rockford's (James Garner) stings. Their seesaw relationship sometimes brings them to the brink of death. One such instance is *Chicken Little is a Little Chicken*. It is a tale of mistaken identity, false accusations, grim outcomes, and freedom gambits. The slant of things always pins Rockford down but his keen wit and masochistic forbearance enable him to overcome the odds.

Rockford's solution to the problem created by Angel is a shell game to be played at the con-man's fake memorial service. Angels' obit sets the stage for bringing two mobsters, Chester Sierra (Ray Danton) and Martin Freschette (Joe Campanella),together for the sting. An empty suitcase, a suitcase full of money, and a suitcase with forgers' plates will pass hands until the mobsters wind up with incriminating evidence when they are busted by Sgt. Dennis Becker (Joe Santos). The trouble is that the sting is bungled and Rockford is left holding the suitcase with the plates.

Ray Danton's portrayal of Chester Sierra is more comical than menacing. In the warehouse meeting, he is seated at a table, enjoying a pizza dinner. His critique of the pizza is pointed: good crust but not enough anchovies. The Danton touch is there when he force feeds Angel a taste of the pizza. He is also cold and remote when he orders the executions of Rockford and Angel.

Matt Helm, like Derek Flint, was an American runner-up to the British James Bond. Dean Martin and James Coburn played the original spies. By the time they made it to the small screen, Helm and Flint were glorified insurance investigators.

In *The Game of the Century* ('75), the game is a winner-take-all Las Vegas poker game with a four million-dollar payoff. Three Texas

Chester Sierra (Ray Danton) attends a phony wake for Angel Martin (Stuart Margolin) and becomes part of an entrapment sting that will take him and a rival mobster (Frank Campanella) down. 1975, Roy Huggins-Public Arts Productions, Cherokee Productions, Universal Television.

millionaires sponsor Prof. Shannon (Biff McGuire), a mathematics professor in a high-stakes poker match. His lucky charm is Cherokee (Betty Ann Carr), a mysterious beauty with a murky past.

Frank Saxon (Ray Danton) is ostensibly the owner of the hotel where the game is to be played. He is near financial ruin and has become a front man for the unscrupulous Eric Frank (Logan Ramsey). Frank will do anything to ensure that his man, Saxon, wins the game; that includes murder and kidnapping Mrs. Faro (Patricia Crowley), a friend of Helm's. Matt Helm prevents this from happening.

Saxon is a low-key character, a shill who mumbles few pleasantries here and there. He is one of the card players and all he does is grimace, raise the stakes, and speak a couple of lines. He is an old friend of Helm's but this means nothing because he is owned by the mob and has to do its bidding, even if it means killing Matt Helm.

A formal Raymond Danton was also the executive producer of *The Manchu Eagle Murder Caper Mystery*, a clever spoof of gumshoe movies. It uses clichés to create an original movie with a cast of greats like Gabriel Dell, Huntz Hall, Jackie Coogan, Dick Gautier, Vincent Gardenia, Barbara Harris, Anjanette Comer, Nita Talbot and Joyce Van Patten.

Malcolm (Gabriel Dell) runs a chicken hatchery and his project is to genetically manipulate the chickens so they can lay colored eggs. His real ambition is to become a private eye and he begins his career when he receives a diploma from a mail-order school. His first case is to solve the bizarre murder of the milk man (Dick Gauthier), who was killed by an arrow while he sought Malcolm's help in solving the mystery of the Manchu Eagle.

In this case, the Manchu Eagle is not the stuff that dreams of made of; instead, it is a nightmarish descent into depravity. Bestiality, incest, nymphomania, psychosis and dissolution are the themes touched on in this bizarre independent movie. What is so remarkable is that it is an original comedy even though it has all of the earmarks of a 70's low-budget movie.

Despite the lurid and perverse premise, the movie is actually very funny and enjoyable, if only because of the cast of familiar faces that successfully portrays the depressing life styles of an obscure desert community. They diffuse the weirdness by making their behavior seem normal and the movie becomes a portrait of a community living on the edge of nowhere. It is the one time that Gabriel Dell was able to star in a movie and he carries the weight admirably as the clueless gumshoe. He also co-wrote the script.

Raymond Danton also co-wrote his third horror effort as a director— *Psychic Killer*. It is a paranormal thriller about an innocent man confined to an insane asylum because of a wrongful murder conviction. Upon his release after the real murderer confesses, Arnold Masters (Jim Hutton) develops the power of astral projection and wreaks all manner of bloody and ghastly revenge on those responsible for the death of his mother and his wrongful imprisonment.

The 70's Nostalgia Bust | 367

Poster for *Psychic Killer*, a violent paranormal horror film starring familiar stars from the Late Show years. 1975, Lexington Productions, Syn-Frank Enterprises.

Arnold Masters is a soft-spoken mama's boy imprisoned for the murder of the doctor who refused to perform a vital operation on his mother (Diane Deininger). He is confined to an insane asylum and is under the watchful care of Dr. Laura Scott (Julie Adams). He maintains his innocence and refuses to confess to anything that he has not committed.

When he is transferred to the section on criminally violent patients, he makes the acquaintance of Emilio (Stack Pierce), a man convicted of

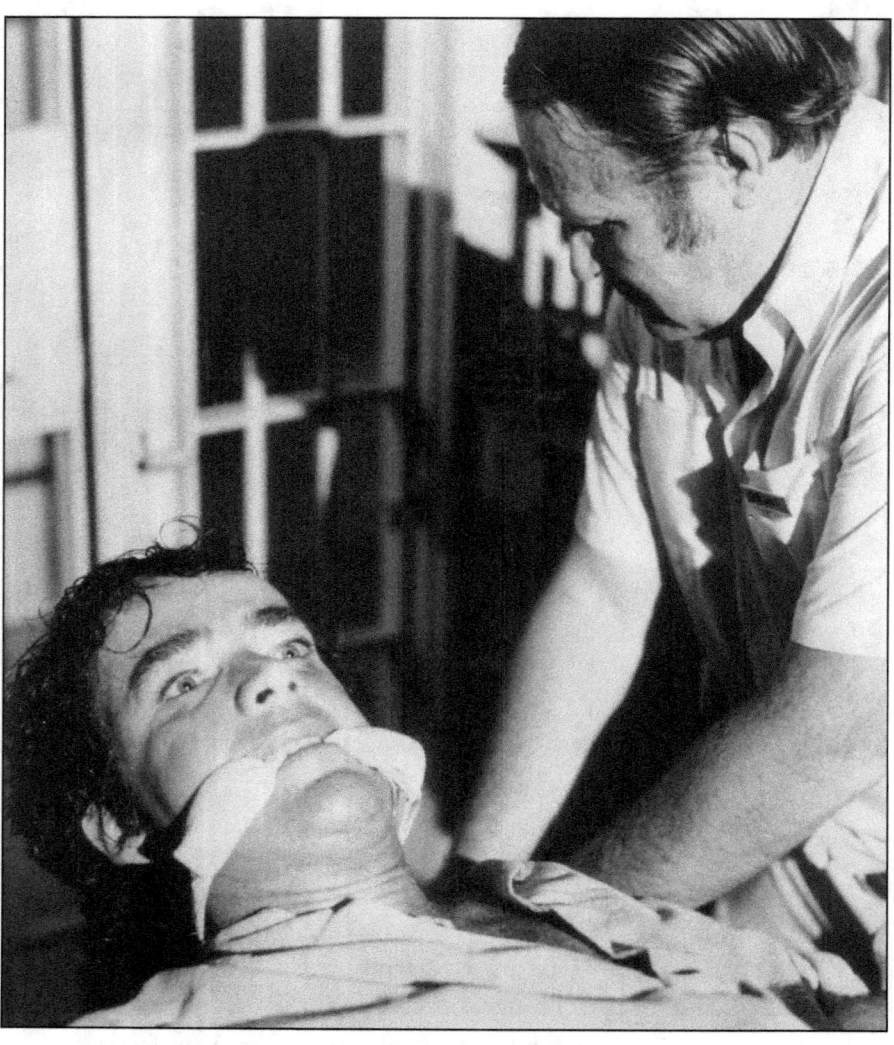

Arnold Masters (Jim Hutton) is subdued by an orderly (John Dennis) as he is transferred to a ward for the criminally insane. 1975, Lexington Productions, Syn-Frank Enterprises.

murdering his daughter when she became a prostitute. Arnold and Emilio form an instant rapport and Emilio cryptically tells Arnold that he will help him get revenge the day following his own death. Astral projection is the answer to this mysterious promise and Arnold learns about it through Emilio's effects, which have been bequeathed to him.

There is a mystic medallion and an arcane book and-before you know it!-Arnold is able to use the force that has taken the ancients years and even lifetimes to master. Astral projection is the ability of the astral body to leave the body to travel spiritual realms for soul edification and holy revelations. In this movie, it is a vehicle for Masters to kill the people he holds responsible for his mother's death and his incarceration: a doctor, a nurse, a police sergeant and a police man.

What follows is a series of gruesome-and, at times, graphic-murders. It does not take the detective on the case, Lt. Jeff Morgan (Paul Burke), long to make the connections between the victims and Arnold Masters. It is the M.O. that stymies the cop. It is not until Dr. Scott becomes involved with the cop that psychic phenomenon is suspected. It happens when Arnold's ethereal self talks to the doctor after she has made love to the cop. She consults Dr. Gubner (Nehemiah Persoff), a professor of paranormal psychiatry, for his help and the hunt is on for the psychic killer. It leads to a fiery climax that is as brutal as any denouement in any low-rent 70's horror thriller and that's saying a lot considering the level of sadism prevalent in this disturbing genre.

Psychic Killer is a combination of crime drama, revenge play, paranormal gore show, and elephant's graveyard for the stars of yesteryear. It is a nasty concoction, as crude and brutal as they came on the 1975 independent circuit. This definitely qualifies as a requisite Seventies horror film for Fifties stalwarts like Paul Burke, Aldo Ray, Whit Bissell, and Rod Cameron. A star turn for Jim Hutton and a cameo by Della Reese absolve them of any guilt. Nehemiah Persoff provides an odd connection to *The Death of Manolete* and *Dan August: The Color of Fury*.

Julie Adams automatically rises above any dubious project she has appeared in because of her greatness but the 'pity-of-it all' award goes to Neville Brand, who played Al Capone in the Desilu television production of *The Untouchables* and Allied Artists' *The George Raft Story*, plus many memorable roles in crime dramas and westerns of the 50's and 60's. In *Psychic Killer*, he is eviscerated in his own butcher shop and winds up as a bloody slab of beef on a meat hook!

Lt. Jeff Morgan (Paul Burke) and Dr. Laura Scott (Julie Adams) bond over dinner and a serious talk about malevolent demonic machinations in the Arnold Masters case. 1975, Lexington Productions, Syn-Frank Enterprises.

Despite being low rent, *Psychic Killer* is enjoyable (in a perverse way) because it is cheaply made and sleazy to the hilt. Dr. Paul Taylor (Whit Bissell) is killed with his own shotgun while conducting an adulterous affair with one of his patients. Nurse Burnson (Mary Wilcox) is scalded to death in the shower after she performs a nude boogie for no apparent reason. A crooked lawyer named Harvey B. Sanders (Joseph Della Sorte) is crushed to death by a cornerstone dropped from a crane after hitting a high note in his favorite aria. Sergeant Marv Sowash (Graydon Clark [the film's associate producer]) loses control of his car and plummets off of a cliff and parts of Lemonowski (Neville Brand), the butcher, wind up in a meat-grinding machine while the rest of him is hacked into prime cuts.

It is the haphazard way that it is edited and shot that makes the movie a typical cheapie circuit flick; that, and the amount of over-acting that keeps the action going. The chief culprit is Paul Burke, a fine actor who made his name in television with two great shows, *Naked City* and *12 O'Clock High*. Here, he is always screaming and ranting and it is strident. His sidekick, Lt. Dave Anderson, played by Aldo Ray, is at the other end of the emotional register. He grunts and groans, making a feeble attempt to emote, but all he does is gurgle and sputter when he is not making faces.

Neville Brand and Della Reese have an amusing scene where Lemonowski harangues Mrs. Gibson (Della Reese), a stereotypical welfare recipient who gets on his nerves. The comical tone of the scene changes when he closes shop and goes into the backroom, where he joins the cow carcasses on display.

Rod Cameron is a shadow of his former self as Dr. Commanger, the director of the sanitarium and Joseph Della Sorte has an absurd scene as an operatic lawyer and real estate maven who becomes acquainted with a concrete slab that silences his high notes forever. Whit Bissell maintains his integrity as the adulterous psychiatrist and Mary Wilcox is miscast as a supposedly sexy nurse doing the obligatory nude scene that was endemic in 70's horror flicks.

Only Julie Adams and Nehemiah Persoff escape unscathed from this histrionics hell. Their scenes together are played with professionalism and are the only noteworthy performances in the movie aside from Jim

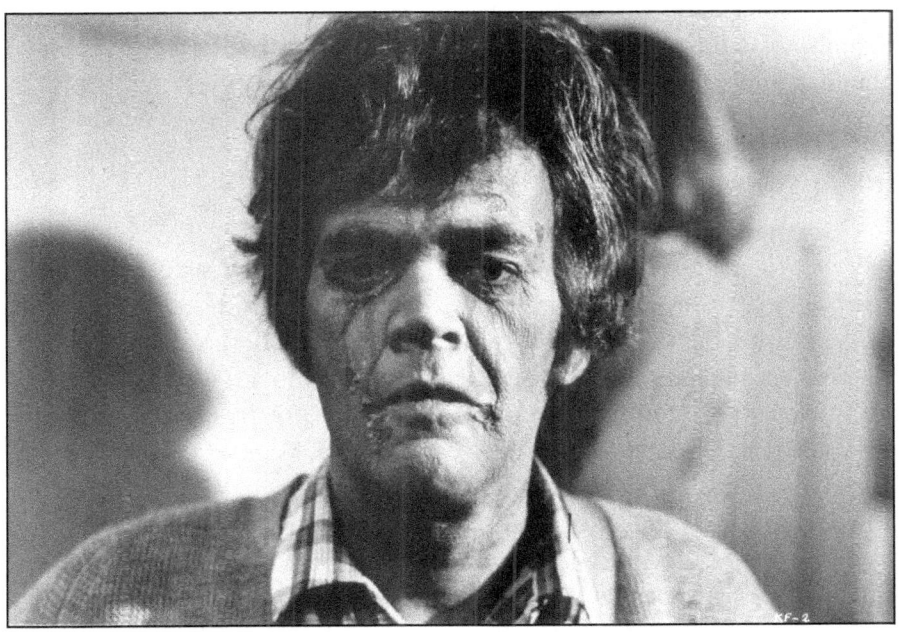

Arnold Masters (Jim Hutton) has transcended the world of sidereal time and exists as a vengeful demon in a parallel dimension. 1975, Lexington Productions, Syn-Frank Enterprises.

Hutton's acting. Unfortunately, Persoff's professor has his throat slit near the end of the movie. Jim Hutton's performance is low-keyed but deadly so it is no crime that he sleep walks through most of the movie. His only scenes of agitation are at the beginning and end of the movie. He has a breakdown in the sanitarium and bursts into hysterics at the end when he finds himself in a coffin going through a crematorium conveyor belt.

Ray Danton's shows a little bit of the style that he will perfect in his television direction. He has his cameraman reel the camera in haphazard fashion when Dr. Taylor loses control when he confronts his invisible nemesis. There is a nice use of the rack focus when Masters lies on his bed and contemplates his revenge. It is used to make a connection between the voodoo paraphernalia and Master's acknowledgement of his mission.

The best visuals are the brief scenes that precede the murders. Arnold Masters goes into a trance and visualizes each victim harassing his mother. The fantasy sequences are shot in faded black and white and are quite effective, if unintentionally funny. They are followed by the gruesome murders. However, the best shots in the movie occur during the opening credits when examples of Kirlian photography are shown as the credits flash. The eerie music that plays also enhances the otherworldliness of the visuals. The unsettling score by William Kraft also adds a creepiness to the murder scenes.

The Last Picture Show

Psychic Killer did reasonably well at the box office and successfully rode the wave of the brutal horror films. Sadism, cruelty and gore were staples of the waning but still lucrative genre and it was not unusual to see themes taken from real crime cases. Slice 'em-dice 'em movies were still the rage and when Ray Danton began preparations on *The Trunk Killer* for Viva Productions. It was based on the ax murderess, Winnie Ruth Judd, who murdered her friends and put their body parts in trunks. This seemed like the perfect premise for this grisly type of entertainment.

The project never went beyond the pre-production phase because the blockbuster had been reborn, thanks mainly to the phenomenal success of Steven Spielberg's *Jaws*. That's when crass commercialism returned to dominate the industry and moviemaking concentrated on the big money stakes.

Ray Danton returned to what he had been doing on television: playing mobsters. He plays Ralph Carson, another mobster caught in a sting in *Switch: Big Deal in Paradise* ('76). Unlike Chester Sierra, he is not comical and a lack of anchovies would be the least of his problems.

Robert Wagner played Pete Ryan, a con man gone straight and his sidekick was Eddie Albert as Frank McBride, a retired detective in *Switch*. They took on cases that required stings to bring down their marks and were aided by Malcolm (Charlie Callas), a retired small time con artist who opened a restaurant and Maggie (Sharon Gless), a Girl Friday and a Mistress-of-all Trades. The show ran from 1975 to 1978.

In *Big Deal in Paradise*, mobster Ralph Carson contacts Pete Ryan (Robert Wagner) and accuses him of having engineered the theft of laundered money. He gives him twenty four hours to return it. Ryan's scheme is to raise the money by gambling with Ralph Carson's partner, Phil Saunders (Peter Mark Richman) in the Bahamas. The scheme includes Laurie (Anne Archer), a vivacious con artist with the figure of a poolside Venus and the voice of a phone sex temptress. She will be the bait that lures Saunders into the game.

At this point of his career, all Ray Danton had to do was phone in his part. Menacing phone calls and threats of broken bones fit the bill for a 70's crime figure from central casting. Ralph Carson is a case in point. 1976, Glen A. Larson Productions; Universal Television.

Ray Danton had settled into his requisite mob personality by now. Ralph Carson is all attitude and menace-that's what befits an enforcer. Danton has a few menacing shots: slamming down the phone after threatening Ryan; dressed in black turtle neck and shadows while waiting in a tree to shoot Ryan; and bringing Ryan and MacBride to their knees on their yacht. He also gets beaten up and subdued by Mac (Eddie Albert), a rude come down to *I'll Cry Tomorrow* and *The Longest Day*.

In the late 70's, Canadian film productions were making deals with American studios and television networks. One of them was Canawest Film Productions, a division of KVOS-TV (B.C.) Ltd. They pitched the idea of filming a 90 minute TV movie in six days using videotape instead of film and inked a deal with 20th Century Fox television to produce two movies.

The licensed the rights to Derek Flint and hired Ray Danton to play him in *Dead on Target* and *Ultimatum*. It is ironic that, after playing so many James Bond clones, that Ray Danton would up playing the best Bond imitator: Derek Flint. The only thing is that Danton's Derek Flint isn't even a footnote to the secret agent roles he played in Europe. He's not even Derek Flint.

In a plot that was inspired by the oil crises of the Seventies, the looming power of the Arab world underlies the menace that threatens the

Ray Danton's Derek Flint is more like an international insurance investigator than a cool secret agent. 1976, 20th Century Fox television.

stability of capitalism. Actually, it is the duplicitous capitalists that are the villains but that is not revealed until the ending; that is, if you're not aware of clichés and standard plot solutions.

Wendell Runzler (Lawrence Dane), an oil executive for Southern Hemisphere Oil Co., is drugged and kidnapped by Sandra Carter (Sharon Acker), his secretary. Two bearded revolutionaries dressed in workmen's overalls cart him out of the building in a filing cabinet. By the time it is discovered that Runzler is missing, the kidnappers are gone. A shot of an overturned coffee cup dissolves into ultra-cheap credits backed up by a lively disco theme.

Poorly animated shots of a silhouetted Flint-in-motion dart across the screen. The credits roll while the silhouette flips villains, hang glides, and awkwardly runs around. This is an early indication of the film's low budget.

Simon Della Ciaza (Fran Russell), the chairman of SH Oil Co., has called in Derek Flint to act as an intermediary. Flint starts impressively by pointing out the defects in the company's security. He does so in a dramatic fashion-by hurling a handful of plastic caps that explode when they hit the wall. Flint also smugly points out the weak points in the entrance's electronic surveillance.

The chairman explains that SH Oil Co. has a contract with the sheik of Bar El Sol for drilling rights to the untapped oil reserves that lie beneath his kingdom. This doesn't rest too well with the Bar El Sol Liberation Army (BESLA), a revolutionary group. They have supplied the muscle in the kidnapping and have yet to make known their demands.

Leaden acting, scripting, directing, and editing combine to make the movie a sleeper, although not in the usual sense of the word. To awaken at various points of the movie actually makes for better viewing because the confusion adds an existential quality to the plot.

There aren't any peaks and valleys of action. Flint's challenges are a booby-trapped filing cabinet that fizzles when he shoots it and going undercover as a telephone repairman who drives a Rolls Royce. The only worthwhile thing about the movie is its soundtrack. It's a lively Seventies' disco score worthy of a 42nd Street exploitation theater movie because it is filled with fuzz and wah-wah guitars, r'n'b horns, slap bass playing, and syncopated percussions.

Why the filmmakers decided to call the main character Derek Flint is a puzzle because he doesn't have anything to do with the original character. He isn't even a secret agent; instead, he is more like an international

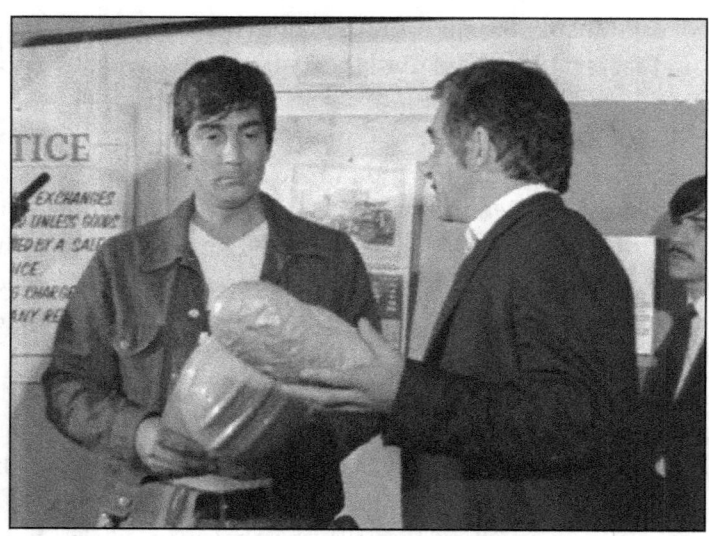

An incognito Flint (Ray Danton) learns the lesson of the bread loaf from a grim and determined La Hood (Donelly Rhodes). 1976, 20th Century Fox Television.

insurance investigator. In a role that would have been perfect for him at one time, Danton is as flat as the video tape look of the movie.

Danton's Flint is void of the irony and tongue-in-cheek humor vested in the original screen character played by James Coburn. Almost humorless to the point of catatonia, a cardboard cutout of himself might as well have played him. The telephone repairman and the filing cabinet scenes show Danton at the end of the road as the heroic tough guy. Still, his performance towers over the acting of the supporting cast.

Benita Rogers (Gay Rowan), his sidekick, is dorkish and Sandra Carter (Sharon Acker), the co-conspirator, is stilted. Runzler (Lawrence Dane) is a dummy, even though he plays the boss. Chairman Della Ciaza's (Fran Russell) sleaziness gives him personality, and Mrs. Runzler (Susan Sullivan) is a wallflower that has a couple of flat lines. LaHood (Donnelly Rhodes), the BESLA operative, is the most interesting supporting character because he has a nonchalant seediness to him.

LaHood, trying to instill fear in Flint, tells him that the people of Bar El Sol handle their enemies without mercy. He illustrates his point by slicing off a chunk of French bread with precision. He holds half a loaf up to Flint's face and says: "It is a tradition and we people of Bar El Sol are a traditional people."

If the criteria of secret agent films are applied to this film, it quickly gets flushed down the hopper. There aren't any challenges, romantic interludes, action sequences, or menacing villains unless you count the archery match, the massage, the filing cabinet scene, and LaHood's lesson of the bread loaf as qualifications.

Our Man Flint: Dead On Target was shelved and eventually shown on the summer anthology series, ABC's *Wide World Mystery*, a nightly challenge to the supremacy of *The Tonight Show*, starring Johnny Carson. At least, *Dead on Target* had a better fate than *Ultimatum*. Although Canawest went three days over schedule to produce *Dead on Target*, it had to postpone production on *Ultimatum* when Ray Danton became ill on the fifth day of filming. The original word was that the picture was on hiatus for three weeks but production was never resumed.

Ray Danton recovered from his ailment and returned to work, however brief his return may have been. He rounded off his acting career playing a hoodwinked crime boss and a store front stooge. They are Big Jim in *The Feather and Father Gang: The Apology* ('77) and Nick di Marcos in *Barnaby Jones: Duet for Danger* ('77). In both cases, he looks pale and wane.

Big Jim is Ray Danton's last mob boss impersonation. He is a supporting role in *The Feather and Father Gang: The Apology* ('77), a feeble sting episode. His identity is purloined by a father and daughter

Flint (Ray Danton) and Benita Rogers (Gay Rowan) use the element of surprise to break up a terrorist band. 1976, 20th Century Fox Television.

con team, Toni "Feather" Danton (Stephanie Powers), a lawyer, and Harry Danton (Harold Gould), an ex-con. They want to avenge the death of Charley (Eddie Firestone), their close friend, by a shipping magnate, Joe Generales (Gene Barry).

Using mistaken identity, phony radio reports, and government ringers, Toni and her father hoodwink Generales into confessing his involvement in Charley's murder. All along, Big Jim, having been released from prison, is a dupe who shows up at the wrong times in the sting and doesn't have any idea of what's going on. The best thing about the episode is that Ray Danton appears with Eddie Fontaine (rockabilly singer and star of the *Gallant Men*) as his bodyguard. Ray Danton plays the part as if he is in pain but he is balanced out by the grim-faced Eddie Fontaine so it's a sense of gangland style stoicism.

Ray Danton repeats the type in *Barnaby Jones: Duet for Danger* ('76). The only variations are that he is a mid-level club owner and he reads a couple of notices using aviator glasses. Barnaby Jones is another unlikely Quinn Martin hero. He is a homespun, geriatric private investigator. How he manages the stamina and musters to survive weekly bouts with the scum of the earth is beyond the realm of logic. Public popularity doesn't require logic, only star status. With Buddy Ebsen, it was a matter of cultural recycling to get Jed Clampett to come out like a Seventies' private eye.

In *Duet for Danger*, Barnaby Jones is the only character who has a Zen like calmness to the chaos created by Pearl Connors (Mary Ann Chinn) and Ruby Connors (Cassie Yates), otherwise known as the Starshine Sisters. He has dealt with them before in *Duet for Dying*. They were imprisoned for manslaughter at the end of that episode. Now, they dance their way out of prison as The Dream Girls when they are forced to participate in a jail break.

They use Lester Gibson (Bryan Montgomery) a love struck geek from the past to help them acquire money to jumpstart their non-existent careers. After a card sharp scam goes haywire, The Dream Girls are exploited by Nick di Marco (Ray Danton), a racketeer. He is the sinister and ill-tempered manager of a restaurant fronting for a secret gambling den run by the mob. The mobster uses the women when he catches them in a play-for-profit scheme with one of his dealers. He has long range plans for the sisters as lures for his card sharp operation. The low-level thug has plans to use them on the international gambling circuit, with the big payoff being a Monte Carlo scam.

Ray Danton is finally at his wit's end as the typecast mobster, an ironic closure to the glory days of Warner Brothers. His heart is not in the role, even though he gets to utter a 70's Las Vegas gangster's best line: "Waste them...and bury them in the desert." The scene of Nick di Marco putting down his rifle and surrendering to Barnaby Jones is the sad end of the line for the descendants of Pete Corder from *The Looters*. Leslie H. Martinson, the director of some of Ray Danton's best television work at Warner Brothers, directed *Duet for Danger*.

One of Ray Danton's assets was a strong-iron will to survive and dominate, possibly a quality of his iron-willed ego. That is why he did

The cover for the cast album of Selma. 1976, Cotillion Records.

not allow himself to be diminished by the end of his acting career. The stage had always been the bedrock of Ray Danton's acting career and he returned, once more, to the boards; only this time it was as a director.

He directed the stage musical, *Selma*, based on the life of Martin Luther King. Tommy Butler played Martin Luther King and composed the songs and the musical soundtrack. Denise Erwin portrayed Coretta Scott King. Janice Barnett and Betty Waldrom alternated in the role of Rosa Parks. The musical styles of the songs are a collection of genres that includes Afro-Cuban rhythms, southern gospel, rhythm and blues and 70's-styled disco-funk. Snippets of Dr. King's speeches are interspersed throughout the soundtrack.

The play was the brain child of Tommy Butler, who was inspired to create it in nine months in 1972 after he saw a special on Dr. Martin Martin Luther King that contained his I Had a Dream vision. The play starts with the assassination of Dr. King and his life is recounted in flashbacks recollected by his widow, Coretta Scott King. It covers the powerful mass transit boycott in Montgomery, Alabama after Rosa Parks was arrested after she sat in a 'whites only' section on a city bus. The play progresses through the famous Freedom marches and concludes with a rousing tribute to the freedom fighter.

Tommy Butler explains his vision this way: "In *Selma*, I didn't want to be guilty of doing the same thing that other people have done to us. You know, if a black person commits a crime, they say we are all alike-that's not so. I didn't want to be guilty of the same thing in portraying bigots in the play-I didn't want to give the impression that all white people are bigots, because not all people are bigots. So the way I deal with that in the play is that if the person playing the role of a bigot-if he's a white actor or a black actor-he wears a mask. Bigotry, after all, hides behind a mask, so they wear a mask."[7]

Financial backing was slow in coming and desperate times gave Butler the chance to perform and perfect his play in places like the basement of a church and local civic center. He eventually presented the play to Redd Foxx, who became the show's angel and it premiered at the Huntington Hartford Theatre in Hollywood.

Selma was a sobering recollection of Martin Luther King's vision. Dr. King insisted that his movement be non-violent as he was a minister who preached the gospel of Christ. The miracle that he achieved is that his life and death defeated the segregated South, a modern Babylon that defied the spirit of the American Constitution.

It was Martin Luther King and his Freedom Marches that forever changed the course of American history, not only for the future but by rewriting the past and this musical pays tribute to the man. It was a bare bones musical, the complete opposite of many of the over-indulgent techno-wonders that besot modern Broadway, but the message is what makes it stand tall and proud. *Selma* is one of Ray Danton's finest moments as a director because it was done on a shoestring budget and performed to SRO audiences.

Portrait of Ray Danton, circa 1976. 1985,
Hollywood Studio Magazine (Vol. 18. No. 8).

Law and Order

BEHIND THE TV EYE

By the late Seventies, Ray Danton's acting career had come to a standstill. Roles like Yellow Shirt and Derek Flint would have been handled with ease earlier in his career. Instead, he offered indifferent performances. Aside from that, as the Seventies progressed, these types of characters seemed outdated. The *Star Wars* phenomenon had just started and the youth market was reinvented. Ray Danton's career as an actor folded but, instead of becoming a Fifties' actor who fizzled in parody mode during the Seventies, he found a new path that led him to success behind the scenes as a television director.

The website archivists have created museums that provide technical info-logs about the history of television shows. It is among the vast reams of knowledge that one can spot Ray Danton's name in the television credits for director, writer, producer, and supervising producer from the mid-70's to the late 80's. To the average viewer, his name is a meaningless credit in an endless rerun caught in the syndication loop. For others, it is a vestige of an earlier time when the electronic eye belonged to the triple late night shows of the Cyclops' Network.

Ray Danton summed up his transition from actor to director in a 1979 Variety profile, "Ray Danton Has Not Quit Acting-He's Just Busy Directing Television."

The article quotes Ray Danton as saying that he, " hasn't quit acting, but I don't have time to do more because I'm busy directing. I like directing, that's what I'm doing and enjoy. It's a good opportunity. I couldn't create an atmosphere as an actor, but I can as a director. I try to create a convivial atmosphere, but it isn't easy. Still, I never had so much fun In my whole life."

"There are problems, however", he comments. "There is never enough time in TV. It's not fair. TV Is a tight squeeze, restricted in time and money."

With all that, he finds himself moving more and more to directing. Danton in recent years was before the cameras in 11 motion pictures in Europe and for five years did no TV.

"I was afraid to do TV. I thought the demand and velocity of the medium."

He felt that it worked against real quality. At one point, he was asked to direct a "Columbo" segment, but declined. As an actor, also, he found himself typed as a heavy, something he tried to avoid. "

"It didn't bother me when I was 30-31, but then I found I couldn't get out of it. I was determined to beat the mold," he remarked in the interview."[8]

Ray Danton's experience as an actor is reflected in his respect for the craft from a director's point of view. He uses technical devices to make a point but knows when to get out of the performers way so they can act. It's the acting that makes the final point, with the use of techniques adding the accents.

The thematic and technical threads that connect his different projects with each other give his work a personality. The devices and techniques used to express the familiar themes and attitudes comprise his visual style. From *Senza Via D'Uscita* to *John Henry*, there are consistencies among the evolution of his style. Another dimension to his technique is subject matter and personality quirks. His narrative is stronger and his command of the action is steady.

Rage, the search for identity and finding comfort in nostalgia are recurring themes in many episodes. Identity of the self is often a spoke in the familial wheel. His romance with the past is sometimes expressed through the use of photographs. Ray Danton's bag of tricks, from stunning camera shots to action scenes handled with finesse, had grown considerably since his schlock horror days. Some of his favorite devices are slow pans, fading lights, double exposures, slow motion and triple cuts.

He uses slow pans to express extremes: emptiness and dejection or excess and grandiosity. Fading lights often suggest absence and loss. Double exposures create moving montages that hide ironic conclusions. Slow motion creates tension; and triple cuts heighten drama by viewing an action from three different angles edited together to create a quick tempo and sudden shift in locale.

Ray Danton's directing portfolio is a mixture of crime dramas, syndication and cable television projects. He became a television director when the influence of *The Godfather* was still strong. The movie's influence was pervasive in 70's movies and television and still resonated in the 80's.

He honed his directing skills with regular assignments for *Quincy, M.E.* and broadened his talent with *Mickey Spillane's Mike Hammer* and *Cagney and Lacey*. His method and style with *Quincy, M.E.* was stark and to the point; he becomes a nostalgic romanticist with the Mike Hammer series; and he combines the best of both styles with *Cagney and Lacey*.

QUINCY, M.E. (PART ONE)

Quincy (Jack Klugman) was a medical examiner with the instincts of a detective. When an autopsy suggested foul play, he used the corpse's side of the story to unravel the mystery and expose the perpetrator. His assistant, Sam Fujiyama, was played by Robert Ito. John S. Ragin played Quincy's officious boss, Dr. Robert Asten. They were the satellites that revolved around Quincy when it came to his laboratory domain.

Quincy's connection to the police department was the cantankerous Lt. Frank Monahan (Garry Walberg), whose sidekick was Sgt. Brill (Joseph Roman), a stone wall with little dialogue. Their relationship was volatile in a friendly way and provided the basis for many conflicts and comic

Jack Klugman lent his coarse charm to *Quincy, M.E.*, a successful crime show about a dogged forensics medical examiner who was part sleuth, much to the dismay of the police department. 1977, Universal Television.

resolutions. That was the case with everyone that Quincy dealt with, including restauranteur Val Bisoglio, who played the owner of Danny's Bar and Grill, where the main players often spent their down time. *Quincy, M.E.* ran from 1976 to 1983.

Ray Danton's residency at *Quincy, M.E.* allowed him to tighten his style and eliminate the redundant and clumsy aspects that were apparent in his big screen horror films. The pace of television production imposed a discipline that resulted in a style that grew from curt and deliberate to poetic and commanding.

Jack Klugman had a demanding and domineering acting approach and this provided the setup for fireworks in every episode. Ray Danton helmed the action with an unobtrusive directing style that enhanced the cast's acting by observing their conflict instead of intruding on their space. He was developing his style so he concentrated on an almost static presentation to let the players unfold the drama. It was rare that he added artsy camera angles and, then, it was to promote perspective as opposed to affecting a grandiose baroque vision.

Ray Danton's *Quincy, M.E.* episodes featured familiar actors and actresses who worked with him in the past. The most notable is Julie Adams, who starred in three episodes. Rudy Solari, who played Rabbit Stockings in *The Four Thumbs Story,* appeared in four episodes. Fifties' actors Neville Brand, Whit Bissel, Cameron Mitchell and Judson Pratt had parts. Former stars from the Warner Brother years were Carolyn Jones, Edd Byrnes, Madlyn Rhue, Donald May and Peter Brown. Jose Ferrer and Jane Greer also had supporting roles, as did former *Peter Gunn*, Craig Stevens.

Many of the twenty-three *Quincy* episodes that Ray Danton directed can be divided into three categories: crime dramas, crusading causes and faded glory exposes.

The crime dramas are old-fashioned who-done-its?, thrillers, and revenge sagas. The crusader episodes are indictments of social abuses that are partial polemics dressed in plot and characters. The faded glory exposes are reminiscent of *Sunset Boulevard* because of their grotesque beauty and twisted romanticism of screen iconography.

The first *Quincy, ME* episode Ray Danton directed is called *A Question of Time.* Rudy Solari plays a quack psychologist named Bridges who blots the name of the respected Thaler Institute with his angst-ridden antics. Patients devolve to the womb via hot tubs and verbal harassment. The doctor incites them to rebel against their complacent identities.

Quincy (Jack Klugman) witnesses one of Bridges (Rudy Solari) primal therapy sessions at the Thaler Incident in *A Question of Time*. 1977, Universal Television.

They lose touch with their societal inhibitions and become slaves to primal self-hatred. Shouting resentments like slogans, they use adrenaline as a drug of choice.

The scheme falls apart when Tom Holloway (John Alderman), a solitary patient, dies and attempts to make the death look natural are revealed by Quincy to have been caused during a phase of hot tub hysterics.

Mrs. Holloway (Brenda Scott), the man's widow, is trying to get an insurance settlement but the institute is too strong to challenge. Walter Kingman (Peter Mark Richman) is a slippery high-priced lawyer whose expertise protects the organization's sterling reputation. Quincy's specialty is tilting at windmills and his impetus is talking to the founder of the institute, Ruth Thaler (Irene Tedrow), an old friend who rues the impersonal expansion of her clinic into a series of impersonal franchises.

This episode reflected the explosion of pop-psychology regimes that flooded the 70's psyche. Societal and religious identities were considered archaic and detrimental to the development of the true self. A new narcissism was slowly crowding out altruism and the common weal. It was an outgrowth of the spiritual awakening of the late 60's with its influx of eastern gurus and yogis. Psychology was slowly edging out psychiatry and one did not need an accredited degree, only a good line of rhetoric and a dynamic personal presentation, like Bridges, a man who did not have verifiable credentials and failed to get para-medical help for one of his patients for fear of exposing his non-existent reputation.

There are some nice uses of the camera to achieve moods and rhythms in *A Question of Death*. When Holloway loses control of his senses, he rocks in a slow motion rant that borders on the horrific as the steam engulfs his flailing body.

Menacing shots look downward at the spa where patients rant and rave while Bridges motivates them to lose their inhibitions. A quick cut takes Quincy from telling Monahan that he will get the answer from the corpse to him and Sam standing over the body and studying test results.

In another scene, the camera focuses on the Holloway children swaying back and forth on their swings while a conversation between their mother and Quincy dominates the soundtrack. The camera tracks to the left to some bushes and focuses on garden steps where the conversers come into view to finish their talk.

Craig Stevens appeared in *Tissue of Truth*. He plays Bill Stoddard, the father of a kidnapping victim whose live burial becomes a certain death sentence when the kidnapper is killed in a car accident. Quincy must use deductive reasoning to pinpoint the burial location by examining a collection of disparate clues, including teeth impressions in a partially eaten apple and a puddle in the desert located from a bird's eye view of a helicopter in the middle of the night.

Stevens has enough screen time to show an array of emotions from helplessness to total control. He develops a hands-on approach to locate his missing son. A betrayal to his heart disrupts his world and unleashes the hidden primal man in him when he hits the field to dig for the secret compartment that holds the teenager with the limited oxygen supply.

This episode bows to one of the popular conventions of 70's pop entertainment: the car chase. *Bullitt* with Steve McQueen created a new craze in the late 60's with its breathtaking case chase sequence. The kidnapper's attempt to escape an overzealous yahoo sheriff results in his mountainside dive after a long and winding car chase. Royal Dano has a small part as Holsang, a disgruntled farmer whose reluctant clues help solve the puzzle of the buried missing kidnap victim.

In *Main Man*, Julie Adams plays Mrs. Daniels, the estranged wife of Walter Daniels (Eugene Roche), a man whose obsession with his sons' success on the gridiron wreaks havoc on his family. The self-perception of being a lifelong number two causes the football fanatic to push his sons to the limits of greatness as gridiron heroes.

Frank (Michael F. Kelly), the older brother, is a college football star and Steve (Scott Columby), the younger star, is deemed to have greater potential than his sibling.

The mania has fatal consequences when the older boy dies after a tackle during a game. Quincy's examination reveals the cause of death: a brain cyst. Because it is congenital, the medical examiner has to convince the hard-headed father that it would be catastrophic if he lets his son play in the big game on Friday, when the boy will have a chance to break an old record and become the high school's greatest player.

The father is a self-confessed loser who cannot accept his part in alienating his wife. He blames her for the family's dysfunctional behavior because of her walking out on them. It takes relentless hounding by Quincy and Mrs. Daniels to get him to change his mind, which he does, right in the middle of the big game. Peter Brown, from *Lawman*, plays a

Mrs. Daniels (Julie Adams) and Quincy (Jack Klugman) are relieved when Walter Daniels (Eugene Roche) takes his son Steve (Scott Columby) out of the 'big game' rather than risk his life in *Main Man*. 1977, Universal Television.

coach at the school. This episode was based on a story by Ray Danton who, again, shows his love of football and his knowledge of the Pop Warner football circuit. It also showcases brilliant acting by Eugene Roche, which is something you always got from him.

In *Last of the Dinosaurs*, Carolyn Jones plays the shadow wife of Will Prestin (Chuck Robertson), a Hollywood Western legend whose death was part of a scenario that was more suited to a murder mystery. Quincy has to go beyond the screen legend's invincible image to piece together his case when he investigates the mysterious death of the iconic cowboy star who was one of the coroner's childhood celluloid heroes. Quincy, an ardent fan of the western star, is stunned when he is contacted to examine the earthly remains of his hero, especially when he receives the call at Danny's, where he is watching one of the legend's movies on the bar's television set.

The crime scene suggests robbery and manslaughter, but Quincy believes that the scenario is a phony meant to mislead the police, which it does. Lt. Monahan and Quincy butt heads about suspects and motives. The detective insists on railroading two drifters who claim they are victims of circumstance. Quincy believes the vagrants are innocent and is convinced that the murderer is someone closer to home, especially when he discovers that reports of the actor stumbling like a drunk turn out to be a diabetic going into a coma.

Quincy's investigation into the face behind the mask leads to a belief in his addiction to drugs; instead, it is found out that Will Prestin was a diabetic.

Quincy proves that Prestin was severely weakened by his need for an insulin shot and would have eventually died. The person who replaced his insulin with water and was also the one struck him with his Oscar before going into a coma because of the placebo.

The Last of the Dinosaurs is a tragic Hollywood expose, a variation of the face behind the mask premise. The man behind the myth rides south by way of the west in a cautionary tale of hero worship and the danger of trusting jealous sycophants. Cameron Mitchell plays Granger, a gopher under suspicion before he is arrested for the murder of the western icon. The former stunt man's career was ruined when he was injured performing a stunt for the western hero. Disability insurance is being on the payroll as a major domo-gopher.

He makes a better suspect than the drifters, who have an alibi in the missus, Sylvia Prestin (Carolyn Jones), a sad wall flower who harbored her husband's dark secrets in exchange for the privileges of being married to a screen legend. It was her burden that absolved her husband of his guilt until betrayal freed her from being crowded out by a starlet with less mileage.

The emptiness of fame is the remnants of the past captured in photographs of Will Preston's heyday. They cover a table in the foreground and dominate a shot of Quincy and the widow meeting for the first time. Another contrast between reality and illusion is a stunned Quincy looking at the Will Prestin cowboy movie on the bar television after he has received the call from Monahan informing him of his idol's death. A somber analysis of the contradictory information in a darkened lab adds to the ambivalent relationship of star-struck fans and their clay idols. In this episode, John Anderson appears as a movie director and John Dennis has a part of a bartender selling information to Quincy.

Images is another episode based on a short story written by Ray Danton. Quincy's credibility is lost when his death notice of Jessica Ross (Jessica Walter), a famous TV journalist, is contradicted by her appearance at the press conference. The empirical facts of his autopsy are negated by her presence yet he is convinced that he is right in his pronouncement.

Corporate power, individual scruples and the evil monozygotic twin figure in a story that pits media stardom against a majority of one. DNA never had it so hard because of individual rights but, in the end, it is the evil twin who is carted away while the charred corpse of her sister, the celebrity, remains in cold storage.

Jessica Walter gives a convincing portrayal as a psychotic fraud who tries to recreate the personality that she has destroyed, consumed and been reborn as. She fiercely guards her territory after it has been invaded by Quincy. Her breakdown at the end of the story is a dam bursting under pressure and she elicits sympathy from the audience even though she is a killer.

The settings range from a sleazy motel where the celebrity reporter often prepared her stories (no reason for this idiosyncrasy is ever given) to a convent/orphanage where she kept her out-of-wedlock daughter hidden from media scrutiny.

Fading light is one of Ray Danton's visual devices for denoting loss. After Quincy exposes the evil twin in *Images*, the technical crew on her show shuts down the set when the program is pre-empted because of technical difficulties. The icon's death is symbolized by a slow zoom on her chair as the studio lights dim. The zoom stops when the last studio light

Dr. Asten (John S. Ragin) is relieved to find that TV news icon Jessica Ross (Jessica Walter) is still alive despite having been pronounced dead by Quincy (jack Klugman) who is still stands by the signature on his death certificate. 1978, Universal Television.

goes out and the camera focuses on a close-up of an empty chair half-lit in shadows. The same episode shows a twilight laboratory after Quincy has been suspended for the seemingly wrongful death charge. Whit Bissell has a small part as the journalist's doctor, Dr. Miles Thornton.

Even Odds is a powerful episode where compelling acting takes center stage. Quincy, Sam, Lt. Monahan and Sgt. Brill are investigating a crime scene where a bar owner was shot to death. Quincy has some doubts about the scenario and refers to a similar case that he investigated where the clues did not point to the obvious suspect. It takes convoluted steps to unravel that mystery but before he can voice his doubts he is shot during a melee when the suspect is brought in and grabs the murder weapon from Lt. Monahan, prompting a wild shootout.

Quincy's chances for survival are slim but even in his comatose state he solves the case when Dr. Asten, Sam and Lt. Monahan use past tactics and strategy to piece together a murder that is not as routine as it appears to be. Four flashbacks recreate the eureka! moments of the previous cases that will crack this case, much to the consternation of Lt. Monahan, who believes that he has an open and shut case in both shootings. He is wrong on both counts.

The actors realize a well-written script that could only come off with gut wrenching emotion. No one goes overboard in an emotionally-charged episode. It is one of Danton's best *Quincy, ME* episodes, possibly because the focal point is a comatose Quincy, who dominates the proceedings even in his absence.

Ed Grover, who often appeared in Ray Danton's *Quincy, ME* episodes, plays Dr. Richards, the not-too-optimistic physician in charge of Quincy's case. He has a strong scene with John S. Ragin as Dr. Asten. They are debating whether or not to remove the bullet which is located in a sensitive area. Either decision could mean death for Quincy and the actors ably illustrate the gravity of making life and death decisions relative to their professions.

A Question of Death is a moral tale that deals with the ethical dilemma of life support systems and the moral obligation of organ donation. It also touches on the legal bottom feeders who capitalize on the grief and

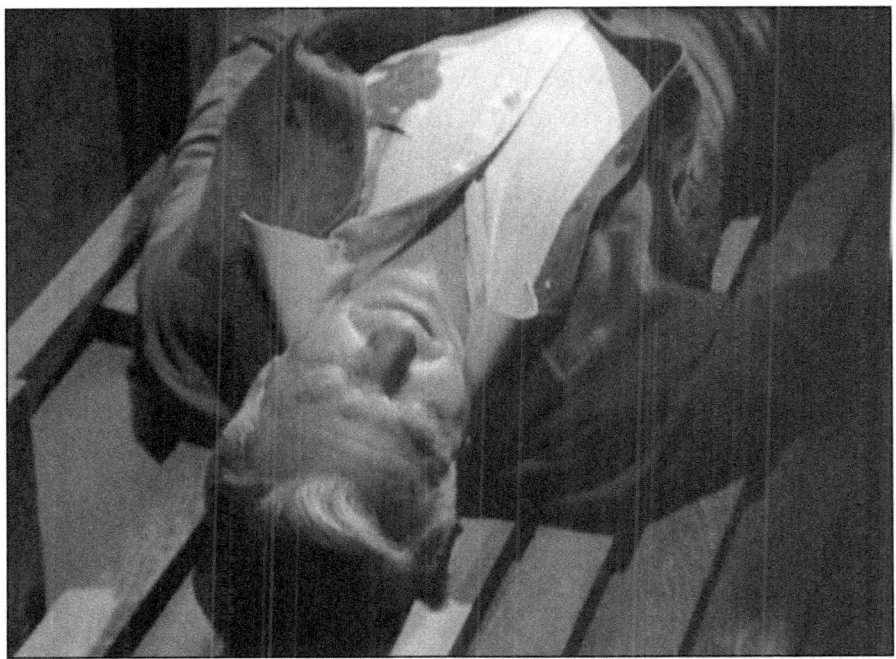

In *Even Odds*, Quincy's life hangs in the balance when he is shot during the investigation of a robbery and shooting death in a bar. 1978, Universal Television.

sorrow of the survivors. Raymond Morrison (Granville Van Husen) is an ambulance chasing lawyer who convinces the bereaved parents (Judson Pratt and Jeanne Bates) of a young man killed in a motorcycle accident that he was not clinically dead when his life support system was turned off. He persuades the parents to sue the hospital and Quincy for damages. Royal Dano plays Dr. Williams, an expert on brain injuries and clinical death, who is totally discredited on the witness stand which results in the charges against Quincy being dropped.

This episode is also an examination of today's health care system where the bottom line is money and paper work sustains the machinery that keeps brain dead people alive. The bureaucracy is portrayed as an unemotional tyrant that toys with the emotions of individuals whose credence is established by money or insurance. The case in point is the sub-plot regarding a man waiting for a kidney transplant. He was next in line for the donor's organ but is bumped down the list because a wealthy contributor to the hospital is considered more deserving of the life saving procedure. The agony of living on a dialysis machine is presented in living color and it was something that had relevance for Ray Danton, who suffered from kidney disease and had to rely on such a support system.

Medical malpractice by a Dr. Butcher-type prompts Quincy to seek a federal indictment of the fiend in *The Depth of Beauty*. The episode begins with a bird's eye view of the night in flight. The lit windows of the massive buildings make the scene look like a panoramic night skyline but a slow zoom focuses on trouble in paradise when a disfigured woman in a silk nightgown jumps to her death from the roof of one of the buildings.

Quincy's autopsy brings attention to her facial scars. He investigates and finds that they were the result of a botched chemical peel by Dr. Emile Green (Garnett Smith), a gynecologist who performs plastic surgery on the sidelines and hides behind legal loopholes.

Rudy Solari plays Baker, the District Attorney who goes out on a limb for Quincy when he brings charges against Dr. Green. The lawyer is humiliated when his case is thrown out of court and he blames Quincy for not providing substantial evidence to justify a trial. Quincy was never one to be rebuffed by paper chases or brick walls nor did he ever cease to plead his case or seek any means to prove his point.

Donald May, from *The Roaring Twenties* and *Colt .45*, appears as Dr. Walt Mitchell, a successful and reputable plastic surgeon who aids Quincy in his campaign against the fraudulent surgeon. Through dogged assurance Quincy manages to enlist the support of Dori Larkin (Jane Greer), a former screen legend who lives in seclusion after she was harmed by the surgeon. She is a recluse who surrounds herself with publicity photos that preserve her legendary beauty.

Her past glory lives on the walls that guard her privacy. The movie star reluctantly lends her public support to Quincy's attempts to shut down the practice of an unlicensed butcher who works as a plastic surgeon. The final shock is the once-beautiful movie star removing her mask on television. Her clout sways public opinion after she appears on television and reveals her new face.

Dark Angel is PCP, popularly known as Angel Dust. It is a hallucinogenic drug that gives its user super human strength and psychotic reactions, often to the detriment of the body. PCP is the real culprit in the accidental death of Billy Harris (Richard Stanley) a violent car thief (and murderer), not the cop, NYPD officer Tommy Bates (Neville Brand), who subdued him.

Tommy Bates was Lt. Monahan's former partner and the two share some wild memories after they have been suspended. Bates has been crucified by Internal Affairs because of the testimony of several hostile witnesses and the lieutenant was given two weeks administrative leave after he roughed up the surviving suspect.

It takes Quincy's relentless efforts to clear the cop of a departmental castigation and public smearing by Charlie Trusdale (William Daniels), a social activist who has a vendetta against cops because his son was shot to death by a cop. Quincy is able to link the suspects to the murder of a butcher and prove that a blow suffered during that altercation was responsible for the fatal injury incurred in the scuffle with the police.

The episode is a social heads-up to a serious problem of the time, the rise in use of PCP among teenagers. The usual scare tactics are videos of recovering addicts trying to make sense of it all through addled wits and paranoid perceptions. However, the frightening statistics offered by the episode's expert, Dr. Herb Tarlton (Paca Thomas), are enough to justify the preaching.

Marshall Thompson plays Mr. Harris, the father of the murder victim. He belongs to the generation that survived the Great Depression and World War II only to enter an alien world populated by psychotic teenagers plagued by hallucinogenic demons.

No Way to Treat a Flower is another cautionary tale warning teenagers about the peril of marijuana grown with a gout medicine called colchicine. The super herb was developed by the Army during WW II so it could create a durable hemp from which a stronger type of rope could be made. In the 70's, it causes a violent death in whoever smokes it.

Kathy Campbell (Karlene Crockett) is the first victim and she is soon followed by her boyfriend. His on-screen death is intense as his pale corpse is found sitting under tree by the roadside. Paca Thomas returns as the voice of reason, this time named Dr. Mark Lieber.

Quincy is in familiar territory when he comes up against a bureaucracy that is hampered by Catch-22 type of statutes. Drug magazines can advertise forbidden products so long as the wording is protected by the law. It takes Quincy's skill in toppling windmills to get things done. Whit Bissell has a small part as a botanist who explains the purpose of colchicine.

Dead Last is about a horse racing scam run by Ron Henner (Joseph Sirola), a small time stable owner who uses ringers and dope to fix races. It takes the deaths of two jockeys—Julio Ruiz (Daniel Faraldo) and Billy McGinn (Lou Wagner)—and the autopsy of a horse to make Quincy investigate the scheme and expose the scam: using second-rate ringers and amphetamines to create larges purses for long shot jackpots.

Joseph Sirola plays Ron Henner (l), a race horse owner who tries to advance his standing in the big league through doping and fixed races. 1979, Universal television.

Slow motion is used to portray an antic horse as it jumps up and down in its stable. The action is cut with a scene of two jockeys arguing with each other about stolen opportunities. Later, one of the jockeys is found dead in the horse's stable, seemingly stomped to death. Quincy's autopsy comes to another conclusion.

Quincy and Dr. Asten conflict on a voucher for horse's hooves and it is not until the supervisor hears Quincy's rationale that he reverses his stance and supports the coroner when it leads to exposing the killer. The exchange is humorous and well-directed.

A satisfied Dr. Asten leaves the lab and the camera tracks him through the glass window. Lt. Monahan and Sgt. Brill pass him in the hall and the camera backtracks to follow them as they enter the lab to badger Quincy. Without skipping a beat, he uses the same logic to make his case with the detectives. It is a scene that is smooth and well paced.

QUINCY, M.E. (2)

Ray Danton established himself as a gifted director by the time the 80's began. He was a resident director for *Quincy, M.E.* and also directed a couple of other shows, too. There were other changes in store for him, as well. He and Julie Adams finalized their divorce, although they remained friendly and continued to work together. There was also another downturn in Ray Danton's health when he received his first kidney transplant in 1981. He had to temporarily relinquish his *Quincy, M.E.* director's schedule to George Fenady until he regained his strength.

As *Quincy, M.E.* continued it run, the show began to veer more towards a soapbox format. There were still good murder mysteries and some of the socially relevant storylines were successful from a dramatic standpoint. However, overt sentimentality and statistical interludes diluted the effect of some of the causes. The eventual spokesperson for the cause of the week was Dr. Emily Hanover (Anita Gilette), initially Quincy's love interest and ultimately the shrill voice of doom. Before Dr. Gilette's part grew to that point, the facts and motives were spelled out with statistics and slide shows from various experts.

Never a Child is a sickening look at pedophiles who prey on runaway children. It is a forceful drama about the seedy Uncle Harry (Alan Manson), a chicken hawk who victimizes young runaway girls. At the bus station, he stands out among the pimps because he is dressed like a

Uncle Harry (Alan Munson) is a sick pedophile who preys on underage runaways in *Never a Child*. Here, he details his plans on having Amanda (Melora Hardin) star in a porn movie. Terri (Tara Buckman) is an enabler who is about to turn the tables on the pervert. 1979, Universal Television.

suave middle-aged bachelor whose pickup line is being concerned about runaways because his daughter is one of them. Finances force him to produce a child porno movie and he graduates to murder when he pushes one of his former victims off a rooftop.

Quincy has to cut through a lot of red tape again as he tackles the sordid issue of teenage runaways, kiddie porn and predators like Uncle Harry. Alan Munson plays the revolting Uncle Harry and Amanda (Melora Hardin) is a naïve runaway who almost falls prey to the monster. Terri (Tara Buckman) is a young woman trapped by years of servitude before she finds redemption by saving Amanda, and Carol Trager (Cassie Yates) is the avenging angel who guides the young women out of their private hells with her persistent struggle against the system. Father Tony Hamilton (Kene Holliday) and Councilman Becker (Walter Brooke) are two faces of the system that eventually see eye-to-eye when tackling the problem at hand.

Hot Ice has all of the ingredients of a good thriller: diamond smuggling, beauty contests, Las Vegas gangsters, manipulative Feds, a sexy bodyguard and a debonair assassin with a poison-tipped umbrella. It is also a suspenseful episode leavened with laughs.

It all comes together in a story that has a reluctant Quincy playing secret agent when his life takes a turn for the exotic after he performs an autopsy and finds a small cache of mob diamonds on the corpse. Quincy is used by two bumbling federal agents to sting the mobsters in Las Vegas, where he is to judge a Miss Coroner's Contest.

Guest stars include Elaine Giftos as FBI Agent Roxie Adams, Quincy's glib and alluring FBI bodyguard; John Karlen and Edward Grover are Customs Agents Rice and Niven, two the inept feds; George Loros is Bernie Evans, a crime lackey posing as the boss to retrieve the diamonds.

Nicholas Georgiade (Rossi on *The Untouchables*) is Lew, an even lower-mob underling. His presence in the cast adds meaning to Quincy's jibe that the feds don't need him, they need Elliot Ness. Elsa Raven plays a frumpy coordinator of the pageant and Katherine Moffat is the wide-eyed winner. Veteran character actor Robert Cornthwaite has a small role as Dr. Evans, a physician who attends to Quincy after the medical examiner is poisoned by Eddie Parker, the umbrella assassin, played with composure and derring-do by Tom Williams.

Diplomatic Immunity is a compelling murder drama involving South American politics. Armando Sarejo (Rudy Solari) is a dictator who visits the United States for life-saving surgery. Sarejo is a proud iron-handed despot who regales his wife, Isabella (Ana Navarro), with his criticism of America's First Amendment privileges when they view the television news' account of the protestors picketing his stay at the hospital.

Isabella later offers an apologia for a totalitarian regime run by men like her husband, whom she looks upon as being a hero-savior who saves the people from themselves. She shares her husband's opinion that democracy gives rise to the riff-raff who are incapable of determining what is right for their lives.

Sarejo is well-guarded in his hospital room when some of his staff members are murdered. It is deemed that he is the target and the suspects are the protestors who detest his repressive regime. The suspicion is correct to a certain extent because they have trained an assassin to impersonate a hospital orderly. He only succeeds in killing the wrong targets and his eventual slip-up leads to a police raid of the revolutionaries' squalid headquarters.

The bust does not end the attempts on the dictator's life. Quincy uses his medical expertise to discover that the real threat is one of his entourage, a doctor who has been bribed by the dictator's brother-in-law, the acting potentate who wants to be more than a guest dictator.

His method of operation is to inject an anti-coagulant into one of the feed bags that will be used during the procedure. He is foiled by Quincy just as the patient is about to go into a coma because of a loss of blood. The bag is replaced, the potentate is saved and the bitter doctor is arrested.

Honor Thy Elders is a cautionary tale about growing old in America, where the race goes to the swift and the strong and there is no runner-up prize for experience and wisdom. It starts with an old man, a victim of abuse, looking at old photos of himself and his abusive son as a child. He puts away the memories and takes out a small box where he has hidden his sleeping pills, the cache he uses to commit suicide in the nursing home the night before his release to return to his family.

Tim Morgan (Joby Baker) is the son whose failing business drives him to harass his family. His mother (Susan French) rues the day when her son became the parent, a responsibility he is not fit to accept. He was physically abusing his father and strikes his mother in a heated argument. Quincy's dogged persistence brings the situation to a head.

A tragic example of negligence is the case of Muriel (Estelle Winwood) and Edna (Jessamine Milner), two elderly sisters whose assets have been siphoned off by their avaricious nephew. They are indigent and live in squalor, their house a rundown tenement populated by cats.

It is the rage within that creates monsters out of ordinary people and no one knows this better than Sharon Ross (Julie Adams), the director of a center where abused elders can share their skills with young people. She reinvigorates the senior citizens by having them share talents, memories and patience with the younger members of the community.

It is hard not to be affected by the message of this episode because it shatters many stereotypes about the elderly. The character who has this epiphany is a politician (Leonard Stone) who refuses to staff a new youth center with seniors until he sees the wonders achieved by Ms. Ross' facility.

Madlyn Rhue was a contract player at Warner Brothers and starred with Ray Danton in *A Majority of One*, along with many television episodes. She plays Ann Asten-Stedman, a distraught mother-in-denial in *Unhappy Hour*, a polemic about teenage alcoholism. It is a sobering study considering the statistics of teenagers who are destroyed by the disease. The plot centers around possible manslaughter charges against Melanie Stedman (Karlene Crockett), Dr. Astin's niece, after her boyfriend is killed in a car accident while she is driving under the influence.

Honor Thy Elders is a sobering study of elder abuse. It also depicts the contribution elders can make as mentors to the young, a point driven home by Sharon Ross (Julie Adams), an activist shows Quincy her philosophy in action. 1980, Universal Television.

Dr. Asten has an ethics crisis because the parents expect him to sweep any incriminating evidence under the rug. Quincy believes that his boss' moral character is too strong to give into the pressure but Dr. Asten is not so sure. What makes the burden so great is that Quincy and Dr Asten have switched jobs temporarily because each man thinks that he has the heavier work load. The deadly car accident is Dr. Asten's first job and it rattles his nerves and emotions.

The most interesting technical aspect of the case is the then-revolutionary computer re-enactment of the accident. It is crude by today's standards and shows how far computer technology has advanced. Still, it shows the computer as a diagnostic tool in its infancy.

In *Stain of Guilt*, an old Hollywood murder is reopened and solved a la *Hollywood Story* when Quincy is the advisor on a movie based on the evidence of the original case, a passion killing where Victoria Sawyer (Carolyn Jones) murdered her husband, Harland. Quincy examines the evidence and is convinced that she is innocent and has wrongfully spent the last six years in prison.

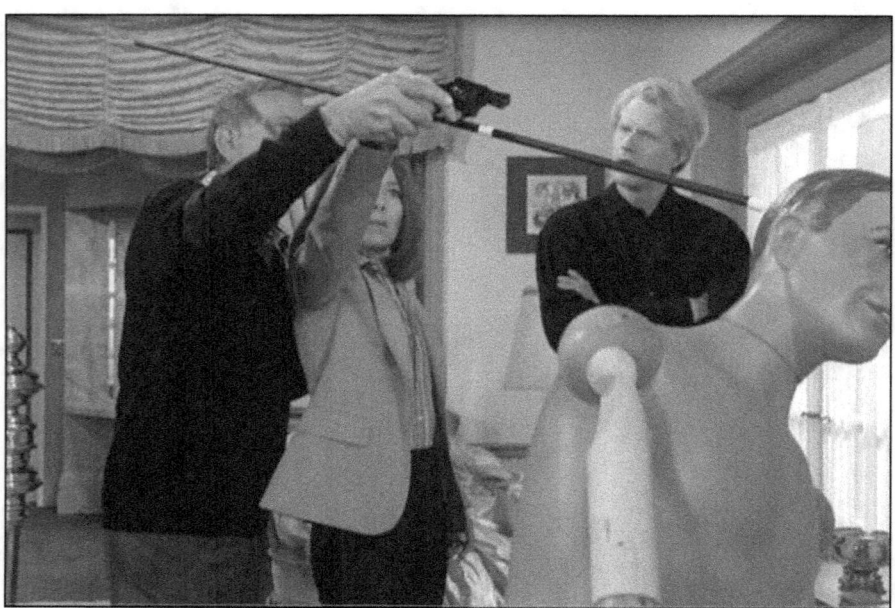

Stain of Guilt is another behind-the-scenes of Hollywood mythmaking as Quincy uses his crime fighting methods to re-open a murder case that will exonerate Victoria Sawyer (Carolyn Jones), an innocent woman convicted of murder. 1981, Universal Television.

His initial findings and suspicions are rejected by D.A. Harrison (William Sylvester) but he makes his case with a recreation of the murder. Friends, strangers and lovers are transported to the past where blackmail and deceit take a modern life of their own. Illusion and reality meet on a Hollywood set and the real murderer is revealed.

Stain of Guilt is a fascinating police procedural where Quincy earns the top honors as a sleuth. He trumps Hollywood and the judicial system with his expertise and frees an innocent woman. The technical aspects of his profession only enhance the curiosity value of the story and he weaves in and out of show business illusion and bureaucratic delusion with ease.

Susan Powell plays Cassie Spencer, an advocate for Victoria Sawyer, her onetime mentor. William Sylvester plays the skeptical D.A. and Sid Haig is Hatch, one of the accomplices whose new sideline is blackmail until he asks for one payment too many. Ed Begley, Jr. plays Kit, Victoria's nephew, a terrible aspiring comedian who now lives in the murder house. Ezra Stone applies his rough-throated style to the role of Judge Simon. Bobbi Jordan and Ed Rudy are the Newlands, the next door neighbors, one of whom harbors a guilty secret that turns into two counts of murder.

Paul Tanner (Luke Askew) garrotes his kindly Uncle Jason (Paul Fix) in the desert and pours a liquid on the dead man's face to attract coyotes for a midnight feast in the opening scene to *For Want of a Horse*. His unscrupulous deed is witnessed by Gabe (Ronnie Scribner), an autistic child who remains mute until the story's climatic scene. Before that happens, Paul tricks his ailing aunt into signing papers that will close down the Institute of Equestrian Therapy, which helps disabled children adjust to the world at large.

In this episode, John S. Ragin showcases his acting chops. He portrays Dr. Asten as a humorless fussbudget worried about efficiency and not stepping on bureaucratic toes. Beneath the porcelain exterior is a rational and caring individual who allows Quincy enough rope to tie up the loose ends…or hang himself. In this episode, familial ties prompt him to push Quincy into keeping the institute open and bring Tanner to justice. It is because his foster son Andy (Brian Andrews) is one of the children at the institute.

The feel good factor of this episode is watching physically and mentally challenged children overcome obstacles through will power and courage. The program that enables them to achieve is the brainchild of Jack Lafollette (Lonny Chapman), who uses equestrian therapy and nature to help the children overcome their limitations. This noble pursuit only makes Paul Tanner appear to be more evil because he wants to confiscate the land so he can sell it to a large corporation to use for its commercial ends. He brought down by two of the children who regain their self-confidence after they turn the tables on him.

The illegal hauling and dumping of toxic wastes is examined in *Dead Stop*, an episode that utilized the backdrop of the trucker phase and C.B. craze of late 70's. Quincy becomes aware of the problem when he performs an autopsy on Hank Cheznell (Sandy McPeak), a trucker who was killed when his eighteen-wheeler jackknifed on a road and tumbled down a cliff. The startling conclusion of the autopsy reveals that the trucker had died before the accident, a victim of toxic poisoning.

Quincy is aided by the trucker's wife (Salome Jens) and they try to enlist the aid of other truckers in finding the dump site. The encroaching danger is that the toxins produce lethal gas, especially if activated by water. It is a race against time as Quincy tries to pinpoint the location before an impending downpour. They succeed in finding the location and covering the barrels with a tarp before the storm starts.

Salome Jens plays the wife of a trucker who was killed while illegally transporting toxic chemicals. She can handle a rig just as well as the toughest truckers. 1981, Universal Television.

This episode was an echo of the many trucker themed storylines that were prevalent in late 1970's television. CB jargon, trucker codes of honor and the rugged individualistic ethos were the staples of the genre. *Dead Stop* is true to the genre but goes a step further by examining the perils of modern transport. Economics and stringent commerce laws create a gray area for desperate drivers to make extra money doing illegal hauls. It is informative without being preachy.

Salome Jens (*Terror from the Year 5000*) adds a feminine sensibility to her trucker instincts and she is accepted on the circuit as a legitimate trucker. She is the one who rallies the reluctant truckers to help Quincy to find an illegal dumping site and prevent a lethal combustion from an oncoming storm.

A Ghost of a Chance is a riveting story about ghost surgery, a procedure that involves a surgeon standing in for the scheduled doctor. Dr. Stanley Royce (Jose Ferrer) is a celebrated heart surgeon who was supposed to perform a simple bypass procedure on Harold Markham (Tom Stuart). His intern performed the routine operation but complications set in and the patient dies.

The victim's brother Ted (Nicholas Coaster) does not buy Dr. Royce's explanation of his brother's death and pays money for an autopsy to be performed. Quincy uses his investigator's acumen to discern that the surgical technique used for the operation differed from Dr. Royce's revolutionary method. After it is revealed that Dr. Royce did not perform the operation, Quincy sets out to solve and rectify the ethical questions posed by ghost surgery.

Jose Ferrer is overpowering in his understated performance as Dr. Royce. His calm confrontations with the accusatory Quincy create a tense battlefield where reputations are challenged and put on the line. The hospital and the medical establishment back the revered doctor. Their official positions are upheld by the Deputy DA Jim Barnes (James A. Watson, Jr.), Dr. Panucci (Phillip Pine), an overburdened bureaucrat of an oversight committee, and the hospital director, Dr. Herb Martin (Harry Townes), who does not want to alienate the cash cow that is the legendary Dr. Stanley Royce.

It is when Al Werbin (Frank Marth), an insurance investigator, gives Quincy Dr. Royce's insurance records of the last six months that the coroner realizes that unsupervised interns have been performing a couple of unsuccessful procedures in the surgeon's absence. Quincy challenges Dr. Royce, who has a crisis of conscience when he is forced to abandon a scheduled operation in favor of flying to Washington to perform surgery on a brigadier general. Dr. Royce's reputation remains intact when he changes his mind and returns to instruct his intern (Jonathan Frakes) in his techniques and medical philosophy.

Science for Sale tackles the question of genetic engineering, a subject that posed grave philosophical misgivings in the 70's. The story takes on the worst possible scenario of bio-genetics when Dr. Paul Lynn (Lane Smith) has created a killer virus. The episode is a critique of the crass commercialization of bio-genetic research for pharmaceutical profit. Greed and blind ambition clash with bold vision and traditional ethics.

Dr. Paul Flynn's (Lane Smith) revolutionary cancer treatment program is jeopardized by the freak deaths of one of his patients. Somehow, the delusional terminally ill woman escaped the hospital and was found dead in a nearby alleyway. The real scandal is the genetically-created virus that she spread to the susceptible hosts she may have come in contact with. They include a sympathetic elderly hospital orderly, a derelict who stole her necklace when she collapsed in the alley where he lived and a little boy whose lips she touched in the hospital waiting room when she was

Quincy lends a sympathetic ear to Dr. Chris Winston (Julie Adams) as she discusses the lack of ethics behind the funding of a questionable genetics programs at her hospital in *Science for Sale*. 1982, Universal Television.

making her getaway. All but the boy died because of the virus, a side effect of the serum created by Dr. Flynn.

Julie Adams is Dr. Chris Winston, the director of the hospital where Dr. Flynn's patient escaped from. She creates a rift between Dr. Flynn and herself when she refuses any further work on human guinea pigs. Dr. Winston is adamant about putting a stop to the program if only for the sake of good public relations for the hospital. Dr. Flynn feels betrayed and bolts for the competition, headed by the evil Garfield Calhoun (Dennis Patrick), an almost demonic wheeler-dealer and smooth hustler. He charms Dr. Flynn with a state of the art laboratory and a *carte blanche* budget before imposing an impossible schedule on him as wild promises about a possible cure cause the company's stock to jump in value.

This is where the study of greed and personal ambition is played out. The dangerous side effects cause Calhoun to withdraw his support and Dr. Flynn to find his moral compass. The story ends with Dr. Flynn giving a face saving mea culpa speech to the press while Dr. Winston welcomes him back into her administration.

The episode, for the most part, contains strong scenes that range from the bizarre to the stark and frightening. The contagion is a genetically created zombie who contaminates the vulnerable, those with weak immune systems like the intrusive old orderly who insists on visiting the off limits patient and contracts the virus only to die in a gruesome scene. The bum who accosts her and steals her necklace is found dead by his drinking buddies, who are horrified by his death grimace. Only the little boy with the angel face is spared when he is given the antidote in time.

Next Stop, Nowhere is a heavy-handed warning to youngsters about the perils of punk rock. A teenager is stabbed to death with an ice pick while slam dancing in a mosh pit. He was not the only one raving; so was his killer…on pills. The murder suspect is Abigail 'Abby' Garvin (Melora Hardin), a straight-A student who has gone to seed because of punk rock and pill popping. Her descent into Hell is really due to her best friend (?) Molly Howard (Karlene Crockett), the real murderer, who is making the suspect consume codeine pills, something that she is allergic to. Hopefully, the pills will finish her before her memory returns and she realizes that she is not the real killer.

Adding to the peril is the hysterical Dr. Emily Hanover (Anita Gillette), Quincy's new girl friend and basically the new speech making statistics orator for a crusader episode. In *Next Stop, Nowhere*, she is adamant about exposing the fallacies of the punk rock philosophy of nihilism and youthful death. She does this to anyone who will listen, including going on a talk show with Quincy to confront punk rockers about their alleged madness.

The episode's title is also the name of the song played by Mayhem, the house band in the punk club. Yes, the lyrics include admitting stealing pencils from a blind man and not giving a damn and this is enough to make Emily and Quincy roll their eyes as they listen and wonder what is happening to the nation's youth? Not to mention the Goth makeup and nihilistic slogans.

A subtle irony is that the club is run by the apathetic Vince Laska, played by Nicholas Georgiade, the actor who played Rossi on *The Untouchables*, a group of federal agents battling Prohibition. Contrast the club scene with the opening scene of the pill popping Stan Hess in *The Beat Generation*, made more than twenty years prior to this episode. It would have been great if there was a glassy-eyed tattooed guru in this episode. There isn't; instead, you get 80's prime time television version of an anti-MTV video. The nether-punks are too polished and well-coiffed, as is usually the case in teenage angst TV episodes or movies. This has been the case since the 50's and Hollywood's depiction of the beatniks; such is the case with *Next Stop Nowhere* and that is what gives it a certain camp value. There is also the usual mistrust of adults and abdication of responsibility along with the diminution of self-worth and the abolition of ambition.

The episode ends at Danny's, where Quincy and Emily share a romantic slow dance to Glenn Miller's, *Moonlight Serenade*. Their rationale is who would want to listen to music that makes you want to kill when you can listen to music that makes you want to love? Who can argue with that?

In *Sword of Honor, Blade of Death*, an international dope-for-guns deal sets the stage for a blending of cultures. A young cop is killed in the Little Tokyo section of Los Angeles while investigating a dope smuggling ring. He was an old friend of Sam's, who takes a personal involvement in the case. The crime kingpin's son was also a close friend of Sam and the murder victim and this complicates things because of the Japanese code of honor, justice and business.

Sword of Honor, Blade of Death is a well-made episode about ancestral Japanese honor and American tradition. Here, Nakatama (John Fugioka), a Yakuza kingpin prepares to do battle with Morishima (Mako) a man intent on avenging the murder of his son, a police officer. 1982, Universal Television.

It appears that the Yakuza was behind the murder and this riles the victim's father, John Morishima (Mako). Ancestral honor and personal obligation are the two ends of a cultural bridge when the samurai code and the rule of law become one. The New World's way of preserving and assimilating worldly customs bring Nakatama (John Fugioka), the Yakuza kingpin, to his knees by the weight of a promise made by Morishima, a strict traditionalist who vows to avenge his son's death.

Sam walks a fine line between his cultural heritage and the western law ethics when he seeks justice for his friend. Quincy tries to honor this understanding and his respect keeps him out of the way of Morishima. The elder's triumph of honor is the outcome of this challenge to dignity scenario where eastern ancestral honor trumps western justice.

Mako and John Fugioka are two veteran actors who often played these roles on television and in the movies. Their styles are direct and straight to the point and they make good adversaries. Soon-Teck Oh has a good guy role for a change as Captain Bob Nishimura, head of the Asian Task Force.

Sword of Honor, Blade of Death covers familiar territory, including Sadalko (Donna Kei Benz), the Americanized daughter-in-law who eschews tradition in favor of modern America. It perturbs her father-in-law, who cannot believe that one uncaring generation can undo three thousand years of tradition.

Tradition is also what motivates Nakatama, who has no problem separating business from personal matters. He is a traditionalist who bristles at the low-class, boorish business styles of two Mafia thugs (Ed Grover and George Loros). He can kill the cop for intruding on his business but can spare the father's life because he is in debt to Sam for once saving his son from a riptide.

Guilty Until Proven Innocent is a dramatic treatise on judicial improprieties within the Federal Grand Jury system. Ted Locke (Rudy Solari), the estranged son of a Mafia capo, is presumed guilty of arson and murder when his business burns and his foreman is reduced to a cinder. Howard St. Johns (Eugene Roche) is an overzealous federal prosecutor who repeatedly brings his charges before the grand jury. Each time, Locke is absolved but that doesn't satisfy St. Johns' blood lust. The prosecutor maintains that Locke, whom he refers to as Tony Locaselli (his birth name), is a point man for the Mafia and he vows to protect the community from him.

The Grand Jury system comes off like the Spanish Inquisition in *Guilty Until Proven Innocent*. Eugene Roche plays Phillip St. Johns, a

D.A. whose relentless harassment of a businessman makes him look like Torquemada. It is implausible that the social crusading side of this show actually shows the American Grand Jury system as being totalitarian. It is a system where ordinary citizens-not the judiciary-decide what cases go to trial based on the merit of evidence presented by the D.A.'s office.

It is an entertaining story mainly because of Eugene Roche's fascistic D.A. and Rudy Solari's Kafkaesque Everyman lost in a legal labyrinth. Both actors play their parts well and their interplay creates a dynamic tension that ends with a declaration of principles by St. Johns, who vows to continue fighting Locke until he is brought down.

On Dying High is an examination of the crack cocaine epidemic that plagued the country during the 1980's. J.J. Chandler (Roger Miller) is a reckless singer and comedian whose pro-drug act contains tasteless drug jokes. His act backfires when it goes up in smoke after he freebases near a lit cigarette, an incident inspired by Richard Pryor's

Edd Byrnes plays the manager of J.J. Chandler (Roger Miller), a pro-drug country-western singer whose career goes up in smoke when he is immolated by an exploding crack pipe. 1983, Universal Television.

tragic accident around the same time. It was also the cause of pop star Rick Nelson's death. Edd Byrnes plays his concerned manager and Dr. Emily Hanover gets a chance to give another hysterical public service polemic.

Edd Byrnes, who played Kookie on *77 Sunset Strip*, plays Bud Auerbach, Chandler's manager. He is an enabler and procurer, except when it comes to encouraging an underage groupie. She is a witness to Chandler's immolation and visits him regularly at the hospital. She also becomes a victim of a drug overdose. Quincy convinces Chandler to become an anti-drug crusader, something that the singer resists until he realizes that he has no career without his damaged vocal cords and missing fingertips, injuries incurred by the fire.

Like *Next Stop Nowhere*, *On Dying High* focuses on the effects that pro-drug stances have on impressionable fans. The crusader tactics of episodes like these seem heavy-handed but they are well meaning. Perhaps, if Dr. Emily Hanover was not the apologist, the message would get across instead of sinking like a lead weight.

Besides directing the show, Ray Danton also contributed two stories that teleplays were based on: *Welcome to Paradise Palms* and *Requiem for the Living*. After *Quincy, M.E.*, Ray Danton went on to direct several episodes of *Cagney and Lacey* and *Mickey Spillane's Mike Hammer* (later retitled *The New Mike Hammer*). The two shows would have made credible contestants on a game show about the war of the sexes where macho ethics challenged female resilience.

CAGNEY AND LACEY

Ray Danton blends s *Quincy, ME*'s stark reality with a new poetic justice for *Cagney and Lacey*, a groundbreaking television series. Created by Barbara Avedon and Barbara Corday, *Cagney and Lacey* is a unique police drama with a rocky history and an evolution tempered by popular demands. It was produced by Barney Rosenweig, whose vision, tenacity and persistence (or insistence!) kept the series going through a sea of troubles and dead ends.

In the Tele-Film, Loretta Swit played Christine Cagney. During the first season, Meg Foster played the part. In the long run, the role belonged to Sharon Gless. The show was cancelled twice and successfully rose from the ashes. It also produced three television movies in the 90's.

Sharon Gless and Tyne Daly's portrayal of *Cagney and Lacey* gave the show a three-dimensional soul that liberated the show from the usual cops and robbers pattern that crowded the small screen. The show tapped into the feminist psyche and created a legion of loyal fans that helped the show weather a series of tempests created by nervous network executives. CBS (Columbia Broadcasting System).

The tales of New York City are the stories of *Cagney and Lacey*. In that respect, the show is like many of the best urban police dramas that preceded it. However, the classic tough guy crime shows had an ancestral lineage with hard-boiled origins and macho philosophies. What made *Cagney and Lacey* unique is that it dramatizes female power in the male citadel of law and order. Cagney and Lacey are tough enough to be New York City detectives yet the show's episodes are sensitive portraits of the female psyche, a stark contrast to the macho world of cops and robbers.

An underlying premise of the show is the work ethic and moral turpitude of a working class that no longer exists. The blue collar sensibility of a male dominated world is successfully challenged by a new generation of women because they were raised in this world and have assimilated the underlying values of their parents' generation. The difference is that the women strive to assume responsibilities that were traditionally reserved for men. That is why the men in the precinct can't compete with Cagney and Lacey; they would be destroying the values that were instilled in them.

Like so much of Ray Danton's work as a director, many of his *Cagney and Lacey* episodes deal with the meaning of the self. Identity is either seen through the nostalgia of the past or from the perspective of one about to make a desperate leap into an uncertain future. Ray Danton directed three episodes in the series first season. It was when Christine Cagney was played by Meg Foster. Her character was actually found objectionable by the buffoonish network executives and the renewal of the show was dependent on her replacement. Nevertheless, she created a strong and somber character in the six episodes that she appeared in.

A simple synopsis of *Street Scene* would be Cagney and Lacey investigate the shooting of a gang member by an elderly retiree. Was the shooting justified or unprovoked? Who was the real victim? The gang member who was Puerto Rican and a member of the underclass or an old man forgotten by society to become a relic of the former migration from eastern Europe? This being a Cagney and Lacey episode meant that there was much more to the plot than the anatomy of a crime. Besides dealing with the investigation of a shooting, *Street Scene* investigates the parameters of turf, not only on the street but in the squad room. It also examines the weight given to ethnic identity and gender politics.

The detectives deal with the opposing worlds of the Old World Europeans and the New World Hispanics. They also have to contend with power within the police precinct. They also have to survive the street beat and, ironically, the close knit world of police wives, where they are perceived to be threats to their husbands. Cagney and Lacey negotiate the terrain successfully and maintain their own identity by establishing their individualism. It comes at a price, such as drunken interludes and fights with each other but they are worth it because Cagney and Lacey succeed to bringing down two rival gangs and dissolve the stereotype of police

In *Better Than Equal*, Cagney (Meg Foster) and Lacey (Tyne Daly) are assigned to guard anti-feminist Helen Granger (Julie Adams) against a deranged stalker who torments his would-be victim with violent threats. 1982, CBS (Columbia Broadcasting System).

force home wreckers. They also prove the innocence of the old man, who was protecting himself from a viable threat to his life.

Better Than Equal stars Julie Adams as Helen Granger, an anti-feminist based on Phyllis Schafly, a conservative opponent of the ERA amendment. Granger is on a nationwide lecture tour when she is threatened by a series of threatening phone calls. They start out as obscene calls but become more intense as the tour continues. The crank has entered her hotel room and ransacked her bedroom, including mutilating her lingerie. He has now graduated to death threats.

Granger requests police protection and is upset when Cagney and Lacey are assigned to her case. She has a dim view of women working outside of their traditional domestic perimeters and is not shy about showing her contempt for the female detectives. Old fashioned detective work, including call traces and a spot-on description of the suspect, help the detectives to corner the lethal pervert. He turns out to be a mama's boy and former Eagle Scout. It is not discerned why Granger ticked him off or turned him on.

Better Than Equal was made early in the series run when the other cops were still going through their Neanderthal phase, making anti-female comments and still resisting having two women work in the squad room. That is why the Helen Granger character seems to be so obtuse because she is in league with the male chauvinists. Julie Adams broadened what could have been a stereotypical outline into a full bodied personality. Ms. Adams is fine and her curt resoluteness creates the conflict between her and the cops. Her facial expressions say just as much as the best written dialogue. The look of stunned amazement she shows when Cagney cajoles the lunatic caller into dropping his guard nullifies all of her previous condescension towards the female cops.

The professional writing, direction and acting in this episode save it from being a polemic. It is a crime drama that packs a whallop, because of the social points it scores. It also hit a raw nerve with conservative groups, who picketed the show with demands that the episode be removed from future syndication. On a technical note, the scene in the auditorium of the crank defacing the banner welcoming Ms. Granger is impressive if one is a lover of old film noir movies. Even though it is shot in color, the cinematography and the editing captures the dreamy ambience of the best black and white moodiness of the old crime classics.

Suffer the Children is a harrowing story of child abuse. Cagney and Lacey rescue a little girl from a fourteenth story ledge and their heroics highlight the cowardice of an angry husband and father. In this case, identity means finding out whether or not the little girl had a sister and, if so, what happened to her? The parents claim that she was given up for adoption, although they can't remember any of the details. Forensics tell another story when the skull of a dead child is examined and given a face.

This is a brutal episode that successfully captures the fear and intimidation of a family dominated and abused by a broken man. At first, he appears to be docile and slightly disoriented, mainly due to a faltering economy. He admits that lack of money forced him to give up his daughter for adoption.

Cagney and Lacey piece together tidbits of information until they come to the shocking realization that the girl was murdered. They finally get the truth from his wife, a stone faced woman whose face is a monument to resignation. Gail Strickland's performance is the most unsettling thing about the episode because she embodies the fear and self-loathing of an abused woman. Her pain has made her numb and she is on the verge of catatonia. The subplots deal with a stakeout at a ritzy hotel to nab

Suffer the Children is a powerful episode about child abuse and delves into the many perspectives that involve neglect, frustration and-when taken to its extreme-murder. 1982, CBS (Columbia Broadcasting System).

a thief and Cagney's inability to have a successful relationship with a dashing lawyer, who turns out to be married.

Ray Danton directed one episode of the newly revamped series when it returned to the fall schedule. Sharon Gless's assumption of the Christine Cagney role changed the show's dynamics and expanded the realm of expression and possibilities. She was tough and somber like her predecessor but also possessed a unique kinetic energy and sense of humor.

Beauty Burglars centers on a series of beauty salon robberies committed by two phony cops. They eventually branch out into home invasions and molestations. Cagney and Lacey are appointed heads of a task force to bring the perpetrators to justice. The sub-plots deal with the second marriage of Lacey's childhood chum to a well-heeled doctor and a robbery victim's loss of social skills after the first salon invasion, a crime that claimed the life of her friend after she suffered a heart attack from being beaten by one of the robbers.

The episode shows that pain-staking step-by-step progress of solving a criminal investigation that in includes false leads, dead ends and fuzzy clues. Perseverance and a connect-the-dots approach lead to the apprehension of the criminals, but not without a price. The sub-plot deals with working class roots, blasts from the past and friendship ties from the past do not have any binding to the present.

It also shows the frustrations of moving up the economic ladder. John Karlen gives an excellent performance as Harvey, an old-fash-

A gang of phony cops targets beauty salons for their hit and run robberies. They cross the line when a customer dies from a heart attack. 1982, CBS (Columbia Broadcasting System).

ioned working class stiff who wonders if he is worthy enough to be married to Lacey because of the groom's well-heeled professional life. Harvey is the best supporting character on the show because of Karlen's sincere portrayal.

It would be three years before Ray Danton returned to the show. In the interim, he wrapped up his residency at *Quincy, M.E.*, bringing the total of his episodes to twenty three. He also directed a couple of successful primetime dramas and started his involvement with *The New Mike Hammer* series starring Stacey Keach.

1985 was a benchmark year for Ray Danton, as well as a milestone. Ten years previously, his career was in a transitional phase. His acting career had hit the skids with two dreadful movies that proved to be twin swan songs. He struggled to be recognized as an independent director and producer but his European achievements were not taken seriously in the States. Now, he was a successful television director, in-demand and well-respected. In April, he signed on with Shapiro-Lichtman Talent Agency for directorial representation. As was the case with Ray Danton, there was always a touch of the old during a change. He recorded his first voiceover in fifteen years for Lawrence Kasdan's, *Silverado*.

Besides directing an episode for William Shatner's successful cop show, *T. J. Hooker*, Ray Danton directed three episodes for the successful pop musical, *Fame*. He also returned to *Cagney and Lacey and* directed three episodes, one of them a two-part story line. The stories deal with family matters and, consequently, the search for identity and the meaning of self. It was the same theme he tackled in the *Fame* episodes and—to some extent—in the *T.J. Hooker* episode.

The mother and child reunion is the focal point of *Mothers and* Sons, wherein a perpetrator finds sanctuary in his mother's alibi. She lies for her son and provides a concrete lie to ensure his freedom. Her perjury means freedom to commit crime. Cagney and Lacey try to convince the mother to stop fending for her child. Lacey is somewhat sympathetic because she is a mother. She is also going through a crisis with her own son. The child successfully defended himself against a bully but is accused of hurling bricks through a shop owner's window. The son denies it and she feels that he may be lying. Her husband accepts his alibi without question.

The episode deals with the immutable bond between her mother and child. In this case, the odd man out is a father who does not believe in excuses. The man (Charles Aidman) was raised in a poor family and does not believe that it is a crime to be poor. He also does not believe that it is an excuse to break the law.

The father counter balances the mother when he gives the detectives a pocket watch that the kid left behind. It turns out that the watch figures big in a robbery rap that the son beat two years earlier when the mother once again provided an alibi for him.

The comedic subplot is Cagney being used by the guys as a ringer to beat the new detective at poker. He humiliated them in a game so they want to get even by having her dupe him the way she fooled them in their first game together. The problem is that her reputation precedes her because the detective knows her father and has heard the old man boast about his little girl's massive knowledge of card playing.

In *The Psychic*, a desperate family hires a psychic to help locate their missing loved one. Madame Zal (Elizabeth Ashley) uses the media to publicize her search and this infuriates the detectives who have been ordered by the commissioner to co-operate with her. The subplots are marital fidelity and a thief who steals Elvis memorabilia. Lacey is pregnant and she worries that she and her husband are not spending enough time with each other. She also becomes suspicious of every woman who calls her husband at work. She is also very sensitive and irritable, something her husband attributes to the missing person's case, a matter that reminds Lacey of the father who walked out on his family.

Madame Zal (Elizabeth Ashley) is a savvy huckster who has perfected the crime-psychic routine in *The Psychic*. Her cleverness leads to her unmasking. 1985, CBS (Columbia Broadcasting System).

Chuck McCann plays the owner of an Elvis memorabilia shop in the sub-plot of *The Psychic*. 1985, CBS (Columbia Broadcasting System).

The detectives begin their investigation with skepticism but slowly change their minds when Madame Zal's clues pan out. She says that the woman is on the run from danger; that she will be found near the city but in a field of horses; and to be aware of a man in a white coat. Eventually, the woman is found dead by the carousel in Central Park and their main suspect is a mentally unbalanced man who wears a white smock as part of his job as a supermarket produce clerk.

It turns out the psychic is an expensive fraud and it appears that she was correct because the husband was the murderer and he used her clues to cover his crime. He was upset because his wife was missing on purpose and they fought when she returned. The husband then disposed of the body in ways that would coincide with the psychic's predictions.

Lacey's dilemma is solved because the other woman is Harvey's mother, Muriel, who calls once a week to see how things are going. The Elvis memorabilia thefts go unsolved, a tribute to the mystique of the man. Chuck McCann has a small part as an obsessed fan who runs an Elvis memorabilia shop. He has an exaggerated pompadour to match his girth and describes the missing jumpsuit with affectionate and historical accuracy.

This is another excellent episode, well-written, well-acted and well-directed. There is the perfect blend of drama and humor and the

Cagney and Lacey prove to be three-dimensional personalities. They are tough and equal to the task of being New York City cops but also have vulnerable sides to them as expressed through their personal lives with family, relations and friends. This perfect balance shows why there was such a strong fan base to this show.

Who Says It's Fair? is a critically-acclaimed two-part drama dealing with Mary Beth Lacey's cancer scare. Her world is turned upside down when she finds a lump on her breast. The road to a negative diagnosis is a drama of despair and alienation. There is the expected denial and hostile outbursts towards her loved ones' concern.

The episode starts with Harvey looking at a mantle full of photographs of his family. From there, everything is played out in real time so that it takes a gradual unraveling of Lacey's will and the nerves to confront the challenge. Denial, defiance, acceptance and confrontation are the stages of development that Lacey experiences and it is a wildly emotional performance by Tyne Daly that makes it seem so real that it appears that you are dealing with a loved one's problem.

Part of the challenge is continuing to deal with her life and Lacey's schedule seems like the tasks of Hercules when you see her living under the gun. The strength it takes to deal with her family and partner eventually wears her down to the point where she is an emotional wreck yet her strength never wavers.

The episode is really an evaluation of the cancer treatments available to women and the social attitudes that encapsulate the beauty myth, especially with the way women view themselves because of social mores. Unlike the Quincy episodes that deal with social issues, there are no polemical speeches because of the brilliant writing. Facts and statistics are woven into the script and the story never wavers away from making a point through strong acting.

One salient point that is underscored is how everyone is a hub that supports the spokes that are the lives around them. We take ourselves for granted and it is not until an emergency occurs that we realize how important we are to other people. The emotional output of this episode is intense but it is never maudlin. The credit goes to the actors who portray their characters as real people. Excellent writing and savvy direction also play a strong part of telling the story.

The point of carrying on with daily life is brought home in the subplot of the search for a missing child. Racial implications are emphasized when the mother insists that the cops would try harder if the child were white.

Law and Order | 421

Who Says It's Fair? is an example of a show dealing with a sensitive and relevant topic without being preachy or stereotypical. One of the unbelievable elements of the show was the principals' ability to portray real people within the confines of a scripted situation. 1985, CBS (Columbia Broadcasting System).

It is a difficult situation to comprehend because the mother is one of the rare instances when an individual is a victim of circumstances and dealt a bad hand by society.

Lynne Whitfield gives an impassioned performance of a woman who tries desperately to provide a good life for her son but encounters difficulties because the ghetto life has a stronger effect on her child than she does. The pertinent point that covers both plot lines is that the family bond can weather any storm, no matter how damaging the aftermath.

People Magazine was doing a profile on the show when this episode was being filmed. The article for its Feb. 11th issue presented a curious portrait of Ray Danton as a director:

"The boredom inherent in any filming of a television program stalks this episode of *Cagney and Lacey*. In the best of times, there are endless takes and retakes. This episode is directed by Ray Danton, a brooding, sallow man known in the trade as "Midnight Ray," partly because of the long hours he demands, partly because his temperament on the set seems to resemble the color of the sky in dead of night. Danton is largely on good behavior in this episode-charming, rarely moved to ire, often avuncular with his actors. Still, filming one courtroom scene takes the best part of a day, with endless breaks to change camera positions. One

A photo of Ray Danton on the Cagney and Lacey set. 1985, CBS (Columbia Broadcasting System).

take needs to be redone because Danton notices that Christine Cagney's watch has run almost an hour ahead of its position from the last scene. "As Stanislavsky said, " he bellows in a guttural Russian accent, "*Kak pozhivayete!*-God is in the details." He uses the phrase at least a dozen times a week, proving that the people on the set are either unversed in Russian or in unusually generous spirits. *Kak pozhi-vayete* means, roughly, "How 'ya doing?"⁹

He didn't have to worry about how he was doing with *Cagney and Lacey*. He explained his technique to producer Barney Rosenweig: "You put the camera at the eye level of the women, say action, and get the hell out of the way."¹⁰

Too bad casting with other shows wasn't that amendable. Ray Danton was a firm, hands-on director. He was committed to his craft and outspoken about it, as was the case with The ABC's of a casting, a 1985 Variety interview with Ray Danton.

"Network execs sometimes "force casting on you which destroys a show," charged director Ray Danton, who added: "They are people who do not know much about casting. They are not qualified. I dislike people like Lou Erlicht and Jordan Kerner of ABC making casting decisions. They are neither qualified nor really aware of the kind of talent that is out there. There are exceptions, and the most obvious is Tony Barr of CBS, an accredited judge of acting talent. He was an actor and currently runs an acting school in the Valley. He is such an important exception that he deserves to be mentioned."

Danton remarked: "TV wants instant hits. They don't want to take a chance. They try to do a show like one that was successful."

Still, he has no sympathy for those within TV who have a condescending attitude toward the medium, remarking: "If I hear another guy saying, 'It's just TV,' I will throw up. They should have more of a sense of responsibility to the medium. I think they are not capable of doing better work as writers and/or producers.

Those of us who work in TV have an enormous influence on the acting styles and standards of our time. We have no national theater, and movies are a hit and miss affair. More people watch us, night after night, than any other form of entertainment, and we should be aware of this and do the best we can under the circumstances."¹¹

It was an attitude that he would use for two more episodes of the show as he became more involved in the Mike Hammer show as a director, supervising producer and writer. The next year, he directed *Culture Clash*, besides directing four Mike Hammer shows and a television movie. On top of that, he fit in a *Dallas* episode.

Culture Clash had a topical American storyline with variations due to ethnicity, time and circumstances. In 1986, the Diaspora is due to the Russian invasion of Afghanistan. A young woman from a devout Islamic family wants to eschew family custom in *Culture Clash*. Her desire is to move to Malibu and enjoy the lifestyle of a young American woman. Her choice results in her death.

Explaining her death to a family whose mores are in a different culture presents the detectives with the awkward pretext of justifying a challenge to their beliefs. Co-existence is a matter of course in American society, although most of us do not realize it. The death of the young woman highlights traditions and religious attitudes. Here, the old and the new usually rumble through time without incident but in the case of the young woman it results in a violent death.

It is not the American boyfriend, whose respect puts him on par with Islamic self-discipline. However, the family cannot see that and it blinds them to the prejudice that exists within them. They hide behind Islamic tradition and do not realize that they are guilty of the decadence they accuse American society of fostering. That the murderer is the brother is an accepted fact because he did it to save her soul. The subplot deals with the politics of being women in a man's world when Cagney and Lacey are considered for a task force.

Ray Danton's last episode for *Cagney and Lacey* is *To Sir with Love* , a story done with affection and humor. It is a light hearted episode where Lacey is nudged into being the Chairperson of the Committee Dinner. Event planning is not her specialty and realizes that she is out of her league. Lacey resorts to asking members of the squad to help with the decorations, catering and entertainment. Adding to the burden of planning is the task of catching up on cold cases to achieve the best clearance rates in an intra-precinct competition. On top of that is the care given to planning the first birthday party for Cagney's daughter.

This is not to mention the normal case loads. In this week's episode, it is the senseless feuding of alienated lovers on how to split up their possessions. The breakup, too, is portrayed to comical effect as the couple are obviously two schmucks in love. What starts out as mass confusion turns into a successful dinner, which is appropriate because the recipient of the Honors Award is Lt. Samuels, the squad leader. It ends with Cagney and Lacey dressed as two gaudy and bawdy cabaret entertainers.

Culture Clash is a searing drama where Mid-Eastern ethics and American values become a moot point when the younger sister of a devout Muslim is murdered seeking the American dream. Honor becomes a fine line between life and death. 1985, CBS (Columbia Broadcasting System).

To Sir with Love could have been overdone and silly but is saves the episode is the performers who play it naturally instead of campy. The other event planners are steering business to their relatives and they play it off in an understated, a-matter-of fact way. The detectives are tapped to provide the entertainment and they act the way any amateur would when given a chance to step into the limelight.

The best example of playing it natural is the way Cagney and Lacey get on each other's nerves. Many of their situations—from buying party decorations to making the cannolis—is screwball comedy but made believable because of the pressure and frustration they feel because of their multi-tasking.

This show is an example why Cagney and Lacey was more than just a successful cop show. The show is more than excellent writing and production values, which is saying a lot for any show. In the long run, all the best direction, professional writing and first rate production values is nothing if the actors cannot add flesh and blood to the bones and real emotions to the nervous system.

Everyone, from the leads down to the ensemble cast is well honed and works like clockwork. It is to Ray Danton's credit that he can handle intimate scenes as well as he can handle group scenes. The ensemble scenes are seamless as the camera pans along the squad room, picking up individual conversations to create a total environment of order among chaos.

That is evident by the next female sidekicks movie that Ray Danton directed. It was called *Leg Work* and starred Margaret Colin and Frances McDormand . They worked well together but the show's writing lacked the depth and sociology of *Cagney and Lacey*. This show was merely a crime drama show and the two buddies happen to be women.

Ray Danton would work with the stars of the show again. He directed Tyne Daly in the 1986-87 production of William Inge's *Come Back, Little Sheba* at the Los Angeles Theatre Center. He was also a creative consultant for Sharon Gless's show, *The Trials of Rosie O'Neil*.

MICKEY SPILLANE'S MIKE HAMMER

In the Eighties, Mike Hammer returned to television in a new incarnation. Any popular icon with Mike Hammer's longevity ultimately becomes a franchise where the drawback is the newer entries are invariably compared to the classics, usually ensuring failure. The new Mike Hammer was still aided by his resolute Girl Friday, Velda (Lindsay Bloom) and assisted by his close friend and war buddy, Captain Pat Chambers (Don Stroud). This time around, the war was Vietnam

ADA Barrington (Kent Williams) hounded and harassed Hammer at every turn, hoping for the day when he could send the detective up the river to the Big House. A clever addition to show was The Face, an enigmatic mystery woman played by Donna Denton. She made a cameo every show, appearing out of nowhere, only to disappear into the crowd. Her brief appearance was accompanied by a mystical musical passage that highlighted the entranced Hammer's amazement at her unexpected appearance.

The self-conscious attitude of the show already made Mike Hammer a parody of the original but Stacy Keach's portrayal saved the new version from being a hollow copy. Stacy Keach was a third generation knockoff, a successful blend of hard-boiled Fifties machismo and Eighties self-conscious smugness. He clicked because he embodied the qualities that were endemic to the role of the private eye: being a rough and tumble sort of guy who sanctified the sleaze in his soul with a stiff sense of righteousness. That might not have been the original Mike Hammer but Stacy Keach gave the character a new face, a cool style and renewed life in a network show and a syndicated version. Combined, he played Mike Hammer for seventy episodes.

Stacey Keach created a unique image for Mike Hammer by replacing the character's misogyny and misanthropy with poetic sarcasm and righteous indignation. He succeeded because of his impressive acting ability. 1984, Jay Bernstein Productions.

Ray Danton's work on *Mickey Spillane's Mike Hammer* has a different style than his *Quincy, M.E.* and *Cagney and Lacey* shows. The Hammer episodes have a poetic elegance, partly due to the romantic premise of the character. Danton's technique had expanded and he was able to direct and produce a series of well-made shows.

His episodes are tinged with nostalgia, where lost identities, squandered lives, and deferred rewards find their way into the storylines. The common link to the episodes is Mike Hammer's dedication to aiding the powerless. His clients are portraits of still lives in motion. The characters belong to the past but they cling to the present to ensure a future.

In *A Death in the Family,* Hammer is drawn into a mob war when his friend, Mama Z (Twyla Littleton), is wounded in a mob hit at her Italian restaurant. The chief suspect is racketeer Vincent Randolph (John Ireland). Convoluted family lines twist the meaning of family obligation for the mob widow (Barbara Bain) and her daughter (Susan Walden) because of a Randolph secret.

The real architect of the mob war is Vincent Acker (Dan Hamilton), adviser to the family whose head he has eliminated in the restaurant massacre. He plans to unite the two major crime families under his rule. Acker's intentions are to start a mob war and claim the spoils of victory after Randolph is destroyed. A torch duel atop an unfinished skyscraper

Donna Denton played The Face, a recurring fantasy image that was finally explained in the series' last episode. 1984, Jay Bernstein Productions.

sets the night on fire. Hammer and Acker set each other aflame in a fight that sends Acker over the top in a downbeat reversal of blazing glory.

Ray Danton pays his respects to the dark masters with a scene that has a flare for the past. It is a poignant variation on the neon-splashed office scene between the detective and the blonde. Susan Walden is the blonde and her liquid skin reflects the light, even in the shadows.

A Bullet for Benny is a sad nod to the two-cents plain and the candy stores of the past. Once again, Mike Hammer treats the past with reverence when he hunts the murderer of Benny Winslow (Martin Rudy), the beloved owner of a 3rd Ave. candy store. Hammer's trip down Memory Lane is filled with false identities, senseless murders, and the collateral damage of greed.

Benny's ill-fated association was formed during his Army days. The war is often a common point for different destinies. Benny became a candy store owner and O'Malley, his Army buddy, became a successful mob accountant whose loophole becomes a leak in the witness protection program. Wartime bonding became free book keeping for Benny, which turned into a fatal shooting by a mob enforcer intent on collecting the million dollar bounty on the accountant's head.

Abe Vigoda plays Arthur Ziegler, an old friend wounded in the mob hit. He is later murdered in the hospital. Leslie Wing has a pivotal role as Monica, a deceitful player who poses as Tina, Benny's daughter, so she can collect the million dollar bounty for herself. The slain candy store owner's memory is preserved in his phony daughter's photo of him in front of the store.

Monica is a clever hit woman who accrued a collection of bodies to cover her motive for killing O'Malley. She almost succeeds but one body she can't collect is Mike Hammer; instead, she substitutes her own. The scene of the showdown at the episode's climax is set in an abandoned building doubling as a safe house for O'Malley. The multiple shootout and final face off between Hammer and Monica is set in dark shadows.

Another nice touch to the show is a fight in a movie theater where Hammer battles two thugs against a black and white backdrop of Rita Hayworth doing her famous musical number in *Gilda*. Hammer does not know it as he fights the men but he is being drawn into Monica's tease, unaware that she is not Benny's daughter.

Mike Hammer has another showdown with three men whom he believes are criminals but who are really federal agents. This fight is handled using another style: slapstick knockabout comedy. The foils are a cleaning crew and glaziers carrying a sheet of glass. Mops, buckets, and two-by-fours are used to create havoc like sliding across soap water floors and being hit in the face with a block of the wood. The confrontation combines the violent style of The Three Stooges with the comic precision of Buster Keaton. The action is orchestrated by a breezy big band arrangement and the angles and editing make it work.

Deidre is *Pygmalion* meets Jack the Ripper with a veneer of *Laura*. Despite the obvious references it is also a poetic well-crafted funeral song to mystery and romance. Mae (Leslie Wing) is a plain Jane is groomed to emulate a 'model-type' in order to entrap Reverend Blessing (John S. Ragin), a Tele-Evangelist with feet of clay.

Incriminating sex tapes cause a blood trail that leads Mike Hammer to a wire tap that plucks the wings of the fallen angel. Throw in a female Svengali (also played by Leslie Wing) whose blackmail payoff is a berth at the bottom of an air-shaft and a false identity created by a wall of photographs and you have a mystery where the clichés add up to an original presentation.

The story begins with the murder of the mystery woman. Two champagne glasses drop in slow motion; so does the body, followed by a street shot of the top floor apartment's light going out. The difference is the slow speed of the triple cut. It is done at a graceful pace to imply the death of elegance. It still covers time and distance in a compact way.

Leslie Wing, again, plays a woman with a dual identity who misleads Mike Hammer because of his trusting nature. The difference is that her character is psychotic and her breakdown is truly ugly and a fine piece of acting on Ms. Wing's behalf. It is also good, if unsettling, to see John S. Ragin apply his craft. He is charming in a superficial way. His magnetism is a fitting cover for a phony, if charismatic, public personality.

Deirdre begs for simpler times when innocence has yet to be spoiled. Hammer becomes lost in a myth created by a wall of photos of Deirdre, a woman who never really existed. The woman he hunts is a phantom because Deidre is the product of an insane woman's revenge fantasy. Her identity is a transfer of guilt, a disguise for Mae, who disowns herself by becoming her own conqueror.

Golden Lady is a echo of the code of yesterday's working man. All that remains of honor is a dockworker's widow (Julianna McCarthy) who seeks justice in the murder of her husband. Hammer tackles union corruption when he tries to recover the missing pension of Sam Bailor (David Carlile), the murdered dockworker.

What Hammer uncovers is a pension fraud that wiped out the members' holdings while paying dividends to the stockholders. The mastermind of the embezzlement scheme is Mildred Hofsteder (Nina Foch), a well-respected matron of the arts and sciences, who has set up a series of shell accounts to circulate her fortune without being detected by the IRS.

She is a powerful women who owns three department stores, two square blocks of Manhattan real estate and a dozen banks. Her true love is her collection of rare coins, some dating back to the Roman Empire. It satisfies her lust for power in a way that would have made Lucretia Borgia

Mildred Hofsteder (Nina Foch) is a rich matriarch whose life is enriched by her rare coin collection. 1986, Columbia Pictures Television.

Ray Danton's poetic use of dissolves and double exposures gives one scene a haunting quality by creating a dream world where Mildred Hofsteder (Nina Foch) escapes the mundane. 1986, Columbia Pictures Television.

envious. So would her cavalier attitude about the murders committed to protect her fortune.

There is a satisfying twist ending when Hammer recovers the pension in the form of a fistful of Mrs. Hofsteder's rare coins. The face value of the coins is equal to the stolen pension fund; oblivious to what they are, the widow is instructed by Hammer to cash them in for their numismatic value. Her dividends make her a rich woman.

A striking visual touch is the use of dissolves and double exposure to illustrate Mrs. Hofsteder's infatuation with her coin collection. She studies a coin through a spyglass in a dreamy sequence that resembles the movements of a Bavarian clock due to the way the twin images blend because of the slow dissolves and camera pans.

Another poetic use of dissolves is illustrated in a scene when Mike Hammer breaks a window to let fresh air into a room filled with gas fumes. The window shatters in slow motion and the shards of glass dissolve into ripples of water in the bay where a yacht is anchored in dry dock. Ray Danton also uses the slow motion effect in two scenes where characters are tossed off boats by Mike Hammer.

Harlem Nocturne is the closest thing to Ray Danton in total control. The script is based on his collaboration on a short story. He also served as the supervising producer. The episode is cliché television at its best. It is natural for the 80's Hammer to walk a mile in Philip Marlowe's shoes. The terrain is *Farewell, My Lovely*. After the murder of the modernized Lindsay Marriott, it is a trip to the music business to bring the viewer up to speed with the Eighties. In this version, Ray Danton directs a music video with George Benson.

The Raymond Chandler copy is successfully handled and the alteration is a rhythm 'n' blues interpretation. Moose Malloy becomes Bubba Crown (Samm-Art Williams); his long lost girlfriend is Bess Irving aka Delia Marvel (Lynne Whitfield), not Velma, and the woman who has the girlfriend's photo and the background story to her past is not a slovenly drunken recluse but the worldly Hot Mama Vibes (Isabel Sanford). Finally, Lindsay Marriott, the polished dandy, is replaced by Digger Love (Ernie Hudson), a colorful hipster given to exaggeration.

After Digger Love follows Marriot's lead to become an auto casualty while parked in neutral, the story takes an uptown turn, thanks to a

Bubba Crown (Samm-Art Williams) is just as deadly and determined to find his lost love as his prototype, Moose Malloy. 1986, Columbia Pictures Television.

Law and Order | 433

Delia Marvel (Lynne Whitfield) is the modern Velma and just s deadly as her predecessor. 1986, Columbia Pictures Television.

borrowed cliché-the Lady in Red (Jeannie-Marie Austin). Hammer sees her on the bridge after he and Digger Love park the car. The detective glimpses her through a hazy fog before he is clubbed upon discovering Digger Love's corpse. Later, he sees her at a recording session for the blind rhythm 'n' blues star, Billy Marvel (George Benson).

The real connection between the two worlds is the woman who uses the Lady in Red, Delia Marvel (Lynne Whitfield), the wife of the music icon. She is the real Bess Irving and has been carrying out a vendetta to eliminate the witnesses to her past, such as Digger Love and Hot Mama Vibes, among others. Bubba Crown and, through association, Mike Hammer are next on her list. She is stopped by a bullet from her husband's gun.

Action shown from three different angles in a series of quick cuts is one of Ray Danton's techniques for heightening drama and covering distance. In *Harlem Nocturne*, he and Bubba make a hasty escape from a group of beat cops thanks to three jump cuts. The first shot is them running up the avenue. The cut is to them running up the stairs to the el and the final shot shows the two men out of breath on the train platform.

Ray Danton also uses slow-motion to create tension, as evidenced by a scene where Mike Hammer runs interference for Bubba Crown as a group of cops try to bring him down. It is also another reference to Ray Danton's affection for football in the way the scene is choreographed.

The use of old photographs to create a nostalgic atmosphere is used in a scene where Hot Mama Vibes proudly shows Mike Hammer here glory days with images of the Harlem greats: Count Basie, Louis Armstrong, Cab Calloway, Billie Holiday and Duke Ellington. They are the saintly ghosts of the past who ruefully watch the body count mount before the last body that falls is the mystery woman who started it all in the first place.

The Return of Mickey Spillane's Mike Hammer, a 1986 Tele-Film, is Ray Danton's last film as a director. The movie has interesting characters, a tried and true premise, an intriguing subplot, rich cinematography and fluid direction.

The kidnapping of movie star Diana Lake's (Lauren Hutton) daughter, Megan (Emily Rose Chance), unfolds into an exotic adventure that includes Hollywood filmmaking, suicide commandoes in Viet Nam, a million dollar orphan-for-sale operation, and a collection of tattoos that tells the whole story in a series of beautiful pictograms.

Diana Lake's super cop movie is the movie-within-the movie. It is the segue that allows the viewer to peek at quasi-stars like Bruce Boxleitner and Dabney Coleman as they appear filming the movie or Dionne Warwick as she whizzes by in her car. The Hollywood angle actually detracts from the story whose chief interest lies in the sub-

Mike Hammer is hot on the trail of a child-kidnapping ring after he prevents the snatching of a movie star's (Lauren Hutton) daughter. 1986, Columbia Pictures Television.

plot and the minor characters, mainly the kidnappers.

The key point of concern is the undercover suicide unit turned kidnapping merchants. The field unit is led by a Neville Brand look alike named DAK (Michael Preston), and they are united by tattoos that, when combined, tell of their mission in Vietnam. It is a story that tells itself every time a member of the unit winds up on the coroner's table and it becomes a case of connecting tattoos to understand the plot. The command does are aided by the mistress who tattooed them in Viet Nam. She serves her purpose before they do but her tattoo of a Buddhist temple leads Hammer to Chapel (John Karlen), whose front for his child-for-sale ring is a child rescue organization.

A TV reporter (JoAnn Pflug) tries to interview Diana Lake (Lauren Hutton) about the attempted kidnapping of her daughter. 1986, Columbia Pictures Television.

John Karlen stands out as the crusader turned crazed child marketer. His loyalty to his special unit is life binding and he does everything he can to protect them. It ends when he convinces DAK to pack it in when the mute assassin holds a child hostage in his kidnap lair. The crazed vet has it out with Hammer on his property, which has been booby-trapped with mines. DAK is summarily dismissed and Hammer enjoys tossing his dog tags into the pit created by a Claymore mine.

Stacy Keach is his usual sardonic self, sated with caustic wit and keen observations, along with a sharp preservation instinct and a charming bedside manner. He is a gentleman 'til the end, when his date with Diana Lake is attending a theatre to view her movie. Lauren Hutton, as the movie star, has her effective emotional moments and Mickey Rooney has a great cameo as Jack Bergin, a legendary Hollywood agent still full of wit and tricks.

Vince Edwards plays Frank Walker, a grim F.B.I. agent who is contemptuous of Hammer. Leo Penn is Leo, the beleaguered director of Lake's film and Stephen Macht plays Nick Anton, the actress' dissipated husband. He is heavily in debt because of his gambling problem and helps to mastermind the kidnapping of his daughter so he could use the money to pay off his creditors. His payoff is a death on a desert plateau.

Tom Everett is exceptional as Orville, a cemetery troubadour. He strums his guitar and sings Beatles songs to the head stones. Orville is the only disoriented member of the unit but, at least, he is safe because he lives in his own world. Hammer cracks the case when Orville's tattoo and his renditions of "Hey Jude" and "Strawberry Fields Forever" tell the detective the story of DAK and the Dragon. That's when he learns that a Temple is really a Chapel.

The series regulars are also on hand, such as Lindsay Bloom as Velda, Don Stroud as Capt. Pat Chambers, Kent Williams as ADA Barrington, Danny Goldman as Ozzie the Answer and Donna Denton as The Face.

Ray Danton uses an effective triple jump cut in the when the private eye saves the movie star's daughter from being run over, he careens over

Veteran actor Vince Edwards plays a hard-bitten F.B.I. agent who does not disguise his contempt for Mike Hammer. 1986, Columbia Pictures Television.

the car's hood in the process and the action is accentuated from three angles.

The Return of Mickey Spillane's Mike Hammer was the third television movie about the iconic detective and was sort-of-made as a second pilot to test the waters after Stacy Keach's notorious sabbatical in a London jail for what could have been a career ending bust. The series was renewed and lasted for another season. Keach revived the character for a short-lived syndication version in the 90's. The only returning original cast member was Kent Williams as ADA Barrington. Even the Face had changed!

Ray Danton resigned as a direct and supervising producer of the *New Mike Hammer*, effective December 8, so he could work on the preproduction on William Inge's play, *Come Back, Little Sheba*. Originally meant as a PBS special it was postponed and resurrected as the season opener for the Los Angeles Theater Center.

General Directory

THE CRIME CLUB

The rest of Ray Danton's directing credits are a mixture of crime shows, syndication series and cable productions. He was one of the resident directors of three popular and critically-acclaimed television shows but also worked independently, as was his want as an actor in the 50's and 60's.

Crime shows are abundant in Ray Danton's portfolio and his first outside *Quincy, M.E.* show was *The Hardy Boys,* co-directed with Jack Arnold. It was an odd link to *Outside the Law*, made twenty one years previously with Arnold as the director and Danton as the star.

The Hardy Boys was Franklin W. Dixon's popular book series about the crime-busting exploits of two juvenile sleuths, Frank and Joe Hardy, the sons of a private detective. Walt Disney first brought the duo to the small screen during the 1950's and it was given new life in the 1980's. It was first part of a revolving series where it alternated with another teen detective, Nancy Drew (Pamela Sue Martin), who was first given screen life by the popular actress Bonita Granville in the late 1930's and early 1940's. *The Hardy Boys* took center stage when the Nancy Drew shows were dropped.

Death Surf is the search for a mystery woman (Maren Jensen) claimed by the waves when she has an accident wind surfing in Hawaii. Frank (Parker Stevenson) witnesses the calamity and tries to rescue her but has no success. Later, he is detained by the police but is released and he seeks to learn the girl's identity.

Frank meets her father, who tells the young sleuth that he has not seen his daughter in two years. The usual American dysfunctional family alienation is the reason and dad is overcome by guilt and remorse. He hires Frank to piece together the two years and find out what happened to his daughter during their estrangement. Frank and his brother, Joe (Sean Cassidy), tail the illusion and come up with someone who faked her own death because she was on the run from gangsters.

It is hard to tell which scenes were directed by Ray Danton or Jack Arnold. It is a laugh to credit Arnold with the underwater scenes of Frank making like a pearl diver looking for the girl who went under the waves and disappeared. Parker Stevenson is reminiscent of the Creature from the Black Lagoon because of his agile aquatic style. The Hawaiian locale is always a winner and it outshines the two adolescent Tiger Beat pin-up kids. Maren Jensen plays the mystery woman and Jack Jones plays Sam 'Hubba' Hubblemeyer, a sinister over-the-hill surfer boy. Tara Buckman has a small part.

Ray Danton returned to *Switch* as a director for two episodes, *Death Tong* and *Photo Finish*. He had previously appeared as a gangster in an episode titled, *Big Deal in Paradise*. In *Death Tong*, Wang (James Hong), Malcolm's (Charlie Callas) cook is involved in a murder that may presage war among Chinese clans. Pete, Frank and the gang are mortified to learn that Wang is a revered elder of the Tong. He says that it is a hereditary honor and that no underhanded clandestine activities motivate his life. He is embroiled in murder when a smuggler is killed and his scroll is stolen.

Sgt. Lee (Barbara Luna) is a San Francisco cop who is an expert on Tong history and genealogy. She witnessed the murder and saw Wang kneeling over the victim after he was murdered and robbed. He later tells Frank and Pete that the scroll has inflammatory information that could upset a fifty year old peace pact between two Tong families. Wong claims that a young upstart wants to wage war to increase and consolidate his power.

The truth is that the smuggled goods were fragments of Chairman Mao's diary. They were brought into the country by Nin Tung Fat (John Fujioka), the owner of a fast food emporium. He has hired Charlie Kuang (Phillip Ahn), an expert forger, to insert some seditious passages that would cause revolution and social unrest across the world. Wang clears his name when he assists his friends and the police in bringing down the revolutionaries.

They have no trouble getting the truth from the conspirators, whom they believe will confess rather than being extradited to Communist China for punishment. The episode is noteworthy because it has Barbara Luna as the star and noted Asian actors James Hong, John Fujioka and Phillip Ahn in supporting roles.

Photo Finish was the last episode filmed for the show; in it, Mac and Pete aid Cluny Young (Sherry Mathis), a woman whose sister Jacy (Anne-Marie Martin) has disappeared. The trail leads to a murderous politician and an extremist environmentalist group. Arthur Gilmore (Edward Power) is a State Senator with an eye on the governor's mansion. He hopes that a deal to build a nuclear reactor will be a hit with his constituents. The Earth Liberation Movement (ELM) does not consider its members to be among his constituents and their plan is to sway his vote with a sexual blackmail scheme.

It backfires when the state senator arrives a meeting with the blackmailers accompanied by Dokovic (Rudy Solari), his procurer and enforcer. They use explosives to obliterate the pair in an attempt to frame the couple for attempting to blow up a government restricted site. Mac and Pete don't buy the explanation and dig deeper into their case. Their investigation takes them to eccentric escort services and the farm hideaway of ELM.

Pete disguises himself as Scorpion, the group's leader, but he tips his hand because the real deal is on the premises. He is given a free pass because he is not a narc and has been trying to locate Jaycee. This leads to the kidnapping of the state senator and his sidekick and they are taken to the ELM's hideout, where Pete and the gang coerce a confession out of the men by threatening to blow them up.

The best things about the episode are a musical number and a confrontation with cult idol Sig Haig. Cleo is a group member who uses her cabaret act as a cover. She sings "Ain't Nobody's Business if I Do" in a cleverly staged video that includes double exposures to create an on-the-spot night life montage. The other scene is when Pete is dressed like Scorpion, affecting a 70's disco-pimp disguise. It does not fool the farmer, played by Sid Haig. Haig gets to go into his borderline-psycho-on-the boil routine when he interrogates Pete about his real identity. The real Scorpion gives Pete a free pass and lets him live.

The Incredible Hulk was considered a sci-fi program although it had a basic police manhunt premise, like *The Fugitive* on steroids. Jack McGee (Jack Colvin) was an investigative reporter for a tabloid newspaper who was pursuing Dr. David Banner to link him with The Incredible Hulk, his super-human alter-ego.

Killer Instinct is a subconscious impulse that gives John Tobey (Denny Miller), a star quarterback, the same energizer that turns David Banner (Bill Bixby) into the Incredible Hulk (Lou Ferrigno). David Banner's task

John Tobey (Denny Miller) is a football player whose repressed hatred of his father creates a rage akin to David Banner's (Bill Bixby) *Killer Instinct*. Only one of them turns into *The Incredible Hulk*. 1978, Universal Television.

is to get a psychologist to convince a football to bench its star player. John Tobey has been playing rough and dirty, apparently motivated by an unconscious urge to destroy all cheaters!

Two of Ray Danton's devices—rage as a theme and the use of photographs—are used in this intense episode. In this episode, a childhood photo of football hero John Tobey (Denny Miller), is folded in half to block out the memory of his cheating father. His rage is traced to a childhood incident when he witnessed his father cheating to win a game. He transfers his guilt into a desire to hurt his opponents. Tobey is cured when he is confronted by someone with a rage greater than his: The Incredible Hulk! References to Ray Danton' past as a high school quarterback and the coach of his son's football team are used in an episode that uses the sport as a metaphor of rage.

Much of the 1980's crime shows were cut and paste premises culled from the staples and-by then-cliché trademarks of the genre. Ray Danton helmed the pilots for two cop shows: *Bender's Force* ('80) and *Feel the Heat* ('83). *Bender's Force* was produced by Carroll O'Connor and Terry Becker's production company and starred Harry Guardino and Joseph Burke as the veteran cop and his cocky sidekick.

Harry Guardino played Bender, a tough, streetwise New York City cop who seeks a change in his life after his wife dies of cancer. He leaves the concrete jungle for the land of palm trees when he becomes the chief-of-police in a California desert resort community. Much of the show's premise rests on the sharp contrast between the vociferous Bender and his laid back team, including a sidekick played by Joseph Burke.

Ray Danton said Bender, "…is the last of the angry men."

The pilot episode dealt with Bender fending off threats made by Ben Piazza, a land developer who is a front for the syndicate. He is trying to pull a land grab on one of the residents, Will Hare. Perhaps the most notable thing about *Bender's Force* was Joseph Burke's anecdote about star Harry Guardino having to stand on a box to match Burke's height. According to Burke, this lead Guardino to complain, "Who the f--k am I, Mickey Rooney?"

Ray Danton also directed another pilot for a cop show. *Feel the Heat* ('83) starred Nick Mancuso as a foot loose and fancy free ex-cop now working as a P.I. in Key Blanco, Florida. His aim is to take down drug runners a la *Miami Vice* and he is aided and abetted by his chief nemesis, the worldly wise and overly confident Bouldon County D.A., Honor Campbell (Lisa Eichhorn), whom he happens to be in love with.

They form an uneasy alliance to find the murderer of a vicious drug dealer whose death has made a group of influential and powerful citizens concerned and panicky.

Robert Hooks played Barney Hill, the name of the character Hooks father played on *Mission: Impossible*. Paula Kelly and Hector Elizondo were also in the cast.

Ray Danton directed *Love Story*, an episode of William Shatner's *T.J. Hooker*, which also starred Heather Locklear and James Darren. 1985, Columbia Pictures Television, Spelling-Goldberg Productions.

The show was a cross between *Miami Vice* and *Moonlighting* but without the staying power of either show. Mancuso, unfortunately, also did not click with his previous effort, the excellent *Stingray*, based on the superb T.V. movie of the same name.

That, too, was inspired by *Miami Vice* but stood on its own. Too bad it did not find its deserved success on the network schedule. Fortunately, it found renewed life in the age of DVD.

T.J. Hooker was Wiliam Shatner's successful star turn in a 80's cop show. It ran for five seasons and featured Adrian Zmed and Heather Locklear as Hooker's sidekicks as they dealt with high speed car chases and depraved psychos on the loose. The forever-youthful James Darren also starred in the series and looked the same as he did in the early 60's teenage romp movies and his late 60's television show, *The Time Tunnel*.

Ray Danton directed *Love Story*, another quest for phantom justice story that starred Michelle Philips as Teri Sherman, a witness to her friend's assault by a quartet of depraved misfits who have been committing a series of rapes and robberies. Her cooperation with T.J. Hooker targets her as the gang's next victim.

Hooker falls in love with Teri but there is no room for romance in their lives because of their careers and the tragic underlining feeling of inadequacy on both their behalves. Tara Buckman and Miguel Ferrer portray half of the gang that is pursued and tracked down by the overbearing Hooker. Atmosphere is provided by the stereotypical gang and scenes filmed in Chinatown, where a piece of scrimshaw leads to identifying one of the punks.

Ray Danton continued his crime drama assignments with *Leg Work*, a short-lived crime comedy-drama starring Margaret Colin as Claire McCarron, a private detective and Frances McDormand as Willie Pipal, her contact on the police force. Patrick James Clark played her brother, Lt. Fred McCarron, also a law enforcement officer.

The show's writing is amateurish and the humor is strained. How it made it to the fall schedule is a mystery but its short shelf life was the solution. It only served to give Frances McDormand a credit for her resume and Ray Danton a chance to perfect his directing technique. *Leg Work* was a feeble attempt to create a female buddy dichotomy show and its main grace is the lead, Margaret Colin.

Things That Go Bump in the Night is a Mafia send up stuffed with stock mob stereotypes. Claire is asked by a lawyer-friend to help exonerate his client, a hot-headed man who was threatening a low-level gangster before the goon was injured in a car bombing. Illegal explosives were found at the suspect's garage and this gives the D.A. plenty of momentum to steam roll the defendant.

Claire infiltrates the mob world by patronizing a beauty salon where mob wives and mistresses go. This gives her the opportunity to ingratiate herself to them, especially after she has hair transformed into a wildly teased hair-do. Mob gossip, coupled with info obtained from an annoying friend who is a mob expert, help Claire uncover the motive behind the car bombing.

Margaret Colin was one of the stars of *Leg Work*, which also featured Frances McDormand. 1987. 20th. Century Fox Television.

It seems that the victim was consoling the wife of an impotent mobster and this infuriated his spouse. She was the one who performed the dirty deed and Claire discovers this by going through the woman's garbage and discovering a cache of paramilitary magazines. The suspect is freed and is reunited with his son, the only love of his life.

In *Mystery Woman*, Claire is hired to work undercover at a nursing home by an ambitious assemblyman who wants to become the D.A. His aim is to uncover shading business dealings and abusive behavior by the staff towards the residents. Trouble ensues when the media misinterprets the private meetings he has with a mystery woman.

The media infer that the married assemblyman is having a love affair. The mystery woman is really Claire who is secretly meeting with him to give updates on her investigation. The episode is a lesson on using people for personal profit and the pitfalls of being misjudged by those around you.

Magnum, P.I. was a popular private eye show that ran for eight seasons (1980-1988). It had all of the ingredients that made a show a hit: a handsome and likeable star, appealing supporting characters, popular guest stars, strong writing, excellent direction and an exotic location that gave the show a magic aura.

Hawaii was the setting of the show that made Tom Selleck a household name, mainly because he presented a new type of hero: a macho protagonist with a sensitive side that was not threatening to women. He was a fighter and a lover who was faithful to his friends and his principles.

He also had the perfect foil in Higgins, one of the best supporting characters ever written. John Hillerman played the English snob to perfection but, like Magnum, he was a contradiction because he was just as tough as he was effete. He was a WW II vet having served the mother country besides possibly being the unseen Robin Masters, writer of pulp novels and owner of the estate that Magnum lived on as the security specialist. His friends, Rick (Larry Manetti) and T.C. (Roger E. Mosley) are Vietnam buddies and run a club and Island Hoppers, a helicopter tour service.

The turning point in the series came when Magnum was shot in the last episode of season seven. It was unsure whether or not he was going to continue in the role so he wound up in Limbo, as did his fans. Tom Selleck decided on one more season and it was a change of pace as the episodes were more reflective and were based on the fact that he had survived the shooting and had reached 40 years of age. Identity crisis was the dominant theme of *Magnum, P.I.* during its last season and it figures big in the two Ray Danton directed episodes: *The Great Hawaiian Adventure Company* and *The Love that Lies*. It is also a theme for many of the show's that he directed.

In the first episode, Magnum has developed a great idea for a new tour business. It involves making a deal with the local airlines to prepare a tour package that will be handled by Magnum and his friends. He tries to curry support from Higgins, Rick and T.C. but they seem to be too involved in their lives to take him seriously. Higgins has developed a new approach to his memoirs, Rick has fallen in love with Cleo (Phyllis Davis), a call girl who is stuck on Magnum, and T.C. is trying to keep his son out of jail because he has fallen under the influence of a motorcycle gang.

The crux of the drama lies in the subplot, where T.C.'s son is experiencing growing pains and has to carve out a niche for himself without being dominated by the dimwitted hoods on wheels. Juvenile antics such as joy riding and plundering land the son in jail a couple of times but it is a rough ride of sea that is his rite of passage.

The episode is mellow by the show's standards and even the prospect of dealing with a motorcycle gang seems lackluster because they are teenage model types and could be taken down a couple of notches with a couple of slaps to their faces. Some humor is evident in Magnum's attempt to sell his idea to a female executive, who promises to present it to a board

The Love That Lies is something that Thomas Magnum (Tom Selleck) and Brenda Babcock (Eileen Brennan) have to deal with in a sensitive story about love, abandonment, and reclamation. 1987, Belasarious Productions, Glen A. Larson Productions, and Universal Television.

meeting but Magnum misses his chance to make his pitch because he is busy helping T.C. rescuing his son when he experiences a crisis at sea.

The Love That Lies deals with facades and blood ties when Magnum is hired by Brenda Babcock (Eileen Brennan) to find the child she gave up 30 years ago. The child turns out to be Magnum's friend, Carol Baldwin (Kathleen Lloyd), an attorney who has often represented him when he got into legal jams. It is an extremely tense time for Carol as she is in the middle of a murder trial involving a much admired businessman. She is threatened by his adoring public and Magnum convinces her to stay with her mother, Abigail (Celeste Holm) for safekeeping. Abigail finds out about Magnum's client and tries to find the right time to tell Carol but it is brought out into the open one night when she witnesses an argument between the two women who are, in fact, her mother.

Soul-searching, lashing out at others and a reevaluation of values turn Carol's life upside down when the news causes her to have a raging fit at her adoptive mother but the butt of her disappointment is directed at her deceased father. It is not so much that he cheated on his wife but that he concealed the truth from her. It takes Magnum's understanding to help

Carol realize the magnitude of her parents' love and that resolution adds meaning to love and discretion.

This episode shows the undercurrents to our lives that exist in an alternate universe and create havoc when they cross over to our waking states. It takes a super-human emotional makeup to unite the two and remain sane. Carol and Abigail have achieved this because they have each other. Brenda achieves the same end because she no longer has a choice. She gives up her daughter a second time when she realizes there is no place for her in Carol's life.

Ray Danton's last crime show (other than Cagney and Lacey) was *Beverly Hills Buntz*, which wasn't exactly a crime drama but a show that it was spun off of was a very successful cop series, *Hill Street Blues*. Norman Buntz (Dennis Franz), a cynical cop who has been poisoned by a career of chasing and arresting criminals, makes the move to Beverly Hills to open up his own private detective agency. He is aided by *Hill Street Blues*' former snitch, Sid Thurston (Peter Jurasik) as his leg man.

Buntz implicates himself in a gangster's revenge when he aids Nora Saynes (Kathryn Dowling), the object of a mob hit in *Umbrella in the Water*. She can spoil his life-saving alibi and that marks her for death. Buntz becomes involved in her plight when his car is caught between the hit man's vehicle and her wheels on the freeway as she escapes the first attempt on her life.

The detective loses his driver's license at a bail hearing because he is accused of firing the shots and he tracks her down through her license

Beverly Hills Buntz was a short-lived comedy show about a transplanted big city detective (Dennis Franz) and his former snitch turned spacey leg man (Peter Jurasik). 1988, MTM Enterprises.

plates, Tapped Out. Buntz is taken along for a one way ride when the hit man (Seth Jaffe) shows up at her office and escorts them to his car. Luckily, Sid is watching and follows them, enlisting the aid of a witless surfer in calling 911. The umbrella in the title refers to the murder weapon in a dream Sid has where he killed Buntz. This episode reminds the viewer of the *T.J. Hooker* episode, *Love Story*, because of the unfortunate involvement of an innocent bystander.

Whoever gave the green light to this series forgot to hire clever writers to compliment the chemistry of the leads. The stories are okay but they are not up to the talents of the two main characters. Dennis Franz plays like an exasperated straight man to the manic and mercurial lunacy of Peter Jurasik. Together, they solve a bevy of crimes in spite of themselves. The only crime they couldn't solve was how to get better writers.

FAMILY VALUES

Miniseries became popular with the success of *Roots* in 1977. They were still popular in the 80's when Ray Danton directed the last installment of *The Contender* starring Marc Singer. Singer played Johnny Captor, a college student who became a boxer to support his mother and younger brother after his father, an Oregon lumberjack, committed suicide. His decision causes a rift with his girlfriend, Jill, who is a teacher who preferred that Captor stayed in college and earn a degree. She has a distaste for the sweet science and does not want to see him risk life and limb every time he steps into the ring. Captor believes that he is championship material and allows his career to be handled by George, his trainer, and a mobster named Harry.

The mini-series ran for six weeks and Ray Danton directed the last installment, *Mission at Moscow*. In the episode, Johnny's Olympic dreams are threatened when he has a less-than desirable encounter with Russian police. He becomes a product of bureaucratic red tape but is released from the totalitarian labyrinth and free to pursue his dream.

Marc Singer portrayed Johnny Captor, a college dropout turned boxer in the mini-series, *The Contender*. 1980, CBS.

Family values also figure big in the next domestic drama Ray Danton directed, *American Dream*. A shift in family fortune causes the Novak family to downscale their lifestyle when they give up their comfortable suburban life and return to urban Chicago.

The short-lived series (only five of the eight filmed episodes were aired) dealt with the pressures that the Novak family had to deal with because of their economic downturn.

Stephen Macht and Karen Carlson played the parents, Danny and Donna. Michael Hershewe and Tim Waldrip played their sons, Todd and Casey. Veteran actors John McIntire and Hans Conreid also starred as Sam and Abe, two old timers from the new neighborhood.

Ray Danton directed two episodes, *Crossing Patterns* and *California Dreamin'*. In *Crossing Patterns*, he deals with a familiar subject-his love for football-when Danny acts as a substitute coach for the football team. He enjoys the work until he finds out that one of his players in an undercover narcotics officer. It is another drug-tinged episode, a subject Danton dealt with a couple of times in his tenure as one of the directors of *Quincy, M.E.* His next directing assignment for the show was the unaired *California Dreamin'*. The title is a reference to the Mamas and Pappas first hit single and it deals with Casey thinking about leaving the nest and moving to California.

Ray Danton went from examining the trials and tribulations of a suburban family that returned to its working class roots to two families where such a change in fortune would be as unthinkable as being middle-class or working class. How could such a thing be contemplated when the heads of the clans were J.R. Ewing and Blake Carrington? That was the case with *Dynasty* and *Dallas*, companion studies on the lives of the rich and famous.

Dallas was a blockbuster nighttime soap opera that centered on the evil machinations of J.R. Ewing (Larry Hagman), a Texas oil man who lacked scruples and made up for it with a ruthless will to power. 1980, Lorimar Productions.

Primetime soaps were the rage of the Eighties and *Dallas* was the progenitor of the craze. Larry Hagman created one of television's most memorable villains with J.R. Ewing, the oil magnate and scion of a family of dysfunctional power brokers. *Offshore Crude* is about the rivalry between J.R. and Cliff as they try to outbid each other on an offshore drilling operation. They are two snakes in the grass and use everything and everyone at their disposal to undermine each other. The subplots revolve around the ever-changing romantic entanglements of the secondary characters.

Dynasty was another nighttime soap created in the wake of *Dallas*. The star of this drama was John Forsythe, who had his own television series in the early 50's with *Bachelor Father* and provided the voice of Charlie in *Charlie's Angels* during the late 70's. In *The Trial*, Blake Carrington fights for his reputation when he is accused of participating in an illegal weapons deal. This comes on the heels of a near-fatal car accident in Natumbe, Africa. His political campaigned may be ruined unless his children can solve the mystery frame which they do before the closing credits.

SYNDICATION AND CABLE:

In the Eighties, syndication and the nascent cable industry offered alternative ways for the production and marketing of television programs. In 1981, Ray Danton formed Malada International, Ltd. with international financier Bob Graf. The company's intention was to develop and produce films but nothing came of it. Instead, Ray Danton mined the new syndication and cable market. Two of the syndicated programs that Ray Danton directed for are *Tales of the Unexpected*, a horror anthology and *Fame*, a high school musical.

Quinn Martin was the executive producer for the first incarnation of *Tales of the Unexpected*, a suspense anthology that lasted for a year. Roald Dahl created the second version and hosted most of the anthology program's episodes, which frequently included scripts written by him. John Houseman replaced Dahl after he died. Ray Danton directed three episodes, *Bird of Prey* for Quinn Martin and *The Best Policy and Turn of the Tide* for the second version.

In *Tales of the Unexpected: Bird of Prey*, a slow pan crosses a desert panacea, where the only sign of life is a bungalow that belongs to a couple about to be cursed by the visit of a demonic bird. At the start, it's three human players plus a parrot and its monstrous offspring. By the end, it is just the grotesque bird.

Jack (Frank Converse) and Edna (Sondra Locke) are a couple whose lives are dominated by isolation and boredom. Frank works at a desert facility, drives home, has a drink and cracks jokes with his parrot while silently bristling at Edna having a good time drinking and listening to

Frank Converse and Sondra Locke are a couple cursed by the *Bird of Prey*, a demonic offspring of their lovable parrot. 1981/1984, Angela Productions.

Charlie (Charles Hallahan), his co-worker, play the piano. Charlie is the third wheel who is a friend who appears to be too friendly. Edna insists that there is no hanky-panky involved and they are just wiling away the time until Frank comes home from work.

The unlucky couple is claimed by desert madness after their parrot gives birth to a monstrous bird. All that remains is the offspring of madness and a jealousy blessed by the noonday sun and cursed by the midnight moon when Edna announces that she is pregnant. Jack wonders whether he is the father of the good news or the bearer of bad tidings? According to the bird, it's both and that spells doom for the couple and a timely transfer for the jovial friend, whom the bird suggests is the real father of Edna's child. Sacrifice and doom is the final stage of the parents-to-be self-imposed judgment as good news of the family way elicits cigars, champagne and a murder-suicide.

Ray Danton depicts the loneliness of a desert habitat and the tension that mounts between a couple whose only human friend is the husband's co-worker. The playful parrot and the huge black monster it gives birth to are the extremes that symbolize the pressure that builds within the sedate marriage that ends in a tragedy instead of a celebration.

General Directory | 453

The Best Policy is a macabre comedy about a bank's computer expert, Flock (Gary Burgdoff), who becomes the acting manager after the boss unexpectedly dies when he chokes on a piece of meat loaf. The head office begins to receive a series of anonymous letters alleging improprieties at the bank. Soon, Flock is being audited for suspicions of embezzlement and possibly murder.

The allegations and the ensuing investigation unsettle him and he goes to the main branch and confronts the bank manager (Logan Ramsey). The matter is cleared up, Flock's reputation is restored and restitution is becoming the bank manager. The catch to the story is that Flock's wife (Deborah Harmon) was sending the letters in an attempt to get the head office to recognize her husband's efficiency. The couple-avowed vegetarians-celebrate by eating a dinner of greasy fast food which sends them into throes of ecstasy.

The Best Policy makes an appealing contrast to *Senza Via D'Uscita* because of the bank backdrop. There are similarities to the cold machinations of the financial institutions, the only difference being the levity in the television episode. Gary Burgdoff is first-rate as the bespectacled milquetoast on the verge of ruin. His wife is weird as a wholesome natural food fanatic.

Turn of the Tide stars Richard Basehart as Slade, a celebrated retired criminal attorney. He is on the verge of financial ruin and needs an extension of a case he is working on but his colleague, Spalding, refuses to help because of the unethical nature of the request. Slade had just given an interview where he claims that many people have committed the perfect murder because their victims were never found.

He has an opportunity to test his theory when he murders Spalding and tries to dispose of him with the morning tide. The only thing he overlooked was the power of rigor mortis and how such an oversight would make him a victim when he carries the corpse on his back to the tide and is unable to loosen the dead man's grip. Slade, too, is claimed by the turn of the tide.

Slade's prolonged death by drowning scene is filmed in close-ups with the raging waves swallowing him and the murder victim that clings to him to provide the dead weight that will drag him to the bottom of the deep.

This episode is filmed in a dark creepy fashion that reflects the murderer's frame of mind. The interview between him and the reporter (Gretchen Corbett) is low-keyed and ominous, something out of a horror

Turn of the Tide is karmic payback for Slade (Richard Basehart), a criminal lawyer who thinks that he has committed the perfect murder. 1983, Angela Television.

movie. It has the sedate quality of the pre-dawn hours, something that relates to the rest of the episode. Light and shadows dominate the story until the raging tide is highlighted by the breaking dawn. It ends with the sunrise and a family that arrives on the scene to enjoy the new morning. The daughter sees Slade's metal garrote lying on the beach and uses it as a whip and her parents laugh at her playful attitude.

Fame is based on the 1980 movie of the same name. It chronicles the trials and tribulations of the students and teachers at New York's High School of the Performing Arts. Originally a 1982 NBC show, it was produced for syndication after the network cancelled it a year and a half later. New members were added to the cast, which included originals from the movie, Debbie Allen, Albert Hague and Gene Anthony Ray.

In *Selling Out*, Jesse (Jesse Borrego), a young song-writer, enters the "A Song in Your Heart" contest and must compete with his fellow students in a chance to sing his song and perform in a video. He has problems putting a handle on his song and Nicole (Nia Peeples) suggests that he may be looking in the wrong places. Jesse goes to Spanish Harlem and encounters a street musician playing a guitar in the style of his beloved grandfather, the man who inspired him to become a musician. The encounter turns into a musical number where Jesse is encouraged by his Latino heritage.

He writes the winning song and promises to include his friends in the video but things begin to sour when the producers make changes to his song and its ideal to the point where it has become unrecognizable. An immigrant's dream has become a boy-meets-girl storyline and the choreography is glitzy and hedonistic.

Jesse must decide whether or not to change his prize-winning song to please the request of the contest's promoters. He is introduced to the cold, hard world of the music business where contract law holds sway over creative integrity. The hook to success is the accouterments of fame but is it compromising or selling out that snags the prize?

In the end, Jesse shocks the producers when he reverts to the low keyed but emotional ballad about his grandfather's dream when he performs the song to the audience. They give him a standing ovation but

Selling Out is not an option for Jesse (Jesse Borrego), an aspiring song writer who returns to the old neighborhood for inspiration and the courage to deal with commercial minded music producers. 1985, MGM/UA Television.

it does not mollify the producers' anger. Jesse does not care because he did it his way.

Principles of the moral kind also challenge Mr. Shorosky (Albert Hague), a music teacher, in a conflict over new musical equipment. The school's budget has no room for musical equipment but he may get the financial backing from one of the city's art patrons. The problem is that his worst violin candidate is the grandson of the patron and he is at a crossroads when he wants to tell the kid that he is hopelessly untalented. In the end, the student is accepted and Mr. Shorofsky gets his new brass section. To the teacher, the difference between selling out and compromising is what you get or lose in return.

Ray Danton utilizes several shadings and emotional pitches for this episode. The flashback to Mexico when Jesse was a child taking guitar lessons from his grandfather is done with low-key lighting to give the scene an almost reverential tone to it, especially with the religious altar in the background. The music number in Spanish Harlem is on the opposite scale with its lively *barrio* rhythms. Both scenes deal with unfulfilled promises and frustrated hope and the common link is Jesse and what values have been instilled in the young man because of his heritage.

Ray Danton also uses the school and the producers' offices as springboards to illustrate the meaning of show business. He shows us the naïve optimism of the aspiring artists and the cold hearted cash register mentality of the school principal and the music producers. He also successfully shows the tug-of-war between artistic ideals and practical economics in the soul searching of Jesse and Mr. Shorofsky.

A Place to Belong is the theme song for adjustment. Dusty (Loretta Chandler) sings it in a private rehearsal at her new school as Leroy (Gene Anthony Ray)—a former student who tries to adapt to being a faculty member—listens in the wings. He has graduated the year before and feels unsure about the transition to the "so-called" real world. The street environment is not conducive to creativity because it is a track for the work horses to chomp at the bit to fill their feed bags. Is it graduating that worries Leroy or being surrounded by people for whom being an artist means nothing?

Lydia Grant (Debbie Allen), the school's dance instructor, suggests that he become her assistant so that she can take a sabbatical to be in a Broadway musical. He agrees that an intermediary step to adjustment is becoming her assistant dance teacher. This gives him a couple of life lessons when his friends try to manipulate him into winning an audition

Leroy (Gene Anthony Ray) is a former student who is at a crossroads in his life. *A Place to Belong* is a coming-of-age tale about artistic ambition and brass tacks reality. 1985, MGM/UA Television.

for the school musical. Chief among them are Nicole (Nia Peeples) and Holly (Cynthia Gibb), who compete with each other for a lead in the play.

Being a member of the faculty also turns out to be a drag because Leroy has little patience to deal with executive meetings. This leads him to taking a job as a busboy at the local pizzeria. Trying to get an audition for the musical CATS sets his sights straight as he realizes that teaching is not a bad way to go until he gets his big break. At least, he can share his knowledge with the fledgling dancers and mentor them the same way he was when he first arrived at the school. It is better than bussing tables and making pizza.

Two subplots also deal with the change of adjustment. Dusty has to overcome the rites of passage at her new school and also become acclimated to the big city. She is a preacher's daughter and she carries her parents' disapproval into the new phase of her life.

Her song may have inspired Leroy to temporarily leave but his return meant that he could inspire her to audition for the musical. Danny (Carlo Imperato) and Chris (Bill Hufsey) also deal with the change of adjustment when they are given the project of acting in a two-act play about two women being in love with the same man. At first, it is an affront to their macho sensibilities but it becomes a life lesson in empathy and character development.

There are two musical production numbers in this episode. The first is a splashy street dance production that celebrates the first day of school and the other is a recreation of a number from the hit musical, CATS, wherein Leroy imagines himself dancing with the feline cast members.

Ray Danton shows his ability to weave subplots into the main storyline. It is a talent that he will perfect with his tenure on *Cagney and Lacey*. His directing is as fresh as the young faces in the cast, delineating the character traits of the older players to create a perfect balance. He also handles Dusty's musical number with sensitivity. The scene begins with Leroy walking onto the empty stage and going through some dance moves, unaware that Ms. Grant is watching. She gives some advice to him before leaving. He stands in the wings and listens to Dusty singing "A Place to Belong." In a sense, it is her coming out scene.

A birth mother uses her photography as a means to get acquainted with the daughter she gave up for adoption in *Who am I, Really?*, an insightful study about finding an identity when you are adopted. Nicole (Nia Peeples) is composing a song for the student show when she becomes the focus of a visiting photographer's photo essay of the students. Diane Petit (Julie Carman) uses her camera to create order out of turmoil, in this case it is the frenzied environment of the artistic school.

Nicole's world is turned upside down when she senses that Diane might be her birth mother after a brief conversation on why Diane is focusing on her. The scene where they become acquainted with each other is handled with care. They walk down a dimly lit avenue, where the lights from the lampposts and the stores are reflected off the puddles that have formed after a rainfall. As they walk, the camera focuses on their reverse images in a street puddle that stretches halfway down the block. The visuals mirror Nicole's topsy-turvy world and the camera cuts to a normal shot of them once the conversation becomes grounded in the women's acceptance of each other.

Diane's return comes at a time of change in Nicole's life and this is awkward for her adoptive parents. The usual questions about the rights of birth parents and adoptive parents clash and there is resolution only through understanding. Diane teaches Nicole about artistic vision and cautions her about pushing her art until it smothers her passion. She uses her photographs to teach Nicole about understanding the world around her. This impresses Nicole, who is developing wanderlust because she is at an age when maturity demands that she spread her wings like the bird in her song.

Diane's suggestion that Nicole accompany her to an annual arts festival in Taos, New Mexico creates tension between her adoptive parents and her biological mother. They resent Diane's return and consider it an intrusion. This leads to bad feelings between them and Nicole. Fear of separation creates challenges for all involved but it is resolved through love and understanding. It takes Nicole's stirring rendition of her song at the student show to create a connection between the warring factions and the insecurities of loss turn into the strengths of gain.

Nia Peeples gives a moving performance about a young woman whose life is turned upside down when her birth mother re-enters her life and causes a rift with her adoptive parents. 1985, MGM/UA Television.

This episode is a definite must for Nia Peeples' fans because it showcases her singing and dancing abilities. Her showcase number is stirring but it is her two scenes practicing her dance moves that are breathtaking to behold.

In the early Eighties, the burgeoning cable industry gave rise to a side of Hollywood that had more latitude than network television and an intimacy that the movie theaters lacked. Two of Ray Danton's best efforts are cable offerings: The *Home* segment of *Vietnam War Story* and *Shelley Duvall's American Tall Tales and Legends: John Henry*.

HBO was a trailblazer in the early days of cable television when they began to produce their own series and movies. *Vietnam War Story* was a limited series that featured a trio of stories each week that dealt with the Vietnam War. Every perspective of the war, from in-country hell to the purgatory of anti-war America was handled with great skill and sensitivity. Ray Danton directed *Home*, his most personal work as a director. It is the flip side of *Empire:The Four Thumbs Story*, his most sensitive performance as an actor. Both episodes have the insurmountable challenges of tormented war veterans as their themes.

The short drama focuses on the therapy that is needed to help the veterans cope with their crosses and enable them to function in a society that will have little or no need for them because of their participation in an unpopular war. It is 1969 and the tide of public opinion was overwhelmingly against the Vietnam War and much of the resentment was directed at the returning vets.

The tortured adjustment of wounded Marines to the civilian world is the struggle of this war-themed drama. It is about sharing an anger that rips apart the boundaries that are borders of the past. The hospital ward of a Marine base is a halfway house for disabled Vietnam War vets about to return to their old worlds. They are coming to grips with their dilemma, which is accepting loss of a way of life. The society they fought for is about

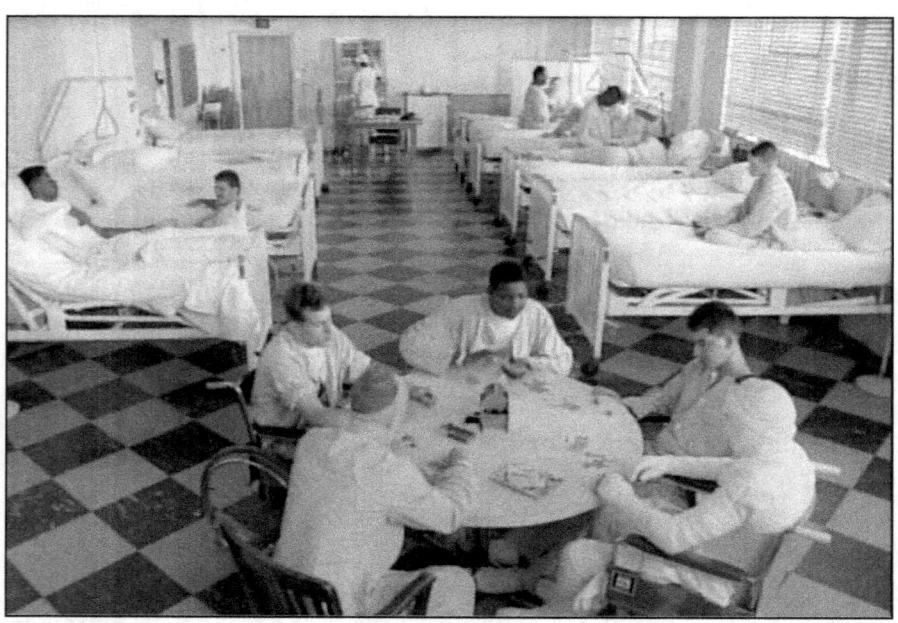

This is the hospital ward for wounded Marines trying to recover from the devastating wounds they received in Vietnam. 1987, HBO.

to reject them because they won't look like the cartoon heroes of popular war fiction.

The hospital ward would make Dante's Inferno seem like Paradise if not for the bravery of the men who deal with their personal losses with an inner strength that most people would seem unfathomable. The shock of losing parts of their bodies and the trauma of reliving the experience of war has not dimmed their will to succeed.

The catalyst in their recovery is Zadig (Nicholas Cascone), a standup-comic in the despair ward. Everybody resents him to an extent because his efforts to ease their pain with his sarcasm and oft-told pig joke interrupt their attempts to revel in self-pity. One of the soldiers who won't allow him to make a joke out of his pain is Harris (David Harris).

Harris is wheelchair bound and has to accept the pain of knowing that his girlfriend is now his ex and she is about to marry someone else. He is the alienated figure of resistance in the ward so much that he does nothing to prevent a fellow vet from trying to kill himself before his very eyes while everyone else is asleep.

His reasoning is that the man is an adult and can accept responsibility for his action. This does not sit well with Zadig, whose humor is a disguise

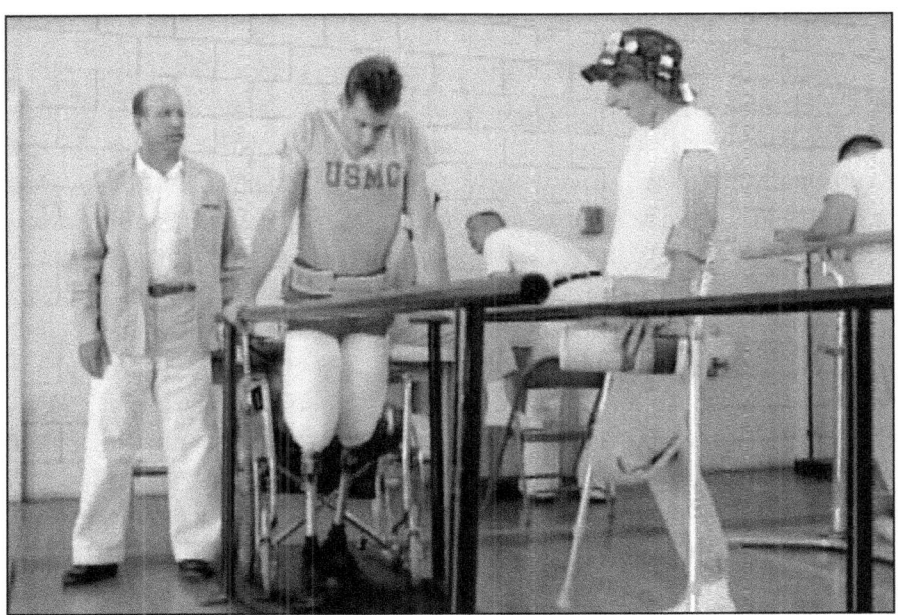

Zadig (Nicholas Cascone) is the motivator who gets on everyone's nerves until his optimism is muted by a cruel twist of fate. 1987, HBO.

for profound wisdom developed when he took charge of a unit under fire and held out until the enemy retreated. He lost a leg for his heroics and that started a new battle for him

Zadig provides the encouragement to continue living and face the world outside of their ward. As Harris says, "Everyone in here is so f*#ked up that you feel normal." The truth is they know that the world that sent to fight their war will not feel the same way about them. That is the cause of the underlying depression, resentment and hopelessness.

It is Zadig's senseless death after a routine operation that gives the men the strength to resurrect their lives. After a ceremony to present Zadig with a posthumous Silver Star, Harris assumes the hero's burden by becoming the ward's motivating influence for a new group of recovering Marines. The episode ends with him regaling a group of new recruits with his version of the pig joke as they sit around a table playing poker.

Ray Danton's sensitive direction does not shy away from the hard-hitting truth that twists the emotions to reveal the senselessness of war. The irony is that-for the wounded Marines-the war continues because they will be viewed as less than whole human beings because of their lost limbs. They are the true heroes that one rarely sees in war movies. What is heroic is that the vets consider their injuries secondary to the sacrifice of all their buddies who never made it home.

Home is arguably Ray Danton's best work as a director. It is an ensemble piece, which is one reason for its exuberant energy and Danton's use of the camera keeps up with the hectic pace of the players. In the emotionally charged drama, he achieves a perfect balance between acting and technical devices. He uses cross-cutting, pans, dissolves, and tracking shots to achieve a soft poetic focus in a harsh setting.

Cross-cutting from different angles gives greater depth and emphasis to conversations. A simple pan turns a shot of a cab full of drunken young men into a focus of disabled vets returning to their marine base. The use of dissolves and double-exposures show the soldiers awaiting Zadig's return after surgery and increases their anxiety but also exemplifies their need for him.

A stunning overhead shot of Harris sitting at the base of an anti-aircraft gun becomes frenetic when the camera glides down the barrel to focus on his pensive face as he contemplates a major change in his life while Zadig's award ceremony is conducted inside the ward. Everything about this drama is perfect; that includes the acting, directing, cinematography,

John Henry was an installment of *Shelly Duval's Tall Tales and Legends*. 1987, Showtime Network.

music and editing. Ray Danton won the cable Ace Award of 1988 for Directing a Theatrical or Dramatic Special.

Another type of man who resurrects lives is *John Henry*, a freed slave who rises to legendary status by becoming the greatest steel driver in the land. He is a physical marvel but it is his spirit that is gargantuan as it enables him to challenge the Industrial Age and win. John Henry is part of American folklore, a collection of tall tales about the men and women who created of the United States out of an expansive wilderness. They are literally people of the land and are as natural as the frontier they tamed.

Shelley Duval's Tall Tales and Legends was another cable series and it illustrated the tales that was once required learning for school children from another era. In 1867, John Henry (Danny Glover) is a freed slave turned migrant worker. He heads to West Virginia and arrives at the C&O Railroad Work Camp, where he meets Miss Polly-Ann (Lynn Whitfield), the woman who makes him realize his destiny.

John Henry is a proud, determined man whose physical strength is matched by his compassion. "I'm a natural born man; nothing more, nothing less", is how he describes himself. He is always assisting those less fortunate than him. The first example is Quinn (Thomas Hulce), the Irish indentured servant he has known since childhood on the plantation. Henry sends him money to buy out his contract for his freedom. He also aids Jim Wallace (Lou Rawls), who is incapacitated by a work-related injury. John Henry's greatest act of charity is saving the jobs that would have been lost by the newly invented mechanical steel driver.

Beneath the benign surface, the tale also recounts the travails of slavery, indentured servitude, manual labor and the changes brought about by the Industrial Revolution. Challenging the steel driver is John Henry's greatest confrontation. His super human strength humiliates the machine but the sad fact is that the machines will win in the end and the working man will become a thing of the past.

John Henry is brought to life by vivid performances, imaginative stage design, and an experienced director at the helm. As John Henry, Danny Glover is determined, enthusiastic and full of passion. He is superhuman, as befits the legendary character. Simple and honest but tough and resilient, he is the personification of the country he helped to define.

Lynn Whitfield is beautiful and alluring as Polly-Ann. She is sophisticated and elegant and has social pretences about her, even though her current beau was cheating on her. Upon meeting John Henry, she looks down at him and considers him a country bumpkin but his charm and honesty eventually win her over. Thomas Hulce is the leprechaun-like Quinn. He is short in stature but strong in his soul and has weathered the hardships of the Irish indentured servants who worked off their contracts on the southern plantations. Barry Corbin is steel willed as Mr. Jenkins, the foreman of the work camp. He is the craven, entrepreneurial spirit that turned a bucolic country into an urbane waste and through industrialization.

Lou Rawls and Thelma Houston play Jim Wallace and his wife, Edna. Jim is a worker who is injured for life due to a cave-in in the mountain. Edna is a kitchen worker who lends her considerable singing voice to the story for inspiration. Julian Christopher [James Louis Watkins] plays Spike, the best steel driver in the camp until he is dethroned in a contest with John Henry. He was Polly Ann's original beau, although it is found revealed until later that he is a barnyard pimp because of his pecking prowess. He leaves the camp with his bawdy women at his side, only to return later (with an extra one in tow) to assist John Henry in his contest with the steam driven steel driving machine.

John Henry has the fresh look and feel of a filmed stage play, with the exception of technical effects like John Henry's face beaming like the sun

Danny Glover gives a powerful performance as *John Henry*. He embodies all of the characteristics that turn a man into a legend. 1987, Showtime Network.

in the sky at the end of the story. Ray Danton also uses his dissolve-double exposure combo during John Henry's final contest. He had perfected the technique to the point where this scene is the best example of this device. Majestic is the only way to describe the way the anxious faces blend with the mammoth sinewy John Henry pounding steel and the warmly lit sky changing colors as dusk turns into night which stretches into the dawn.

That's how long the contest between man and machine lasted and when it is over, an exhausted John Henry is a sweat-covered giant more ominous and powerful that the mountain he cracked wide open. His triumphant laugh finishes the job by blowing a hole through the rocks so the victory light can shine through.

The warm colors of the set design also add to the glorious mood of the scene. The overall stage design and the lighting are magical and lend a rustic warmth to the folk tale. The overall effect is the culmination of Ray Danton's experience as a film and theater director. He combines the conventions of both mediums to create an uplifting story leavened by the musical arrangements of Andrae Crouch and accentuated by a theme song and blues musings sung by Thelma Houston.

Afterword

Towards the end of the Eighties, Ray Danton's activity became restricted by a severe kidney ailment.

Unable to direct, he served as a supervising producer for *The New Mike Hammer* and a creative consultant for *The Trials of Rosie O'Neil*, starring Sharon Gless.

The show's last episode, *Role Reversal*, was dedicated to Ray Danton, who, at the age of 60, died from complications following a kidney transplant on February 11, 1992.

Hawaii was Ray Danton's last home and his ashes became part of the coral reefs, lava flats and underwater rainbows.

List of Credits

MOVIES AS AN ACTOR

Chief Crazy Horse (1955 - Universal - International - 86m -C)
Chief Crazy Horse: Victor Mature. *Black Shawl*: Suzan Ball. *Major Twist*: John Lund. *Little Big Man*: Ray Danton. *Conquering Bear*: Morris Ankrum. *Flying Hawk*: Keith Larson. *Lieutenant Colin Cartwright*: David Janssen. *Aaron Cartwright*: Donald Randolph. *Jeff Mantz*: Robert F. Simon. *Caleb Mantz*: James Westerfield.   *Director*: George Sherman. *Producer*: William ALand. *Screenplay*: Franklin Coen and Gerald Grayson Adams. *Director of Photography*: Harold Lipstein, ASE. *Editor*: Al Clark. *Music*: Frank Skinner.

The Looters: (1955-Universal-International-87m)
Jesse Hill: Rory Calhoun. *Sheryl Gregory*: Julie Adams. *Pete Corder*: Ray Danton. *George Parkinson*: Thomas Gomez. *Stan Leppich*: Frank Faylen. *Major Knowles*: Russ Conway. *Red*: Rod Williams. *Stevenson*: John Stephenson. *Director*: Abner Biberman. *Producer*: Howard Christie. *Screenplay*: Richard Alan Simmons. *Story*: Paul Schneider. *Cinematography*: Lloyd Ahern. *Editor*: Russell Schoengarth. *Music Supervision*: Joseph Gershenson.

The Spoilers: (1955-Universal-International-84m-C)
Cherry Maloote: Anne Baxter. *Roy Glennister*: Jeff Chandler. *Alex McNamara*: Rory Calhoun. *Bronco Blackie*: Ray Danton. *Dextry*: John McIntire. *Helen Chester*: Barbara Britton. *Judge Stillman*: Carl Benton Reid. *Flapjack Sims*: Wallace Ford. *Banty Jones*: Forrest Lewis. *Duchess*: Ruth Donnely. *Director*: Jesse Hibbs. *Producer*: Ross Hunter. *Screenplay*:

Oscar Brodney, Charles Hoffman, and James MacArthur. *Based on the novel by* Rex Beach. *Cinematography:* Maury Gertsman. *Editor:* Paul Weatherwax. *Score:* Henry Mancini.

I'll Cry Tomorrow: (1955-MGM-117m)

Lillian Roth: Susan Hayward. *Tony Bardeman:* Richard Conte. *Burt McGuire:* Eddie Albert. *Katie Roth:* Jo Van Fleet. *David Tredman:* Ray Danton. *Wallie:* Don Taylor. *Director:* Daniel Mann. *Producer:* Lawrence Weingarten. *Screenplay:* Helen Deutsch and Jay Richard Kennedy. *Based on the book, "I'll Cry Tomorrow", by* Lillian Roth, Mike Connely, and Gerold Frank. *Cinematography:* Arthur E. Arling. *Editor:* Harold Kress. *Score:* Alex North.

Outside The Law: (1956-Universal-International-81m)

Johnny Salvo: Ray Danton. *Maria Craven:* Leigh Snowden. *Don Kastner:* Grant Williams. *Alec Conrad:* Onslow Stevens. *Phillip Boorman:* Raymond Bailey. *Maury Saxon:* Judson Pratt. *Phil Schwartz:* Jack Kruschen. *Milo:* Mel Welles. *Mama Gomez:* Amapola Del Vando. *Director:* Jack Arnold. *Producer:* Albert J. Cohen. *Screenplay:* Danny Arnold. *Story:* Peter R. Brooke. *Cinematography:* Irving Glassberg. *Editor:* Irving Birnbaum. *Original music:* Henry Mancini and Stanley Wilson.

The Night Runner: (1957-Universal-International-87 min.)

Roy Turner: Ray Danton. *Susan Mayes:* Coleen Miller. *Loren mayes:* Willis Bouchey. *Amy Hansen:* Merry Anders. *Hank Hansen:* Harry Jackson. *Ed Wallace:* Robert Anderson. *Dr. Crawford:* John Stephenson. *Dr. Royce:* Alexander Campbell. *Director:* Abner Biberman. *Producer:* Albert J. Cohen. *Screenplay:* Gene Levitt. *Short Story:* owen Cameron. *Cinematography:* George Robinson. *Editing:* Albrecht Joseph..

Too Much, Too Soon: (1958-Warner Bros.-121m)

Diana Barrymore: Dorothy Malone. *John Barrymore:* Errol Flynn. *Vincent Bryant:* Efrem Zimbalist, Jr. *John Howard:* Ray Danton. *Robert Wilcox:* Ed Kemmer. *Director:* Art Napoleon. *Producer:* Henry Blanke. *Screenplay:* Art Napoleon. *Based on the autobiography by* Diana Barrymore. *Cinematographer:* Nick Musuraca. *Editor:* Owen Marks. *Music:* Ernest Gold.

Onionhead: (1958-Warner Bros.-110m)
Al Woods: Andy Griffith. *Stella:* Felicia Farr. *"Red" Wildoe:* Walter Matthau. *Ensign Higgins:* Ray Danton. *Jo Hill:* Erin O'Brien Moore. *The "Skipper":* James Gregory. *Gutsell:* Joey Bishop. *Poznicki:* Claude Akins. *Doc O'Neal:* Joe Mantell. *Director:* Norman Taurog. *Producer:* Jules Schermer. *Screenplay:* Nelson Giddon. *Based on the book by* Weldon Hill. *Cinematography:* Harold Rosson. *Editor:* William H. Ziegler. *Music:* David Buttolph.

Tarawa Beachhead: (1958-Columbia Pictures-77 mins.)
Sgt. (Lt.) Tom Sloan: Kerwin Mathews. *Ruth Nelson Campbell:* Julie Adams. *Lt. (Cpt.) Joel Brady:* Ray Danton. *Paula Nelson:* Karen Sharpe. *Gen. Nathan keller:* Onslow Stevens. *Casey Nelson:* Russell Thorson. *Lt. Lou Gideon:* Eddie Ryder. *Johnny Campbell:* John Baer. *Director:* Paul Wendkos. *Producer:* Charles H. Schneer. *Screenplay:* Richard Alan Simmons. *Cinematography:* Henry Freulich. *Editing:* Jerome Thoms.

The Beat Generation: (1959-MGM-95m) *aka This Rebel Age*
Sgt. Dave Culloran: Steve Cochran. *Georgia Altera:* Mamie Van Doren. *Stan Hess:* Ray Danton. *Francee Culloran:* Fay Spain. *Jake Baron:* Jackie Coogan. *Art Jester:* Jim Mitchum. *Louis Armstrong:* Himself. *Cameos:* Vampira, Maxie Rosenbloom, Charles Chaplin, Jr., Sid Melton, Grabowski, Dick Contino, Ray Anthony. *Director:* Charles Haas. *Producer:* Albert J. Zugsmith. *Screenplay:* Richard Matheson and Lewis Meltzer. *Cinematography:* Walter Castle. *Editor:* Ben Lewis. *Songwriters:* Louis Armstrong, Albert Glasser, Walter Kent, Louis Meltzer, and Tom Walston.

The Big Operator: (1959-MGM-91m) *aka Anatomy of a Syndicate*
Little Joe Braun: Mickey Rooney. *Bill Gibson:* Steve Cochran. *Mary Gibson:* Mamie Van Doren. *Fred McAfee:* Mel Torme. *Oscar Wetzel:* Ray Danton. *Tony Gibson:* Jay North. *Cliff Helden:* Jim Backus. Director: Charles Haas. Screenplay: *Allen Rifkin and Robert Smith.* Based on a short story by *Paul Gallico.* Producer: *Albert J. Zugsmith.* Cinematography: *Walter H. Castle.* Editor: *Ben Lewis.* Music: *Van Alexander.*

Yellowstone Kelly: (1959-Warner Brothers-91m-C)
Luther "Yellowstone" Kelly: Clint Walker. *Anse Harper:* Edward Byrnes. *Gall:* John Russell. *Seipai:* Ray Danton. *Wahleeah:* Andra Martin.

Sergeant: Claude Akins. *Major Townes:* Rhodes Reason. *Leutenant:* Gary Vinson. *Soldier:* Warren Oates. *Riverboat Captain:* Harry Shannon. *Direction:* Gordon Douglas. *Screenplay:* Burt Kennedy. *Based on the book by* Clay Fisher (Heck Allen). *Original Music:* Howard Jackson. *Cinematography:* Carl E. Guthrie. *Editor:* William H. Ziegler.

Ice Palace: (1960-Warners Brothers-143m-C)
Zeb Kennedy: Richard Burton. *Thor Storm:* Robert Ryan. *Dorothy Kennedy:* Martha Hyer. *Dave Husack:*
Jim Backus. *Bridie Ballantyne:* Carolyn Jones. *Bay Husack:* Ray Danton. *Christine Storm:* Diane McBain. *Director:* Vincent Sherman. *Producers:* Henry Blanke and Harry Kleiner. *Screenplay:* Harry Kleiner. *Based on the novel by:* Edna Ferber. *Cinematography:* Joseph F. Biroc. *Editor:* William H. Ziegler. *Music:* Max Steiner.

The Rise and Fall of Legs Diamond: (1960-Warner Brothers-101m)
Jack "Legs" Diamond: Ray Danton. *Alice Shiffer:* Karen Steele. *Monica Drake:* Elaine Stewart. *Arnold Rothstein:* Robert Lowery. *Leo Bremer:* Jesse White. *Lt. Moody:* Simon Oakland. *Fats Walsh:* Judson Pratt. *Eddie Diamond:* Warren Oates. *Sergeant Cassidy::* Gordon Jones. *Chairman:* Frank De Kova. *Dixie:* Dian Cannon. *Little Auggie:* Sid Melton. *Direction:* Budd Boeticcher. *Screenplay:* Joseph Landon. *Producer:* Milton Sperling. *Associate Producer:* Leon Chooluck. *Cinematography:* Lucien Ballard. *Editor:* Folmar Blangsted. *Music:* Leonard Rosenman.

A Fever In The Blood: (1961-Warner Brothers-117m)
Judge Leland Hoffman: Efrem Zimbalist, Jr. *Cathy Simon:* Angie Dickenson. *Dan Callahan:* Jack Kelly. *Senator A.S. Simon:* Don Ameche. *Marker:* Ray Danton. *Governor Thornwall:* Herbert Marshall. *Laura Thornberry:* Andra Martin. *Mickey Beers:* Jesse White. *Director:* Vincent Sherman. *Producer:* Roy Huggins. *Screenplay:* Roy Huggins, Harry Kleiner, and William Pearson. *Cinematography:* J. Peverell Marley. *Editor:* William H. Ziegler. *Music:* Ernest Gold.

Portrait Of A Mobster: (1961-Warner Brothers-108m)
Dutch Shultz: Vic Morrow. *Iris Murphy:* Leslie Parrish. *Frank Brennan:* Peter Breck. *Bo Wetzel:* Norman Alden. *Legs Diamond:* Ray Danton. *Michael Ferris:* Robert McQueeny. *Lt. D. Corbin:* Ken Lynch. *Director:* Joseph Pevney. *Screenplay:* Howard Browne. *Based on the book*

by: Harry Grey. *Cinematography*: Eugene Polito. *Editor*: Leo H. Shreve. *Music*: Max Steiner.

The George Raft Story: (1961-Allied Artists-106m)
George Raft: Ray Danton. *Lisa Lang*: Jayne Mansfield. *Shiela*: Julie London. *June*: Barry Chase. *Texas Guinan*: Barbara Nichols. *Moxie*: Frank Gorshin. *Sam*: Herschel Bernardi. *Benny Siegal*: Brad Dexter. *Ruth*: Margo Moore. *Al Capone*: Neville Brand. *Director*: Joseph Newman. *Producer*: Ben Schwalb. *Screenplay*: Daniel Mainwaring and Crane Wilbur. *Cinematography*: Carl E. Guthrie. *Editor*: George White. *Music*: Jeff Alexander.

A Majority of One: (1961-Warner Brothers-153m-C)
Mrs. Jacoby: Rosalind Russell. *Koichi Asano*: Alec Guinness. *Jerome Black*: Ray Danton. *Alice Black*: Madlyn Rhue. *Director and Producer*: Mervyn LeRoy. *Screenplay and Play*: Leonard Spigelglass. *Cinematography*: Harry Stradling, Jr. *Editor*: Philip W. Anderson. *Music*: Max Steiner.

The Longest Day: (1962-20th Century Fox-180m)
Stars: Eddie Albert, Paul Anka, Arletty, Jean-Louis Barrault, Richard Beymer, Hans Christian Blech, Bourvil, Richard Burton, Wolfgand Buttner, Red Buttons, Pauline Carton, Sean Connery, **Ray Danton**, Irina Demick, Fred Dur, Fabian, Mel Ferrer, Henry Fonda, Steve Forrest, Gert Frobe, Leo Genn, John Gregson, Paul Hartmann, Peter Helm, Werner Hinz, Donald Houston, Jeffrey Hunter, Curd Jurgens, Alexander Knox, Peter Lawford, Fernand Ledoux, Christian Marquand, Dewey Martin, Roddy McDowall, Michael Medwin, Sal Mineo, Robert Mitchum, Kenneth More, Richard Munch, Edmond O'Brien, Leslie Phillips, Wolfgang Preiss, Ron Randell, Madeleine Renaud, Georges Riviere, Norman Rossington, Robert Ryan, Tommy Sands, George Segal, Jean Sevais, Rod Steiger, Richard Todd, Tom Tryon, Peter van Eyck, Robert Wagner, Richard Wattis, Stuart Whitman, Georges Wilson, John Wayne and a supporting casts of hundreds. *Directors*: Ken Annakin, Andrew Marton, Gerd Oswald, Bernhard Wicki, and Darryl F. Zanuck. *Writers*: Romain Gary, James Jones, David Pursall, Cornelius Ryan and Jack Seddon. *Book*: Cornelius Ryan. *Producer*: Darryl F. Zanuck. *Associate Producer*: Elmo Williams. *Cinematography*: Jean Bourgoin, Pierre Levent, Henri Persin, and Walter Wottitz. *Editor*: Samuel E. Beetley. *Music*: Maurice Jarre. *Theme Song*: Paul Anka.

The Chapman Report: (1962-Warner Brothers-125m-C)
Sarah Garnell: Shelley Winters. *Kathleen Barclay:* Jane Fonda. *Naomi Shields:* Glynis Johns. *Paul Radford:* Efrem Zimbalist, Jr. *Fred Linden:* Ray Danton. *Dr. George C. Chapman:* Andrew Duggan. *Ed Kraski:* Ty Hardin. *Frank Garnell:* Harold J. Stone. *Director:* George Cukor. *Screenplay:* Gene Allen, Wyatt Cooper, Dpn Mankiewitz, and Grant Stuart. *Based on the novel by:* Irving Wallace. *Producers:* Darryl F. Zanuck and Richard D. Zanuck. *Cinematography:* Harold Lipstein. *Editor:* Robert L. Simpson. *Music:* Leonard Rosenman, Frank Perkins, and Max Steiner.

F.B.I. Code 98: (1963-Warner Brothers-94m)
Robert P. Cannon: Jack Kelly. *Fred Vitale:* Ray Danton. *Alan W. Nichols:* Andrew Duggan. *Inspector Leroy Gifford:* Phillip Carey. *Special Agent Fox:* William Reynolds. *Deborah Cannon:* Peggy McKay. *Marian Nichols:* Kathleen Crowley. *Grace McClean:* Merry Anders. *Walter Mcklin:* Jack Cassady. *Joseph Peterson:* Vaughn Taylor. *Lloyd Kinsel:* Eddie Ryder. *Director:* Leslie H. Martinson. *Producer:* Stanley Niss. *Screen-play:* Stanley Niss, based on his short story, "Headquarters, F.B.I." *Cinematography:* Robert Hoffman. *Editor:* Leo H. Shreve. *Music:* Max Steiner.

Sandokan Against the Leopard of Sarawak: *Original Title: Sandokan contro il leopardo di Sarawak; aka Throne of Vengeance* **(1964-Eichberg-Film GmbH [Ger]/Liber Film [It]-94m-C)**
Sandokan: Ray Danton. *Yanez:* Guy Madison. *Princess Somoa:* Franca Bettoia. *Charles Druk:* Mario Petri. *Director:* Luigi Capuano. *Screenplay:* Luigi Capuano and Arpad De Riso. *Novel:* Emilio Salgari. *Producer:* Ottavio Poggi. *Cinematography:* Bitto Albertini. *Editor:* Antonietta Zita. *Music:* Carlo Rustichelli.

Sandokan Fights Back (1964-Eichberg-Film GmbH [Ger]/Liber Film [It]-94m-C) *Original Title: Sandokan alla riscossa; aka The Conqueror and the Empress*
Sandokan: Ray Danton. *Yanez:* Guy Madison. *Princess Somoa:* Franca Bettoia. *William Druk:* Mario Petri. *Director:* Luigi Capuano. *Screenplay:* Luigi Capuano and Arpad De Riso. *Novel:* Emilio Salgari. *Cinematography:* Bitto Albertini. *Editor:* Antonietta Zita. *Music:* Carlo Rustichelli.

List of Credits | 475

Code Name "Jaguar": *Original Title: Corrida pour un espion. Aka as The Spy Who Went Into Hell* (1965) (Hans Oppenheimer Film [Ger]-Midega Film [Es]-Trans-Atlantic Prod. S.a.r.l.[Fr] 105m-C)

Jeff Larson: Ray Danton. *Pilar Perez:* Pascale Petit. *Bob Stuart:* Roger Hanin. *Louis Moreno:* Conrado San Martin. *Miss Calderon:* Helga Sommerfield. *Parker:* Wolfgang Preiss. *Director:* Maurice Labro. *Screenplay:* Maurice Labro, Jean Meckert, Claude Rank, and Louis Velle. *Story:* Claude Rank. *Producers:* Miguel De Echarri and Hans Oppenheimer. *Editor:* Georges Arnstam. *Music:* Michel Legrand.

Secret Agent Super Dragon: *aka New York Calling Super Dragon;*(1966) (Films Borderie [Fr]-Fono Roma [It]-Gloria-Film GmbH [Ger]-Ramo Film[It]-95m-C)

Bryan Cooper: Ray Danton. *Charity Farrell:* Marisa Mell. *Cynthia Fulton:* Margaret Lee. *Baby Face:* Jess Hahn. *Fernand Lamas:* Carlo D'Angelo. *Verna:* Adriana Ambesi. *Professor Kurge:* Marco Guglielmi. *Elizabeth:* Solvi Stubing. *Coleman:* Gerard Herter. *Ross:* Jacques Herlin. *Director:* Calvin Jackson Padget (Giorgio Ferroni). *Screenplay:* Bill Coleman, Remigo Del Grosso, Giorgio Ferroni, and Mike Mitchell. *Producer:* Roberto Amoroso. *Cinematography:* Antonio Secchi. *Editor:* Antonietta Zita. *Music:* Benedetto Ghiglia.

How To Win A Billion and Keep It!: (1966-Augusta [It]-92m-C) *Original Title: Ballata da un miliardo*

Joe Martin/Big Smiley: Ray Danton. *With:* Kitty Swann, Gianni Serra, Jacques Herlin, and Aldo Berti. *Director:* Gianni Puccini. *Screenplay:* Bruno Baratti, Bernardo Bertolucci, and Gianni Puccini. *Producer:* Gugliermo Simon. *Cinematography:* Mario Parapetti. *Editor:* Lucian Benedetto *Music:* Luis Enriquez Bacalov.

Man Only Dies Once: (1967-Italcid-90m-C) *Original Title: Si muore una sola volta [It]; Man Stirbt Nur Einmal [W. Ger]*

Mike Gold: Ray Danton. *Ingrid:* Pamela Tudor. *Jane:* Silvia Solar. *Malsky:* Marco Guglielmi. *Gloria:* Rosella Bergamonti. *Archeopculos:* Mario Landoni. *Directors:* Mino Guerrini and Giancarlo Romitelli. *Screenplay:* Augusto Caminito, Jose Luis Dibildos, Joaquin Romero Hernandez, and Don Reynolds (Renato Savino). *Producer:* Fernando Alivermimi. *Cinematography:* Carlo Carlini, Aldo Greci, and Julio Ortaz. *Editor:* Magdalena Pulido. *Music:* Carlo Savina. *"Che Uomo Sei":* sung by Ammarita Spinaci.

Lucky The Inscrutable: *Original Title: Lucky el intrepido; aka Agente speciale L.K. (1967)* (Atlantida Films S.A.[Sp]-Explorer Films '58 [It]-Fono Roma [It]-91m-C)

Lucky the Inscrutable: Ray Danton. *Michael:* Dante Posani. *Yaka:* Rosalba Neri. *Goldglasses:* Marcelo Arroita-Jauregui. *Cleopatra:* Teresa Gimperal. *Messenger with Knife in the Back:* Jesus Franco. *With:* Beba Loncar, Barbara Bold, and Patty Shepherd. *Director:* Jesus Franco. *Screenplay:* Julio Buchs, Jose Luis Martinez Molla, Jesus Franco. *Story:* Julio Buchs and Jose Luis Martinez Molla. *Cinematography:* Fulvio Testi. *Editor:* Antonietta Zita. *Music:* Bruno Nicolai.

Jamaica Calling, Mr. Ward: (1968-Orbita Films-105m-C) *Original Title: Llaman de Jamaica, Mr. Ward; aka Flatfoot*

Glen Ward: Ray Danton. *Liz Taylor:* Pamela Tudor. *Mulligan:* Luis Davila. *Rickers:* Jorge Rigaud. *Sra. Parker:* Carroll Brown. *Lefty:* Allan Collins. *Martinelli:* Beni Deu. *Director:* Julio Salvador. *Screenplay and Story:* Ricardo Ferrer and Julio Salvador. *Executive Producer:* Jorge Ferrer. *Cinematography:* Gino Santini. *Editor:* Emilio Rodriguez. *Music:* Alessandro Alessandroni.

The Last Mercenary: (1969-Orbita Films-100m-C) *Original Title: Die Grosse Treibjagd* (W.Ger); *aka El Mercenario*(Sp)

Mark Anderson: Ray Danton. *Steinman:* Carl Mohner. *Isabel:* Pascale Petit. *Manuel de Lagos:* Georges Rigaud. *Silent Killer in Black:* Gunther Stoll. *Little Girl:* Inma de Santis. *Director:* Mel Welles. *Screenplay:* Ricardo Ferrer and Julio Salvador. *Story:* Ricardo Ferrer. *Producer:* George Ferrer. *Cinematography:* Jose Climent and Juan Gelpi. *Editor:* Edith Schuman. *Music:* Bruno Nicolai.

Triangle: (1971-Commonwealth Entertainment,Inc.w/Federal Film Corp-87m-C)

Todd: Charles Robinson. *Sharon McClure:* Tiffany Bolling. *Carlo di Fundi:* Ray Danton. *Headmistress Olive:* Dana Wynter. *School Shrink:* Paul Richards. *Director and Producer:* Bernard Glasser. *Screenplay:* Howard Berk, Gloria Elmore, and Jim Barnett. *Associate Producer:* Lynn Raynor. *Cinematography:* Jacques Marquette, A.S.C. *Editor:* B. Richard Connors, A.C.E. *Music:* Raoul Krasseur.

Will Our Hero Find The World's Largest Diamond? *Original Title:Riuscira il nostro eroe a ritovar piu grande diamante del mondo?* (1971-Ameican Motion Pictures of Italy-87m-C)

Jimmy Logan: Ray Danton. *Arianne:* Agnes Spaak. *Prof. Froyd:* Lewis Jordan. *Desire:* Luciana Gilli. *Lolita:* Monica Pardo. *Gladis:* Pamela Tudor. *Dalmann:* Daniele Vargas. *Gran Capo:* Francesco Mule. *Lulu Nise:* Seyna Seyn. *Shiela:* Gieriela Minicardi. *Director:* Guido Maletesta. *Screenplay:* Guido Malatesta and Piero Sciume. *Producer:* Michelangelo Ciafre. *Montage:* Giancarlc Cappelli. *Cinematography:* Luciano Rasatti. *Music:* Gianni Rosompagni.

Banyon: (TVM-1971-Warner Brothers-100m-C)

Myles Banyon: Robert Forster. *Lt. Pete Cordova:* Darren McGavin. *Lee Jennings:* Jose Ferrer. *Diane Jennings:* Anjanette Comer. *Harry Sprague:* Herb Edelson. *Peggy Revere:* Hermione Gingold. *Ruth Sprague:* Leslie Parrish. *Victor Pappas:* Ray Danton. *Carl Horner:* Joseph Ruskin *Elderly Waitress:* Florence Lake *Doorman:* John Craig. *Director:* Robert Day. *Screenplay:* Ed Adamson. *Producers:* Richard Alan Simmons and Ed Adamson. *Cinematography:* Lamar Boren. *Editor:* Jamie Caylor. *Music:* Leonard Rosenman.

The Ballad of Billy Blue: (1972-American Video-90m-C) *aka Jailbreakin'; Starcrossed Roads*

Billie Blue: Jason Ledger. *Harvey Trip:* Marty Allen. *Carl:* Ray Danton. *With:* Renny Roker, Sherry Bain, Erik Estrada, Bob Plekker and Sherry Miles. *Director:* Kent Osborne. *Original Story and Screenplay:* Kent Osborne, Ralph Luce, and Robert Dix. *Producer:* Dr. Robert Plekker and A.F. Raigosa. *Cinematography:* Ralph Phaddo. *Editor:* Renn Reynolds. *Music:* Richard Wess.

The Sagittarius Mine: (1972)

Stars: Richard Basehart, Diane Baker, Ray Danton and Steve Forrest. -no other credits available-

A Very Missing Person: (TVM-1972)

Hildegarde Withers: Eve Arden. *Oscar Piper:* James Gregory. *Aleatha Westering:* Julie Newmar. *Captain Westering:* Ray Danton. *Sister Isobel/ Leonore Gregory:* Skye Aubrey. *James Malloy:* Bob Hastings. *Judge:* Ezra Stone. *Delmar Faulkenstein:* Pat Morita. *Director:* Russ Mayberry.

Screenplay: Philip H. Reisman, Jr. *Novel(Hildegarde Withers Makes The Scene):* Fletcher Flora and Stuart Palmer. *Producer:* Edward Mantagne. *Executive Producer:* Richard Irving. *Cinematography:* William Margulies. *Editor:* Richard M. Sprague. *Music:* Vic Mizzy.

Runaway: (TVM-1973-C)

Holly Gibson: Ben Johnson. *Lee Reever:* Ben Murphy. *Nick Staffo:* Ed Nelson. *Ellen Staffo:* Vera Miles. *Carol Lerner:* Darleen Carr. *Mark Shedd:* Lee Montgomery. *John Shedd:* Martin Milner. *Prof. Jack Dunn:* Ray Danton. *Fireman:* Bing Russell. *Travers:* Judson Pratt. *Director:* David Lowell Rich. *Teleplay:* Gerald Di Pego. *Producer:* David Lowell Rich. *Executive Producer:* Harve Bennett. *Cinematography:* Bud Thackery. *Editor:* Douglas Stewart. *Music:* Hal Mooney.

The Centerfold Girls: (1973-General Films Corporation-88m-C)

Clement Dunne: Andrew Prine. *Jackie:* Jaime Lyn Bauer. *Ed Walker:* Aldo Ray. *Miss January:* Charlie. *Melissa:* Francine York. *Perry Sutton:* Ray Danton. *Detective:* Jeremy Slate. *The Caretaker:* Mike Mazurki. *Charley:* Jennifer Ashley. *Vera:* Tiffany Bolling. *Pam:* Anneka De Lorenzo. *Walden:* Himself. *Director:* John Peyser. *Screenplay:* Robert Peete. *Story:* Arthur Marks. *Producer:* Charles Stroud. *Executive Producer:* William Silberkleit. *Editor:* Richard Greer, A.C.E. *Music:* Mark Wolan.

Pursuit: (1975-Lighthorse Productions-92m-C) aka *Apache Blood*

Yellowshirt: Ray Danton. *Sam Glass:* DeWitt Lee. *Director:* Tom Queillen. *Screenplay:* DeWitt Lee and Jack Lee. *Producer:* Vern Piehl. *Executive Producer:* Rowd Sanders.

Six Pack Annie:(1975-American-International/United Producers-88m-C)

Six Pack Annie: Lindsay Bloom. *Mary Lou:* Jana Bellan. *Aunt Tess:* Danna Hansen. *Mr. O'Meyer:* Ray Danton. *Sheriff:* Joe Higgins. *Bustis:* Larry Mahan. *Mr.O'Meyer:*Ray Danton. *Jack Whittlestone:* Richard Kennedy. *Carmeilo:* Pedro Gonzales-Gonzales. *Bobby Joe:* Bruce Boxleitner. *Angelo:* Sid Melton. *Flora:* Louisa Moritz. *Hank:* Doodles Weaver. *Louis Danton:* Oscar Cartier *Mr. Bates:* Stubby Kaye. *Director:* Graydon F. David (John C. Broderick). *Screenplay:* Wil David, David Kidd, and Norman Winski. *Story:* Norman Winski. *Producer:* John C. Broderick. *Cinematography:* Daniel Lacambre. *Editor:* John H. Arrufat. *Music:*Raoul Krauschaar.

Our Man Flint: Dead On Target: (TVM-1975-20th Century Fox-78m-C)
Derek Flint: Ray Danton. *Sandra Carter:* Sharon Acker. *Benita Rogers:* Gaye Rowan. *LaHood:* Donnely Rhodes. *Runzler:* Lawrence Dane. *Delia Ciaza:* Fran Russell. *Director:* Joseph Scanlon. *Producer:* R.H. Anderson. *Screenplay:* Norman Klenman. *Story:* Jim McGinn. Based on the character created by Hal Binberg.

TELEVISION AS AN ACTOR

Danger: "Marley's Ghost" (1950)
Guest Star: Ray Danton. *Director:* Yul Brynner.

Starlight Theater: An Act of God Nonwithstanding Out There: "Misfit" (11.18.51)
Guest Stars: Wendell Phillips, Gene Saks, Thomas Cole, Eddie Hyans, Jerry Paris, Arthur Batanides, Ray Danton and John Sylvester.

Hallmark Hall of Fame: "The Pirate and the Lawyer" (3.13.55)
Jean Laffite: Ray Danton. *Edward Livingston:* Herbert Rudley. *Governor Claiborne:* Doublass Dumbrille. *Louise Livingston:* Loretta King. *Devised and directed by* Albert McCleery. *Teleplay:* Helene Hanff.

Lux Video Theatre: "An Act of Murder" (04.21.55)
Calvin Cook: Thomas Mitchell. *Cathy Cook:* Ann Harding. *Charles Dayton:* Lewis Martin. *Judge Ogden:* Howard St. John. *David Douglas:* Ray Danton. *Ellie:* Sally Brophy. *Dr. Lewis:* Dayton Loomis. *Mrs. Russell:* Ruth Warren. *Director:* J. Walter.

Studio 57: "Always Open and Shut" (4.16.57)
Guest Star: Ray Danton.

Matinee Theater: "Eye of the Storm" (6.07.57-NBC)
Stella: Marian Seldes. *Ben:* Ray Danton. *Annie:* Gloria Talbott. *Sheriff:* Robert Karnes. *Lonnie:* Dick Gardner. *Paw:* William H. Vedder. *Devised and Produced by* Albert McLeery. *Teleplay:* Norman Jacob. *Producers:* Ethel Frank and Winston O'Keefe. *Music:* by Edward Truman.

Playhouse 90: "The Death of Manolete" (9.12.57)

Manolete: Jack Palance. *Camara:* Nehemiah Persoff. *Perea:* Robert Middleton. *Tani:* Suzy Parker. *Antonito:* Ray Danton. *Augustias:* Esther Minicotti. *Director:* John Frankenheimer. *Adapted by* Paul Monash and Barnaby Conrad. *Producer:* Martin Manulos. *Associate Producer:* Peter Kortner.

Sugarfoot: "Bunch Quitter" (10.29.57-ABC)

Tom Brewster: Will Hutchins. *Blacky Rude:* Ray Danton. *Yam Dooley:* George O'Hanlon. *Dale Jardine:* Cathy Case. *Slim Jackson:* Tyler McVay. *Otto Jardine:* Frank Ferguson. *Cowboy:* Bob Steele. *Director:* Leslie H. Martinson. *Teleplay:* Wells Root. *Based on a story by* Jess Linford. *Producer:* Carroll Case. *Executive Producer:* Wm. T. Orr. *Theme Song:* Mack David and Jerry Livingston.

Trackdown: "Sweetwater, Texas" (11.08.57-CBS)

Hobey Gilman, Texas Ranger: Robert Culp. *Sheriff:* Paul Birch. *Doc:* Arthur Space. *Saloon Girl:* Chana O'Brien. *Clem, the gambler:* Ray Danton. *Traveling Salesman:* Paul Richards.

Climax: "Sound of the Moon" (1.23.58-CBS)

Guest Stars: Vera Miles, Hoagy Carmichael, Royal Dano and Ray Danton. *Director:* Anthony Barr. *Writers:* Gwen and Irwin Gielgud.

Studio One: "Tired of Corruption" (2.17.58-CBS)

Guest Stars: Amanda Blake, Ray Danton, Patricia Neal, Barry Sullivan and Murvyn Vye.

Climax: "The Disappearance of Daphne" (5.15.58-CBS)

Guest Stars: Mona Freeman, Ray Danton , Elaine Stritch, Irene Pappas and Eduardo Cianelli. *Director:* Anthony Barr. *Writer:* Robert Blees, based on a serial in the Saturday Evenin Post by Nancy Rutledge.

Wagon Train: "The Monte Britton Story" (6.11.58-NBC)

Major Seth Adams: Ward Bond. *Flint McCollough:* Robert Horton. *Monte Britton:* Ray Danton. *Sarah Britton:* Mona Freeman. *The Reverend:* John Hoyt. *Redmond:* Claude Akins. *Army Captain:* Walter Wolf King. *Director:* Mark Stevens. *Teleplay:* Thomas Thompson. *Producer:* Howard Christie. *Executive Producer:* Richard Lewis.

Decision: "The Danger Game" (unsold pilot) (7.20.58-NBC)
Star: Ray Danton.

Bronco: "Quest of the Thirty Dead" (10.07.58-ABC)
Bronco Lane: Ty Hardin. *Col. Bill Macrider:* Ray Danton. *Paco:* Jay Novello. *Irene Lang:* Beverly Tyler. *Pearson:* Willis Bouchey. *Mohler:* Tol Avery. *Director:* Lee Sholem. *Teleplay:* Tom Blackburn. *Producer:* Arthur W. Silver. *Executive Producer:* Wm. T. Orr. *Theme Song:* Mack David and Jerry Livingston.

77 Sunset Strip: "A Nice Social Evening"(10.24.58-ABC)
Stu Bailey: Efrem Zimbalist, Jr. *Jeff Spencer:* Roger Smith. *Kookie:* Ed Byrnes. *Senor Velazquez:* Ray Danton. *Marilyn:* Arlene Howell. *Betty:* Dorothy Provine. *The Frankie Ortega Trio:* Themselves. *Director:* Stuart Heisler. *Teleplay:* Frederic Brady. *Producer:* Howie Horwitz. *Executive Producer:* Wm. T. Orr. *Theme Song:* Mack David and Jerry Livingstone.

Yancy Derringer: "An Ace Called Spade" (10.30.58-ABC)
Yancy Derringer: Jock Mahoney. *John Colton:* Kevin Hagen. *Pahoo:* X Brands. *Stuart Spade:* Ray Danton. *Lavinia Lake:* Joan Taylor. *Director:* Richard Sale. *Teleplay:* D.D. Beauchamp and Richard Sale. *Created and Produced by* Mary Loos and Richard Sale. *Theme Song:* Henry Russel and Don Quinn.

The Millionaire: "Erik Lodek" (12.17.58-CBS)
Michael Anthony: Marvin Miller. *Nick Slade:* Ray Danton. *Marika Franz:* Chana Eden. *Erik Lodek:* Stephen Bekassy. *Director:* James Sheldon. *Teleplay:* Jack Hadley. *Producer:* Don Fedderson. *Executive Producer:* Fred Henry.

Desilu Playhouse: "Chez Rouge" (2.16.59-CBS)
Guest Stars: Janis Paige, Harry Guardino and Ray Danton.

Behind Closed Doors: "The Meeting" (3.05.59-NBC)
Commander Matson: Bruce Gordon. *Guest Stars:* Ray Danton, David Opatoshu, Judith Braun, Virginia Gregg, Robert Warwick, Booth Colman, Wolfe Barzell, and an appearance by Rear Admiral Ellis Zacarias (ret). *Director:* John Peyser. *Teleplay:* Robert C. Dennis. *Producer:* Sidney Marshall. Jane Gallu Productions, Inc: Screen Gems.

77 Sunset Strip: "A Bargain In Tombs" (4.24.59-ABC)

Stu Bailey: Efrem Zimbalist, Jr. *Johnny Manetti:* Ray Danton. *Julia Maltby:* Louise Fletcher. *Marta:* Lisa Gaye. *Sebastian:* Al Ruscio. *Guido Orsini:* Bart Bradley. *Delphine de Janville:* Linda Watkins. *Director:* Reginald Le Borg. *Teleplay:* Charles Hoffman. *Novel:* Aaron Marc Stein. *Producer:* Howie Horwitz. *Theme Song:* Mack David and Jerry Livingston.

Bat Masterson: "The Romany Knives" (7.22.59-NBC)

Bat Masterson: Gene Barry. *Antonio:* Ray Danton. *Gypsy King:* Frank Silvera. *Leda:* Chana Eden. *Mischa:* Robert Carricart. *Emma:* Eve Cotton. *Director:* Walter Doniger. *Teleplay:* Barney Slater. *Producers:* Frank Pittman and Andy White.

Sugarfoot: "The Wild Bunch" (9.29.59-ABC)

Tom Brewster: Will Hutchins. *Jenny Markham:* Connie Stevens. *Ken Savage:* Troy Donahue. *Duke McGann:* Ray Danton. *John Savage:* Morris Ankrum. *Director:* Leslie Goodwins. *Teleplay:* Dean Riesner. *Producer:* Harry Tatelman. *ExecutiveProducer:* Wm. T. Orr. *Theme Song:* Mack David and Jerry Livingston.

Lawman: "Lily" (10.04.59-ABC)

Marshal Dan Troup: John Russell. *Johnny McKay:* Peter Brown. *Lily:* Peggy Castle. *Annette:* Nan Peterson. *Director:* Leslie H. Martinson. *Teleplay:* Dean Reisner. *Story:* Claire Hoffaker. *Producer:* Jules Schermer. *Executive Producer:* Wm. T. Orr. *Theme Song:* Mack David and Jerry Livingston.

The Alaskans (11.29.59-9.25.60-ABC)

Stars: *Silky Harris:* Roger Moore. *Rocky Shaw:* Dorothy Provine. *Reno McKee:* Jeff York *Nifty Cronin:* Ray Danton (occasional). *Fantan:* Frank DeKova (occasional). **Directors:** Leslie Goodwins, Richard Gordon, Charles F. Haas, Jesse Hibbs, Leslie H. Martinson, William A. Seiter, Richard Sinclair, Robert Sparr, Herbert L. Strock, Jacques Tourneur, and George Waggner. **Producers:** William T. Orr (Executive Producer), Barry Ingster, Harry Tatelman, and Charles Trapnell. **Music Supervisors:** Mack David and Jerry Livingston (theme): Howard Jackson, Heinz Roemheld, Hans J. Salter, Paul Sawtell, Bert Shefter, and Max Steiner. **Film Editors:** David Wages and Robert B. Warwick, Jr.

1. "Cheating Cheaters" (10.11.59): *Brother Bowers:* Frank Ferguson.
2. The Blizzard" (10.18.59): *Jenks:* Walter Burke. *Cornish:* John Dehner. *Duchess:* Andrea King.
3. Petticoat Crew" (10.25.59): *Madeleine Rondolet:* Peggy McKay. *Capt. Smithers:* Dwight Marfield. *Miranla:* Cathy Case.
4. "Starvation Stampede" (11.01.59): *Stella:* Allison Hayes. *Dick Gray:* Joe De Reda.
5. "The Big Deal" (11.08.59): *Soapy Smith:* John Dehner. *Bbbb:* Jesse White.
6. "Contest at Gold Bottom" (11.15.59): *Jackson.* I. Stanford Jolley. *Sara:* Monty Margetts.

Hawaiian Eye: "Murder, Anyone?" (4.13.60-ABC)

Tom Lopaka: Robert Conrad. *Tracy Steele:* Anthony Eisley. *Cricket Blake:* Connie Stevens. *Sara Crane:* Julie Adams. *Barry Logan:* Ray Danton. *Mike Cornell:* Richard Garland. *David Crane:* Herbert Rudley. *Kim:* Poncie Ponce. *Director:* William J. Hale, Jr. *Teleplay:* Robert C. Dennis and W. Hermanos. *Story:* Jerry Davis and Jim Barnett. *Producer:* Jerry Davis. *Theme Song:* Mack David and Jerry Livingston.

Bourbon Street Beat: "Last Exit" (5.02.60-ABC)

Rex Randolph: Richard Long. *Duke Powell:* Ray Danton. *Amanda Hale:* Joan Marshall. *Nita Roulas:* Madlyn Rhue. *Raoul Roulas:* Damien O'Flynn. *Director:* Leslie H. Martinson. *Teleplay:* W. Hermanos. *Story:* Douglas Heyes. *Producer:* Charles Hoffman. *Executive Producer:* Wm. T. Orr. *Theme Song:* Mack David and Jerry Livingston.

Colt .45: "Bounty List" (5.31.60-ABC)

Christopher Colt: Wade Preston. *Sam Colt, Jr.:* Donald May. *Kane:* Ray Danton. *Harriet Potts:* Janet Lake. *Tommy Potts:* Ron Foster. *Harp McGuire:* J. Edward McKinley.

Hawaiian Eye: "I Wed Three Wives" (9.14.60-ABC)

Tracy Steele: Anthony Eisley. *Tom Lopaka:* Robert Conrad. *Mark Hamilton:* Ray Danton. *Mavis Hamilton:* Kasey Rogers. *Sharon Hamilton:* Lenore Roberts. *Nora Hamilton:* Jeanne Baird. *Cy Bliss:* Tommy Farrell. *Henry Bunker:* Barney Phillips. *Sturat Bailey:* Efrem Zimbalist, Jr. *Jeff*

Spencer: Roger Smith. *Director:* Alvin Ganzer. *Teleplay:* Hugo Walters. *Producer:* Stanley Niss. *Executive Producer:* Wm. T. Orr. *Theme Song:* Mack David and Jerry Livingston.

Surfside 6: "Country Gentleman" (10.03.60-ABC)
Dave Thorne: Lee Paterson. *Sandy Winfield:* Troy Donahue. *Marty Hartman:* Ray Danton. *Paula Gladstone:* Janet Lake. *Stinger:* Frank De Kova. *Allan Abbot:* Fred Wayne. *Commodore Gladstone:* Robert Burton. *Roger Fielding:* John Hubbard. *Director:* Irving J. Moore. *Teleplay:* Anne Howard Bailey and M.L. Schuman. *Story:* M.L. Schuman. *Producer:* Jerome L. Davis. *Executive Producer:* Wm. T. Orr. *Theme Song:* Mack David and Jerry Livingston.

Lawman: "Yawkey" (10.23.60-ABC)
Marshal Dan Troup: John Russell. *Yawkey:* Ray Danton. *Johnny McKay:* Peter Brown. *Lily:* Peggy Castle. *Jake:* Dan Sheridan. *Director:* Stuart Reisler. *Teleplay:* Richard Matheson. *Producer:* Jules Schermer. *Associate Producer:* Wm. T. Orr. *Theme Song:* Mack David and Jerry Livingston.

The Roaring 20's: "The White Carnation" (12.03.60-ABC)
Pinky Pinkham: Dorothy Provine. *"Dandy" Dan Brady:* Ray Danton. *Pat Garrison:* Donald May. *Sammie:* Adam Williams. *Ben Dorechal:* Frank De Kova. *Director:* Robert Altman. *Teleplay:* Laszlo Gorog. *Producer:* Boris Ingster. *Executive Producer:* Wm. T. Orr. *Theme Song:* Mack David and Jerry Livingston.

Surfside 6: "The Frightened Canary" (12.12.60-ABC)
Sandy Winfield: Troy Donahue. *Danny Rome:* Ray Danton. *Nina Landis:* Nina Shipman. *Eddie:* Robert Ridgely. *Moran:* Hal Baylor. *Director:* Charles H. Rondeau. *Teleplay:* Sonya Roberts. *Producer:* Jerome Davis. *Executive Producer:* Wm. T. Orr. *Theme Song:* Mack David and Jerry Livingston.

Cheyenne: "Savage Breed" (12.19.60-ABC)
Cheyenne: Clint Walker. *Marshal Lestrade:* Ray Danton. *Nora Henton:* Patricia Huston. *Lily Lestrade:* Shirley Ballard. *Paul Henton:* Robert Clarke. *George Naylor:* Walter Coy. *SenatorLeland Carr:* Carlyle Mitchell. *Dull Knife:* Michael Keep. *Director:* Robert Sparr. *Teleplay:* Pete

B. Germano. *Based on the novel by* Joseph Chadwick. *Producer*: Sidney Biddell. *Associate Producer*: Wm. T. Orr. *Theme Song*: Mack David and Jerry Livingston.

Maverick: "A State of Siege" (1.01.61-ABC)

Bart Maverick: Jack Kelly. *Don Felipe*: Ray Danton. *Soledad Lazarro*: Lisa Gaye. *Don Manuel Lazarro*: Joe De Santis. *Don Roberto*: Raoul De Leon. *Yaquito*: Ref Sanchez. *Mamocita*: Bella Bruck. *Stagecoach Driver*: Slim Pickens. *Director*: Robert C. Sinclair. *Teleplay*: Larry Welch. *Story*: Robert Louis Stevenson. *Producer*: Coles Trampnell. *Associate Producer*: Wm. T. Orr. *Theme Song*: Mack David and Jerry Livingston.

Bronco: "The Buckbrier Trail" (2.20.61-ABC)

Bronco Lane: Ty Hardin. *Deputy Larkin*: Ray Danton. *Blyden*: Mike Road. *Ruth Gillespie*: Gale Bettin. *Norton Gillespie*: Denver Pyle. *Marshal Kilgore*: Paul Birch. *Director*: Robert Sparr. *Teleplay*: William Bruckner. *Story*: Ray Hogan. *Producer*: Sidney Biddell. *Executive Producer*: Wm. T. Orr. *Theme Song*: Mack David and Jerry Livingston.

The Roaring 20's: "The Vamp" (3.04.61-ABC)

Pat Garrison: Donald May. *Harry Shayne*: Ray Danton. *Helen Collins (Mara Nari)*: Grace Gaynor. *Zelda Valmy*: Mari Blanchard. *Max Felix*: Alex Jerry. *Candy Candell*: Lewis Charles. *Pinky Pinkham*: Dorothy Provine. *Charles Higbee*: Gary Vinson. *Director*: Leslie H. Martinson. *Teleplay*: Edwin Blum. *Producer*: Boris Ingster. *Executive Producer*: Wm. T. Orr. *Cinematographer*: Robert Hoffman. *Theme Song*: Mack David and Jerry Livingston.

The Dick Powell Show: "The Hook" (pilot for Attorney General [3.06.62-NBC])

Collin Maese: Robert Loggia. *Magnus Repp*: Ray Danton. *Mac Thane*: Ed Begley. *Lt. Juan Gonzales*: Tony Caruso. *Director*: Joseph H. Lewis. *Teleplay*: Christopher Knopf. *Producers*: Jules Levy, Arthur Gurdner, and Arnold Lavin. *Score*: Joseph Mullendore.

Laramie: "The Fortune Hunter" (10.09.62-NBC)

Slim Sherman: John Smith. *Jess Harper*: Robert Fuller. *Vince Jackson*: Ray Danton. *Kitty McAllen*: Carolyn Craig. *Fred McAllen*: Parley Baer. *Hutch Davis*: Peter Witney. *Daisy Cooper*: Spring Byington. *Mike Williams*:

Dennis Holmes. *Opal:* Pat Krest. *Harvey Doads:* Willis Bouchey. *Director:* Joe Kane. *Teleplay:* Buckley Angell. *Story:* John Champion. *Producer:* John Champion. *Associate Producer:* Dan Ullman. *Theme:* Cyril Mockenridge.

The Virginian: "Riff-Raff" (11.07.62-NBC)
The Virginian: James Drury. *Trampas:* Doug McClure. *Steve:* Gary Clarke. *Molly:* Pippa Scott. *Lt. Drex:* Ray Danton. *Cpt. Langhorne:* Don Durant. *Colonel Roosevelt:* Karl Swenson. *Harry:* Judson Pratt. *Betsy:* Roberta Shore. *Director:* Bernard Girard. *Teleplay:* Jon Booth. *Producer:* Warren Duff. *Associate Producer:* Charles Marquis Warren. *Theme:* Percy Faith.

The Wide Country: "The Bravest Man in the World" (12.06.62-NBC)
Mitch Guthrie: Earl Holliman. *Andy Guthrie:* Andrew Prine. *Warren Price:* Ray Danton. *Anita Callahan:* Yvonne Craig. *Mike Callahan:* Ford Rainey. *Lorenzo:* Harold Fong. *Captain Ainslee:* Bob Steele. *Director:* Ted Post. *Teleplay:* Margeret and Paul Scneider. *Producer:* Frank Telford. *Associate Producer:* Doug Benton. *Theme:* Johnny Williams.

Solitaire: (1962-unsold pilot)
Guest Star: Ray Danton

Entre Nous: (1962-unsold pilot)
Guest Star: Ray Danton.

Empire: "The Four Thumbs Story" (1.08.63-NBC)
Jim Redigo: Richard Egan. *Four Thumbs:* Ray Danton. *Rabbit Stockings:* Rudy Solari. *Constance Garrett:* Terry Moore. *Lucia Garrett:* Anne Seymour. *Tal Garrett:* Ryan O'Neal. *With:* Barry Atwater, George Gaynes and Don Diamond. *Created by:* Hathleen Hite. *Director, Producer and Writer:* Frank Pierson. *Theme:* Johnny Green.

The Gallant Men: "Operation Secret" (2.16.63-ABC)
Hugo Petra: Ray Danton. *David Storm:* Earl Hammond. *Contessa Loren:* Maria Machado. *General Kile:* Albert Paulsen. *Major Neumann:* George Gaynes. *Giadennza:* Vito Scotti. *Cpt. Jim Benedict:* William Reynolds. *Director:* Richard C. Sarafia. *Teleplay:* Richard Landau. *Magazine Story:* Elton Floring. *Producer:* Richard Bluel. *Executive Producer:* Wm. T. Orr. *Music:* William Lava and Frank Perkins.

List of Credits | 487

Kraft Mystery Theater: "Talk To My Partner" (8.28.63-NBC)
Guest star: Ray Danton, Scott Brady.

Wagon Train: "The Molly Kincaid Story" (9.16.63-ABC)
Chris Hale: John McIntire. *Cooper Smith:* Robert Fuller. *Kate Crowley:* Barbara Stanwyck. *Molly Kincaid:* Carolyn Jones. *Rome:* Fabian. *John Kincaid:* Ray Danton. *Martha Kincaid:* Brenda Scott. *With:* Pamela Austin, Harry Carey, Jr., Richard Reeves, Frank McGrath and Myron Healey. *Director:* Virgil Vogel. *Teleplay:* Gene L. Coon. *Producer:* Howard Christie. *Associate Producer:* Frederic Shorr. *Theme:* Jerome Moross.

Redigo: "The Thin Line" (12.03.63-NBC)
Jim Redigo: Richard Egan. *Mike:* Roger Davis. *Frank Martinez:* Rudy Solari. *Gerry:* Elena Verdugo. *Linda Martinez:* Mina Martinez. *Jeff Burton:* Ray Danton . *Deputy Sheriff:* Jim Drum.

Temple Houston: "The Case for William Gotch" (2.06.64-NBC)
Temple Houston: Jeffrey Hunter. *George Taggart:* Jack Elam. *Gotch:* James Best. *Martin Royale:* Ray Danton. *Coley:* Richard Jaekel. *Phineas Fallon:* Denver Pyle. *Bryce:* Gordon Westcourt. *Director:* Abner Biberman. *Executive Producer:* Wm. T. Orr.

Death Valley Days: "The Wooing of Perilous Pauline" (2.22.64-syn)
Jere Fryer: Ray Danton. *Pauline:* Paula Raymond. *Frank:* Eddie Ryder. *Doc:* Loyal Lucas. *Tom:* Jeff Davis. *Carmela:* Tita Marsell. *Director:* Tay Garnett. *Teleplay:* Joanna Lee. *Producer:* Robert Stabler. *Associate Producer:* Stephen Lord.

Arrest and Trial: "The Black Flower" (3.01.64-ABC)
Det. Anderson: Ben Gazzara. *John Egan, Esq.:* Chuck Connors. *Rick Tobin:* Dewey Martin. *Ellen Tobin:* Patricia Crowley. *Jess Malloy:* Ray Danton. *Ben Chalice:* Andrew Duggan. *Director:* Earl Bellamy. *Teleplay:* Don Brinkley. *Producer:* Arthur H. Nadel. *Executive Producer:* Frank P. Rosenberg. *Production Executive:* Jon Epstein. *Theme:* Bronislaw Kaper.

Wagon Train: "The Stark Bluffs Story" (4.06.64-ABC)
Christopher Hale: John McIntire. *Cooper Smith:* Robert Fuller. *Duke Shannon:* Scott (Denny) Miller. *Zeb Stark:* Ray Danton. *Suzy Dunphy:* Jean Hale. *Judge Pike:* Stanley Adams. *Sheriff Pincus:* Peter Whitney. *Director*

and Teleplay: Allen H. Miner. *Producer:* Howard Christie. *Associate Producer:* Frederick Shorr. *Theme:* Jerome Moross.

Honey West: "The Swingin' Mrs. Jones" (9.17.65-ABC)

Honey West: Anne Francis. *Sam Bolt:* John Ericson. *Sonny:* Ray Danton. *Ma/Masseuse:* Winnie Coffin. *Joe Steele:* Marvin Brody. *Aunt Meg:* Irene Hervey. *Direction:* Paul Wendkos. *Teleplay:* Gwen Bagni and Paul Duboo. *Producer:* Richard Newton. *Executive Producer:* Aaron Spelling. *Associate Producer:* Don Ingalis. *Music:* Mullendore. *Based on the Honey West novels by:* Skip and Gloria Fickling.

The Man From U.N.C.L.E.: "The Discotheque Affair" (10.15.65-NBC)

Napoleon Solo: Robert Vaughn. *Illya Kuryakin:* David McCallum. *Alexander Waverly:* Leo G. Carroll. *Vincent Carver:* Ray Danton. *Tiger Ed:* Harvey Lembeck. *Sandy Tyler:* Judi West. *Farina:* Evylyn Ward. *Director:* Tome Gries. *Teleplay:* Dean Hargrove. *Story:* Leonard Stadd. *Producer:* David Victor. *Executive Producer:* Norman Felton. *Series Developed by:* Sam Rolfe. *Theme:* Jerry Goldsmith.

The Big Valley: "Devil's Masquerade" (3.04.68-ABC)

Victoria Barkley: Barbara Stanwyck. *Jarrod Barkley:* Richard Long. *Nick Barkley:* Peter Breck. *Heath Barkley:* Lee Majors. *Audra Barkley:* Linda Evans. *Reed Clayton:* Ray Danton. *Nancy:* Anne Helm. *Jim North:* John Doucette. *Maia:* Argentina Brunetti. *Creators:* A.I. Bezzerides and Louis Edelman. *Director:* Paul Henreid. *Teleplay:* Sasha Gilien and Mel Goldberg. *Producer:* Lou Morheim. *Associate Producers:* Jules Levy, Arthur Gardner and Arnold Laven. *Music:* Elmer Bernstein. *Theme:* George Dunnz.

The Name of the Game: "The Inquiry" (1.17.69-NBC)

Glen Howard: Gene Barry. *Senator Preston Collins:* Barry Sullivan. *Scretary Folwer:* Jack Kelly. *Colonel Shotz:* Fritz Weaver. *Renata:* Gia Scala. *Bertelli:* Ray Danton. *Sgt. Ernest Maxwell:* Gene Evans. *Cesare Moreno:* Ed Asner. *Director:* Sutton Riley. *Teleplay:* Harold Livingston. *Producer:* Richard Irving. *Associate Producer:* Dean Hargrove. *Theme:* Dave Grusin.

Ironside: "A Drug on the Market" (3.06.69-NBC)

Robert Ironside: Raymond Burr. *Det. Sgt. Ed Brown:* Don Galloway. *Eve Whitfield:* Barbara Anderson. *Marc Sanger:* Don Mitchell. *Karen*

Martin: Betsy Jones-Moreland. *Avery Martin:* Ray Danton. *Judith:* Victoria Shaw. *Dr. Braven:* Fred Beir. *Zuppus:* Nick Dennis. *Creator:* Collier Young. *Director:* Barry Shear. *Teleplay:* Arthur Weingarten. *Producer:* Douglas Benton. *Executive Producer:* Cy Chermak. *Associate Producer:* Jeannot Szwarac. *Theme:* Quincy Jones.

It Takes A Thief: "The Baranoff Timetable" (3.18.69-ABC)
Alexander Mundy: Robert Wagner. *Noah Bain:* Malachi Throne. *Laurie Brooks:* Jessica Walter. *Secretary Ramon Ortega:* Ray Danton. *Diego:* Nico Minardos. *Director:* Michael O'Herlihy. *Teleplay:* Carey Wilbur and Mort Zarcoff. *Story:* Carey Wilbur. *Producer:* Mort Zarcoff. *Executive Producer:* Jack Arnold. *Creator:* Roland Kibbee.

Love, American Style: "Love and the Mr. Nice Guy" (1.12.70-ABC)
Peter: Wally Cox. *Kane Walker:* Ray Danton. *Erica:* Alexandra Hay. *Director:* Bruce Bilson. *Teleplay:* Bud Freeman. *Producer:* William D'Angelo. *Executive Producers:* Jim Parker and Arnold Margolin. *Associate Producers:* Gregg Peters and Don Boyle. *Theme:* Arnold Margolin and Charles Fox.

Dan August: "The Color of Fury" (10.28.70-ABC)
Det. Lt. Dan August: Ray Danton. *Sgt. Charles Wilentz:* Norman Fell. *Sgt. Joe Rivera:* Ned Romero. *Chief George Untermeyer:* Richard Anderson. *Jimmy Barlow:* Raymond St. Jacques. *Councilman Leo Cassoni:* Nehemiah Persoff. *(Andy) Androtti:* Ray Danton. *Mr. Marsden:* Richard O'Brien. *Director:* Harvey Hart. *Teleplay:* William Wood. *Producer:* Anthony Spinner. *Associate Pproducer:* Robert Lewin. *Supervising Producer:* Adrain Samish. *Executive Producer:* Quinn Martin. *Music:* Pat Williams. *Theme:* Dave Grusin.

Hawaii Five-O: "The Last Eden" (11.18.70-CBS)
Det. Steve McGarrett: Jack Lord. *Det. Danny Williams:* James MacArthur. *Det. Chin Ho Kelly:* Kam Fong. *Det. Kono Kalakaua:* Zulu. *Jimmy Nuanu:* Ray Danton. *Colfax:* Paul Stevens. *Eddie:* Tom Fujiwara. *Lyons:* Bruce Wilson. *Bartender:* Terry Plunkett. *Director:* Paul Stanley. *Teleplay:* Jerry Ludwig and Eric Bercovivi. *Producer:* Robert Stamliler. *Associate Producer:* James Heinz. *Theme:* Morton Stevens.

The F.B.I.: "The Inheritors" (12.27.70-ABC)
Inspector Lewis Erskine: Efrem Zimbalist, Jr. *Special Agent Tom Colby:* William Reynolds. *Temple Alexander:* Suzanne Pleshette. *Glen Frye:* Ray Danton. *Harlan Franciscus:* Gene Raymond. *George Fransicus:* Lawrence Linville.

The Young Lawyers: "And The Walls Came Tumbling Down" (2.24.71-ABC)
Attorney David Barrett: Lee J. Cobb. *Aaron Silverman:* Zalman King. *Pat Walters:* Judy Pace. *Guest Stars:* Nan Martin, Julie Adams, Ray Danton, Kathy Cannon, and D'Urville Martin.

Nichols: "Deer Crossing" (10.21.71-NBC)
Nichols: James Garner. *Ma Ketchum:* Neva Patterson. *Ketchum:* John Beck. *Mitch:* Stuart Margolin. *Ruth:* Margot Kidder. *Juan Garcia:* Ray Danton. *Durand:* Gene Evans. *Creator:* Frank R. Pearson. *Director:* William Wiard. *Teleplay:* Shimon Wincelberg. *Story:* Frank R. Pearson. *Producer:* Frank R. Pearson. *Executive Producer:* Meta Rosenberg. *Music:* Bernardo Seagall.

Night Gallery: "The Miracle at Camefeo" (1.19.72)
Joe Melchior: Ray Danton. *Gay Melchior:* Julie Adams. *Rogan:* Harry Guardino. *Priest:* Richard Yniguez. *Bartender:* Rodolfo Hoyas. *Mother:* Margarita Garcia. *Boy:* Thomas Trujillo. *Host:* Rod Serling. *Short Story:* C.B. Gilford. *Director:* Ralph Senensky. *Teleplay:* Rod Serling. *Producer:* Jack Laird. *Theme:* Gil Melle.

Hawaii Five-O: "Cloth of Gold" (2.08.72)
Det. Steve McGarrett: Jack Lord. *Det. Danny Williams:* James MacArthur. *Det. Chin-Ho Kelly:* Kam Fong. *Det. Kono Kalahua:* Zulu. *Wallis:* Jason Evers. *Fred Akamai Loy:* Ray Danton. *Mingo:* Jay Robinson. *Manoa:* William Valentine. *Doc:* Al Eben. *Director:* Michael O'Herlihy. *Teleplay:* Bennett Foster. *Story Consultant:* Will Lorin. *Producer:* William Finnegan. *Associate Producer:* James Heinz. *Supervising Producer:* Bob Sweeney. *Theme:* Morton Stevens. *Music:* Robert L. Morrison.

McCloud: "The New Mexican Connection" (10.01.72)
Sam McCloud: Dennis Weaver. *Peter B. Clifford:* J.D. Cannon. *Sgt. Joe Broadhurst:* Terry Carter. *Chris Coughlin:* Diana Muldaur. *Sgt. Grover:*

Ken Lynch. *Hollis:* Jackie Cooper. *Jimmy Ray Taylor:* Rick Nelson. *Adrian Becker:* Murray Hamilton. *Marshal Ben Melendez:* Gilbert Roland. *Stokes:* Ray Danton. *Wilkes:* Gary Vinson. *Sgt. Maggie Clinger:* Sharon Gless. *Creator:* Herman Miller. *Directors:* Hy Averbrook and Russ Mayberry. *Teleplay:* Glen A. Larson. *Producer:* Michael Gleason. *Executive Producer:* Glen A. Larson. *Associate Producer:* Arthur E. McLaird. *Music:* John-Andrew Tartglia. *Sunday Mystery Movie Theme:* Henry Mancini.

The Streets of San Francisco: "Before I Die" (10.04.73-ABC)

Dt. Lt. Mike Stone: Karl Malden. *Inspector Steve Kelly:* Michael Douglas. *John T. Connor:* Leslie Nielson. *Royce:* Ray Danton. *Based on characters created by:* Carolyn Werton. *Developed for tv by:* Edward Hume. *Director:* William Hale. *Teleplay:* Albert Ruben. *Producer:* John Wilder. *Executive Producer:* Quinn Martin. *Music:* Duane Tatro. *Theme:* Pat Williams.

Cannon: "Trial By Terror" (11.21.73-CBS)

Frank Cannon: William Conrad. *Judge Haines:* Simon Scott. *Julie Haines:* Kelley Miles. *Len Francisco:* Keith Andes. *Earl Dakin:* Ray Danton. *Les Vernon:* Stuart Moss. *Maggie Marshall:* Anne Randall. *Director:* Robert Douglas. *Teleplay:* Larry Brody. *Producer:* Winston Miller. *Executive Producer:* Quinn Martin. *Theme:* John Parker.

Police Story: Countdown (Pts. 1&2 [1.15,1.22.74-NBC])

La Frieda: Vic Morrow. *Jenny:* Laraine Stephens. *Sally Pickle:* Joe Santos. *Blodgett:* Tige Andrews. *Johnnny Landros:* Ray Danton. *Martin Landros:* Tony Caruso. *Constantina Landros:* Anjanette Comer. *Lorraine:* Jennifer Billingsly. *Vinny:* Scott Brady. *Eddie Parent:* Michael Callan. *George Morris:* John Randolph. *Terry:* Scott Marlowe. *Vicki:* Domanique Pinassi. *Marta:* Ina Balin. *Pollard:* Paul Stevens. *June Lang:* Lana Wood. *Lloyd Adams:* Frank Costellano. *Created by:* Joseph Wambaugh. *Director:* Richard Benedict. *Writer:* Mark Rodgers. *Executive Producer:* David Gerber. *Producer:* Stanley Kallis. *Associate Producer:* Christopher Morgan. *Music:* Jerry Goldsmith. *Director of Photography:* Emmett Bergolz.

McCloud: "This Must Be The Alamo" (3.24.74-NBC)

Sam McCloud: Dennis Weaver. *Chief Peter B. Clifford:* J.D. Cannon. *Sgt. Joe Broadhurst:* Terry Carter. *Sgt. Grover:* Ken Lynch. *Dan Kiley:* Van Johnson. *Shannon Taylor:* Lorraine Stephens. *Chet:* Ray Danton. *Manny*

Donner: Jack Kelly. *Elton Packer:* XXX. *Lazar:* Eugene Roche. *Harris:* Della Reese. *Sgt. Norton:* Teri Garr. *Creator:* Herman Miller. *Director:* Bruce Kessler. *Teleplay:* Glen A. Larson. *Producer:* Michael Gleason. *Associate Producer:* Ronald A. Satlof. *Executive Producer:* Glen A. Larson. *Music:* Stu Phillips. *Theme:* Henry Mancini.

Toma: "Pound of Flesh" (4.19.74-ABC)

Det. David Toma: Tony Musante. *Patty Toma:* Susan Strasberg. *Inspector Spooner:* Simon Oakland. *Jimmy Toma:* Sean Manning. *Donna Toma:* Michelle Livingston. *Jack Angelis:* Joseph Hindy. *Al Dancer:* Ray Danton. *Edie Angelis:* Hildy Brooks. *Limpy:* Val Bisoglio. *Crackers:* Pepper Martin. *Lucius Careon:* Joseph Della Sorte. *Waitress:* Marisol Del Rio. *Director:* Jeannot Szwarc. *Teleplay:* Edward Hume. *Producer:* Stephen J. Cannell. *Associate Producer:* Jo Swerling, Jr. *Executive Producer:* Roy Huggins. *Theme:* Mike Post and Pete Carpenter. *Production Consultant:* David Toma.

The Manhunter: "The Man Who Thought He Was Dillenger" (9.18.74-CBS)

Dave Barrett: Ken Howard. *Lizabeth Barrett:* Hilary Thompson. *James Barrett:* Ford Rainey. *Sheriff Tate:* Robert Hogan. *Jeffrey Donenfield:* David Hedison, *Tom Bailey:* Mitchell Ryan, *Homer:* Ray Danton. Alexandra Hay, *Blueprint Kelly:* Robert Emhardt.

Cannon: "The Hit Man" (9.18.74-CBS)

Cannon: William Conrad. *Bishop Harrigan:* Richard Kiley. *Chief Ames:* Richard O'Brien. *Alex Brennan:* Ray Danton. *Lester Cain:* Paul Stewart. *Leo Carruthers:* Val Avery. *Savini:* Michael Bell. *Father Joseph:* Christopher Connelly. *Director:* William Wiard. *Teleplay:* Robert Haverly. *Producer:* Anthony Spinner. *Associate Producer:* Leigh Vance. *Executive Producer:* Quinn Martin. *Theme:* John Parker.

Hawaii Five-O: "Steal Now...Pay Later" (10.01.74-CBS)

Det. Steve McGarrett: Jack Lord. *Det. Danny Williams:* James MacArthur. *Dt. Chin Ho Kelly:* Kam Fong. *Ron Colby:* Ray Danton. *Swift:* Casey Kasem. *Charley Portman:* Jacques Aubuchon. *Rogers:* Howard E. Gottschalk. *Duke:* Herman Wedemeyer. *Director:* John Peyser. *Teleplay:* Jerome Coopersmith. *Producer:* William Finnegan. *Associate Producer:* James Heinz. *Theme:* Morton Stevens. *Music:* Richard Shores.

Nakia: "No Place To Hide" (10.18.74-ABC)
  Nakia: Robert Forster. *Archie MacIntosh:* Gabe Dell. *Norm:* Ray Danton. *Half Cub:* John Tenorio, Jr. *Sheriff Jericho:* Arthur Kennedy. *With:* George Loros, Marc Singer and Gloria de Haven. *Created by:* Christopher Trumbo and Michael Butler. *Director:* Nicholas Colasanto. *Teleplay:* Jim Byrnes. *Producers:* Ernest Losso and George Sunga. *Executive Producer:* Charles Nelson. *Music and Theme:* Leonard Rosenman.

Caribe: "The Plastic Connection" (2.17.75-ABC)
  Lt. Ben Hogan: Stacy Keach. *Sgt. Mark Walters:* Carl Franklin. *Dpt. Cm. Walters:* Robert Mandan. *Guest Stars:* Jack Ging, Paul Jenkins, Julie Adams, Ellen Weston, Ray Danton, and Harvey Jason.

Matt Helm: "The Game of the Century" (x.xx.75-xxx)
  Matt Helm: Tony Franciosa. *Claire Kronski:* Lauraine Stephens. *Mrs. Faro:* Patricia Crowley. *Professor Shannon:* Biff McGuire. *Cherokee:* Betty Ann Carr. *Frank Saxon:* Ray Danton. *With:* Fred Bior, Rudy Diaz and Logan Ramsey. *Developed for television by:* Sam Rolfe. *Based on characters created by:* Donald Hamilton. *Director:* Reza Badiya. *Teleplay:* Steve Fisher and Edward De Blasio. *Producers:* Charles B. Fitzsimmons and Ken Pettus. *Theme:* Morton Stevens.

The Rockford Files: "Chicken Little is a Little Chicken" (11.14.75-NBC)
  Jim Rockford: James Garner. *Angel:* Stuart Margolin. *Rocky:* Noah Beery, Jr. *Sgt. Becker:* Joe Santos. *Chester Sierra:* Ray Danton. *Martin Frishette:* Frank Campanella. *Tom Little:* Angelo Gnazzo. *Kessler:* Nicholas Worth. *Director:* Lawrence Doheny. *Teleplay:* Stephen J. Cannell. *Producer:* Lane Slate. *Associate Producer:* Chas. Floyd Robinson. *Executive Producer:* Meta Rosenberg. *Supervising Producer:* Stephen J. Cannell. *Creators:* Roy Huggins and Stephen J. Cannell. *Theme:* Mike Post and Pete Carpenter.

Joe Forrester: "Target: Mexican Syndicate" (11.25.75-NBC)
  Joe Forrester: Lloyd Bridges. *Georgia Cameron:* Patricia Crowley. *Sgt. Bernie Vincent:* Eddie Egan. *Guest Stars:* Rosemary Forsyth, Ray Danton, Lloyd Battista, Armand Alzamora, Erik Estrada, and Milt Kozun.

Switch: "Big Deal in Paradise" (2.24.76-CBS)
  Pete Ryan: Robert Wagner. *Frank MacBride:* Eddie Albert. *Saunders:* Peter Mark Richman. *Laurie:* Anne Archer. *Ralph Carson:* Ray Danton.

Malcolm Argos: Charlie Callas. *Director:* Bruce Kessler. *Teleplay:* Lou Shaw. *Producer:* Gene R. Kearney. *Supervising Producer:* Joe L. Cramer. *Creator/Theme/Executive Producer:* Glen Larson. *Music:* Stu Phillips. *Director of Photography:* Ben Colman.

The Feather and Father Gang: "The Apology" (3.07.77-ABC)

Toni "Feather" Danton: Stephanie Powers. *Harry Danton:* Harold Gould. *Lou:* Lewis Charles. *Joe Generales:* Gene Barry. *Big Jim Morgan:* Ray Danton. *Musleman:* Eddie Fontaine. *Barbara:* Linda Foster. *Michael:* Monte Landis. *T.V. Producer:* Marcus J. Grapes. *Director:* Ernie Pintoff. *Teleplay:* Calvin Clements, Jr. *Producers:* Bill Driskill and Robert Mintz. *Associate Producer:* Bert Gold. *Executive Producer:* Larry White. *Creator:* Bill Driskill. *Music and Theme:* George Romanis.

Barnaby Jones: "Duet for Danger" (5.22.77)

Barnaby Jones: Buddy Ebsen. *Jedediah Jones:* Mark Shera. *Ruby Connors:* Cassie Yates. *Pearl Connors:* Mary Ann Chin. *Nick Di Marcos:* Ray Danton. *Lester:* Bryan Montgomery. *Stan Toland:* Paul Picerni. *Director:* Leslie H. Martinson. *Teleplay:* Gerald Sanford. *Producer:* Phillip Sanford. *Associate Producer:* Robert Sherman. *Executive Producer:* Quinn Martin. *Theme:* Jerry Goldsmith.

Movies as a Director

Devil's Ransom (Senza via d'uscita)- 1.25 min. (1970) American Motion Pictures of Italy / Orbita Films)

Michele: Marisa Mell. *Gilbert:* Philippe Leroy. *Britt:* Lea Massari. *Kurt:* Roger Hanin. *Bergman:* George Rigaud. *Director:* Ray Danton. *Teleplay:* Tiziano Cortini. *Story:* Ricardo Ferrer, Julio Salvador and Peiro Sciume. *Producer:* Pier Luigi Torri. *Music:* Piero Piccioni. *Cinematography*: Cecilio Paniagua. *Editor*: Renato Cinquini.

Deathmaster-American-International-1.24 min. (1972) AIP

Khorda: Robert Quarry. *Pico:* Bill Ewing. *Rona:* Brenda Dickson. *Pop:* John Fiedler. *Kirkwood:* Bob Pickett. *Esslin:* Betty Ann Rees. *Monk:* William Jordan. *Barbado*: Le Sene Hilton. *Mavis*: Tari Tabkin. *Director*: Ray Danton. *Screenplay*: R.L. Grove. *Producer:* Fred Sadoff. *Music:* Bill Marx. *Cinematography*: Wilmer C. Butler. *Editor:* Harold Lime.

Hannah, Queen of Vampires 1 hr. 15 m.-Orbita Films(1973)
Chris Bolton: Andrew Prine. *Peter*: Mark Damon. *Mary*: Patty Sheppard. *Hannah*: Teresa Gimpera. *The Wild Man*: Ihsan Gedik. *Prof. Bolton*: Mariano Rey. *Abduk Hamid (The Blind Sailor)*: Frank Brana. *Ali, Adnan's Father*: Edward Walsh. *Adnan*: Jack LaRue, Jr. *Zora, the Little Girl*: Shera Osman. *Directors*: Julio Salvador, Ray Danton. (augmentation). *Original Screenplay*: Julio Salvador. *Original Story*: Ricardo Ferrer. *U.S. Screenplay*: Lou Shaw. *U.S. Story*: Lois Gibson. *Producer*: Lou Shaw. *Music*: Phillip Lambro. *Cinematography*: Juan Gelpi. *Editor*: Alberto G. Nicolau and David Rawlins.

Psychic Killer-1.29 min.-Avco-Embassy Films (1975)
Police Lt. Jeff Morgan: Paul Burke. *Arnold Masters*: Jim Hutton. *Dr. Laura Scott*: Julie Adams. *Dr. Gubner*: Nehemiah Persoff. *Lemonowski*: Neville Brand. *Lt. Dave Anderson*: Aldo Ray. *Dr. Paul Taylor*: Whit Bissell. *Dr. Commanger*: Rod Cameron. *Mrs. Gibson*: Della Reese. *Nurse Burnson*: Mary Wilcox. *Frank*: John Dennis. *Emilio*: Stack Pierce. *Narrator (Intro)*: Ray Danton. *Director*: Ray Danton. *Screenplay*: Greydon Clark, Mikel Angel and Ray Danton. *Producer*: Mardi Rustrum. *Music*: William Kraft. *Cinematography*: Herb Pearl. *Editor*: Michael Brown.

TELEVISION AS A DIRECTOR

QUINCY, M.E:
   Regulars: *Quincy*: Jack Klugman. *Lt. Frank Monahan*: Garry Walberg. *Dr. Robert Asten*: John S. Ragin. *Danny Tovo*: Val Bisoglio. *Sam Fujiyama*: Robert Ito. *Sgt. Brill*: Joseph Roman. *Eddie*: Ed Garrett. *Waitress*: Dinah Manoff. *Creators*: Glen A. Larson and Lou Shaw. *Theme*: Glen A. Larson and Stu Phillips.

"A Question of Time" (10.14.77)
Walter Kingman: Peter Mark Richman. *Bridges*: Rudy Solari. *Mrs. Holloway*: Brenda Scott. *Dr. Ruth Thaler* Irene Tedrow. *Rossi*: Michael Lane. *Tom Holloway*: John Alderman. *Director*: Ray Danton. *Teleplay*: Irving Pearlberg. *Producer*: Christopher Morgan. *Executive Producer*: Jud Kinberg.

"Tissue of Truth" (10.28.77)
Robert Stoddard: Craig Stevens. *Amanda Stoddard*: Lenka Peterson. *Louis banfield*: Sheilah Wells. *Holsang*: Royal Dano and Ivor Francis.

Director: Ray Danton. *Teleplay:* Max McClellan. *Producer:* Christopher Morgan. *Associate Producer:* George E. Crosby. *Executive Producer:* Jud Kinberg.

"Main Man" (11.11.77)
Walter Daniels: Eugene Roche. *Steve Daniels:* Scott Colomby. *Coach Bodine:* Peter Brown. *Mrs. Daniels:* Julie Adams. *Director:* Ray Danton. *Teleplay:* Irv Pearlberg. *Story:* Ray Danton. *Producer:* Christopher Morgan. *Executive Producer:* Jud Kinberg.

"Last of the Dinosaurs" (12.16.77)
Sylvia Prestin: Carolyn Jones. *Movie Director:* John Anderson. *Dan Granger:* Cameron Mitchell. *Will Prestin:* Chuck Robertson. *Director:* Ray Danton. *Teleplay:* Leonard Stadd. *Producer:* Edward J. Montagne. *Executive Producer:* Richard Irving. *Creators:* Glen A. Larson and Lou Shaw.

"Images" (11.02.78)
Jessica Ross: Jessica Walter. *Ron Gordon:* Jack Hogan. *Bert:* Robert Ellenstein. *Dr. Miles Thornton:* Whit Bissell. *Director:* Ray Danton. *Teleplay:* Aubrey Solomon and Steve Greenberg. *Story:* Ray Danton. *Associate Producer:* William Cairncross. *Executive Producer:* Peter J. Thompson.

"Even Odds" (11.09.78)
Dr. Monroe: Edward Grover. *John Holmes:* Richard McKenzie. *Billings:* Dennis Madalone. *Director:* Ray Danton. *Teleplay:* Pamela Glasser. *Associate Producers:* William Carroll and William Cairncross. *Executive Producer:* Peter J. Thompson.

"A Question of Death" (1.04.79)
Raymond Morrison: Granville Van Husen. *Dr. Williams:* Royal Dano. *Dr. Monroe:* Ed Grover. *Mr. Murphy:* Judson Pratt. *Director:* Ray Danton. *Teleplay:* Aubrey Solomon and Steve Greenberg. *Story:* Peter J. Thompson, Robert Crais, Aubrey Solomon and Steve Greenberg. *Producers:* William Cairncross and Charles E. Dismukes. *Executive Producer:* Peter J. Thompson.

"The Depth of Beauty" (1.25.79)
Dori Larkin: Jane Greer, *D.A. Baker:* Rudy Solari.*Dr. Walt Mitchell:* Donald May. *Harry Chase:* Walter Brooke. *Eddie Carlton:* Joey Foreman.

Director: Ray Danton. *Teleplay:* Robert Crais. *Story:* Robert Crais and Barbara Evans. *Associate Producers:* William Cairncross and Charles E. Dismukes. *Executive Producer:* Peter J. Thompson.

"Dark Angel" (2.13.79)

Charlie Trusdale: William Daniels. *Officer Tommy Bates:* Neville Brand. *Mr. Harris:* Marshall Thompson. *Dr. Herb Carlton:* Paca Thomas. *Director:* Ray Danton. *Teleplay:* Robert Crais. *Associate Producers:* William Cairncross and Charles E. Dismukes. *Executive Producer:* Peter J. Thompson.

"No Way to Treat a Flower" (9.20.79)

Kathy Campbell: Karlene Crockett. *Joey Campbell:* Charles Bloom. *Mrs. Campbell:* Joan Freeman. *Botanist:* Whit Bissell. *Director:* Ray Danton. *Teleplay:* Jeff Freilich and Christopher Trumbo. *Producers:* William Cairncross and Charles E. Dismukes. *Executive Producer:* Donald Bellasario.

"Dead Last" (9.27-79)

Ron Henner: Joseph Sirola. *Charlie:* Red West. *The Farrier:* Red West. *Penny:* Howard Payton. *Director:* Ray Danton. *Teleplay:* William T. Zacha and E. Nick Alexander. *Producers:* William Cairncross and J. Rickley Dumm. *Executive Producer:* David Moessinger.

"Never a Child" (10.11.79)

Carol Trager: Cassie Yates. *'Uncle' harry Simkins:* Alan Manson *Terri:* Tara Buckman. *Amanda:* Melora Hardin. *Father Tony Hamilton* Kene Holliday. *Councilman Becker:* Walter Brooke. *Director:* Ray Danton. *Teleplay:* Sam Egan. *Producers:* Charles Dismukes and William Cairncross. *Associate Producer:* Maurice Klugman.

"Hot Ice" (10.18.79)

Agent Niven: Edward Grover. *F.B.I. Agent Roxie Adams:* Elaine Giftos. *Bernie Evans:* George Loros. *Agent Brice:* John Karlen. *Miss Coroner Supervisor:* Elsa Raven. *Director:* Ray Danton. *Teleplay:* Robert Crais. *Story:* Ralph Wallace Davenport. *Pro-ducers:* William O. Cairncross and Charles Dismukes. *Associate Producers:* Maurice Klugman, Lester William Berke and Richard E. Rabjohn.

"Honor Thy Elders" (1.10.80)

Sharon Ross: Julie Adams. *Tim Morgan:* , Joby Baker. *Tim Morgan's Mother:* Susan French. *Muriel Prentiss:* Estelle Winwood. *Director:* Ray Danton. *Teleplay:* Sam Egan. *Producers:* Charles Dismukes and William Cairncross. *Associate Producers:* Maurice Klugman, Lester William Berke, and Richard E. Rabjohn.

"Diplomatic Immunity" (1.17.80)

Armando Sarejo: Rudy Solari. *Agent Niven:* Ed Grover. *Isabella Sarejo:* Anna Navarro. *Dr. Allermo:* Rene Enriquez. *Director:* Ray Danton. *Teleplay:* Steve Greenberg and Gregory Crossman. *Producer:* William O. Cairncross. *Executive Producer:* R.A. Cinader.

"Unhappy Hour" (2.14.80)

Melanie Stedman: Karlene Crockett. *Ann Asten Stedman:* Madlyn Rhue. *Mr. Polk:* Joseph Sirola. *Robert Waite:* Lonny Chapman. *Eric:* Scott Columby. *Director:* Ray Danton. *Teleplay:* Sam Egan. *Producers:* William O. Cairncross and Lester William Berke.

"Stain of Guilt" (1.14.81)

Victoria: Carolyn Jones. *Kit:* Ed Begley, Jr. *Director:* Stewart Moss. *Inspector:* William Sylvester. *Cassie Spencer:* Susan Powell. *Judge Stone:* Ezra Stone. Blackmailer: Sid Haig. *Director:* Ray Danton. *Teleplay:* Sam Egan.

"For Want of a Horse" (12.09.81)

Paul Tanner: Luke Askew. *Jack LaFolle:* Lonny Chapman. *Jason Randall:* Paul Fix. *Cicely Randall:* Susan French. *Gabe:* Ronnie Scribner. *Director:* Ray Danton. *Teleplay:* Jeri Taylor. *Producer:* Sam Egan. *Executive Producer:* David Moessinger.

"Dead Stop" (12.23.81)

Mrs. Cheznell: Salome Jens. *Mickey Langford:* Jack Ging. *Hank Cheznell:* Sandy McPeak. *Trucker Harwood:* Red West. *Starvin' Marvin:* Tony Burton. *Will Case:* John Dennis. *Director:* Ray Danton. *Teleplay:* Linda Cowgill. *Producers:* Sam Egan and Michael Braverman. *Associate Producer:* John Hart.

"Science for Sale" (11.24.82)

Dr. Paul Flynne: Lane Smith. *Dr. Chris Winston:* Julie Adams. *Garfield Calhoun:* Dennis Patrick. *Mr. Lifton:* Stack Pierce. *Director:* Ray

Danton. *Teleplay:* Erich Collier. *Story:* Diana Marcus, Chris Abbott and Nancy Faulkner. *Producers:* Michael Braverman and Jeri Taylor. *Executive Producer:* Sam Egan.

"Next Stop, Nowhere" (12.01.82)

Abigail Garvin: Melora Hardin. *Molly Howard:* Karlene Crockett. *Mrs. Susan Garvin.:* Barbara Cason. *Skip:* Kelly Ward. *Club Owner:* Nick Georgiade. *Director:* Ray Danton. *Teleplay:* Sam Egan. *Producers:* Michael Braverman and Jeri Taylor. *Supervising Producer:* Sam Egan. *Songs:* "Next Stop, Nowhere" and "Give Up" by Sam Egan and Irving Kramer.

"Sword of Honor, Blade of Death" (12.15.82)

Mr. Nakatoma: Soon-Teck Oh. *John Moroshima:* Mako. *Nishimura:* John Fujioka. *Sadako:* Donna Kei Benz. *Mafia Drug merchants:* Ed Grover and George Loros. *Director:* Ray Danton. *Teleplay:* Michael Braverman. *Producers:* Michael Braverman and Jeri Taylor. *Executive Producer:* David Moessinger.

"Guilty Until Proven Innocent" (1.12.83)

Philip St. John: Eugene Roche. *Ted Locke:* Rudy Solari. *Hannah Locke:* Susan-Plantt Winston. *Director:* Ray Danton. *Teleplay:* Allison Hock. *Producers:* Michael Braverman and Jeri Taylor. *Supervising Producer:* Sam Egan.

"On Dying High" (2.09.83)

J.J. Chandler. Roger Miller. *Ginger Reeves:* Kelly Palzis. *Red Auerbach:* Edd Byrnes. *Dr. Emily Hanover:* Anita Gilette. *Director:* Ray Danton. *Teleplay:* Michael Braverman. *Producers:* Michael Braverman and Jeri Taylor. *Supervising Producer:* Sam Egan.

As a writer

"Main Man" (11.11.77)

(check above listings for credits)

"Images" (11.02.78)

(check above listings for credits)

"Requiem for the Living" (3.10.78)
   Guest Stars: John Vernon, Val Avery, Ina Balin, Max Showalter, Larry Gelman, and Terry Lynn Wood. *Director:* Rowe Wallerstein. *Teleplay:* Irving Pearlberg. *Story:* Ray Danton. *Producer:* Peter J. Thompson. *Executive Producer:* Richard Irving.

"Welcome to Paradise Palms" (12.17.80)
   Dr. Paul Monongye: Ronald Joseph. *Roberta:* Silvana Gallardo. *Shaman:* Dehl Berti. *Charles Curtis:* Dennis Patrick. *Director:* Georg Fenady. *Teleplay:* David Mossinger. *Story:* Jon Dalke and Ray Danton.

CAGNEY AND LACEY:

"Street Scene" (04/15/'82)
   Regulars: Mary Beth Lacey: Tyne Daly. *Chris Cagney:* Sharon Gless. *Victor Isbecki:* Martin Kove. *Guests: Esteban:* Panchito Gomez. *Polaski:* George Petrie. *Mario:* Danny De La Paz. *Director:* Ray Danton. *Teleplay:* Claudia Adams. *Producer:* Richard M. Rosenbloom. *Cinematography:* Hector R. Figueroa. *Editor:* Geoffrey Rowland.

"Better Than Equal "(4/29/'82)
   Regulars: Mary Beth Lacey: Tyne Daly. *Chris Cagney:* Sharon Gless. *Victor Isbecki:* Martin Kove. *Guests: Helen Granger:* Julie Adams. *Mike Walker:* John Walter Davis. Mr. Aparicio: as T.J. Castronova. Mrs. Walker: . *Director:* Ray Danton. *Teleplay:* Bud Freeman. *Producer:* Richard M. Rosenbloom. *Cinematography:* Hector R. Figueroa. *Editor:* Art Seid.

"Beauty Burglars" (11.08.82)
   Theresa: Christine Belford. *Elizabeth Moran:* Barbara Cason. *Francois:* Henry Polic II. *Director:* Ray Danton. *Teleplay:* April Smith and Robert Crais. *Story:* Patt Shea and Harriett Weiss.

"Who Says Its Fair?" (Pts. 1 & 2 [2.11-18.85])
   Eleanor Taggert: Lynn Whitfield. *Kevin Taggert:* Bumper Robinson. *Corelli:* Joseph Della Sorte. *Lucky:* Martin Davis. *Willie Smoke:* Theoplas Forsett. *Director:* Ray Danton. *Teleplay:* Patricia Green. *Story:* Barbara Avedon, Barbara Corday, Claudia Adams, and Patricia Green. *Associate Producer:* P.K. Knelman.

"The Psychic" (10.21.85)

Michelle Zal: Elizabeth Ashley. *Howard Tanner:* Michael Alldridge. *Deputy Inspector Knelman:* Michael Fairman. *Eli Leavitt:* Richard Frank. *Lynn Sutter:* Janet MacLachlan. *Jim Lundsford:* Chuck McCann. *Dorothy Gantney:* Eve McVeagh. *Director:* Ray Danton. *Teleplay:* Debra Frank and Scott Rubenstein. *Producer:* Steven Brown. *Co-Producers:* Ralph Singleton and P.K. Knelman.

"Mothers and Sons" (11.25.85)

Mr. Carruthers: Charles Aidman. *Officer Santiago:* Danny De La Paz. *Officer Johnson:* Al Fann. *Owen Kessler:* Carl Franklin. *Mrs. Carruthers:* Peggy McKay. *Director:* Ray Danton. *Teleplay:* Frank South. *Producer:* Steven Brown. *Co-Producers:* Ralph Singleton and P.K. Knelman.

"Culture Clash" (10.06.86)

Abdullah: Robert Hallak. *Director:* Ray Danton. *Teleplay:* Frank South. *Producer:* Ralph Singleton. *Co-Producer:* P.K. Knelman.

"To Sir With Love" (2.16.87)

Margeret Moeller: Cassie Yates. *Muriel Lacey:* Penny Santoni. *Director:* Ray Danton. *Teleplay:* Sandy Sprung and Marcy Vosburgh. *Producers:* Georgia Jeffries and Ralph S. Singleton.

MICKEY SPILLANE'S MIKE HAMMER:

Regulars: *Mike Hammer:* Stacy Keach. *Velda:* Lindsay Bloom. *Capt. Pat Chambers:* Don Stroud. *Asst. D.A. Barrington:* Kent Williams. *Ozzie the Answer:* Danny Goldman. *Moochie:* Ben Powers. *The Face:* Donna Denton.

"A Death in the Family" (11.24.84)

Julia Huntley: Barbara Bain. *Vincent Randolph:* John Ireland. *Carol Huntley:* Susan Walden. *Vincent Acker:* Dan Hamilton. *"Little" Ed Huntley:* John Lansing. *Mama Z:* Twyla Littleton. *Director:* Ray Danton. *Teleplay:* B.W. Sandefur. *Story:* Marvin Paul Kupfer. *Producers:* Christopher Seiter and Stephen Kandel. *Supervising Producers:* Lou Gallo and Jack B. Sowards.

"A Bullet for Benny" (12.08.84)
   Tina/Monica: Leslie Wing. *Arthur Ziegler:* Abe Vigoda. *Benny Winslow:* Martin Rudy. *Ray Marlan:* Brian Libby. *Jenny:* Lee Benton. *Director:* Ray Danton. *Teleplay:* Paul Bernbaum and Jack B. Sowards. *Story:* Chester Krumholz. *Producers:* Christopher Seiter and Stephen Kandel. *Supervising Producers:* Lou Gallo and Jack B. Sowards.

THE NEW MIKE HAMMER:

"Deirdre" (9.27.86)
   Leslie Wing. Peter Iacangelo. John S. Ragin. Michael Delano. *Sara Rose:* Jeannie Marie Austin. *Director:* Ray Danton. *Teleplay:* Herman Miller. *Producers:* B.W. Sandefur, Ed Sharlach and Jon Andersen. *Supervising Producers:* Ray Danton and Howard Berk.

"Golden Lady" (10.11.86)
   Mildred Hoffstedder: Nina Foch. *Kate Wilkins:* Shelley Smith. *Ruth Baylor:* Juliana McCarthy. *Director and Co-Producer:* Ray Danton. *Teleplay:* Duke Sandefur. *Producers:* B.W. Sandefur, Ed Sharlach and Jon Andersen.

"Harlem Nocturne" (11.26.86)
   Bubba Crown: Samm-Art Williams. *Billy Marvel:* George Benson. *Delia Marvel:* Lynne Whitfield. *Digger Love:* Ernie Hudson. *Hot Mama Vibes:* Isabel Sanford. *Rubin Washington:* Leonard Lightfoot. *Lady in Red:* Jeannie-Marie Austin. *Director:* Ray Danton. *Teleplay:* Howard Berk. *Story:* Ray Danton and Ed Sharlach. *Producers:* B.W. Sandefur, Ed Sharlach, and Jon Anderson. *Supervising Producers:* Ray Danton and Howard Berk.

The Return of Mickey Spillane's Mike Hammer (TVM-1986-Columbia Pictures Television-94m-C)
   Mike Hammer: Stacy Keach. *Joanna Lake:* Lauren Hutton. *Frank Walker, F.B.I.:* Vince Edwards. *Captain Pat Chambers:* Don Stroud. *Jack Bergin:* Mickey Rooney. *Megan:* Emily Rose Chance. *Velda:* Lindsay Bloom. *Barrington:* Kent Williams. *Nick Anton:* Stephen Macht. *Chapel:* John Karlen. *Dak:* Micheal Preston. *Leo:* Leo Penn. *Cameos:* Bruce Boxleitner, Dabney Coleman, and Dionee Warwick. *Director:* Ray Danton. *Teleplay:* Larry Brody, Janis Hendler, and James M. Miller. *Producer:* Gray Frederickson. *Associate Producer:* Jeffrey Morton. *Executive Producer:*

Jay Bernstein. *Cinematography:* Hector R. Figueroa. *Editor:* Richard E. Rabjohn. *Score:* Earle H. Hagen.

As a Supervising Producer

"Murder in the Cards (12.03.86)-"Requiem for Billy" (12.10.86)

"Little Miss Murder" (1.07.87) - "Kill John Doe" (1.21.87)

"Elegy for a Tramp" (1.28.87) "Body Shot" (2.04.87)

SWITCH:

"The Tong" (1/09/78)
 Stars: Pete T. Ryan: Robert Wagner. *Frank MacBride:* Eddie Albert. Malcolm Argos: Charlie Callas. Maggie Philburn: Sharon Gless. *Sgt. Ellen Lee, SFPD:* Barbara Luna. *Nin Tung Fat:* John Fujiyoka. *Charlie Kuang:* Philip Ahn. *Wang* James Hong. *Director:* Ray Danton. *Teleplay:* Peter Allan Fields. *Story:* David Carren. *Producer:* John Peyser. *Cinematography:* Frank A. Beascoechea. *Editor:* John Arthur Davies.

"Photo Finish" (7/02/78)
 Stars: Pete T. Ryan: Robert Wagner. *Frank MacBride:* Eddie Albert. Malcolm Argos: Charlie Callas. Maggie Philburn: Sharon Gless. *Dokovic:* Rudy Solari. *Cluny Young:* Sherry Mathis. *Arthur Gilmore:* Edward Power. *Krupich:* Ken Lynch. *Farmer:* Sig Haig. *Cleo Johnson:* Sheila DeWindt. *Elvira Windsor:* Irene Tedrow. *Monica:* Sheila Rogers. *Scorpion:* Scott B. Wells. *Director:* Ray Danton. *Teleplay:* Cynthia A. Cherbak. *Producer:* Leigh Vance. *Cinematography:* James Di Pasquale. *Editor:* David Howe.

TALES OF THE UNEXPECTED:

"The Best Policy" (1980-syn)
 Harry Flock: Gary Burgdorf. *Daisy Flock:* Deborah Harmon. *Philbert:* Logan Ramsey. *Simpson:* William Boyett. *Director:* Ray Danton. *Teleplay:* David Scott Milton. *Executive Producer:* Quinn Martin.

"Bird of Prey" (1981-syn)

Edna: Sondra Locke. *Jack:* Frank Converse. *Charlie:* Charles Hallahan. *Director:* Ray Danton. *Producer:* Norman Lloyd. *Executive Producer:* John Fleming Ball.

The Turn of the Tide (9/03/'83)

Slade: Richard Basehart. *Martha Parker:* Gretchen Corbett. *John Spalding:* Nicholas Hormann. *Fred:* Harry Northup. *Fred's Wife:* Maggie Peach. *Fred's Daughter:* Angie McCright. *Director:* Ray Danton. *Teleplay:* Ross Thomas. *Short Story:* C.S. Forester. *Producer:* Norman Lloyd. *Cinematography:* Dean Cundey.

AMERICAN DREAM;

"Crossing Patterns" (4/27/'81)

Danny Novak: Stephen Macht. *Donna Novak:* Karen Carlson. *Casey Novak:* Tim Waldrip. *Todd Novak:* Michael Hershewe. *Jennifer Novak:* Andrea Smith. *Abe Berlowitz:* Hans Conreid. *Sam Whittier:* John McIntire. *Bill Swartz:* George Barrow. *Director:* Ray Danton. *Teleplay:* Ronald M. Cohn. *Executive Producers:* William Blinn and Robert Minkoff. *Cinematography:* Jack L. Richards. *Editor:* Byron Chudrow.

"California Dreaming" (1981-not aired)

Danny Novak: Stephen Macht. *Donna Novak:* Karen Carlson. *Casey Novak:* Tim Waldrip. *Todd Novak:* Michael Hershewe. *Jennifer Novak:* Andrea Smith. *Abe Berlowitz:* Hans Conreid. *Sam Whittier:* John McIntire. *Bill Swartz:* George Barrow. *Director:* Ray Danton.

FAME:

"A Place To Belong" (10.13.85)

Leroy Johnson: Gene Anthony Ray. *Dusty Tyler:* Loretta Chandler. *Christopher Donlon:* Billy Hufsey. *Danny Amatullo:* Carlo Imperato. *Nicole Chapman:* Nia Peeples. *HollyLaird:* Cynthia Gibb. *Peggy Persky:* Randee Heller. *Director:* Ray Danton. *Teleplay:* Paul and Sharon Boorstin. *Theme:* Michael Gore and Dean Pitchford. *Sung by:* Erica Gimpel.

"Selling Out" (11.03.85)

Jesse Valesquez: Jesse Borrego. *Mr. Benjamin Shorofsky:* Albert Hague. *Alan Stewart:* Christian Clemonson. *Mitch Randall:* Robert Fieldsteel. *Joshua Cadman:* Bradley Eliot, Jr. *Director:* Ray Danton. *Teleplay:* Joanne Pagliaro. *Theme:* Michael Gore and Dean Pitchford. *Sung by:* Erica Gimpel.

"Who am I, Really?" (5/11/'85)

Nicole Chapman: Nia Peeples. *Diane Petit:* Julie Carman. *Joyce Chapman:* Jennifer Rhodes. *Ted Chapman:* Ted Sorel. *Director:* Ray Danton. *Teleplay:* Michael McGreevey. *Producer:* David De Silva. *Theme:* Michael Gore and Dean Pitchford. *Sung by:* Erica Gimpel.

LEG WORK:

"Things That Go Bump In The Night" (10.10.87-CBS)

Willie: Frances McDormand. *Fred:* Patrick James Clarke. *Jeffrey:* Robert Dorfman. *Judy:* Deborah Rush. *George Liakos:* Victor Bevine. *Carmen:* Tracy Kollis. *Angelo Norelli:* John DiBenedetto. *Director:* Ray Danton. *Teleplay:* Deborah R. Baron.

"Mystery Woman" ('87-not broadcast)

Claire: Margaret Colin. *Director:* Ray Danton. *Teleplay:* Janis Hirsch.

MAGNUM, P.I.:

"The Love That Lies" (11.18.87)

Carol Baldwin: Kathleen Lloyd. *Abigail Baldwin:* Celeste Holm. *Brenda Babcock:* Eileen Brennan. *Keough Palmer:* Gary Wood. *Director:* Ray Danton. *Teleplay:* Jeri Taylor.

"The Great Hawaiian Adventure Company" (1.27.88)

Clio Mitchell: Phyllis Davis. *Bryant Calvin:* Shavar Ross. *Sarah Amblin:* Shanna Reed. *Budge:* Danny Nucci. *Director:* Ray Danton. *Teleplay:* Jeri Taylor. *Producers:* Jeri Taylor, Stephen A. Miller and Rick Weaver. *Associate Producer:* Mark R. Chilz.

The Hardy Boys/Nancy Drew Mysteries : "Death Surf "(3/12/'78)
    Joe Hardy: Shaun Cassidy. *Frank Hardy*: Parker Stevenson. *Maryann Dalton/Teri Turner*: Maren Jensen. *Mr. Turner*: Jack Hogan. *Bernie Lucas*: Tara Buckman. *Sam 'Hubba' Hubblemeyer*: Jack Jones. *Directors*: Jack Arnold, Ray Danton. *Teleplay*: Robert Earll. *Story*: Joyce Heft Brotman. *Producer*: Joe Boston. *Cinematography*: Jack Woolf. *Editor*: Buford F. Hayes.

THE INCREDIBLE HULK:

"Killer Instinct" (11.10.78-CBS)
    David Banner: Bill Bixby. *The Incredible Hulk*: Lou Ferrigno. *John Tobey*: Denny Miller. *June Tobey*: Barbara Leigh. *Dr. Stewart*: Rudy Solari. *Coach Haggerty*: Pepper Martin. *Director*: Ray Danton. *Teleplay*: Joel Humpreys and William M. Whitehead. *Story*: Richard Landau, William M. Whitehead and Joel Humpreys. *Producer*: James C. Hirsch. *Executive Producer*: Kenneth Johnson.

THE CONTENDER (MINI-SERIES):

"Mission at Moscow" (5/01/'80)
    Johnny Captor: Marc Singer. *Jill Sindon*: Katherine Cannon. *George Beifus*: Moses Gunn. *Rick*: Terrance Michos. *Director*: Ray Danton.

INDIVIDUAL EPISODES:

Bender's Force "Pilot" (1980)
    Stars: Harry Guardino and Joseph Burke. *Director*: Ray Danton. *Executive Producer*: Carroll O'Connor.

Feel the Heat "Pilot" (1983)
    Andy Thorn: Nick Mancuso. *Honor Campbell*: Lisa Eichorn. *Captain Barney Hill*: Robert Hooks. *Sally Long*: Paula Kelly. *Monkey Moreno*: Hector Elizondo. *Emille Sanchez*: Pepe Serna. *Eddie Music*: Lenny Juliano. *Director*: Ray Danton. *Producers*: Ronald I. Cohn and Edward K. Milkis.

Dallas: "Offshore Crude" (1.20.84)

J.R. Ewing: Larry Hagman. *Bobby Ewing:* Patrick Duffy. *Sue Ellen Ewing:* Linda Gray. *Miss Ellie Ewing:* Barbara Bel Geddes. *Cliff Barnes:* Ken Kercheval. *Pamela Barnes Ewing:* Victoria Principal. *Ray Krebbs:* Steve Kanaly. *Edgar Randolph:* Martin E. Brooks. *Director:* Ray Danton. *Teleplay:* David Paulsen. *Producer:* Leonard Katzman. *Cinematography:* Bradford May. *Editor:* Fred W. Berger.

T.J.Hooker: "Love Story" (2.16.85)

Teri Sherman: Michelle Phillips. *Simpson:* Jeffrey Josephson. *Laura Benson:* Susan Walden. *Dorothy Unger:* Tara Buckman. *Sonny Unger:* Miguel Ferrer. *Elizabeth Woods:* Kim Sudol. *Director:* Ray Danton. *Teleplay:* Stephen Downing and Judy Burns. *Producers:* Stephen Downing and Chuck Bowman. *Theme:* Mark Snow.

Vietnam War Story: "Home" (third story) (1987)

Olson: Joshua Cadman. *Zadig:* Nicholas Cascone. *Henderson:* Peter Cohl. *M.P.:* Ernest Dixon. *Stewart:* Alan Duane. *Harris:* David Harris. *Waller:* Amy Van Nostrand. *Orderly:* Chris Robinson. *Taxi Driver:* Dick Stelling. *Director:* Ray Danton. *Teleplay:* Ronald Rubin. *Producer:* Ernest Gold. *Executive Producer:* Georg Stanford Brown. *Score:* Mark Snow.

Shelley Duvall's American Tall Tales and Legends: "John Henry"(1987)

John Henry: Danny Glover. *Quinn:* Thomas Hulce. *Pollie-Ann:* Lynn Whitfield. *Jenkins:* Barry Corbin. *Edna:* Thelma Houston. *Jim Wallace:* Lou Rawls. *Spike:* James Louis Watkins. *Edward:* E'lon Cox. *Director:* Ray Danton. *Teleplay:* Samm-Art Williams. *Producer:* Bridget Terry. *Executive Producer:* Shelly Duvall. *Score:* Ron Ramin. *Vocals arranged and conducted by:* Andrae Crouch. *Title song sung by:* Thelma Houston.

Dynasty: "The Trial" (3/09/'88)

THEATER AS AN ACTOR

Tiger at the Gates (1957)

Sombrero Theatre, Phoenix, Arizona / Ivar Theatre, Los Angeles
Playwright: Giradoux. Director: Harold J. Kennedy. Cast: Robert

Ryan, John Ireland, Mary Astor, Marilyn Erkskine and Ray Danton.

Happy Hunting (1957)
Sacramento Light Opera Theatre
Cast: Ray Danton. Producers: Russell Lewis and Howard Young.

Becket (1962)
Pasadena Playhouse, Pasadena, California
Playwright: Jean Anouilh. Director: Lenore Shanewise. Cast: Ross Martin, Ray Danton, Richard St. Johns, and Morri Ankrum.

110 in the Shade (1963)
The Broadhurst Theatre, New York City
Book: N. Richard Nash. Music: Harvey Schmidt. Lyrics: Tom Jones. Producer: David Merrick. Choreography: Agnes de Mille. Cast: Inga Swenson, Ray Danton, Will Geer, Lesley Ann Warren and Gretchen Cryer.

Carnival (1964)
Regional Music Tour
Director/Choreographer: Rudy Toronto. Producer: John Kinley. Libretto: Michael Stewart. Song Writer: Bob Merill. Cast: Ann Blyth, Ray Danton, Helen Blount and John Smolko.

THEATER AS A DIRECTOR

South Pacific (1974)
House of Janus, Hawaii
Producer: Don Over. Cast: Varoa Tiki, Jocelyn Suan and Les Freed. Choreographer: Scott Michaels. Musical Director and Conductor: Donald Yap.

Selma (1978)
Huntington Hartford Theatre, Los Angeles
Playwright/Star: Tommy Butler. Producer: Redd Foxx. Choreographer: Elimu Goss abd Marie Bryant. Cast: Tommy Butler, Ruth Brown, Denise Erwin, Bhetty Waldron, Ernie Banks, Fred Tucks and

Rubert Williams.

Return to Paradise (1979)
    Honolulu Dinner Theater
    Producer: Don Over.

Come Back, Little Sheba (1987)
    Los Angeles Theatre Center
    Playwright: William Inge. Cast: Tyne Daly, Charles Hallohan, Zoaunne LeRoy and Al Rossi.

Acknowledgements

ARCHIVISTS

Fabio Di Angelis, Mon Ayash, Bob Benedek, Doc Blake, Paul Carr, Barbara Cole, Sharon Daniels, Barbara Douglas, Vern Duel, Mike Egerton, Dr. Ron Evans, Don Harden, Jasage, Jonas, Tom Kleinschmidt, Barbara Lambert, Craig Ledbetter, Boyd Magers, Ray Marerro, Des Martin, Bob McCrea, Norm V. Oyster, J.M. Smith, James Tittermary and Mike White.

BRIEF WORDS AND THINGS:

Chris Alcaide, Budd Boeticcher, Bob Bertrand, Joseph Burke, Yvonne Craig, Will Hutchins, Sara Shane, Mel Welles and Tim Werner.

Endnotes

1. Playhouse 90: The Death of Manolete. Martin Grams. martin grams. blogspot.com/2014/11/playhouse-90-death-of-Manolete.html

2. Ethel Winart Interview/ Playhouse 90/ Archive of American television; www.emmytvlegends.org/interviews/shows/playhouse.90; May 29, 2012.

3. Film Talk: Directors at Work; Wheeler Winston Dixon; Rutgers University Press; July 11, 2007

4. Budd Boetticher and the Westerns of Ranown; Senses of Cinema; Bruce Hodson; Feb. 2006, Issue 38

5. Robert Altman: Jumping Off a Cliff; Patrick McGilligan; St. Martin's Press, 1989.

6. Warner Bros. Television; Woollery, Lynn; Malsbary, Robert W.; and Strange, Jr., Robert G.

7. A Hit is Happening: Tommy Butler's Selma; Frank Bach and Edwenna Edwards; Associated Press; 1976.

8. I Haven't Quit Acting, says Ray Danton; Daily Variety, March 1, 1979.

9. Cancer, Cagney and Lacey; People Magazine, Feb. 11, 1985.

10. Cagney and Lacey…and Me: An Inside Hollywood Story OR How I Learned to Stop Worrying and Love the Blonde; Barney Rosenweig; iUniverse, Inc., 2007.

11. The ABC's of Network Casting; Daily Variety, April 11, 1985.

Index

A

Adams, Julie 3 (p), 4, 7, 9 (p), 84, 90, 107, 109, 122, 130, 151, 153, 291 (p), 307, 314, 332, 368, 369, 371, 388, 389(p), 400, 401(p), 406(p), 414, 415
Albert, Eddie 59, 61, 208, 373, 374
Alden, Norman 203, 206, 335
Arnold, Jack 98, 103, 440

B

Bancroft, Anne 17, 19,
Barry, Gene 37, 280, 378
Bloom, Lindsay 361, 362, 426
Bolling, Tiffany 342
Boetticher, Budd 12
Bruno, Nicolai 264, 268
Burr, Raymond 22, 282, 283
Byrnes, Edd 56, 157, 159, 386, 410(p),

D

Daly, Tyne 420, 426
Donahue, Troy 143, 175
Duggan, Andrew 20, 80, 142, 200

E

Eden, Chana 33

F

Ferrer, Jose 299, 404
Foch, Nina 430

Forster, Robert 298, 299, 351
Franco, Jesus 1, 263,267
Freeman, Mona 25

G

Garner, James 32, 186, 187, 308, 364
Gaye, Lisa 161, 162, 187
Gimpera, Teresa 266, 328,330
Gless, Sharon 416, 467
Gregg, Virginia 45, 61
Guardino, Harry 35, 307

H

Hay, Alexandra 305, 341, 350, 351

I

Ireland, John 22

J

Jens, Salome 403, 404
Jones, Carolyn 77, 79 (p), 233, 235, 386, 390, 401

K

Karlen, John 416, 435
Keach, Stacey 363, 417, 426, 435, 437
Kelly, Jack 68, 69, 186, 187, 260, 282, 354

L

Long, Richard 142

M

Mansfield, Jayne 132, 134
Manulis, Martin 24, 29
Martin, Quinn 291, 292, 312, 350, 481
Martin, Ross 235, 236, 303
May, Donald 147, 386, 394
Martin, Andra 56, 58, 79
McCann, Chuck 419(p)
Mell, Marisa 240, 250, 252, 254, 319
Miller, Denny 230, 441, 442
Morrow, Vic 203, 204, 346, 348

O

O'Brien, Chana 37, 43

P

Parker, Suzy 30, 31
Parrish, Leslie 204(p), 205, 300
Persoff, Nehemiah 29, 30, 311, 369, 371
Petit, Pascale 247, 269
Pratt, Judson 102, 127, 129, 304, 386, 394
Prine, Andrew 213, 215(p), 328, 330, 340
Provine, Dorothy 147, 160, 193

R

Reason, Rhodes 68, 79
Roche, Eygene 354, 388, 410
Rooney, Mickey 10, 117, 118, 435
Rudley, Herbert 20, 152, 153
Ruscio, Al 161, 162
Russell, John 56, 175, 177
Ryder, Eddie 202, 224, 226

S

Serling, Rod 16, 307, 331, 343
Solari, Rudy 227, 386, 394, 399, 409, 410, 441
Stanwyck, Barbara 233, 277
Stevens, Connie 151, 155 (p), 173, 175

T

Tudor, Pamela 11, 240, 253, 257, 261, 262,

V

Van Doren, Mamie 115, 116, 118, 120,

W

Wagner, Robert 283, 284, 373
Walter, Jessica 284, 391, 392(p)
Welles, Mel 102, 261, 263, 264, 267, 268
Whitfield, Lynn 421, 432, 433,(p), 464

Z

Zimbalist, Jr., Efrem 64, 68, 81, 156, 159, 312

www.ingramcontent.com/pod-product-compliance
Lightning Source LLC
Chambersburg PA
CBHW070158240426
43671CB00007B/481